DATE DUE

MARXISM

MARXISM

The Inner Dialogues

Second Edition

Edited by

Michael Curtis

TRANSACTION PUBLISHERS

New Brunswick (U.S.A.) and London (U.K.)

New material this edition copyright © 1997 by Transaction Publishers, New Brunswick, New Jersey 08903. Originally published in 1970 by Atherton Press, Inc.

This book is printed on acid-free paper that meets the American National Standard for Permanence of Paper for Printed Library Materials.

Library of Congress Catalog Number: 96-52289
ISBN: 1–56000–945–4
Printed in the United States of America

Library of Congress Cataloging-in-Publication Data

Marxism : the inner dialogues / edited by Michael Curtis—2nd ed.
    p.   cm.
  Includes bibliographical references and index.
  ISBN 1–56000–945–4 (alk. paper)
    1. Marx, Karl, 1818–1883. 2. Socialism. I. Curtis, Michael,
1923–   .
HX39.5.C86   1997
335.4—dc21   96–52289
                                                                    CIP

To Joseph Machlis,
matchless musicologist

Contents

Preface, ix
Introduction, 1

PART ONE
POLITICAL THEORY, SOCIAL SCIENCE, OR IDEOLOGY?

From Theory to Ideology, 19

1. GEORGE LICHTHEIM
   On the Interpretation of Marx's Thought, 21
2. LEWIS COSER AND IRVING HOWE
   The Role of Ideology, 32

   Marxism: Consistency or Revisionism?, 37

3. DONALD CLARK HODGES
   The Unity of Marx's Thought, 39
4. CHARLES F. ELLIOTT
   Problems of Marxist Revisionism, 46

   Marxism and Political Modernization, 61

5. RICHARD LOWENTHAL
   The Points of the Compass, 63
6. GEORGE LICHTHEIM
   Marxism, West and East, 75

   Is Marxism a Social Science?, 87

7. DONALD CLARK HODGES
   Marxism as Social Science, 90
8. T. B. BOTTOMORE
   Karl Marx: Sociologist or Marxist?, 97

PART TWO
MARX: MORALIST AND HUMANIST

Marxist Ethics, 107

9. R. N. Carew Hunt
   The Ethics of Marxism, 109
10. Eugene Kamenka
    The Primitive Ethic of Karl Marx, 118

Alienation and Humanism, 129

11. Daniel Bell
    A Critique of Alienation, 131
12. Michael Harrington
    Marx as Humanist, 144

Marxism and Religion, 153

13. N. Lobkowicz
    Karl Marx's Attitude toward Religion, 155
14. Alasdair MacIntyre
    Marxists and Christians, 165

PART THREE
CLASSIC MARXIST THEMES:
PHILOSOPHY, HISTORY, AND ECONOMICS

The Dialectical Process, 175

15. Max Eastman
    Against the Marxian Dialectic, 177
16. Herman Simpson
    In Support of the Marxian Dialectic, 186

The Materialist Conception of History, 195

17. H. B. Mayo
    Marxism as a Philosophy of History, 197
18. J. H. Hexter
    A New Framework for Social History, 207

The Contribution of Marxism to Economics, 213

19. Oscar Lange
    Marxian Economics and Modern Economic Theory, 215

20. WASSILY LEONTIEF
The Significance of Marxian Economics for Present-day
Economic Theory, 229
21. PAUL A. SAMUELSON
Marxian Economics as Economics, 235

PART FOUR
CLASS CONFLICT, REVOLUTION, AND POLITICAL POWER

Class and Class Conflict, 243

22. S. OSSOWSKI
The Concept of Social Class, 245
23. RALF DAHRENDORF
A Sociological Critique of Marx, 254

Revolution or Peaceful Change?, 263

24. HAROLD ROSENBERG
The Proletariat and Revolution, 265
25. S. M. LIPSET
Is Gradual Change Possible?, 275
26. ROBERT TUCKER
Ambivalence about Gradual Change, 280

Is Dictatorship Necessary?, 283

27. HAL DRAPER
The Dictatorship of the Proletariat, 285
28. ROBERT TUCKER
The Proletarian State, 297

The Future of the State, 303

29. CALVIN B. HOOVER
The Soviet State Fails to Wither, 305
30. GEORGE A. BRINKLEY
The "Withering" of the State Under Khrushchev, 315
31. MICHAEL CURTIS
The Asiatic Mode of Production and Oriental Despotism, 326

Selected Bibliography, 377
Index, 381

Preface

THIS second edition of *Marxism* seeks to introduce students of political thought and comparative politics to some of the major contemporary controversies and continuing discussions of the meaning and significance of an important and influential ideology of our time. Since the concept of the Asiatic mode of production has aroused both interest and passion in recent years, a new essay on that subject has been added to the original work.

When the first edition appeared, it could be argued that the study and evaluation of Marxism was logically inseparable from the analysis of politics in the Soviet Union, China, and other Communist countries, and could help understand the debates, sometimes heated, in Communist parties and movements elsewhere. Even then the book concentrated on problems and issues in Marxist studies rather than on political practice and behavior. Now that most of the Communist political systems in the world, with the important exception of China, have been dissolved and Marxism is no longer the ideological base of society and politics in the former Communist countries, it is even more appropriate that Marxism be critically assessed in an objective and dispassionate way.

The articles in the book are both expository and critical in nature. I wish to thank the various authors and publishers for allowing me to use the excerpts included in this volume. I have on a number of occasions removed footnotes, which in no way has detracted from the scholarly nature of the contributions.

I am grateful to the Moshe Dayan Center at Tel-Aviv University for providing financial and logistical assistance allowing me to write the last chapter.

Michael Curtis
December 1996

Introduction

MARXISM is the most intellectually ambitious, systematic, and influential political philosophy in the contemporary world. It not only has affected much of modern culture but has also provided the conceptual framework for powerful political movements and the theoretical basis for the regimes of a substantial number of nations. Marxism comprises a methodological approach to the perception and understanding of phenomena, a scientific study of society, a philosophy of history, a history of economic behavior (especially that of the capitalist system), and a conception of political power.

Philosophically, Marxism is a compound of Hegelianism, positivism, and materialism. Ethically, it is a descendant of the spirit of the Enlightenment. Politically, it derives its inheritance from the revolutionary movements of nineteenth-century France. Economically, it stems from the preoccupations of British political economy. But Marxism is not simply a majestic theoretical structure in which, as Isaiah Berlin has argued, the parts are made to appear from each other and to support each other in a single systematic whole. [1] Marxism is also a call to action, a revolutionary cry to change economic and social conditions. The frontispiece of the *Collected Works* of Marx, the *Gesamtausgabe*, shows the cartoon of Marx as Prometheus, the representative of the oppressed. Marxists claim that theory and action are inextricably connected; for Lenin, "the living soul of Marxism was its revolutionary content."

On one occasion, when confronted with an interpretation of his theory, Marx is reported to have said, "In that case I am not a Marxist." Certainly, interpretations of Marxism are legion, and the true inheritance has been continually disputed. The problem of elucidating the meaning of Marxism stems from a number of factors. Marx and his closest colleague and alter ego, Engels, never wrote any coherently interrelated analysis of all their major ideas, and any synthesis has been provided by their disciples and epigoni. Not surprisingly in an author who wrote so widely during a long career, there is some change of perspective or difference of nuance in parts of the theories. Some of the confusion is due to the reception and selectivity of the Marxist ideas by later theorists or by parties and political movements claiming to be inspired by Marx, but using or emphasizing only those parts of the ideas to which they were attracted.

In addition, Marxism is an intellectual structure which continues to grow as each disciple or interpreter adds his own contribution to the original scaffolding and claims to be the exponent of the true faith. Each student must decide whether Marxists such as Lenin, Trotsky, Stalin, Kautsky, Plekhanov, Luxemburg, Gramsci, Bernstein, Lukacs, Tito, Castro, or Mao are to be included in the intellectual line of succession. Similarly, students must assess the degree to which Marxism is related to other forms of contemporary thought, such as psychoanalysis, existentialism, phenomenology, linguistics, or avant-garde culture.

But the problem of elucidation is compounded when the ideas are deliberately abused or distorted by theorists or by regimes which have bestowed a halo of certitude on their respective versions of the Marxist credo. Even as sympathetic a writer as Jean-Paul Sartre has castigated Marxist intellectuals who have thought to serve the Communist Party by "distorting experience, by overlooking embarrassing details, by grossly oversimplifying data, and above all by conceptualizing an event before studying it."[2] One reason for the conflicting views of Marxism is the inherent complexity and intellectual difficulty, if not the abstractness and turgidity, of some of the writings. But some of the conflicting views are due to the lack of availability of the full Marxist canon; the development of Marx's thought has not been fully apparent. Important works such as the *Economic and Philosophic Manuscripts of 1844* and the *Grundrisse* of 1857–58 only recently became generally available. In 1968, one hundred and fifty years after his birth, there was still no complete edition of Marx's writings, although the 40–volume *Werke*, published in East Berlin, is a close approximation and allows the student to trace the evolution of his ideas.

The Marxist Method

It was primarily to distinguish their thought from that of the socialists of the early nineteenth century—unkindly characterized by Marx as "Utopian Socialists"—that Marx and Engels called themselves scientific socialists, claiming to be scientific in their study of society, economics, and politics. If Marx concluded his years of research in the British Museum as he had begun, by advocating and suggesting the inevitability of revolutionary change, this was due not so much to a belief that the existing social order was inhumane and intolerable, which is implicit in his writings, as to his conviction that he had discovered the laws of historical development which led to revolution. In the Preface to the first edition of *Capital*, Marx wrote that the ultimate aim of the book was "to lay bare the economic law of motion of modern society.... One cannot alter at will the economic reality—one can only shorten the birth pangs."

A cutting comment by Croce was that what Marx called science was really bad Hegelianism.[3] Clearly, the premise of Marxist methodology is the concept of the dialectic which Marx took from Hegel. "Dialectics," Isaac Deutscher said, "is the grammar of Marxist thinking." In *Anti-Dühring*, Engels defined the dialectical process as the science of general laws of motion and development of nature, human society, and thought. For Marx, the dialectic meant the transitory, impermanent character of form, the presence of internal contradictions in phenomena which are always in the process of change, and the inevitability of contradictions between form and content. "All relationships," Marx wrote in *The Poverty of Philosophy*, "coexist simultaneously and are mutually supporting." Hegel had regarded the real world as the external form of the "Idea," and history as the unfolding of the spirit of consciousness of freedom. Marx, claiming to have turned Hegel upside down and set him right side up, treated the "Idea" as nothing but the material world reflected by the human mind, and as the outcome of objective conditions and circumstances. Men were simultaneously the authors and actors of their own history, and the history of men is one of transformation of the world and of themselves.

The Nature of History

The fundamental analytic concept of Marx, resulting from the dialectic approach, was his materialist conception of history. Later Marxists and theorists, especially Stalin, popularized the term *dialectical materialism*, but Marx himself did not use that phrase. Marx, and more particularly Engels, in a number of letters in the later years of their lives, were to qualify and soften the seeming rigidity and determinism in which their conception of history was cast. But the basic theory was that the mode of production of the material means of life in any society conditioned the political, social, and intellectual processes and the relationships among men. The final causes of all social changes and political revolutions were to be sought not in the philosophy but in the economics of each particular epoch.

The mode of production—the way in which a society produces and exchanges its goods and the manner in which it uses techniques, tools, skills, and knowledge—was, for Marx, the ultimately determining element in history. Social being determines consciousness, and not the reverse, as Hegel and the idealists had argued. The ruling ideas of any society are the expression of material conditions or relationships, the ideas of the ruling class. The economic "substructure"—the forces of production and the relations of production—gave rise to the "superstructure," the ideas and beliefs of the society. Yet, the Marxist writings are not always clear or consistent about the exact elements included in the "substructure" and the "superstructure," especially the latter, which at differing times included politics, esthetics, morals, philosophy, law, and theology, and excluded scientific knowledge and linguistics. And the extent to which the "superstructure" could influence, or exist independently of, the "substructure" has been subject to debate.

Students have differed on whether to see Marxism as a deterministic or a voluntaristic philosophy. The Marxist view is that men make their own history, but not under circumstances they choose themselves. For some analysts, this has meant economic determinism or impersonal laws controlling action. Others have stressed the necessity to act, individual responsibility, and the significance of historical accident. For an activist like Lenin, consciousness and will were often independent and decisive factors, necessary to make a revolution. But the logical paradox remains of a Marx devoting his life to fomenting a revolution he believed to be inevitable.

A related problem has been that of the nature of moral values. If the dialectical process implies that ideas are in constant change, and if morality, as part of the superstructure, is the outcome of changing material conditions and the interests of the ruling class, this process suggests an acceptance of moral relativism. Yet many Marxists would be reluctant to acknowledge the absence of absolute moral standards in Marxism or to deny that the future Communist society would embody the right ethical values.

A basic idea of Marxist theory, proclaimed in *The Communist Manifesto*, is that history is propelled by struggles between classes. One curiosity of Marxism is the absence of definition or extensive analysis of the crucial concept of "class," although the Marxist writings are replete with allusions to it. It is clearly apparent that classes were related to each other by the different processes of production. Social relationships arose from the existing forces of production, and the existence of classes was bound up with particular historic phases in the development of production. The essential relationship between the classes was the conflict between those who owned the means of production in any society and those who did not. Illustrative of the operation of the dialectical process, contradictions inevitably arise between the forces of production (the techniques and tools employed) and the relations of production (the manner in which men are related to each other). The forces of production are continually changing because of innovation and technological development, while the relations of production usually remain unchanged. This contradiction, and the ensuing antagonisms it causes, eventually become so acute as to lead to a revolution against the existing social system.

This is the core of the Marxist explanation of the historical process and of the change from one social system to another, each system being characterized by a particular kind of social relationship. In its broad sweep of human history, Marxist theory usually differentiated five successive, general types of social relationships, although sometimes Marx and Engels alluded to four different modes of production—the Asiatic, the ancient, the feudal, and the modern bourgeois types. The five types of social relationships usually mentioned were primitive communism with its condition of general equality; slavery with its slave-owning and slave classes; feudalism with its lords of the manor and serfs; capitalism with its capitalists and proletariat; and the future classless communist society. Since Marx paid little attention to the first three stages of history, and since he regarded any speculation on any detail of the nature or features of a future communist society to be utopian and unprofitable, his basic preoccupation was the analysis of the capitalist system. In this analysis, his empirical material was drawn largely from British sources, and the Marxist theory is grounded in the factual details of nineteenth-century British industrialism, the prototype of the capitalist system.

The Capitalist Society

Marx had high praise for the unparalleled industrial progress and technical advances of the capitalist system, and sometimes waxed lyrical over them. But he also noted the increased role of industry in the economic system, the trend of industrial systems to concentration and monopoly, and the periodic economic crises, ever-increasing in severity. The Marxist economic theory of capitalism was grounded in the concepts of the theory of value and of surplus value, essentially a theory of exploitation. The exchange value of all commodities was derived from the socially necessary labor time embodied in them; the property common to all commodities is that they are products of labor. Since the value of labor power is the amount of socially necessary labor time needed for its production, as is the case with all other commodities, and since labor alone is the source of value, the income obtained by capitalists and land-lords is in fact the surplus value produced by the workers. This value is produced by the proletariat, who make available for the capitalist class the amount of its labor time in excess of that necessary to create the means for its own subsistence. In capitalism, "that laborer alone is productive, who produces a surplus value for the capitalist, and thus works for the self-expansion of capital." [4] This surplus value, the profit of the capitalist, was the source for the accumulation of further capital.

The internal logic of capitalism would lead to industrial expansion, increasing use of machinery, and greater productivity of labor. Thus, the ratio of constant capital (machinery and equipment) to variable capital (labor) in the productive process would be increased; capitalism meant an increasing "organic composition of capital." Unemployment would increase, wages would be held down, and insufficient aggregate demand would occur. At the same time, the relative decline in the use of labor would lead to difficulty in the accumulation of capital and to a tendency for the rate of profits to fall, since profit sprang from the use of labor power. To maintain or increase the total amount of profit, the capitalist was obliged to expand the scale of his enterprise. Accumulation of capital was increasingly accompanied by a concentration of capital and a growing monopolization of industry, and ever-severe business crises. Capitalism thus carried the seeds of its own destruction, since it created an irreconcilable conflict between the increasing centralization of capital and the means of production and the deteriorating conditions of labor, between an increasing production and limited conditions of consumption. There was increasing exploitation of workers through the lengthening of the working day or the increased intensity of labor, the maintenance of wages at subsistence level, a growing reserve army of unemployed, the growing immiseration of workers, the polarization of the capitalist and proletarian classes with the elimination of inter-mediate classes, and the sharpening antagonism between the two classes. This antagonism and the contradictions inherent in capitalist develop-ment would lead the proletariat to revolt against the system.

This analysis of capitalism as necessitating a fall in the rate of profit, industrial expansion, and business crises was applied by later Marxists to the international as well as to individual systems. In *The Accumulation of Capital*, published in 1913, the Polish-German Marxist Rosa Luxemburg held that capitalist expansion created a need for markets in foreign countries and therefore led to competition between the major powers for world markets, and thus to wars.

But Marxists were obliged to explain the existence of powerful trade unions, improved conditions, and higher standards of living, the refusal of crises to take the form predicted by Marx, as well as the political support given by the majority of the proletariat to their governments, above all in time of war. In *Imperialism: The Highest Stage of Capitalism*, a book much influenced by J. A. Hobson, a British non-Marxist, and Rudolf Hilferding, Lenin attempted to explain the non-revolutionary behavior of the proletariat in the major industrial countries as well as the health of the capitalist economies. Imperialism, the monopoly stage of capitalism, was the result of the concentration of capital, and of the creation of national and international finance capital organizations. This stage of capitalism was marked by the export of capital by the leading nations, as well as by the export of consumer commodities at favorable terms of trade. This prevented the rate of profit from falling because the capital was used in industries with a supply of cheap labor or in agriculture. In this way, exploitation was transferred from the home to the colonial country, and the home proletariat, living to some extent on this transferred exploitation, became an aristocracy of the working class. But at the same time imperialism led to the division of the world among the leading nations and financial groups, and would inevitably lead to war between them.

Political Power

The Marxist view of political power is largely confined to the state, paying little attention to other organizations or interests that may affect decision making. State power was regarded as the organized power of one class for oppressing another, and it was generally seen as coercive. In *The Poverty of Philosophy*, Marx spoke of the state as an objective power above the people, as the form of organization which the bourgeoisie adopt for the protection of their property and interests. In the better-known *Communist Manifesto*, the state in a capitalist economy was seen as the executive committee for managing the common affairs of the whole bourgeoisie. Yet Marx also defined the state as the government machine and as "a special organism separated from society through the division of labor."[5] This image has led observers such as Robert C. Tucker to point out[6] the unresolved tension between the Marxist conception of the state as the organ of class domination and as alienated social power.

At the core of politics was the conflict between classes. The struggles within the state between different conceptions of state authority, and between differing political points of view, were merely the illusory forms in which the real struggles of the different classes are fought out among themselves. In the capitalist systems, these struggles would lead to a proletarian revolution which would overthrow the bourgeois state when the conditions were ripe and when all the productive forces for which there was room in any society had developed.

The means by which the revolution was to be accomplished—by violence or by peaceful transition, by unilateral action of the proletariat or by alliance with the progressive bourgeoisie, by the creation of a bourgeois democracy, based on a free parliamentary system, as a necessary historical stage, or by the immediate passage to a proletarian regime— the nature of the transitional political organization between the capture of power and the future society, and the character of the future society itself, were all left ambiguous or were hardly discussed.

In the struggle for power, the proletariat was to be organized into a class conscious of itself both nationally and internationally; the latter because the working class has no country and should unite against the common enemy, the ruling classes of the world. Marx regarded as utopian "the playing with fancy pictures of the future structure of society." [7] But in a handful of references, Marx and Engels hinted that in the political transitional period the state would become the dictatorship of the proletariat. Whether Marx literally believed in the desirability of dictatorship in his later years, or whether his favorable attitude was limited to the period when he was most influenced by French Jacobinism, Babeuf and Blanqui, and for a short time by the experience of the Paris Commune in 1871, has been a continual subject of dispute. Some interpreters have seen a unity and consistency in Marx; others draw a sharp line, occurring in 1850, between the young insurrectionist Marx and the mature scientific socialist who appreciated the possibility of peaceful change. [8]

But the hints about dictatorship were eagerly seized on by Lenin, and the idea of a proletarian dictatorship became a crucial part of his political doctrine. The dictatorship was to be the instrument through which the working class would rule after the successful revolution. Lenin did not believe that the dictatorship would require an oppressive governmental machine or a privileged bureaucracy. In *The State and Revolution*, written in the summer of 1917, Lenin referred often to the example of the Paris Commune which Marx had given as "the political form at last discovered under which to work out the economic emancipation of labor." The proletarian dictatorship would be a state without a standing army and policy, a state which would be a transitional step toward the final classless society.

After the dictatorship of the proletariat had performed its dual function of ending bourgeois power and laying the foundation for the establishment of the new society, the state would no longer be necessary and, logically, political power would not exist, since by definition there would be no class to oppress. The state would, in the words of Engels, "not be abolished: it will wither away." It would be replaced by an association free of class division and antagonism. The political function would be replaced by the economic task of administration. The future society would experience an increase of production to such a degree that the slogan of society could be: "From each according to his abilities, to each according to his needs." The dictatorship of the proletariat would thus have been the transitional stage to socialism, and finally to communism, the society in which classes had been abolished and in which mankind would have made the leap from the realm of necessity to that of freedom. The future Marxist society is one which is not only free of class distinctions but also anarchic in that it is free of political power. In spite of the frequent bitter and personal attacks by Marx on Bakunin and other anarchist writers in the middle of the nineteenth century, the projected future societies of Marxism and anarchism almost coincide. "Man," wrote Engels, "becomes . . . the lord over Nature, his own master, free." [9]

The Appeal of Marxism

Few social theorists or intellectual historians have remained unaffected by, or have neglected to pay some attention to, the Marxist cosmology. But the widespread appeal of Marxism in both developed and developing nations of the world has often seemed to require explanation. One suspects that this appeal is often due less to the incisiveness of its historical, philosophical, or economic analysis than to the aura of certitude and the assurance of ultimate victory that Marxism provides, to the ease with which general laws, propositions, or explanations are supposedly deduced from political and economic phenomena, and to the attractiveness of the future society in which coercion would be unnecessary and from which injustice and oppression would be eliminated.

Engels spoke of "the irony of history." Nothing is more ironic than the fact that Marxism is of much greater import as an emotional creed and as the ideological justification for those engaged in the pursuit of right and justice than as a logical, scientific, or intellectual structure. Many have been attracted by the apparent messianic nature of Marxism, in the conviction that it holds the key to a historic mission, and that its revolutionary theses provide the theoretical foundation for the creation of a political movement which can act as the instrument for the capture of political power. Many appreciate the fundamental optimism in Marxism. In *The Civil War in France*, Marx spoke of the higher life form to which the existing society tends irresistibly by its own economic development; and in *Ludwig Feuerbach and the End of Classical German Philosophy*, Engels wrote that "all successive historical systems are only transitory states in the endless course of development of human society from the lower to the higher." To those impatient or skeptical about the value of gradual reform, the uncompromising Marxist attack on the whole existing system has been admired.[10]

But the existence and power of communist regimes in the world has also made Marxism more appealing. Few today would echo the enthusiasm of a Lincoln Steffens in his comment on the Soviet Union: "I have seen the future and it works," or share the naive views expressed by Sidney and Beatrice Webb in their *Soviet Civilization*. Yet the image of the Soviet Union as a powerful industrial state and the second military nation in the world has exerted a magnetic pull, especially on many in the developing nations who are searching for the way to economic modernization and political development. Moreover, in a world where all regimes have been obliged, to some degree, to engage in economic planning, any lessons to be learned from systems in which state planning has been fundamental will be welcomed.

The interaction between Marxist theory and communist practice has been complex, but fifty years of communist rule has tended to show that action determines the meaning of theory rather than theory determining the nature of action.[11] In the Soviet Union, especially under Stalin's domination, with its control over all sources of political power, physical liquidation of dissenters and rivals, and imposition of ideological conformity, theory has become ideology, an official version of the truth and a support for the regime. While making no theoretical contribution to the Marxist canon, Stalin appears to have ransacked the writings of Marx and Lenin for key phrases or passages to support his major policies, "socialism in one country" and collectivism.

Yet it is just this Stalinist emphasis on the necessity for internal industrial and agricultural development and strong dictatorial powers to control the economy and society that has led some to see Marxism and its communist embodiment as the most useful guide for the modernization of society and as justification for a ruthless policy of forced saving.[12] Writers on political development have at times seen Stalinist totalitarianism as a necessary by-product of rapid industrialization.

The Inadequacies of Marxism

To some extent we are all Marxists now. No one can ignore the importance of economic factors in analyzing past or contemporary societies, or forget that all phenomena are interrelated in a continuing process. Marxism has provided both a plausible conceptual framework and many perceptive insights as by-products of its analysis: the increase in monopoly organization, the inherent tendency to increase industrial production, the alliance of France and Russia and the resultant world war.

Yet Marxism has also proved to be both methodologically deficient and inaccurate in analysis. History, as Marx himself illustrated in *The Eighteenth Brumaire of Louis Bonaparte*, is frequently the story of the absence, rather than the presence, of class struggle. The Marxist concepts of inevitable "contradictions within the economic base," of tensions between "the forces of production" and "the relations of production," of the "determining" or "conditioning" role of the mode of production, of the relationship between property and class, are all riddled with ambiguity. It seems to be most undialectical for the dialectical process to end with the victory of the proletariat. Indeed, the process seems to be possessed of a built-in Marxist bias, and its operation bears out Böhm-Bawerk's criticism of Marxian economics, that it is a case of "putting only white balls in an urn in order to take out a white one."[13] Reading some of the Marxian views—the support for Germany in the war against France in 1870, the argument that Germany could skip the historical stage of bourgeois supremacy, the compromises on the question of nationalism, the equivocal statements on whether Russia was destined to pass through a capitalist stage—it is easy to mistake scientific analysis for political or even sometimes chauvinist prejudice.

Clearly, many of the Marxist predictions about the course of history have not been fulfilled. In developed nations it is far from true that "the proletariat has nothing to lose but its chains." The welfare system, policies that maintain a condition of full employment, social insurance, and the political influence wielded by representatives of labor, all argue the contrary. The condition of the mass of people in industrial countries has been one of greater affluence rather than of increasing immiseration. The degree of class conflict has been reduced, not intensified. The intermediate classes between capitalists and the proletariat have increased as a proportion of the total employed population with the growth of the tertiary sector of the economy. The predicated international solidarity of the working class has never fully recovered from the chauvinistic behavior of workers displayed in support of their governments at the outbreak of World War I.

In countries controlled by communists, the power of the state has greatly increased in scope and intensity rather than withered away. The dictatorship of the proletariat has meant, in reality, party or personal dictatorship, and has produced totalitarian or authoritarian regimes rather than systems without oppression. The experience of these states has shown that there is no Marxist economic theory available for immediate translation to deal with the problems facing those countries.

In most matters, as Daniel Bell has argued,[14] there is a lack of congruity between theory and fact in the Soviet Union. Moreover, the diversity of roads taken by the communist countries in recent years has demonstrated the infinite flexibility of Marxist theory. A sharp irony is that the successful revolutions which have been inspired by Marxist theory have occurred not in the most highly industrialized countries when "the conditions are ripe," as theory suggests, but in the less developed areas of the world. The ultimate paradox exists when, as in China, a "proletarian revolution" occurs in a country almost devoid of a proletariat. This paradox led the German Marxist, Karl Korsch, to regard Leninism as an appropriate theory for the developing nations but as irrelevant for the industrial countries.

Marxists have often claimed that Marxism is not a dogma, but a guide to action. Yet the theory has proved singularly unhelpful in dealing with empirical problems, concrete situations, or contemporary politics. Nothing in Marxist analysis sufficiently explains recent fascist or totalitarian regimes, or allows for the great diversity of political and institutional forms taken by noncommunist nations. Indeed, Marxist thought has often seemed to neglect or underemphasize the importance of political will and action. Changes in political tactics—on whether to ally with social democrats, sponsor candidates, or make electoral alliances—which, in opponents, is termed opportunism, become for the Marxist the objective requirements of the dialectic.

Revolutionary and Moralist

If Marx was a social scientist of undeniable genius, he was also a revolutionary who believed that philosophy should help change the world, and a prophet in the old Hebraic tradition. In his early work, *The Poverty of Philosophy*, Marx wrote that until the classes are abolished, the last word of social science will be "Combat or death, bloody struggle or extinction." In his Address to the Communist League of March 1850, Marx stated, in a passage that profoundly influenced Trotsky and Lenin, that "it is our interest and duty to make the revolution permanent until all the more or less propertied classes are forced from power, and the state power is seized by the proletariat."

Some modern critics have tended to understate the revolutionary nature of Marxism, but it is the fundamental characteristic of Marxism-Leninism. The major Leninist contributions were made in the area of strategy and tactics rather than in theory. For Lenin the working class could not spontaneously develop a class consciousness sufficiently revolutionary to overthrow the capitalist system, since economic struggle, the primary activity of trade unions, did not engender revolutionary consciousness or activity. Only a small, carefully selected party, composed of politically conscious ideologists and dedicated revolutionaries, could solve the necessary theoretical, political, tactical, and organizational questions, instill the needed class consciousness into the workers, and act as the vanguard of the proletariat. In the Leninist view, the party, when it had become a powerful tool, would operate according to the formula of democratic centralism. This meant that there would be discussion at every level of the party and at the election of all party bodies, but there would also be absolute concentration of power at the top, strict party discipline, and the subordination of the minority to the majority. Lenin also emphasized, in a manner in which Marx himself had not done, the desirability of the dictatorship of the proletariat as the political form to be created after the capture of power from the bourgeois state. The history of the Soviet Union has amply fulfilled Trotsky's prophecy that the Leninist conception of dictatorship would successively lead to the domination of the party over the proletariat, the central committee over the party, and the leader over the central committee.

Yet the moral and ethical implications of Marxism are profound. If the proletariat is the dispossessed class destined to end the oppression of the bourgeoisie in capitalist systems, it is also a chosen people given the mission of self-liberation in the journey to the apocalyptic end. "The proletariat," Marx wrote in the introduction to the *Criticism of Hegel's Philosophy of Right* in 1843, "represents the complete loss of man and can only regain itself, therefore, by the complete resurrection of man." This theme, more enunciated in the early writings of Marx but latent in all of them, has led a number of modern commentators to see Marxism as a religious drama, as a compelling myth of sin, suffering, and redemption with the Fall being the transition from primitive communism to a society with class conflict.

The Marxist analysis rests on a tacit humanitarianism. Schumpeter is not alone in seeing Marx as a moralist parading as scientist.[15] Marx is the most formidable critic of the capitalist system, and *Capital* is a devastating indictment of the wretched working conditions, poverty, and savage injustice to which human beings are subjected. Men would free themselves only by revolting against the social system. In the struggle against the system, the nature of man itself would be changed. By changing the system of class relationships, by the very attempt to change it, men might solve the problem of personal integration and freedom, and end the existence of "dehumanized labor."

The problem of "dehumanized labor" and the alienation of man has provoked considerable discussion recently with the publication of some of Marx's early writings. But for the Yugoslavian philosopher Gajo Petrovic, the idea of alienation is the central theme not only in

Marx's early writings but also in his later works.[16] Robert Tucker has also argued that the concept of alienation was central to both the younger and the older Marx, and that in his later works the concept became translated into economic categories. "The myth of the welfare of labor and capital was Marx's final answer to the problem of man's self-alienation."[17]

For Marx, man's own actions helped create an alien power which enslaved him instead of being controlled by him. Alienation was the result of several factors. The worker was separated from his tools; work was not part of man's nature and yet he was dependent on it. "Work does not produce commodities only; it produces itself and the worker as a commodity." The division of labor, entailing specialization, had become an "objective power" to which man must submit: man had thus been reduced to the level of an object. At the same time the objects produced were not the product of the worker. Man had become alienated from other men, while he had created the powerful gods and thus enslaved himself.

The "fetishism of commodities" has meant that social relations between men were really relationships between things, the products of men exchanged with each other. Money had become a "visible Divinity" which had converted all human and natural qualities into their opposites.

Alienation would end when private property was abolished, when men had freed themselves by revolution and had asserted themselves as individuals after overthrowing the state. Only then would self-activity coincide with material life, and man become social, human man. Mythology would disappear when man gained control over the forces of nature. Marx wrote that "The Kingdom of freedom begins only where drudgery enforced by hardship and by external purpose ends." Man becomes a free being, a being of praxis, a creative and self-creative power. Marx the moralist and humanist has joined hands with Marx the social scientist and the revolutionary.

NOTES

1   Isaiah Berlin, *Karl Marx* (London, 1948), p. 13.
2   J. P. Sartre, *Critique de la raison dialectique* (Paris, 1960), pp. 25–26.
3   B. Croce, *Come il Marx Fece Passare il Communismo dall' Utopia alla Scienza, Saggi* (Bari, 1948), pp. 27–28.
4   Karl Marx, *Capital* (New York,1906), p. 558.
5   Karl Marx, *Critique of the Gotha Program*, in Marx-Engels, *Selected Works* (London, 1950), vol. II, p. 31.
6   Robert C. Tucker, "Marx as a Political Theorist," in N. Lobkowicz, *Marx and the Western World* (Notre Dame, 1967), pp. 105–107.
7   Letter to Sorge, Oct. 19, 1877, in Marx and Engels, *Selected Correspondence* (New York, 1942), p. 350.

8 Bertram Wolfe, "Leninism," in M. Drachkovitch (ed.), *Marxism in the Modern World* (Stanford, 1965), p. 60.

9 F. Engels, *Socialism: Utopian and Scientific*, in Marx-Engels, *Selected Works*, vol. II, p. 142.

10 Sidney Hook, *"Marxism in the Modern World,"* in M. Drachkovitch (ed.), *Marxist Ideology in the Contemporary World* (Stanford, 1965).

11 Robert V. Daniels, "What the Russians Mean," *Commentary* (October, 1962), p. 314.

12 Richard Lowenthal, "The Points of the Compass," *Encounter* (September, 1960), p. 25.

13 E. Böhm-Bawerk, *Karl Marx and the Close of His System* (New York, 1949), p. 70.

14 Daniel Bell, "Ideology and Soviet Politics," *Slavic Review*, 24 (December, 1965), pp. 591–603.

15 Joseph Schumpeter, *Capitalism, Socialism, and Democracy* (New York, 1942), part I.

16 Gajo Petrovic, *Marx in the Mid-Twentieth Century* (New York, 1967), p. 32.

17 Robert Tucker, *Philosophy and Myth in Karl Marx* (London, 1961), p. 238.

PART ONE

Political Theory, Social Science, or Ideology?

From Theory to Ideology

ALL political theory has been a response to, or a reflection of, the problems confronting a society, the manner in which social relations are organized, and the way in which power is exercised. Marxism is no exception. It is a theory influenced by a humanistic Western tradition, the political echoes of the French Revolution, the revolutionary struggles of the mid-nineteenth century, and the growth of industrialism. It was one wave, and potentially the most significant wave, in the current of socialist and communist doctrines which began to swell after the third decade of the nineteenth century.

Marxism is also a complex theory which has been subject to multiple interpretations for reasons both internal and external to itself. As a doctrine Marxism is not always completely consistent, nor is it always easily comprehensible. Marx, as Elie Halévy once wrote, spoke in the language of the German philosophers of liberty, and this language, which contains phrases such as the "integral development of the individual" or the "free development of each with the free development of all," has raised problems of elucidation. In addition, it has become difficult to separate the "true" or "classical" Marxism of Marx and Engels from the interpretations provided by their disciples, who have emphasized particular aspects of the original doctrines.

Marxism is also a theory that stresses the need for activism and revolutionary change, and thus forms an unusual combination of social science, philosophical reflection, and polemical advocacy. But Marx's empirical research and historical analyses do not always bear out his sweeping generalizations on political or social matters.

In his article in Part I, George Lichtheim discusses, among other things, the relevance of Marxism to the contemporary world, the

(19)

connection between socialism and technology, the utility of Marxism for societies at early stages in the process of industrialization, and the relation of Marxism to totalitarian systems.

The major problem external to the logic of the doctrine itself arises from the fact that Marxism has become the formal philosophical basis of the political regimes where Communist parties or their allies have captured power. Marxism has therefore become both a supposed guide to action and the defense of the nature of the regime. In Communist countries, understanding of Marxism is inseparable from indoctrination and from acceptance of the actions of the regime.

The existence of Communist systems, ostensibly grounded in Marxist theory, has resulted in an ambiguous relationship between that theory and Communist practice. Many, like Lewis Feuer and Irving Howe, were distressed and disillusioned by the experience of Stalinism in the Soviet Union, and have suggested that theory has been abused and transformed into ideology. This ideology has served the regime by pretending to aid practical activity and by claiming omniscience about the course of history.

Marxism, like all other ideas, is perplexed by the problem of consciousness. Marx himself spoke of ideology as "false consciousness"— the distorted view of material conditions taken by a consciousness which was unaware of real relationships. He argued the need for true consciousness which would enable men to understand their position. In *Capital*, Marx wrote that consciousness may not be able to appreciate "the internal essence and internal form of the capitalist process of production," and that "conceptions formed about the laws of production in the heads of the agents of production and circulation will differ widely from these real laws and will be merely the conscious expression of the apparent movements."

Marxism cannot escape from the problem that individuals may not be able to perceive their true situation or the rationality of history. Nor can it resolve the dilemma that forms of consciousness are said to be related to changing historical situations and ideas shaped by material conditions, while at the same time Marxism is held to be objective analysis, if not the fixed truth. Ironically, Marxism has itself become the tool by which political actions can be defended and rule justified in the Communist world.

I

On the Interpretation of Marx's Thought

George Lichtheim

A CONSIDERATION of the phenomenon called "Marxism" has an obvious starting point in Marx's own reflections on the subject of intellectual systematizations. According to him, they were either "scientific" (in which case they entered into the general inheritance of mankind), or "ideological," and then fundamentally irrelevant, for every ideology necessarily misconceived the real world, of which science *(Wissenschaft)* was the theoretical reflection. Yet it is a truism that Marxism has itself in some respects acquired an ideological function. How has this transmutation come about, and what does it tell us about the theoretical breakthrough which Marx effected and which his followers for many years regarded as a guarantee against the revival of "ideological" thinking within the movement he had helped to create?

Regarded from the Marxian viewpoint, which is that of the "union of theory and practice," the transformation of a revolutionary *theory* into the *ideology* of a postrevolutionary, or pseudorevolutionary, movement is a familiar phenomenon. In modern European history—to go back no further—it has furnished a theme for historical and sociological reflections at least since the aftermath of the French Revolution. Indeed, there is a sense in which Marx's own thought (like that of Comte and others) took this experience as its starting point. In the subsequent socialist critique of liberalism, the latter's association with the fortunes of the newly triumphant bourgeoisie furnished a topic not only for Marxists. But it was the latter who drew the conclusion that the "emancipation of the working class" had been placed upon the historical agenda by the very success of the liberal bourgeoisie in creating the new world

FROM *Survey*, 62 (January 1967), pp. 3–7, 9–14.

of industrial capitalism. Insofar as "Marxism," during the later nineteenth century, differed from other socialist schools, it signified just this: the conviction that the "proletarian revolution" was *an historical necessity*. If then we are obliged to note that the universal aims of the Marxist school, and the actual tendencies of the empirical workers' movement, have become discontinuous (to put it mildly), we shall have to characterize Marxism as the "ideology" of that movement during a relatively brief historical phase which now appears to be closed. The phase itself was linked to the climax of the "bourgeois revolution" in those European countries where the labor movement stood in the forefront of the political struggle for democracy, at the same time that it groped for a socialist theory of the coming postbourgeois order. Historically, Marxism fulfilled itself when it brought about the upheaval of 1917–18 in Central and Eastern Europe. Its subsequent evolution into the ideology of the world communist movement, for all the latter's evident political significance, has added little to its theoretical content. Moreover, so far as Soviet Marxism and its various derivations are concerned, the original "union of theory and practice" has now fallen apart.

This approach to the subject is not arbitrary, but follows from the logic of the original Marxian conception of the *practical* function of *theory*. It was no part of Marx's intention to found yet another political movement, or another "school of thought." His prime purpose as a socialist was to articulate the practical requirements of the labor movement in its struggle for emancipation. His theoretical work was intended as a "guide to action." If it has ceased to serve as such, the conclusion imposes itself that the actual course of events has diverged from the theoretical model which Marx had extrapolated from the political struggles of the nineteenth century. In fact it is today generally agreed among Western socialists that the model is inappropriate to the postbourgeois industrial society in which we live, while its relevance to the belated revolutions in backward preindustrial societies is purchased at the cost of growing divergence between the utopian aims and the actual practices of the communist movement. From a different viewpoint the situation may be summed up by saying that while the bourgeois revolution is over in the West, the proletarian revolution has turned out to be an impossibility: at any rate in the form in which Marx conceived it in the last century, for the notion of such a revolution giving rise to a classless society has now acquired a distinctly utopian ring. Conversely, the association of socialism with some form of technocracy— understood as the key role of a new social stratum in part drawn from the industrial working class, which latter continues to occupy a subordinate function—has turned out to be much closer than the Marxist school had expected. In short, the "union of theory and practice" has dissolved because the working class has not in fact performed the historic role assigned to it in Marx's theory, and because the gradual socialization of the economic sphere in advanced industrial society has gone parallel with the emergence of a new type of social stratification. On both counts, the "revisionist" interpretation of Marxism—originally a response to the cleavage between the doctrine and the actual practice of a reformist labor movement—has resulted in the evolution of a distinctively "post-Marxian" form of socialist theorizing, while the full doctrinal content of the original systematization is retained, in a debased and caricatured form, only in the so-called "world view" of Marxism-Leninism: itself the ideology of a totalitarian state-party which has long cut its connections with the democratic labor movement. While the Leninist variant continues to have operational value for the communist movement—notably in societies where that movement has taken over the traditional functions of the bourgeois revolution—the classical Marxian position has been undercut by the development of Western society. In this sense, Marxism (like liberalism) has become "historical." Marx's current academic status as a major thinker in the familiar succession from Hegel (or indeed from Descartes-Hobbes-Spinoza) is simply another manifestation of this state of affairs. [1]

While the interrelation of theory and practice is crucial for the evaluation of Marx—far more so than for Comte who never specified an historical agent for the transition to the "positive stage"—it does not by itself supply a criterion for judging the permanent value of Marx's theorizing in the domains of philosophy, history, sociology, or economics. In principle there is no reason why his theoretical discoveries should not survive the termination of the attempt to construct a "world view" which would at the same time serve as the instrument of a revolutionary movement. This consideration is reinforced by the further thought that the systematization was after all undertaken by others—principally by Engels, Kautsky, Plekhanov, and Lenin—and that Marx cannot be held responsible for their departures from his original purpose, which was primarily critical. While this is true, the history of Marxism as an intellectual and political phenomenon is itself a topic of major importance, irrespective of Marx's personal intentions. Moreover, it is arguable that both the "orthodox" codification undertaken by Engels, and the various subsequent "revisions," have their source in Marx's own ambiguities as a thinker.

So far as Engels is concerned, the prime difficulty arises paradoxically from his lifelong association with Marx. This, combined with his editorial and exegetical labors after Marx's death, conferred a privileged status upon his own writings, even where his private interests diverged from those of Marx, e.g., in his increasing absorption in problems peculiar to the natural sciences. While Engels was scrupulous in emphasizing his secondary role in the evolution of their common viewpoint,[2] he allowed it to be understood that the "materialist" metaphysic developed in such writings as the *Anti-Dühring* was in some sense the philosophical counterpart of Marx's own investigations into history and economics. Indeed his very modesty was a factor in causing his quasi-philosophical writings to be accepted as the joint legacy of Marx and himself. The long-run consequences were all the more serious in that Engels, unlike Marx, lacked proper training in philosophy and had no secure hold upon any part of the philosophical tradition, save for the Hegelian system, of which in a sense he remained a lifelong prisoner. The "dialectical" materialism, or monism, put forward in the *Anti-Dühring*, and in the essays on natural philosophy eventually published in 1925 under the title *Dialectics of Nature*, has only the remotest connection with Marx's own viewpoint, though it is a biographical fact of some importance that Marx raised no objection to Engels's exposition of the theme in the *Anti-Dühring*. The reasons for this seeming indifference must remain a matter for conjecture. What cannot be doubted is that it was Engels who was responsible for the subsequent interpretation of "Marxism" as a unified system of thought destined to take the place of Hegelianism, and indeed of classical German philosophy in general. That it did so only for German Social Democracy, and only for one generation, is likewise an historical factum. The subsequent emergence of Soviet Marxism was mediated by Plekhanov and Lenin, and differs in some respects from Engels's version, e.g., in the injection of even larger doses of Hegelianism, but also in the introduction by Lenin of a species of voluntarism which had more in common with Bergson and Nietzsche than with Engels's own rather deterministic manner of treating historical topics. In this sense Leninism has to be regarded as a "revision" of the orthodox Marxism of Engels, Plekhanov, and Kautsky. The whole development has obvious political, as well as intellectual, significance. I have dealt with it at some length elsewhere, and must here confine myself to the observation that Soviet Marxism is to be understood as a monistic system *sui generis*, rooted in Engels's interpretation of Marx, but likewise linked to the pre-Marxian traditions of the Russian revolutionary intelligentsia. Unlike "orthodox" Marxism, which in Central Europe functioned for a generation as the "integrative ideology" of a genuine workers' movement, Soviet Marxism was a pure intelligentsia creation, wholly divorced from the concerns of the working class. Its unconscious role has been to equip the Soviet intelligentsia (notably the technical intelligentsia) with a cohesive world view adequate to its task in promoting the industrialization and modernization of a backward country. Of the subsequent dissemination and vulgarization of this ideology in China and elsewhere, it is unnecessary to speak.

In the light of what was said above about the transformation of Marxism from a revolutionary critique of bourgeois society into the systematic ideology of a nonrevolutionary, or postrevolutionary, labor movement in Western Europe and elsewhere, this contrasting, though parallel, development in the Soviet orbit presents itself as additional confirmation of our thesis. The latter assigns to Marxism a particular historical status not dissimilar from that of liberalism: another universal creed which has evolved from the philosophical assumptions and hypotheses of the eighteenth-century Enlightenment. The universal content is, however differently distributed. Liberalism was from the start markedly reluctant to disclose its social origins and sympathies, whereas Marxism came into being as the self-proclaimed doctrine of a revolutionary class movement. The humanist approach was retained in both cases, but whereas liberal philosophy in principle denies any logical relation between the social origin of a doctrine and its ethico-political content, Marxism approached the problem by constituting the proletariat as the "universal" class, and itself as the theoretical expression of the latter's struggle for emancipation: conceived as synonymous with mankind's effort to raise itself to a higher level. Hence, whereas for contemporary liberalism the unsolved problem resides in the unacknowledged social content of its supposedly universal doctrine, the difficulty for Marxism arises from the failure of the proletariat to fulfill the role assigned to it in the original "critical theory" of 1843-48, as formulated in Marx's early writings and in the *Communist Manifesto*. Whereas liberalism cannot shake off the death-grip of "classical," i.e., bourgeois economics—for which the market economy remains the center of reference—Marxism (at any rate in its communist form) is confronted with the awkward dissonance between its universal aims and the actual record of the class upon whose political maturity the promised deliverance from exploitation and alienation is held to depend. There is the further difference that the Marxian "wager" on the proletariat represents an "existential" option (at any rate for intellectuals stemming from another class), whereas liberalism—in principle anyhow—claims to be in tune with the common-sense outlook of educated "public opinion." This divergence leads back to a consideration of the philosophical issues inherent in the original codification of "orthodox Marxism.". . .

The difference between idealism and materialism was seen by Engels to lie in the former's claim to the ontological pre-eminence of mind or spirit, whereas natural science was supposed by him to have established the materiality of the world in an absolute or ultimate sense. The resulting medley of metaphysical materialism and Hegelian dialectics (first described as "dialectical materialism" by Plekhanov) was conserved by Lenin, but his own theory of cognition—which was what mattered to him—was not strictly speaking dependent on it. Matter as an absolute substance, or constitutive element of the universe, is not required for a doctrine which merely postulates that the mind is able to arrive at universally true conclusions about the external world given to the senses. Lenin's standpoint in fact is compatible with any approach which retains the ontological priority of the external world (however constituted) over the reflecting mind. Belief in the existence of an objective reality is not peculiar to materialists. It is, moreover, only very tenuously connected with the doctrine of nature's ontological primacy over spirit, which Lenin had inherited from Engels and which was important to him as a defense against "fideism."

The whole confusion becomes comprehensible only when it is borne in mind that the transformation of Marx's own naturalism into a metaphysical materialism was a practical necessity for Engels and his followers, without being a logical one. It was required to turn "Marxism" into a coherent *Weltanschauung*, first for the German labor movement and later for the Soviet intelligentsia. As such it has continued to function, notwithstanding its philosophical inadequacies, but it has also suffered the fate of other systematizations undertaken for nonscientific reasons. At the same time it has paradoxically served to weaken the appeal of Marx's own historical materialism, since the latter was supposedly derived from a metaphysical doctrine of the universe—or an indefensible theory of cognitive perception—with which in reality it had no connection whatever. . . .

The doctrine sketched out in [Marx's] early writings (notably in the first section of the *German Ideology*), and subsequently given a succinct formulation in the well-known *Preface* to the 1859 *Critique of Political Economy*, was "materialist" in that it broke with the traditional "idealist" procedure wherein ordinary material history was treated as the unfolding of principles laid up in the speculative heavens. The primary datum for Marx was the "real life-process" in which men are engaged, the "production and reproduction of material existence," as he put it on some occasions. In this context, the so-called higher cultural activities appeared as the "ideological reflex" of the primary process whereby men organize their relationship to nature and to each other. Whatever may be said in criticism of this approach, it is quite independent of any metaphysical assumptions about the ontological priority of an absolute substance called "matter," though for evident psychological reasons it was easy to slide from "historical" to "philosophical" materialism. Even so, the grounding of the former in the latter does not necessarily entail the further step of suggesting that human history is set in motion and kept going by a "dialectical" process of contradiction within the "material basis." Such a conclusion follows neither from the materialist principle nor from the quasi-Hegelian picture Marx drew in the 1859 *Preface*, where he referred briefly to the succession of stages from "Asiatic society," via Antiquity and the Middle Ages, to the modern (European) epoch. Marx's own historical research (notably in the *Grundrisse* of 1857–58) stressed the radical discontinuity of these "historical formations." It is by no means the case that the emergence of European feudalism from the wreck of ancient society was treated by him as a matter of logical necessity. Even in relation to the rise of capitalism he was careful to specify the unique historical preconditions which made possible the "unfolding" of the new mode of production. The notion of a dialectical "law" linking primitive communism, via slavery, feudalism, and capitalism, with the mature communism of the future, was once more the contribution of Engels, who in this as in other matters bore witness to the unshakeable hold of Hegel's philosophy upon his own cast of mind.

The reverse side of this medal is the ambiguous relationship of Marx and Engels to Comte, and of Marxism to Positivism. The point has occasionally been made[3] that in dealing with the rise of the "historical school" in nineteenth-century Europe, one has to go back to the intermingling of Hegelian and Comtean strands in the 1830s — mediated in some cases by writers who had actually studied under both Comte and Hegel. It is also arguable that Marx may have been more deeply influenced by Comte than he was himself aware, since some of Saint-Simon's later writings are now known to have been in part drafted by his then secretary. However this may be, it is undeniable that the general effect of Engels's popularization of Marx ran parallel to the more direct influence of Positivism properly so called. With only a slight exaggeration it may be said that "Marxism" (as interpreted by Engels) eventually came to do for Central and Eastern Europe what Positivism had done for the West: it acquainted the public with a manner of viewing the world which was "materialist" and "scientific," in the precise sense which these terms possessed for writers who believed in extending to history and society the methods of the natural sciences. While Marx had taken some tentative steps in this direction, it was Engels who committed German socialism wholeheartedly to the new viewpoint.

At first sight it is not apparent why a Hegelian training in philosophy should predispose anyone in favor of the Comtean approach, which in some respects stands at the opposite pole. Moreover, Marx owed more to the French materialists than did Engels, so that there appears to be a certain paradox in the notion that the fusion of Hegelian and Comtean modes of thought was mediated by the latter. It must, however, be borne in mind that the *Philosophie Positive* had two aspects. Insofar as it stressed the purely empirical character of science and dispensed with metaphysical explanations, it belonged to the tradition of the Enlightenment, in its specifically French "materialist" form (which was the only one Marx took seriously). Insofar as it aimed at a universal history of mankind, its influence ran parallel to that of Hegelianism. Now the peculiarity of Marx's "historical materialism" is that it combines universalism and empiricism. For Marx (e.g., in the *Preface* to the 1859 work), the historical process has an internal logic, but investigation into the actual sequence of socioeconomic formations is a matter for empirical research. The link between the two levels of generality is to be found in the interaction between technology ("forces of production") and society ("relations of production"). This interaction, however, is not uniform, i.e., not of such a kind that the historical outcome can be predicted in each case with reference to a general law abstracted from the principle of interaction. Unlike Hegel, Marx does not treat history as the unfolding of a metaphysical substance, and unlike Comte he does not claim to be in possession of an operational key which will unlock every door. Even the statement that "mankind always sets itself only such tasks as it can solve" is simply an extrapolation from the empirically observable circumstance that in every sphere of life (including that of art) problems and solutions have a way of emerging jointly. A formulation of this kind is at once too general and too flexible to be termed a "law." It is a working hypothesis to be confirmed or refuted by historical experience. Similarly, the statement that socialism grows "necessarily" out of capitalism is simply a way of saying that economic conflict poses an institutional problem to which socialism supplies the only rational answer. Whether one accepts or rejects this, Marx is not here laying down a "law," let alone a universal law. On his general assumptions about history, the failure to solve this particular problem (or any other) remained an open possibility. In such a case there would doubtless be regress, perhaps even a catastrophe. The "relentless onward march of civilisation" is a Comtean, not a Marxian, postulate. If the second generation of his followers understood Marx to have expounded a kind of universal optimism, they thoroughly misunderstood the meaning and temper of his message.

In relation to bourgeois society the Marxian approach may be summarized by saying that this formation contains within itself the germs of a higher form of social organization. Whether these latent possibilities are utilized depends upon historical circumstances which have to be investigated in their concreteness. One cannot deduce from a general law of social evolution the alleged necessity for one type of society to give birth to a more developed one—otherwise it would be incomprehensible why classical Antiquity regressed and made room for a primitive type of feudalism, instead of evolving to a higher level. In fact Marx held that the collapse had been brought about by the institution of slavery, which was both the basis of that particular civilization and the organic limit of its further development. In principle the same might happen again. If Marx makes the assumption that the industrial working class is the potential bearer of a higher form of social organization, he is saying no more than that no other class appears capable of transcending the *status quo*. What might be called the existential commitment of Marxism to the labor movement follows from this assumption. Like every commitment it carries with it the implied possibility of failure. Were it otherwise, there would be no sense in speaking of "tasks" confronting the movement: it would be enough to lay down a "law" of evolution in the Comtean or Spencerian manner. Belief in an evolutionary "law" determining the procession of historical stages was the mark of "orthodox" Marxism, as formulated by Kautsky and Plekhanov under the influence of Spencer and other evolutionists, but also of Engels, whose synthesis of Hegelian and Comtean modes of thought made possible this fateful misunderstanding.

In justice to all concerned, it has to be borne in mind that Marxism and Positivism did have in common their descent from the Saint-Simonian school. It was in the latter that the notion of history as a developmental process subject to "invariable laws" was first adumbrated in confused fashion, later to be given a more adequate formulation by Comte and Marx. The justification for treating these two very disproportionately gifted thinkers under the same heading arises from the evident circumstance that their contemporaries were affected by them in roughly similar ways. In general it might be said that Marx did for the Germans—notably for German sociology and the "historical school" (Schmoller, Weber, Sombart, Troeltsch, etc.)—what Comte had earlier done for Durkheim and his school in France. And this assimilation of Comtean and Marxian modes of thought into the canon of academic sociology was evidently rendered possible by their commitment to the idea of history as the special mode of societal evolution. In saying this one is simply stating the obvious, though on occasion this does no harm. It was Saint-Simon who had first laid it down that the proper business of social science is the discovery of laws of development governing the course of human history. To say that Marx, no less than Comte, remained true to this perspective is simply to say that he remained faithful to his intellectual origins (which in this case antedated the Hegelianism of his student days, since we know that he had come across Saint-Simonism while still a schoolboy). That human history forms a whole—in Hegelian terms a "concrete totality"—was a certainty he never surrendered. There is the same attachment to the original vision in his oft-repeated statement that knowledge of the "laws" underlying historical development will enable society to lessen the "birthpangs" inseparable from the growth of a new social formation. Insight into the regularities of history is, by a seeming paradox, seen as the means of controlling the future course of development.

In all these respects Comte and Marx appeared to be saying the same thing, and it was this similarity which led so many Positivists to describe themselves as Marxists: notably in France, where indeed this identification became a factor in the evolution of the socialist movement. Yet the differences are as important as the similarities. Comte's sociology dispensed with the notion of class conflict, which for Marx was the central motor of historical progress. The Comtean view of society not only posited the latter as the basic reality—over against the state on the one hand, and the individual on the other—but also elevated it to a plane where the "science of society" was seen to consist in the elucidation of an harmonious interdependence of all the parts. From the Marxian viewpoint this is sheer fantasy, a willful disregard of the reality of conflict whereby alone social progress takes place. In the subsequent evolution of the two systems, this difference in approach translated itself *inter alia* into the conflicting doctrines of Russian Populism (heavily impregnated by Comte) and its Marxist rival. There is a sense in which the defeat of *Narodnichestvo* represented the victory of the Marxian over the Comtean school. The Russian Marxists were aware of this situation, and down to Lenin's polemics in the 1890s, the need to differentiate themselves from the Positivist belief in the organic unity of society played an important role in the development of their thinking.

The last-mentioned consideration, however, also served to define the historical context within which the Marxian doctrine could expect to play a role in the formation of a revolutionary movement. When in the 1880s some former Populists turned from *Narodnichestvo* to Marxism, they did so because they found in Marx a convincing statement of the thesis that the economic process would "slowly but unavoidably undermine the old regime," so that the Russian proletariat, "in an historical development proceeding just as inexorably as the development of capitalism itself," would thereby be enabled to "deal the deathblow to Russian absolutism." In other words, what they found was *a theory of the bourgeois revolution*. The latter being a "necessary" process—in the sense that the political "superstructure" was bound, sooner or later, to be transformed by the autonomous evolution of the socioeconomic realm—it was possible to interpret Marx's doctrine in a determinist sense. In *Capital* Marx had indeed done so himself, to the extent that he had treated the "unfolding" of the new mode of production—once it had come into being—as a process independent of the conscious desires and illusions of its individual "agents." Hence the link between the "materialist conception of history" and the notion of "ideology" as "false consciousness."

What his contemporaries, and the first generation of his followers, failed to see was that the entire construction was strictly appropriate only to the evolution of bourgeois society, which in Western Europe was coming to an end, while in Russia the "bourgeois revolution" was about to be carried through by a movement hostile to the traditional aims of the middle class. Marxism as a theory of the bourgeois revolution was destined to celebrate its triumph on Russian soil at the very moment when it began to falter in the postbourgeois environment of Western industrial society. This discontinuity was later to be mirrored in the cleavage between the determinist character of "orthodox Marxism" and the voluntarist strain which came to the fore in the theory and practice of the communist movement. The latter, faced with the evident exhaustion of the revolutionary impulse which had accompanied the great economic gearshift of the nineteenth century, was increasingly obliged to seek fresh sources of popular spontaneity in areas of the world not yet subjected to industrialism (whether capitalist or socialist). At the theoretical level, the uncomprehended necessity to find a substitute for the revolutionary proletariat of early capitalism—an aspect of the bourgeois revolution, for it is only the latter that rouses the working class to political consciousness—found its expression in the doctrine of the vanguard: an elite which substitutes itself for the class it is supposed to represent. This development signifies the dissolution of the Marxian "union of theory and practice": a union originally built upon the faith that the working class *as such* can and will emancipate itself, and the whole of mankind, from political and economic bondage.

NOTES

[1] Cf. *inter alia* the treatment of the subject in *Karl Marx—Selected Writings in Sociology and Social Philosophy*, ed. T.B. Bottomore and M. Rubel (London, 1956), and the recent spate of editions of Marx's early writings. Historically, the interpretation of Marxism as the theory of a revolutionary movement which has now come to an end, goes back to the writings of Karl Korsch; cf. in particular his *Karl Marx* (London-New York, 1938, 1963).

[2] Cf. in particular his letter to F. Mehring of 14 July 1893, and the *Preface* to the English edition of *The Condition of the Working Class in England*.

[3] E.g., by F.A. Hayek, in *The Counter-Revolution of Science* (Glencoe, 1955), especially p. 191 ff.

2

The Role of Ideology

Lewis Coser and Irving Howe

STALINISM grew out of, even as it destroyed, a movement that had been deeply attached to the letter of Marxism. The older leaders of the Stalinist movement, who had once known what it meant to live in a non-totalitarian atmosphere, were trained in a school of exegetics that sharpened wits through prolonged polemics over the meaning of Marxist doctrine. In the world of their youth, a ready capacity to cite Marxist classics, and to cite them with some relevance, could bring prestige and political preferment. But the new Stalinist functionaries, those who were themselves products of Stalinism and had never lived in any other milieu, showed very little interest in Marxist or any other form of speculative thought. They no longer needed to engage in debates with brilliant opposition leaders, as Stalin had once done.

Priding themselves on being practical men, they attached very little prestige to intellectual work and betrayed no desire to emulate Stalin's pretensions as a political theoretician. They looked upon Marxism as a vocabulary useful in controlling followers abroad, a group of symbols that helped cement social loyalty at home, and a body of dogmatics to be guarded by professional scholiasts, who in turn were themselves to be guarded. As Stalinism grew older, its relationship to Marxist doctrine became more manipulative, though seldom to the point of being entirely free of self-deception.

Fascinated as they now were by the mechanics of power, the Stalinist leaders, if they read Marxist works at all, were likely to turn to those dealing with political strategy and tactics rather than those concerned with ultimate goals or values. Lenin's *What Is to Be Done?* or *Left Wing*

FROM *Dissent*, 4 (Autumn 1957), pp. 378–381.

Communism might still be read by them with a certain interest, for while the topics of these pamphlets were not immediately relevant to the problems of Stalinism, they could be regarded as manuals of political warfare rich in suggestion to political strategists of almost any kind. By contrast, Marx's philosophical and economic studies were likely to be neglected by most Stalinist leaders—even though the need to validate their claim to the Marxist heritage, as well as to give themselves satisfactions akin to those felt by patrons of scholarship, prompted the Communist parties to publish these works.

Like one of the dark heretical cults of the Middle Ages which celebrated the devil through the ritual and imagery of Christ, Stalinism missed no occasion for proclaiming its Marxist orthodoxy. It defiled the intentions of Marx, his ethical passion and humanistic prophecy, but it clothed a rejection of his vision in the very language through which he had expressed it. Not for the first time in history, the vocabulary of a great thinker was turned against him, to corrupt his ideas and mock his values. Unlike other totalitarian and quasitotalitarian movements, Stalinism was unable or unwilling to develop its own vocabulary, being an ideologically "dependent" system, an aftermath rather than a beginning.

Yet it would be an error to suppose that this dependence on the trappings of Marx's system was a mere useless survival. For many Stalinists it provided an indispensable means of reassurance: as long as the old words remained it was easier to evade the fact that new ideas had taken over. For the party, it facilitated the strategy of political access. The Stalinist claim to the Marxist tradition enabled it to compete for the allegiance of European workers who had been brought up in the socialist movements, particularly those who were taught to suspect the Social Democratic parties as reformist. To have surrendered the signs and symbols it had appropriated from Marxism would have meant to face the enormously difficult task of trying to establish itself in the labor movement through a new vocabulary and what it would have had to acknowledge as a new set of ideas. Strategically, it proved far more advantageous to appear as the defender of orthodox Marxism even while ruthlessly emasculating it. The humanist elements in Marxism were discarded, the passion for man that animates Marx's writing eliminated, and instead those aspects of Marx's thought were emphasized which might be said to be most tainted by the Hegelian *hubris* of claiming to know what the future *must* be.

So understood, Marxism could provide a feeling of having reached a "total view" which permits one to identify with history and act in accordance with its inner rhythm. The "essence" of history having been grasped, it then became possible to proclaim the primacy of *praxis*. From that point on, since there need be no further desire to question the underlying principle of social existence, strategy and tactics became all-important. The uncritical acceptance of a metaphysical assumption proved in practice to be a shield against any further assaults by meta-physical doubt or contemplative temptations. It was through works that the faith was to be manifested and tested. Theory, even while ritually celebrated, became an object of contempt.

This mixture of knowingness and a pragmatic rejection of abstract thought—a remarkable reflection, by the way, of the profoundly am-biguous feeling of the modern world toward the intellectual vocation—provided the Stalinist leaders and intellectuals with a sense of certainty in a time of doubt. And for the intellectuals it offered the sanction of doing, or seeming to do, something "real."

The elements in Marxism that have proved most attractive to the Stalinists were those most intimately tied to the nineteenth-century progressivism, a mode of thought still powerful in the life of the European "Left." Appearing before the world as fellow progressives—*fellow progressives in a hurry*—the Stalinists were able to utilize many aspects of the liberal tradition and to claim that far from being enemies of Western humanism—as, by contrast, many Nazi ideologues openly declared themselves—they were actually its true heirs.

Precisely to the extent that the left tradition in the West did adhere indiscriminately to a simple optimistic theory of progress, it became most vulnerable to Stalinist infiltration. For if all change tends to be impelled by the logic of history in a progressive direction, those who seemed to stand for the most change would also seem to be the greatest progressives. Put so crudely, the "progressivist" ideology comes close to intellectual caricature; but so, often enough, does political life itself. No Stalinoid intellectual in Paris would have been so unsophisticated as to accept the formula as we have reduced it here, but in the subtle writings of many a Stalinoid intellectual in Paris there was buried exactly this deification of "progress."

And precisely to the extent that modern progressivism committed itself to what might be called technological optimism—the notion that the growth of a society's productive forces automatically renders it "progressive"—did it, in turn, become most vulnerable to Stalinist influence. For the technological optimist, Dnieperstroy is an irrefutable argument.

Ideology in the Stalinist movement was both exalted and degraded as in no other movement: exalted in that it was constantly put to work and accorded formal honor, degraded in that it was never allowed any status in its own right but came to be regarded as a weapon in the struggle for power.

This relationship between Stalinism and its ideology followed from a fundamental attitude of totalitarian movements toward social and personal reality. The most terrifying assumption of the totalitarian mind is that, given the control of terror, anything is possible. In Orwell's *1984* and Milosz's *The Captive Mind* this idea is reiterated again and again, out of a despairing conviction that almost anyone can say the words but almost no one can apprehend their full significance. Given modern technology, total state control, the means of terror, and a rationalized contempt for moral values, you can do anything with men, anything with the past.

Reality is not something one recognizes or experiences; reality is something one manufactures, sometimes in anticipation, sometimes in retrospect. One day Beria is a hero of the Soviet Union, the next day a villain—which is neither bad nor unusual. What is new is that by the third day *he does not exist*. His past has been destroyed, his name removed from the records. Many political movements have claimed to control the present, and others the future; totalitarianism was the first, however, which systematically proceeded to remake the past.

To do this, it was necessary to regard words and ideas as instrumentalities that could be put to any use. Nothing in thought or language need impose any limit. As Milosz wrote: "*What is not expressed does not exist*. Therefore if one forbids men to explore the depths of human nature, one destroys in them the urge to make such explorations; and the depths in themselves slowly become unreal." (*The Captive Mind*, p. 215.) And Orwell, in describing the totalitarian attitude to thought and language, pushed everything to an extreme which helped make the reality all the clearer:

To know and not to know, to be conscious of complete truthfulness while telling carefully constructed lies, to hold simultaneously two opinions which cancelled out, knowing them to be contradictory and believing in both of them, to use logic, to repudiate morality while laying claim to it, to believe that democracy was impossible and that the Party was the guardian of democracy, to forget whatever it was necessary to forget, then to draw it back into memory again at the moment when it was needed, and then promptly to forget it again, and above all, to apply the same process to the process itself— this was the ultimate subtlety: consciously to induce unconsciousness and then, once again, to become unconscious of the act of hypnosis you had just performed. Even to understand the word "doublethink" involved the use of doublethink.

Marxism:
Consistency or Revisionism?

THE fact that neither Marx nor Engels provided a general, over-all synthesis of their doctrines and that Marxism has been an evolving set of theories for more than a century has provoked discussion about the internal or logical consistency of those theories. Though some philosophers, like H. B. Acton, have dismissed Marxism as a "philosophic farrago," and specialists in particular areas have been cautious in assessing the value of Marx's contributions, Marxism has generally been regarded as a remarkable intellectual achievement.

Yet those who accept the view that Marxism is an internally coherent structure face the task of reconciling apparent contradictions or else logically relating the various propositions found in the classical Marxist credo. Among these are the dialectical process in history, the controlling impact of economic factors in society, the nature of change through class struggles, the destined role of the proletariat, and the nature of the future society. But the economic interpretation of history or historical materialism is not necessarily connected with the appreciation of the operation of the dialectic, nor are the laws of the capitalist economy necessarily connected with the inevitable revolution and victory of the proletariat, nor are the humanistic attitudes and concern about alienation necessarily connected with the dictatorship of the proletariat.

On many matters Marx and Engels altered their emphasis or position, such as on true and false consciousness, the nature of classes, economic factors as deterministic, or the need for revolution. One example of the change in emphasis appears in the question of the interrelationship of individual behavior and social structure. Is capitalism to be explained by the profit motive or the acquisitive instincts of men? In his 1844 *Manuscripts*, Marx held that the ethic of capitalism was greed and competition among the greedy. In his later writings, including *Capital*, he held that competitive behavior depended on the market situation and was not to be explained in psychological terms. But, as Daniel Bell pointed out in *The End of Ideology*, "So far no Marxist theoretician has yet detailed the crucial psychological and institutional nexuses which show how the 'personifications' or masks of class role are donned by the individual as self-identity."

Is there a single informing spirit or dominating concept in the Marxist philosophy? Donald Clark Hodges is one of those who views Marx as a consistent writer in that he may have changed his position on occasion, but not his principle. For Hodges the central concern of Marx is his advocacy of the emancipation of labor and the relationship between this and the practice of working-class politics.

A second problem on the consistency of Marx results from the writings of the many disciples and interpreters who debate whether Marxism is an inviolate and closed system, or whether it must evolve in response to social and political needs. In the Soviet Union Marxism has gone through an evolution, changing to Marxism-Leninism, then Marxism-Leninism-Stalinism, and back to Marxism-Leninism. But the possession of political power, which produced these changing formulations, is not to be equated with doctrinal fidelity or true intellectual inheritance. The article by Charles F. Elliott exemplifies one aspect of the transmission of the Marxist inheritance through the differing interpretations taken by three major Marxist figures on the problem of how Marxism should relate to changing social conditions.

3

The Unity of Marx's Thought

Donald Clark Hodges

ALTHOUGH the only works that can accurately be called "Marxist" are Marx's own and the ones he wrote in collaboration with Engels, the question occurs whether there are two Marxisms or one. On the one hand, much has been made of the fundamental difference in orientation in the writings of the young and the later Marx. Scholars believe they have discovered divergent political commitments and corresponding models of social reality, which distinguish "original" from "mature" Marxism. On the other hand, the current fashion among those who argue for the unity of Marx's thought is to interpret his later works in terms of his earlier ones. A superficially plausible argument has been made for the view that Marx in his later works used the terms "oppression" and "exploitation" for specialized political and economic instances of "alienation," the analysis of alienation continuing to be his principal concern despite his abandonment of this term. [1]

Both of these theses disagree with the official Soviet interpretation of Marx's writings, which identifies "Marxism" with the works written after 1847, but proceeds to read back into his earlier writings the elements of his later theory. Although Engels himself mentions that the communist world outlook and dialectical method were first coherently presented in Marx's *Poverty of Philosophy* (1847) and in the *Communist Manifesto* (1848), Engels' authority alone is insufficient evidence for this view. [2] Besides, in a subsequent essay on "The History of the Communist League," he qualified this statement by noting that as early as 1844 in the *German-French Annals*, Marx had already formulated his materialist

FROM *Science and Society*, 28 (Summer 1964), pp. 316–323.

conception of history as the theoretical basis of a communist movement developing alongside that of the League and of Weitling.[3]

Actually, none of these interpretations agrees with Engels' subsequent view that the principal difference between his and Marx's philosophical communism and their later proletarian communism was a matter of strategy rather than of principle. As Engels comments in his 1892 Preface to *The Condition of the Working Class in England in 1844*, it is true enough in the abstract that communism is a theory encompassing the emancipation of society at large, including the capitalist class, from its present narrow conditions. However, his and Marx's youthful formulation of communism as more than a mere party doctrine of the working class was later discovered to be "absolutely useless, and sometimes worse, in practice."[4] For as long as the proprietary classes do not feel the burden of their own condition of alienation, and also strenuously oppose the struggle of the workers to abolish exploitation, "so long the social revolution will have to be prepared and fought out by the working class alone." Although the labor movement stands in need of allies, it cannot reasonably hope for assistance from the class of employers.

In Marx's writings before 1847, there is undoubtedly an emphasis upon social or psychological forms of alienation that are absent from his later works. Presumably, the shift of interest to economic and political forms of oppression meant a revised estimate of the effects of alienation upon the proprietary classes. In contrast to his youthful insistence that man loses his humanity in the process of exploiting his fellow man, Marx subsequently stressed the advantages to a ruling class and corresponding progress of the race resulting from man's inhumanity to man. On this point he would have agreed with Engels' statement in *Anti-Dühring*, that "without slavery, no Greek state, no Greek art and science; without slavery, no Roman Empire . . . [and] without the basis laid by Grecian culture, and the Roman Empire, also no modern Europe . . . [and] no modern socialism."[5] The *Communist Manifesto* itself contains a panegyric to modern industrial capitalism that admits of few rivals. In his youthful writings, concerned as they are with the depersonalization and self-alienation of man, Marx apparently believed that human nature was the principal support of social revolution. Later, he began to rely increasingly upon industrial development as the chief support of revolutionary communism. "No social order ever disappears before all the productive forces for which there is room in it have been developed," he wrote in his Preface of 1859 to *A Contribution to the Critique of Political Economy*. Thus, he eventually gave up his interest in psychological alienation, while ridiculing the philosophical or "true" socialist's efforts to enlist all mankind in the struggle to abolish it.

Although this shift of focus meant the abandonment of his earlier humanism, it did not involve any change of principle. As early as the *Economic and Philosophic Manuscripts of 1844* we find Marx committed to the same principle that continued to guide his theoretical and practical efforts in later life, namely, "the *emancipation of the workers.*"[6] Emancipation from what? The answer is the "laws of estranged labor" or, as he subsequently came to call them, the laws governing the accumulation of capital, surplus value or exploitation. In effect, the basic principle of Marxism is the abolition of wage-labor, forced labor that is not even one's own, but someone else's. Contrary to one widely accepted view, the young Marx was as much concerned with the laborer's low income and corresponding exploitation as with his loss of freedom and self-alienation. The laws of estranged labor express the estrangement of the worker as follows: "the more the worker produces, the less he has to consume; the more values he creates, the more valueless, the more unworthy he becomes. . . . It is true that labor produces for the rich wonderful things—but for the worker it produces privation. It produces palaces—but for the worker, hovels." To be sure, Marx was as much concerned with the subjective immiseration of the proletariat as with its material oppression. However, since the worker's self-alienation was shown to derive from his economic exploitation, the latter and not the former category is basic even to Marx's early writings.

In his earlier works, the term "exploitation" is synonymous with the utilization of natural as well as social resources, including labor. It is used in its most ordinary sense of getting the value out of something for one's own advantage or profit; hence, it did not have the narrowly technical significance that Marx gave to it in his later works. Yet, the question of nomenclature is less important to an understanding of the young Marx than the actual content of his writings. What needs emphasizing is that Marx's commitment to the emancipation of the workers implied a corresponding commitment to struggle against the bourgeoisie. On the one hand, he believed that the emancipation of the workers is a condition of universal human emancipation "because the whole of human servitude is involved in the relation of the worker to production, and every relation of servitude is but a modification and consequence of this relation."[7] Freedom for the workers has a humanist justification that makes it more widely appealing than does a partisan commitment to the working class. On the other hand, Marx was committed to serving the interests of the workers against the proprietary classes and to abolishing bourgeois property as the principal condition of wage-labor. As he described the social struggle in the *Economic and Philosophic Manuscripts of 1844:* "It takes *actual* communist action to abolish actual private property. History will come to it; and this movement . . . will constitute *in actual fact* a very severe and protracted process."

The theme of the emancipation of labor as the goal of revolutionary socialism and communism is reiterated by Marx throughout his historical and political works. This theme, and not the slogans of a "classless society" or the "abolition of private property," is central to a correct understanding of the political foundation of Marxism. It is repeated verbatim in *The Class Struggles in France 1848–1850*, in Marx's "Speech at the Anniversary of the *People's Paper*" (1856), in his *Address and Provisional Rules of the Working Men's International Association* (1864), in his *Critique of the Gotha Programme* (1875), and in his and Engels' "Circular Letter" to Bebel, Liebknecht, Bracke, and others (1879). [8] As Marx wrote in his inaugural address to the First International: "the economical emancipation of the working classes is therefore the great end to which every political movement ought to be subordinate as a means." Moreover, this emancipation must be conquered by the working classes themselves. On at least two occasions Marx equated the emancipation of the workers with the "secret" of the revolution of the nineteenth century. [9] For this emancipation not only depicts the goal of revolutionary socialism, but also points to the proletarian class struggle as the locomotive of change and as the driving force of recent history.

In this light the now fashionable thesis concerning the radical difference in principle that divides the writings of the young Marx from the works of his maturity is hardly tenable. This thesis is based upon the following arguments: (1) "alienation" as originally used by Marx in his *Economic and Philosophic Manuscripts of 1844* and *The Holy Family* was a romantic and basically psychological concept having little relevance to the labor movement; and (2) in these early writings Marx did not regard class struggle as humanity's lever for the achievement of communism. [10] Although these arguments can be supported by numerous quotations from the young Marx, they confuse evidence with illustration. It is true that the young Marx had something to say concerning sexual repression and the corresponding alienation of the self from the human body. But to stress these remarks is to present a caricature of his early thought that slights the central role of the "dismal science" in his treatment of alienation. Marx may have been a forerunner of Freud in contributing to what has recently been called "the unmasking tradition" in modern sociology, [11] but he was hardly an "alienist" concerned with the sexual basis of neurosis. Again, it is simply false that the young Marx founded socialism on love rather than on aggression, on class cooperation to the exclusion of class struggle. Although his early writings stressed the humanistic content of revolutionary communism and the role of the proletariat as the vanguard of an all-human emancipation from the material causes of alienation, their underlying commitment is to the economic and political emancipation of the workers.

The significance of the divergent emphases in Marx's early and later writings has to be sought, then, in a difference of strategy rather than of principle. Originally, the emancipation of the workers was conceived by Marx as the overcoming of alienation as well as wage-labor. Subsequently, he stressed the role of industrial development and capitalist accumulation by means of surplus value. Yet, the principle of the abolition of exploitation, whether formulated in terms of wage-labor or surplus value, is the common thread that runs through all his writings. We have here two fundamental strategies of organized labor: (1) psychological propaganda in the form of ethical humanism designed to win allies for the labor movement from among other social classes; and (2) objective alliance with the forces of technological change and the corresponding political movements supporting their development. The *Communist Manifesto*, for example, underlines the fetters imposed by bourgeois property upon economic growth and the unfitness of the bourgeoisie to manage the industrial process in the face of periodic crises and increasing unemployment. It examines the reactionary, conservative, and progressive roles of the various classes and varieties of socialism in obstructing or forwarding the emergence of new social relations compatible with industrial and technological change.[12] Thus, it completes the transition from a strategy designed to win friends and influence people by ethical suasion to one enlisting the impersonal economic forces of modern society on the side of the proletariat. In place of "alienation," we have "reaction" as the principal strategical concern of the labor movement.[13] In striving to abolish exploitation, Marx is now committed to progress instead of disalienation, to a progressive instead of a humanist political ethic. Communism is no longer motivated by the psychological vision of the completely fulfilled and well-rounded individual, but by the immediate political goal summarized in the slogan, "Workingmen of all countries, unite!" And communism is no longer a positive movement dedicated to the reintegration or return of man to himself, but a fundamentally negative tendency, supporting "every revolutionary movement against the existing social and political order of things."[14]

Typical of current interpretations of Marxism is the confusion of principle and strategy, end and means. The goal of Marxism, the emancipation of the workers, is logically distinct from the overcoming of social and self-alienation or of industrial backwardness and political conservatism. Its ethics of humanism and progress are merely strategical, i.e., means to this particular end. Marx, in other words, was a humanist and a progressive by convenience only. He was committed neither to

the dignity of man in general nor to the progressive ethos of the Enlightenment. Consequently, Marxism is consistent both with violations
of the traditional and "sacred" rights of the individual and with slow-
downs and industrial strikes that hamper the development of the productive forces. On the one hand, the unity of Marx's thought is a function
entirely of its leading principle, all other so-called "principles" consisting rather of rules or techniques for implementing it. On the other
hand, it is convenient to divide Marx's writings into two periods,
the period of original Marxism (1843–1846) and of mature Marxism
(1847–1883). This division, suggested by Engels' observation that
The Poverty of Philosophy (1847) was the first coherent presentation of the
communist world view,[15] corresponds in fact to different strategical
currents in his writings, to his youthful interest in alienation and subsequent concern for industrial and political progress.

Hitherto, we have said nothing about the doctrines of social revolution and proletarian dictatorship in Marx's writings. Although these,
too, have been identified with the leading principle of Marxism, they
are even more frequently confounded with its strategy for the labor
movement. Actually, the question of political reform or revolution is a
tactical rather than a strategical one. Although strategy and tactics are
both concerned with rules of method, strategical questions include the
long-run tasks of leading a party to victory, whereas tactical questions
are directed to the immediate and short-run problems of the struggle
for power. Marxist strategy poses questions involving the strengthening
and disposition of the main forces and reserves of the working class and
its potential allies. In contrast, questions of tactics lead to differences
over the specific forms of socialist struggle and organization appropriate
to comparatively short periods in the ebb and flow of economic life.
One should not be surprised by the absence of any correlation between
the strategical division of Marxism into an earlier and later phase, and its
tactical division into different periods. For, although strategy and
tactics are obviously interrelated, the same strategy may require a variety
of tactics, just as a single tactic may issue from different strategies.

In reviewing the recent literature on Marx, it is surprising how
many works entirely miss the connection between Marxism and the
labor movement.[16] Yet, the conventional interpretations of Marxism in
terms of science, philosophy, history, sociology, or economics are
insufficient to give unity to his thought without one-sidedly sacrificing
some of its content. One would think that the clue to Marx's thinking
would long ago have been discovered in the passage from *The Poverty
of Philosophy* in which he describes, in contrast to the economists or
scientific representatives of the bourgeois class, the socialists and communists as "the theoreticians of the proletarian class." As Marx notes,
the chief concern of these theoreticians is to discover the material con-

ditions necessary to "the emancipation of the proletariat and for the formation of a new society." In a similar vein Engels defined scientific socialism as the theoretical expression of the proletarian movement, whose scientific task is "to impart to the now oppressed proletarian class a full knowledge of the conditions and of the meaning of the momentous act it is called upon to accomplish. . . ." When we recall that it took Marx's two great discoveries, the materialistic conception of history and the theory of surplus value, to transform socialism into a science, is it not abundantly evident that the unity of his thought is to be found not in some liberal art, but in the theory and practice of working-class politics?

NOTES

1   A typical view is that of Fritz Pappenheim, who argues that the alienated or de-humanized human being was Marx's deepest concern and "the central theme even of those writings which on the surface seem to deal exclusively with problems of economic history or economic theory." See *The Alienation of Modern Man* (New York, 1959), pp. 83, 90.

2   See Engels' second preface (1885) to *Anti-Dühring* (Moscow, 1959), p. 14.

3   Lewis S. Feuer, ed., *Marx & Engels: Basic Writings on Politics & Philosophy* (Garden City, 1959), pp. 464–465.

4   *The Condition of the Working Class in England in 1844*, trans. Florence K. Wisch-newetzky (London, 1950), p. x.

5   *Anti-Dühring*, pp. 249–250.

6   *Economic and Philosophic Manuscripts of 1844* (Moscow, 1956), p. 82.

7   *Ibid.*, p. 82.

8   *Selected Works*, ed. V. Adoratsky and C. P. Dutt, 2 vols. (New York, 1933), vol. II, pp. 205, 288, 427–428, 440–443, 560, 568, 570, 633.

9   *Ibid.*, pp. 205, 427.

10 See Lewis Feuer, "What is Alienation? The Career of a Concept," *New Politics* (Spring, 1962), pp. 118-124. Ironically, Robert Tucker agrees in substance with Feuer's arguments, but rejects his conclusion. See *Philosophy and Myth in Karl Marx* (Cambridge, 1961), pp. 144–149, 169–174, 218–241.

11 Irving Louis Horowitz, "Social Science Objectivity and Value Neutrality: Histori-cal Problems and Projections," *Diogenes*, no. 39, pp. 22–25.

12 *The Communist Manifesto* (New York, 1939), pp. 19–20, 32–42.

13 *Ibid.*, pp. 19–20, 32–38, 39, 41.

14 See the *Economic and Philosophic Manuscripts*, p. 101; and *The Communist Manifesto*, p. 44. For other references to communism as a fundamentally negative movement that abolishes the present order of things, there are Marx's comments in "The German Ideology" and "The Civil War in France," in *Marx & Engels: Basic Writings on Politics & Philosophy*, pp. 257, 370.

15 *Anti-Dühring*, p. 14.

16 One of the very few recent interpretations of Marxism as a theory and practice of the labor movement is C. Wright Mills' *The Marxists* (New York, 1962). Although highly critical of Marx's sociology of labor, it at least recognizes "that Marx's model as a whole, and in virtually all of its parts, is built upon and around . . . [its] labor metaphysic . . . [which] provides the central thrust and the major political expectation of classic Marxism . . ." (p. 129).

4

Problems of Marxist Revisionism

Charles F. Elliott

SOME students have maintained that Marxism is nothing more than a critical method for studying society and economic history. In this manner the Hungarian Marxist Georg Lukács wrote that "orthodoxy in questions of Marxism relates exclusively to method."[1] But Marx felt that he had discovered far more than a mere analytical tool for the critical investigation of economic phenomena. He and Engels believed that they had discovered a fundamental social truth, one that was "true" in a sense that rival explanations of economic and social reality were not (e.g., those of the Utopian Socialists, of Proudhon, of John Stuart Mill, and of Bakunin). In his speech at the graveside of Karl Marx in 1883, Engels asserted, "Just as Darwin discovered the law of development of organic nature, so Marx discovered the law of development of human history."[2]

Historical materialism was not itself ideologically conditioned; it was not "false consciousness" as were other theories whose exponents failed to realize the true source of their own thinking: their class position. Thus Engels wrote in a letter to Bebel, ". . . as if a theoretically unsolved *social* question still existed for us." Marx and Engels consistently identified their own theory with "History." In *The Holy Family* they rejected any interest in what the proletariat (falsely) considered to be its goal. Instead, they argued, "the question is *what the proletariat is*, and what, consequent on its reality, it will be compelled to do." In distinguishing between the proletariat's "apparent" and its "real" will Marx and Engels were following the approach of Rousseau and Hegel. Such a distinction already foreshadowed part of the argument Lenin used a half century

FROM "Quis Custodiet Sacra? Problems of Marxist Revisionism," *Journal of the History of Ideas*, 28 (January 1967), pp. 71–86.

later to justify imposing "consciousness" upon the proletariat "from without." And in Volume One of *Capital* Marx immodestly observed, ". . . *world history* took a long time to get at the bottom of the mystery (i.e., the 'mystery' of 'surplus value') of wages. . . ." By attributing to "History" an active role Marx sought to invest his own theory of historical materialism with an aura of scientific certitude.

If Marxism had been merely a tentative economic hypothesis, there would have been no great heat generated over "What Marx Really Meant." The violent polemics over the "correct" interpretation of the many-sided legacy bequeathed by Marx have arisen precisely because Marxism presumes to be an all-embracing explanation of social reality, one that explains the past and the present, predicts the future, provides a general explanation of human suffering and injustice, and holds out the promise of secular "salvation."

The Bolsheviks have righteously decreed that Marxism must be accepted "as a block" and have argued that one cannot be a true Marxist and discard one part of Marx's teachings (e.g., his theory of the dictatorship of the proletariat) while retaining another component (e.g., the concept of the class struggle). Similarly, Karl Radek in his memorial essay on Rosa Luxemburg praised her for the realization that one must either accept or reject the Marxist theory "as a block of granite." But what is the scope of this "block of granite," and who is in charge of interpreting this sacred legacy? *Quis custodiet sacra?* . . . one cannot simply lay the appropriate "proof-text" from Marx or Engels beside the writings of Rosa Luxemburg or Lenin and mechanically decide who was "un-Marxian." The problem is the vastly more complex one of analyzing the basic components of Marx's thought (economic determinism, class state, dictatorship of the proletariat, utopian transcendence of necessity, etc.) and of seeking to determine which of his "successors," and in what manner, have essentially adhered to these basic concepts.

Marx and Engels bequeathed a highly ambivalent legacy, full of many diverse and contradictory elements. These internal contradictions within "scientific socialism," as well as the vexing problem of relating Marxism to the late nineteenth-century European scene led inexorably to the necessity of amending or adjusting the doctrine. How far was this "revision" to extend? In examining this problem this essay restricts its scope to an investigation of three of Marx's and Engels' immediate followers: Eduard Bernstein, Rosa Luxemburg, and Lenin. Each was a major Marxist theoretician and each treated the problem of "Revisionism" in a distinctly different manner, but, this essay will argue, only Bernstein and Lenin arrived at logical and viable political solutions.

A standard Leninist argument is that the death of Friedrich Engels (on August 6, 1895, of cancer of the throat) opened the door to the "betrayal" of the revolutionary content of Marxism. In this vein Paul Frölich wrote that Engels' death "removed a great obstacle to the advance of opportunism in the working-class movement, and it was not long before 'the mature and enlightened Engels' was being quoted as the chief witness in favor of reformism."[3] But, contrary to this interpretation, a strong case could be made that Engels himself, and not Eduard Bernstein, was the "first Revisionist" or the "first Social Democrat."

A central point of dispute in this controversy has been the correct interpretation of the "Preface" written by Engels in 1895 (several months before his death) to Marx's *The Class Struggles in France 1848–1850*. This "Preface"—along with Marx's "Preface" to his *Critique of Political Economy*, Marx's 1872 Address in Amsterdam, the joint Marx and Engels' Preface to the 1872 German edition of the *Communist Manifesto*, and Engels' letters on historical materialism written in the 1890s—became a favorite "proof-text" for the "Revisionists." In his 1895 "Preface" Engels seemed to reject violence in favor of legality and gradualism as the best means to Socialism. In utilizing a Hegelian concept he noted:

The irony of world history stands everything on its head. [*Die Ironie der Weltgeschichte stellt alles auf den Kopf.*] We the "revolutionaries," the "rebels"— we are thriving far better on legal methods than on illegal methods and revolt. The parties of order, as they call themselves, are perishing under the conditions created by themselves.

In a self-critical passage Engels observed, in reference to his and Marx's attitude on historical materialism and causality in 1848–1849, "History has proved us, and all who thought like us, wrong." In this light Engels decided that an entirely new mode of the class struggle was necessary, one which utilized universal suffrage and parliamentarianism. With great enthusiasm he noted the mounting strength displayed in the rapidly increasing Social Democratic vote at the polls in Germany. "To keep this increase growing without interruption until of itself it gets beyond the control of the ruling governmental system . . . that is our main task."

When Engels sent this "Preface" to Germany for publication in *Vorwärts*, the official daily of the SPD, the Central Committee of the SPD decided, in view of the antiagitational law pending before the *Reichstag*, to delete some revolutionary passages from the text. At first Engels was angered at such treatment of his manuscript. He wrote to Paul Lafargue (Marx's son-in-law) on April 3, 1895:

[Wilhelm] Liebknecht has just played me a nice trick. He has taken from my *Introduction* to Marx's articles on France of 1848–50 everything that could serve him to defend the tactics of *peace at any price and of opposition to force and violence*, which it has pleased him for some time now to preach, especially at present when coercive laws are being prepared in Berlin. But I am preaching these tactics only for the *Germany of today*, and even then with an *important proviso*. In France, Belgium, Italy, and Austria these tactics could not be followed in their entirety and in Germany they may become inapplicable tomorrow.[4]

Despite his displeasure, Engels finally consented to the Central Committee's decision to make certain deletions in his "Preface." The result was that, until the publication by Riazanov of the uncut "Preface" in the Soviet Union in 1924, this censored text was considered to be Engels' "political testament."

Was the controversy over Engels' 1895 "Preface" merely a tempest in a teapot? How crucial were these changes made by the SPD Central Committee? Wilhelm Liebknecht (who died five years later in 1900) authorized seven specific changes in Engels' original manuscript. Two of these alterations were quite inconsequential. The remaining five were: deletions of references to the possibility of future street fighting, an omission of the phrase "the day of decision," and an omission of Engels' threat to the "forces of order" not to abrogate the legal constitution of the German Reich on penalty of freeing Social Democracy from the limitations of legality.

Did these changes justify Engels' charge, in his letters to Lafargue and Kautsky, that Wilhelm Liebknecht had "distorted" the essence of his (Engels') "Preface" by cutting out the "essential reservations"?[5] It would seem that Engels' anger was not directed at any real distortion, but rather at the uncomfortable realization that, aside from a few minor modifications (those which Liebknecht had eliminated) his (Engels') own position was precisely that which he and Marx had denounced over the course of many years. There was also, undoubtedly, an element of wounded *amour-propre* at the disciple's (Liebknecht's) insufficient respect for the sacred text of one of the two founders of historical materialism.

It was these serious doubts of Engels about the entire nature of the class state and the need for violent revolution that set the stage for "Revisionism." The main theme of Bernstein's *Voraussetzungen* is well known. Bernstein argued that Marx was wrong on several basic counts: that capitalism was doomed to collapse; that the property owners were growing smaller in number; that the proletariat's lot was growing progressively worse. Marx was also wrong, Bernstein believed, to use a "Blanquist" concept, the "dictatorship of the proletariat"; wrong to ignore the ethical reasons for choosing socialism; wrong to believe that his postulates (e.g., the theory of surplus value) were "scientific"; etc.

Bernstein's challenge to Marx's entire intellectual structure was, therefore, profound and direct, more far-reaching than Bernstein himself probably realized.[6] His negations had emasculated the Marxist pretensions to being an all-inclusive *Weltanschauung*, a messianic as well as a "scientific" truth that provided an "answer" for those "true believers" seeking a sense of commitment in a rapidly changing world where rationalism, empiricism, and skepticism had undermined traditional belief.

Bernstein believed that Marx's theoretical model of capitalism was outdated. Capitalism was being reformed from within by the action of cartels, trusts, and the credit system, all three of which were able to modify the abruptness of the business cycle and to falsify the Marxist assumption of inevitable and total capitalist monopoly. Another crucial factor which prevented the mechanical working out of Marx's economic laws *mit eherner Notwendigkeit* (as Marx had put it in his preface to the first German edition of *Capital*) was the pressure exerted by the trade unions in protecting the industrial workers. The trade unions were able to force the capitalists to pay the workers more than a subsistence wage (thus abrogating the Marxist "law" which decreed that no commodity could be paid more than its "value").

In the political sphere, Bernstein claimed, democracy and parliamentarianism were allowing the working class to advance peacefully their legitimate claims: "In all advanced (industrial) countries we see the privileges of the capitalist bourgeoisie yielding step by step to democratic organizations." This line of reasoning seemed to be a continuation of Engels' 1895 "Preface." Bernstein's claim to represent the logical development of Engels' final intellectual phase was buttressed by the fact that Bernstein was, while living in exile (since 1878) in London, a close associate of Engels during the latter's last years, and by the fact that Bernstein was Engels' literary executor. Another interesting example of the continuity between the attitudes of Engels and Bernstein can be seen in Engels' plea in 1891 to the French proletariat not to "rock the boat" over Alsace-Lorraine, for the German working class would soon come to power (legally, by means of the ballot box) and rectify this injustice. But Bernstein went even further than Engels in his conviction that political democracy was slowly but steadily forcing economic privileges to give way. Bernstein saw no important roadblocks to the steady growth of political and economic democracy. Engels, on the other hand, was more cautious (after all, he was a coauthor of the *Manifesto!*) in his enthusiasm for legal measures; he could not bring himself to believe that the ruling classes would give up their economic privileges without resort to violence.

Marx's picture of capitalism was wrong, Bernstein believed, and this disparity between an incorrect theory and economic reality must be frankly acknowledged. . . . The SPD should emancipate itself from outworn phraseology and come out in its true colors as a "democratic, socialistic party of reform.". . .

Rosa Luxemburg attacked Bernstein's position as *kleinbürgerlich* . . . her onslaught against Revisionism was more uncompromising and uninhibited than was Karl Kautsky's subtle protest. Kautsky criticized Bernstein's "gradualism" and argued that the SPD should pursue a maximum flexibility of tactics: "Social Democracy reckons with crises as with prosperity, with reaction as with revolution, with catastrophe and with slow, peaceful development." Lenin, like Kautsky, argued that the Communists should maintain a maximum flexibility in their tactics. But, as the Bolshevik seizure of power in 1917 and Kautsky's reaction to this event demonstrated, the Russian Marxist really meant what he said while the editor of the *Neue Zeit* drew back from approval of tactics (Lenin's) which "reckoned" very practically "with catastrophe," i.e., the chaos arising in Russia out of the First World War.

Rosa Luxemburg attacked Bernstein's abandonment of what she considered to be the Marxist *Endziel*, the taking of political power by the proletariat. She was very explicit: "And by the final *goal* I do not mean this or that conception of some future State, but that which must necessarily precede the establishment of any future socialist society, i.e., the conquest of political power by the proletariat."[7] Such a goal, she argued, was necessary to give a sense of purpose to the proletariat in its struggle against capitalism. Like Sorel, she understood something of the role of myth in creating proletarian consciousness.

An abandonment of belief in the objective necessity of socialism, Luxemburg maintained, meant a retreat into an "idealist construction" which based socialism on an abstract *Gerechtigkeitsidee*. But here Luxemburg was deceiving herself, for she (and Marx and Lenin), for all her stress on "scientific socialism," assumed an "idea of justice," i.e., the norm of the classless society in which there would be no more exploitation and injustice. The whole dynamic appeal of Marx's theory of surplus value was directed not solely to the intellect but to the moral sense of social justice and to the vision of a better and more humane life for mankind— the ultimate phase of Communism. Volume One of *Capital*, purportedly a dispassionate and objective account of the origins and operation of the capitalist system, not only bristled with such emotion-laden terms of opprobrium as "the shameless manner . . . its brutalizing effect . . . the horrors of this sphere."[8] It also spoke of a future society which would "produce fully developed human beings" and mentioned "a higher form of society, a society in which the full and free development of each individual forms the ruling principle." In addition, Marx asserted—in a passage that was hardly that of an objective social "scientist"—that "On the other hand, constant labor of one uniform kind disturbs the intensity and flow of man's animal spirits, which find recreation and delight in mere change of activity." . . .

Bernstein's theory of capitalism's "adaptation" rested, Luxemburg believed, on the assumption that the increase of democracy was an immutable law. This crucial postulate of "Revisionism" was false, *ein Luftsgebilde*, for the bourgeoisie would only tolerate democracy as long as the proletariat did not seriously challenge its power. She foresaw a decline of parliamentarianism, which, with democracy, would inevitably be discarded by the bourgeoisie. There was no "necessary connection" between capitalism and a democratic republic. Capitalism had historically flourished under a widely differing array of political superstructures, ranging all the way from absolute monarchy to a democratic republic. For, she maintained, "we find democracy in the most varying social forms. . . . Equally we find absolute monarchy and constitutional monarchy under the most widely varying social conditions."

Was such logic by Rosa Luxemburg dangerous to Marxist orthodoxy? What of the problem of the relationship between the mode of production and its corresponding political superstructure? For Marx in Volume One of *Capital* had noted that Don Quixote's utopianism lay in the fact that he did not realize that knight errantry was not compatible with all economic modes of production. But Luxemburg could have argued that there was, according to Marx, always a "lag" in the readjustment of the superstructure to the economic substructure. She also could have cited Engels' work, *The Origin of the Family, Private Property and the State*. In this historical analysis Engels simultaneously argued that: (1) the democratic republic was the highest (i.e., last) form of the state, the one in which the decisive struggle between the bourgeoisie and the proletariat would be fought out; and (2) that the rise of the Athenian city state demonstrated in its "pure form" the transition from the "gentile" form of social organization to the democratic republic. Thus Engels believed that the same political superstructure (the democratic republic) could be produced by two distinct (and quite different) economic modes of production, slavery in fifth-century (B.C.) Athens and capitalism in nineteenth-century Western Europe.

Bernstein had strongly emphasized that democracy was one of the essential *Voraussetzungen* for the development of socialism. *Rote Rosa* denied the validity of his set of priorities and asserted that, on the contrary, democracy depended upon socialism, not vice versa. Bernstein was wrong to equate democracy with socialism, she maintained, for democracy was only a device used by capitalism to conceal its exploitation of the masses. In her last major work, an unfinished analysis of the

Bolshevik Revolution, Luxemburg attacked Kautsky on similar grounds, i.e., that he accepted (bourgeois) democracy *without* socialism. [9]

From Rosa's perspective, Bernstein's faith in social reforms was misplaced, since reforms could not basically change the system. Marx, in his 1864 "Inaugural Address" to the First International, had revealed the same conviction. Bernstein, Luxemburg argued, substituted social reforms for revolution. If Social Democrats worked for social reforms from Bernstein's perspective, they would only strengthen the existing social system, capitalism. Bernstein sought to "blunt" the contradictions of capitalism; Social Democracy should, on the contrary, seek to suppress these contradictions (abolish capitalism). Bernstein's vain attempt to halt capitalism's logical development (by seeking to attenuate its contradictions) was "utopian" and "reactionary." Bernstein, as unrealistic *als ein blaues Auge*, as hopelessly utopian as a Don Quixote, had abandoned the struggle against the capitalist mode of production and sought to achieve a more "equitable" system of distribution within the existing economic order. Social Democracy, Rosa maintained (wrongly, since the "Marxist" parties of Western Europe were becoming increasingly "Revisionist"), realized the hopelessness of Bernstein's cause and sought instead to change the capitalist mode of production—the only way to achieve a more "equitable" distribution of the social product.

Social reforms, *eo ipso*, could not bring about Socialism which, Rosa declared, could only be realized by the *Hammerschlag der Revolution*:

The productive processes of capitalist society approach those of socialism more and more [she wrote], but its political and juridical processes, on the contrary, erect an ever higher wall between capitalist and socialist society. This wall cannot be lowered either by social reforms or by democracy, but, on the contrary, will be further strengthened and consolidated by them. The way to tear down this wall is only through the hammerblow of revolution, that is through the conquest of political power by the proletariat. [10]

Marx and Engels, Luxemburg asserted, had never doubted the necessity of the seizure of political power by the proletariat. Rosa (unaware that Wilhelm Liebknecht had made editorial cuts in Engels' 1895 "Preface") argued that Engels, in his "political testament," had been proposing tactics only for the "daily struggle" and not as a substitute for the proletarian seizure of power.

Luxemburg rejected, in a position almost identical to that adopted by Lenin several years later, "mere trade unionism," that is, the exclusive preoccupation by the trade union leaders with purely economic matters. She wanted, contrary to the German trade union tradition of *Gleichberechtigung* ("equal authority," i.e., between the trade unions and the SPD), to "politicize" the trade unions (as did Parvus), to utilize them not as substitutes for but as catalysts in the class struggle, as devices to energize class consciousness among the working class. She attacked another prominent "Revisionist," Conrad Schmidt, for his tactics which, she believed, reduced the class struggle to a mere fight for higher wages and a shortening of the working day, "d.h., bloss auf die Regulierung der kapitalistischen Ausbeutung." Contrary to the convictions of Bernstein and Schmidt, Luxemburg affirmed that the trade unions could not change the Marxist law of value; they could only fight a temporary, delaying action. The trade unions would not be able to prevent a decline in wages when the general decline (which was inevitable) of capitalism began.

It is of some interest to compare Rosa Luxemburg's polemic against Bernstein with Lenin's attack on the Russian Marxist-Revisionist Madame E. D. Kuskova. Kuskova, deeply impressed by the reformist currents prevalent in West European socialism at the end of the nineteenth century, issued her famous *Credo* (1899), a summons to the Russian Marxists to follow the example of the labor movement in the West and abandon "intolerant Marxism, negative Marxism, primitive Marxism (whose conception of the class division of society is too schematic)" for a "democratic Marxism." The Russian Marxists, Kuskova argued, should cease to talk about an "independent workers' political party," since the oppressive conditions of Tsarist Russia made such a goal impossible. Instead, the Russian Marxists should concentrate on the economic aspects of the class struggle—the organization of trade unions, the striving for higher pay and better working conditions. The socialist intellectuals, she continued, should abandon their sectarian aims and cooperate with the radical and (bourgeois) liberal opposition in a common struggle against the Tsarist autocracy. Her *Credo*, a description of what she considered to be the inevitable trend of the labor movement in the West, was clearly meant to be a model for the Russian Marxists to follow: "(the Western Marxists') striving to seize power will be transformed into a striving for change, a striving to reform present-day society in a democratic direction. . . ."

Kuskova's *Credo* became, like Bernstein's *Voraussetzungen* in Germany, the "Bible" of a major group of Marxist "Revisionists" in Russia. This movement, known as "Economism" because of its members' preoccupation with economic aspects of the class struggle, became very strong in the Russian labor movement at the turn of the last century. Indeed, for a time "Economism" threatened to sweep aside all competing tendencies in the Russian Social Democratic movement. . . .

When Lenin, in exile in the remote Siberian town of Shushenskoe, received Kuskova's pamphlet in 1899, he became furious at her rejection of revolutionary Marxism and immediately wrote and circulated among his fellow revolutionary Marxist-exiles a counterpolemic which, because of the number of its signees, became known as "The Protest of the Seventeen." Lenin's "Protest" strongly attacked Kuskova's rejection of the political struggle and castigated her "attempt to transplant opportunist views to Russia." In opposition to Kuskova, Lenin insisted that the Russian proletariat must strive to form an independent workers' political party, "the main aim of which must be the capture of political power by the proletariat for the purpose of organizing socialist society."

Lenin rightly considered "Economism" as a serious threat to the maintenance of a revolutionary *élan* among the Russian workers. In his famous brochure *What Is To Be Done?* (1902) Lenin set out to annihilate the influence of "Economism" among the Russian Marxists. He asserted that the *Rabochee Mysl'* ("The Workers' Thought": a theoretical organ which, in Lenin's view, expressed the doctrinal quintessence of "Economism") was guilty of a "slavish cringing before spontaneity," i.e., of allowing the workers to take the class struggle into their own hands. Thus, argued the Bolshevik leader, in the Russian Socialist movement, "consciousness was overwhelmed by spontaneity. . . ." Since Lenin believed that "there can be no talk of an independent ideology (i.e., a class consciousness untainted by 'bourgeois ideology') being developed by the mass of the workers," he fanatically opposed "spontaneity" as inimical to the acceptance of revolutionary Marxism by the proletariat. Lenin anticipated his critics on the crucial question of why the workers themselves could not (Marx and Engels, in general, believed they would) achieve revolutionary class consciousness.

But why, the reader will ask, does the spontaneous movement, the movement along the line of least resistance, lead to the domination of bourgeois ideology? For the simple reason that bourgeois ideology is far older in origin than Social-Democratic ideology; because it is more fully developed and because it possesses *immeasurably* more opportunities for becoming widespread.

In his attack on "Economism" Lenin also pointed out the parallels between "Economism" and Bernstein's "Revisionism" and the fact that Socialism (Marxism) did not follow automatically from the trade union struggle. Rosa Luxemburg agreed with these two points made by Lenin. In her critique of Bernstein she recognized that "Socialism, then, does not follow directly from the daily struggles of the working class of itself. . . ." But she would not have assented to Lenin's blunt rejection of "spontaneity," nor would she have agreed that the workers, untutored by professional revolutionary intellectuals, could not achieve "class consciousness."

Bernstein was quite frank to admit that he was fundamentally revising some of the basic Marxist doctrines. He asserted that there should be an open acknowledgment of the "gaps and contradictions" in the Marxist theory. Since Bernstein was an avowed "Revisionist," his position was quite distinct from that of Rosa Luxemburg and Lenin. But even these two "orthodox" Marxists had significantly different approaches to this problem.

Lenin did not admit that he had altered Marx, or that Marx "needed" modification in any fundamental manner. The Bolshevik leader bluntly decreed that all who disagreed with his interpretation of "revolutionary Marxism" were "traitors" (e.g., the "renegade Kautsky") to the "real" Marx. Lenin made some vital additions to Marx's teachings. Such supplements were primarily: the elitist party model, the strategy of using the peasantry as a revolutionary force to facilitate the seizure of power and Lenin's theory of imperialism. Lenin's "voluntarism" and his insistence on the "dictatorship of the proletariat" stressed certain parts of Marx's and Engels' writings and minimized other important passages. Lenin particularly ignored or discounted the trend toward Social Democracy by Engels in the latter's last years.

In part the dissimilarities between Marx and Lenin stemmed from the different situations which each man faced. After the failure of the European revolutions in 1848–1849 and except for the fleeting interlude of the Paris Commune (which, despite Marx's claims in *The Civil War in France*, was controlled by Proudhonists and Blanquists), Marx had to accept the reality of a nonrevolutionary Western Europe. This fact undoubtedly helps to explain why, during the last decade of his life, he increasingly turned his attention to Russia, where there was a vast social ferment in process following the liberation of the serfs in 1861 and where there was also a frustrated ("alienated") intelligentsia with much the same revolutionary frame of mind as Marx himself possessed.

Lenin's political world and revolutionary opportunities were quite different from those which Marx faced. . . .

Because his opportunities were greater, Lenin's political thought was, perhaps, even more action-oriented than was that of the author of the "Eleventh Thesis on Feuerbach." But Lenin's instrumentalist use of Marxism did not impair the doctrine's fundamental postulates. These assumptions were Lenin's own foundations. Without these axioms (laid down by Marx), Lenin could not have forged ahead to shape the revolutionary synthesis that is modern Communist ideology. It is true that without Lenin's rectifications Marx's revolutionary political myth would have receded further and further from political reality. But it is equally true that Lenin without Marx would probably have been merely another member of Russia's radical intelligentsia. Without Marxism to build upon, Lenin probably would have been a Populist, perhaps a member of its terrorist wing as was his older brother Alexander (who was executed for his participation in the unsuccessful plot to assassinate Tsar Alexander III in 1887). Lenin, after praising the "magnificent organization" that the *Narodovol'tsy* (members of the terrorist "People's Will") had created in the 1870s, declared that "Their mistake was that they relied on a theory which in substance was not a [correct] revolutionary theory at all. . . ."[11] In other words, without Marxism as a compelling political myth, Lenin could not have been a successful revolutionary. Without Marxism, Russia in 1917 could have experienced a March but not an October Revolution.

Rosa Luxemburg's treatment of the Marxist legacy was substantially different from that of Lenin. In contrast to the Bolshevik leader, she refused to do verbal obeisance before Marx, and was at times openly critical of him. Luxemburg's two most radical departures from Marx were her refusal to espouse Polish independence and her rejection of Marx's theory of accumulation. She refused to accept the argument of Marx and Engels that the emancipation of Poland (just as the emancipation of Ireland) had to precede the proletarian revolution. Luxemburg and her supporters among the Polish Marxists argued that under capitalist exploitation national "independence" of (a bourgeois) Poland would be a delusion; under socialism it would be superfluous. In her theory of capitalist accumulation Rosa Luxemburg was very explicit that she was revising Marx's "incomplete" formulation of the problem. She noted Marx's "glaring inconsistencies . . . [the] defects [of his reasoning] . . . wrong approach . . . longwinded detours . . . misleading formulation of the problem."[12] She added, "Here, however, we deviate from Marx," and "Marx's diagram of enlarged reproduction cannot explain the actual and historical process of accumulation. . . ." Lenin never made such a frank acknowledgment of a basic theoretical weakness of historical materialism.

But what was sauce for the goose (Rosa) was inevitably sauce for the gander (Bernstein). If she could "deviate" from Marx in her theory of capitalist accumulation, why could not Bernstein do likewise in his theory of reformism and social democracy? It would seem that the Bolsheviks have been far wiser than was Rosa in their denial that they have found any part of the Marxist legacy inadequate. For in criticizing Marx explicitly, as Luxemburg did with her theory of imperialism, she raised questions about the entire political myth of Marxism—issues which Bernstein was very eager to debate but which Rosa Luxemburg, a "true believer," was not.

Lenin and Luxemburg, faced with virtually identical challenges to orthodox Marxism—"Economism" and Bernstein's "Revisionism"—reacted similarly but with this vital difference: The Bolshevik leader was ruthlessly consistent in his conclusion that, in order to save revolutionary

Marxism, something must be done in the face of the workers' obvious reconciliation (mere "trade-union consciousness") to the existing social order. Lenin dealt logically with this situation by retaining revolutionary Marxism and renouncing democracy (since he believed that the proletariat, unaided "from without," could not attain revolutionary "class consciousness"—just as Robespierre believed that "the people" could not, without proper "enlightenment," express their "real will," *la volonté générale*). Bernstein dealt equally consistently with this situation by retaining democracy and renouncing revolutionary Marxism. But Luxemburg did neither. Accordingly, her political solutions (her denial of national self-determination, her concept of the "mass strike," her view of "spontaneity," her theory of imperialism, etc.) were necessarily inadequate to meet the key problem faced by twentieth-century Marxists: the dilemma of the nonrevolutionary proletariat.

Rosa Luxemburg's attempt to forge a new Marxist synthesis was—in contrast to Lenin's doctrinal innovations—a failure. The central reason that Lenin succeeded with his "Revisionism" (and Luxemburg failed with hers) was that he saw (and she did not) the necessity of dealing with a nonrevolutionary proletariat. On the eve of the Spartacus Uprising Rosa declared that the proletariat "needed no terrorism" because it had "historical necessity" on its side. Lenin realized, correctly, that "historical necessity" would be of little assistance in carrying out the seizure of power. He recognized that, since the working class had refused to adopt the Marxist revolutionary myth, this "consciousness" must be thrust upon it "from without." Rosa refused to adopt Lenin's solution for she would not admit—despite the growing evidence pointed out by such "Revisionists" as Eduard Bernstein—that the industrial proletariat overwhelmingly rejected revolutionary Marxism.

NOTES

1   Georg Lukács, *Histoire et Conscience de Classe*, translated from the German (*Geschichte und Klassenbewusstsein*) by K. Axelos and J. Bois (Paris, 1960), 18.
2   Engels, *Werke*, XIX (Berlin, 1962), 333. All references to this East German edition of the works of Marx and Engels will be cited as *Werke*.
3   P. Frölich, *Rosa Luxemburg: Gedanke und Tat* (Paris, 1930), p. 48.
4   *Selected Correspondence*, letter no. 243, pp. 568–569.
5   Cf. Engel's letter to Lafargue, quoted above, see fn. 4. Engels wrote to Kautsky on April 1, 1895 (*Werke*, VII, 623, n. 332), "To my astonishment I see today in *Vorwärts* an extract from my *Introduction* printed without my knowledge and dealt with in such a fashion that I appear as a peaceful worshipper of legality *quand même*. I am therefore so much the more glad that the whole [text] is appearing in its entirety in the *Neue Zeit* so that this disgraceful impression will be wiped out."
6   In his excellent study of "Revisionism" Peter Gay brings out Bernstein's essential

abandonment of Marxism in his observation that "In fact, it was quite possible to remain a Socialist [i.e., as Bernstein did] without being a Marxist." Peter Gay, *The Dilemma of Democratic Socialism, Eduard Bernstein's Challenge to Marx* (New York, 1962), p. 286.

7   Luxemburg, *Sozialreform oder Revolution?*, *Gesammelte Werke* (Berlin, 1925), III, p. 127.

8   *Werke*, XXIII, pp. 486, 487, 489. The quotations in the next two sentences are from the same work, pp. 508, 618, 361.

9   *Die Russische Revolution*, O. K. Flechtheim, ed. (Frankfurt am Main, 1963), p. 51.

10   Luxemburg, *Sozialreform oder Revolution?*, *G.W.*, III, p. 61.

11   *Chto Delat'?*, *Sochineniia*, VI, p. 135.

12   *Die Akkumulation des Kapitals. Ein Betrag zur Erklärung des Imperialismus* [1913] (Berlin, 1922), pp. 122, 269–270, 318.

Marxism
and Political Modernization

AN UNSTATED premise of the original Marxist writings was that they were relevant to regimes which were politically developed and to economies which were undergoing the process of industrialization. Revolution would occur in advanced industrial countries when conditions were ripe. In 1870 Marx wrote that "England alone can serve as the lever of a serious economic revolution. It is the only country where there are no more peasants and where property in land is concentrated in a few hands . . . where the capitalist form . . . has invaded practically the whole of production."

But contrary to this original Marxist view, no revolution based on Marxist theory has occurred in a leading industrial system. A major revision of Marx was made by Lenin and the Russian Bolsheviks, who held that a revolution could occur in an industrially backward country with an immature proletariat if that revolutionary movement were properly organized. Such a movement required not only a revolutionary theory but a party based on strict secrecy, strict selection of members, and the training of professional revolutionaries.

Bolshevism, as C. Wright Mills has argued in *The Marxists*, is not really a theory about advanced capitalist societies, but rather a theory about a backward, predominantly agricultural society that is autocratic. It has justified political ruthlessness, which has enabled the Soviet state to discipline its population in the interests of consolidation and industrialization, and has been a mixture of "progress and tyranny," as Barrington Moore called the Soviet Union. In his article, Richard Lowenthal discusses the relevance of Marxist theory and Communist ideology to underdeveloped societies.

Paradoxically, this revised version of Marxism and the rise of the

Soviet Union to its present industrial and military power have held considerable attraction for societies eager to achieve rapid industrialization and political modernization on national lines. Marxism–Leninism has allowed the defense of regimes in which power has been captured in countries without any substantial proportion of proletarians in its population by a Communist party dominated by intellectuals. A regime such as that of Castro in Cuba has shown that revolutionary adventurism, charismatic personal leadership, and a movement with a vague Marxist orientation are more important for the capture of power in an underdeveloped society than awaiting the maturity of objective conditions.

In his book *Marx against the Peasants*, David Mitrany has pointed out that "In every instance, from 1917 in Russia to 1949 in China, Communism has ridden to victory on the back of disaffected peasantries; in no instance has it come near to victory in industrialized 'proletarian' countries." The dilemma for Marxism in such a situation is amply illustrated by the tortuous fashion in which Mao Tse-tung, without wholly abandoning original Marxism, adapted his theory to meet the needs of China. "The peasants," wrote Mao in 1945, "are the source of our armies. They are the main foundation on which China's democracy rests . . . [but] I would not ignore the working class, politically the most conscious of all classes of the Chinese people and the qualified leader of all democratic movements."

In his article George Lichtheim is concerned with the predicament of Marxism in a situation where Mao is revising the original doctrines to allow "the broad peasant masses to fulfill their historic mission," as Mao put it, where the Soviet Union stands as an example of rapid industrialization and where Western Marxists are inclined to become Social Democrats.

5

The Points of the Compass

Richard Lowenthal

OUR thinking about world affairs has come more and more to revolve around the relation between the familiar East-West conflict and that other complex of problems which somebody has termed the "North-South struggle": the pressure of the underdeveloped have-not nations, with their new pride of independence and their rapidly growing populations, to obtain both more material aid for their own development and more influence on the world stage.

In both cases, we are dealing with the impact of revolutionary social changes and ideologies on the balance of forces in the world and the prospects of peace or war; yet the two movements concerned—totalitarian Communism on one side and revolutionary nationalism on the other—remain distinct in their nature and effect.

Monistic minds, of course, are forever trying to "simplify" the issue by telling us that the one set of conflicts "really" is a part of the other, or at any rate ought to be. To the Communist doctrinaire, the rise of the new nations is just part of the world-wide struggle against capitalist imperialism, and must naturally be carried on under the guidance of the "socialist camp" headed by the Soviet Union. Just so, to some last-ditch defenders of colonial rule and "white supremacy," all movements for national independence and racial equality among the peoples of Asia and Africa appear as the result of "Communist machinations"—at least when they first manifest themselves. Conversely, we may be told by well-meaning Leftists that all our troubles with Communist Russia and China are just due to the natural desire of these late-comer nations for "a place in the sun," which is not basically different from the equivalent desire of,

FROM *Encounter* (September 1960), pp. 22–28.

say, India; while hopeful conservatives (reported to include President de Gaulle) see the tensions between advanced, increasingly comfortable Russia and lean and hungry China as part of the world-wide "North-South" pattern, and look to a re-alignment of Russia with the old industrial nations of the West in a common effort to control and civilize the have-not upsurge.

The common error of all these attempts to reduce all the world's troubles to a single formula, to group all the conflicts along a single East-West or North-South axis, is that they underestimate the effectiveness and persistence of human beliefs fanatically held, and hence the crucial importance of the presence or absence of totalitarian Communist ideology for the nature of any particular conflict. But besides the error, there is in all these simplified ideas of the contemporary world also the perception—now dim, now more distinct—of an important truth: that the Communist and Nationalist revolutions of our time, however different in their nature and impact, originate from broadly similar historical and social situations—that they are, in a sense, alternative responses to these situations.

In fact, all those Communist movements which have conquered power wholly or chiefly by their own efforts—those of Russia, Yugoslavia, China, and Vietnam—have done so in societies which were faced with unsolved development problems in various stages. All of them have conceived Communism not merely as a means to achieve an earthly paradise of social justice, but to catch up with the advanced industrial countries and overtake them; and it is now generally recognized that their methods have proved remarkably successful in approaching the latter though not the former objective. It is, above all, as an engine for the forced modernization of an underdeveloped society that Communism is today admired by large sections of the intelligentsia of the new nations, while it is the peculiar price of using that engine—in ideology, in institutions of permanent totalitarian rule, and in subjection to Soviet imperialism—which repels many of them.

The real link between the future course of the East-West conflict and the rise of the new nations, the key to the influence they are bound to exert on each other, thus lies in the choice of a road of development confronting the Nationalist movements and the intelligentsia as their leading stratum. The crucial questions are: (1) Which are the factors in the situation of an underdeveloped country that favor a totalitarian solution to its problems? (2) What are the practicable alternatives? And (3) What influence is one or the other choice likely to have both on the country's internal evolution and on its relations with the outside world?

These questions form the underlying theme of Professor Hugh

Seton-Watson's study of the postwar world. Contrary to its somewhat misleading title,[1] this is not just another survey of the Cold War, but a thoughtful and original discussion of the totalitarian and Nationalist revolutionary forces which in the author's view now form much of the stuff of world politics. Its reader will not find, e.g., any systematic account of the course and motivations of American foreign policy since the last war, but a wealth of information on the world's crisis areas and the history of revolutionary movements in Asia, Africa, and Latin America as well as on the Soviet Empire.

It would be futile as well as presumptuous for me to attempt to summarize the contents of this storehouse of historical and social facts, or to try to give an idea of the sober independence of judgment and massive good sense which Professor Seton-Watson brings to bear on many concrete and critical issues. I prefer to be unfair to his work, and to concentrate on the argument of those central chapters, dealing with the forces of revolution and the nature of totalitarianism, which have a direct and general bearing on the problem of the crucial choice facing the underdeveloped countries.

This argument centers on the role of the "intelligentsia" in these countries—the group which has been torn from its traditional moorings by a secular, "Westernized" education, but cannot merge its identity, as did their Western predecessors at a corresponding stage of development, in a rising, individualist middle class, because the other elements of that middle class—private entrepreneurs and a modern civil service— are largely lacking. On the contrary, in some of the underdeveloped countries many of the younger, professionally trained officers are by social origin and outlook an extension of this new group, an "intelligentsia in uniform." It is this group which first becomes aware of the backwardness of its country and the poverty of its people, having learned to measure both by the standards of the advanced countries, and which, acting both from a "populist" sense of obligation to the people and from frustrated individual and collective ambition, becomes the leader of revolutionary movements for modernization.

Professor Seton-Watson points out that such a development is not inevitable. Where the ruling group of a country succeeds in combining thoroughgoing modernizing reform from above with the preservation of traditional authority, as in the Japan of the *Meiji* era after 1868, the new intelligentsia may be integrated in the new state and come to form part of a new upper stratum with its bureaucrats and state-licensed capitalists. At the same time, a thoughtful educational policy that takes care to develop elementary village schools at the same pace as the training of the intellectual élite may avoid the yawning gap between the latter and the common people characteristic of so many underdeveloped countries.

But such favorable conditions have only exceptionally been realized under a régime that retained some continuity with the past. In general, the intelligentsia is kept out in the cold as long as possible and correspondingly radicalized, be it by an independent autocracy of the traditional type or by foreign "imperialist" rulers. Hence when it comes to power, it does so at the head of a popular movement directed against the former régime—either after a direct revolutionary clash, or where this is avoided by timely withdrawal of the colonial suzerain, at least with a revolutionary ideology.

In most cases, then, a revolutionary-minded intelligentsia will sooner or later take charge of the modernization of an underdeveloped country, whether ex-colonial or not. Professor Seton-Watson points out that resentment of traditional Western influence and real or alleged exploitation, impatience to catch up and get powerful quickly, and lack of understanding for the importance of limiting the exercise of power by objective legal standards and for the value of tolerance for divergent opinions are likely to exert great influence on the mentality of such a group, and to make it incline toward uncritical admiration of the totalitarian Communist recipe for rapid modernization which has proved so strikingly successful in terms of power. He is, of course, well aware of such nontotalitarian Nationalist revolutions as that which created Kemalist Turkey, and of the fact that the final orientation of the revolutionary régimes created by the "Intelligentsia in uniform" in the Middle East, or of the Nationalist movements that have lately taken over some of the former African colonies, is still open. But he offers no general reasons why a modernistic, "populist" intelligentsia, once it has embarked on the road of revolution, should be likely to reject totalitarianism.

Yet as so much of the future is seen to hinge on this question, it seems worthwhile to inquire whether another approach might not yield a more definite answer. Instead of starting from the intellectual and psychological profile of the Nationalist intelligentsia, let us have a look at the task confronting them—the problem of "development" itself.

An underdeveloped country is not one whose people suffer from an innate, biological lack of aptitude for industry and modern organization; nor is it one, as the opposite legend maintains, whose people have been forcibly prevented from developing these aptitudes by foreign imperialist rule. An underdeveloped country is one whose traditional society did not allow the growth of sufficiently strong independent middle classes—the classes which in the West were the main promoters of the accumulation of capital, the creation of industrial enterprise, and the growth of a spirit of rational industrial discipline.

If such a country is exposed to the impact of Western capitalism from without, as almost all of them were successively in the past two centuries, its traditional social order is disrupted, but no functioning modern industrial society is automatically created in its place. Foreign enterprise may develop some extractive industries or export crops, but there will be no all-round growth of industry or improvement of agriculture. The subsistence economy of the countryside with its cottage industries may be ruined by the need for money payments and the import of cheap industrial goods, but no corresponding employment opportunities arise automatically for the rural overpopulation. Traditional beliefs are undermined by the impact of events rather than by missionary activity, but the ideas imported by Western missionaries or secular educators have no obvious relation to either the traditions of the country or its actual problems. Before, life may have been stagnant and poor if viewed from the outside, but it had a meaning that was understandable in terms of home-grown culture. Now this meaning, the assured role in society, is lost for millions at the same time as their material security. As a result, some may be richer, some poorer than before; most will have a longer life, if a colonial régime introduces modern medical methods; but nearly all will feel more miserable.

These effects are generally worse in countries which are open to the disruptive foreign impact without being colonized, than in countries where the "imperialists" take governmental responsibility: China and India are the classical examples. After the breakdown of the traditional order, the colonial power may ensure public security, health, a measure of education, the training of a civil service. But no colonial power in the age of *laissez-faire* ever dreamt of creating a new social order; none tackled the problem of all-round economic development.

The task of solving that problem, then, devolved on the Nationalist movements. It could, in the circumstances, only be attacked by public action—above all, public action of three kinds:

1. A policy of forced saving to raise funds for development which might in favorable circumstances be combined with foreign loans or aid.

2. A policy of state-directed investment, to ensure placing of these limited funds in such a way that all-round development would result, including such tasks as road-building or canalization as well as immediately profitable tasks, power as well as consumer goods, agricultural improvement as well as technical and administrative training.

3. The promotion of a cultural revolution to make people work-minded and development-minded, to tap human reserves by the emancipation of women, to overcome the countless obstacles to disciplined rational effort resulting from

traditional superstition—in short, to achieve what reformation, counter-reformation, and enlightenment combined achieved over centuries in the West, and to do so in the atmosphere of a demoralizing breakdown of tradition.

The achievement of these tasks is impossible with the methods of a liberal economy: if conditions were such that a liberal economy could work, the country would not have remained underdeveloped in the first place. It is extremely difficult in a liberal democracy, because it requires the concentration of a great deal of economic and social power in the state, and the constant taking of decisions which impose sacrifices and hurt many interests: the less the foreign aid and the greater the need for forced savings, the less likely is democracy to succeed. Finally, it requires the predominant role of an officially-favored ideology, which in the circumstances can only be a secular ideology, to bring about the cultural revolution.

Consider now, in the light of the foregoing, the attractions of Communist totalitarianism for an underdeveloped country. In its Stalinist form, the Communist ideology has been specifically adjusted to deal with the problem of forced modernization. It justifies a ruthless policy of forced savings in the name of "socialist industrialization." It proclaims the superiority of planned investment by the state over *laissez-faire*. Finally, it furnishes the militant faith needed for the cultural revolution, with its materialist attack on traditional superstition, its glorification of dedicated, disciplined work for the community, its emphasis on production as the highroad to national power and individual liberation from misery. It invests the uprooting of traditional life, the frightening impact of social and technical change, the bitterness of years of sacrifice with a meaning. And, last not least, it justifies all the privileges a self-appointed but dedicated élite may require.

Thus, Communist totalitarianism does not only appeal to some of the prejudices and *ressentiments* of the Nationalist intelligentsia: it points a precise path for their modernizing ambitions and offers a ready-made secular faith for enlisting the obedience of the masses. Yet there are also obvious drawbacks: they spring in part from the doctrinaire rigidity inherent in any totalitarian ideology, and in part from its links with Soviet imperialism.

An underdeveloped country that wants to plan for rapid development may need nationalizing *powers* against recalcitrant domestic and foreign capitalists; it will not necessarily *wish* to drive out the few native industrialists it has. It may find the expropriation of absentee landowners vital to its purposes; it will hardly find the experience of collectivization attractive. It may be both proud to get a heavy industry of its own and convinced of its genuine economic necessity; yet it may think twice before giving its development absolute priority over the need to improve agricultural yields or textile supplies for a rapidly growing population. A commitment to Communism would deprive its leaders of much, if not all, of their freedom of choice in these matters.

Again, a "populist" revolutionary intelligentsia about to take power in an underdeveloped country, however sincere in its desire to serve its people and raise their standard of living, may not be anxious to pledge itself to achieve a "classless society." Depending on the background of its national culture, it may find it unnecessary to prepare future trouble for itself by preaching a utopian doctrine. Yet without such a doctrine with its implied need for permanent revolution, it may find it possible to constitute itself openly as a bureaucratic élite while avoiding the specific form of totalitarian party rule, and to conduct the propaganda of the cultural revolution by other means.

Finally, while the Nationalist élites frequently start with a background of anti-Western emotions, nothing in their records suggests that they have an unconquerable aversion to Western economic aid, or even to Western private investments if offered in accordance with their laws and in the framework of their plans. Their natural preference is for taking aid from both sides while rejecting political interference from either. But the Communist dogma, with its basic assumption of irreconcilable conflict with the non-Communist world, justifies modernization by the road of maximum sacrifice—the road of absolute priority for heavy industry—precisely on the ground that every other procedure would entail prolonged dependence on "the enemy." Even now, the Russians accuse the West of trying to keep the new nations backward and dependent by offering them help for agricultural improvement and consumer goods industries. With greater truth, we might suggest that they are seeking to create dependence on their empire, as well as on internal dictatorship, by seeking to commit these countries to lopsided concentration on slowly-maturing goods, and to pre-empt their exports for years ahead as repayment for their loans.

Altogether, the advantages of an undoctrinaire approach to development planning, of an avoidance of egalitarian promises of a utopian type, and of keeping a new nation uncommitted in a divided world, are so striking that they go far to explain why, in most of the new nations, the initial attitude of the majority of the intelligentsia at any rate is *not* a truly totalitarian one—why their admiration for Communist achievements is in fact as eclectic as it is widespread.

It is precisely this eclecticism—the conscious, critical imitation of some features of the Communist model of modernization, coupled with the equally conscious rejection of others—that constitutes the only practicable alternative to full-scale, ideological totalitarianism in many of these countries. Neither traditionalism nor imitation of Western institutions on a different stage of development offer such alternatives.

Traditionalist régimes are in many cases either unwilling or unable to embark on a serious program of economic development; hence they become more vulnerable to revolutionary movements as the disruptive impact of the modern world makes itself felt from outside. Even where such a régime makes a determined effort at economic development with a reasonable degree of efficiency, it may find itself decisively handicapped by inability or unwillingness to enlist the loyal and responsible cooperation of the intelligentsia. And in the exceptional case where the intelligentsia is for a time successfully integrated in a régime combining traditional authority with modernistic policy, the alliance is apt to prove unstable because the roots of authority itself are being eaten away by the growth of a modern, secular society, until they can no longer withstand any serious shock. The vulnerability of social stagnation is illustrated today by the case of Iran that of modernization without cooperation of the intelligentsia by the fate of Nuri's Iraq and the present difficulties of South Vietnam, while the instability of intelligentsia integration under traditional authority is shown by the contrast between the remarkable achievement of the first sixty years of modern Japan (used as an example for successful nonrevolutionary modernization by Professor Seton-Watson) and the prewar and postwar sequel.

As for the attempt to imitate Western liberal democratic institutions under different conditions, it may have a measure of success in the special case where a strong tradition of respect for law and individual rights coincides with the stabilizing force of a virtually uncontested forward-looking national leadership, as in Nehru's India. Even there it is at least an open question whether the use made of these institutions by vested interests to slow down urgent economic and social reform measures will not undermine them to a dangerous degree. Elsewhere, the sincere defenders of Western democratic ideals are apt to suffer the fate of the Mensheviks, like Dr. Sjarihr in Indonesia; while the more power-conscious imitators of Western parliamentary forms tend to create a caricature which is unable either to cope with the problems of modernization or to win and hold the allegiance of the intelligentsia and the masses, as may be seen in South Korea and the Philippines.

Given the magnitude of the problem of modernization, and the obvious weaknesses of most traditional or pseudo-liberal régimes, the remarkable phenomenon is not so much the prevalence of revolutionary ferment in so many underdeveloped countries, but the fact that so comparatively few of the revolutionary movements have been captured by totalitarian ideology. So far from being the "natural" outlook of any revolutionary intelligentsia, totalitarian dogma seems to be adopted by most of its members only as a last resort, when all efforts to gain power with a more independent or eclectic program of modernization have proved obviously futile, and when the rising despair of both the intelligentsia and the masses cries out for a vision of secular salvation.

Indeed, the original attitude with which the Nationalist revolutionary intelligentsia first becomes conscious of its mission, and which we have described as "eclectic" from the viewpoint of the practical tasks of modernization, is based on an ideological outlook of its own—an outlook which Professor Seton-Watson, in a happy analogy with the familiar history of the Russian revolutionary movement of the nineteenth century, has described as "populist." The common characteristic of all populist ideologies and movements is the search for a synthesis between the basic values on which the traditional culture of the society in question was founded and the need for modernization. In contrast to the traditionalist régimes and movements, the populist intelligentsia is aware that these values can only be preserved by a radical reinterpretation and in a transformed institutional framework. In contrast to the bearers of alien, totalitarian ideas or to spiritually uprooted "Westernizers," it feels that those specific values must be preserved if the cultural revolution is not to lead to a nihilistic destruction of the common culture of their society, but is to have the invigorating effect of a true Reformation.

This populist formula covers such diverse attempts at ideological synthesis and practical eclecticism as are represented by the Buddhist-Marxist régime in Burma, the Indonesian Nationalists, or the Egyptian Council of the Revolution. They all correspond to the deeply-felt need to adopt Western rational techniques of production and power while preserving what is viable in the traditional culture—they are attempts to react to the "schism in the soul" brought about by the impact of modern conditions from outside. There is nothing inherently unrealistic in such an attempt, as the example of Russian populism might suggest at a superficial glance; for it may well be argued that the Russian Bolsheviks ultimately succeeded only by accepting the same task and transforming their Western Marxism in accordance with certain specifically Russian traditions. But particular attempts may well fail either because their exponents prove naïve and unrealistic in the execution of their program, or because they are successfully kept from power by the defenders of the old régime until disruption and despair have so far advanced that the totalitarians appear to offer the only solution.

In fact, the earlier the stage in the disintegration of the traditional order in which the revolutionary intelligentsia comes to power, and the smoother its path has been made by the previous régime, the less likely does it seem to embrace totalitarian dogma. Moreover, experience suggests that the Communist type of totalitarian movement can only win power if circumstances permit it successfully to appropriate the Nationalist element in the populist tradition, and if its leaders have gained a degree of tactical independence from Soviet "advice" which has hitherto been exceptional. The only true Communist revolutions which have so far gained power outside Russia's sphere of military domination—those of Yugoslavia, China, and North Vietnam—have all been led by men who, thanks to unusual circumstances, had succeeded in emancipating themselves from Russian leading strings in the actual conduct of their struggle, and who had used this freedom of movement to capture the leadership of a national uprising against invading or colonial powers. The record hardly suggests that such a course is typical, let alone inevitable for the revolutionary movements of underdeveloped countries, or for the intelligentsia as their leading stratum.

This is not to say that the nontotalitarian régimes of the revolutionary intelligentsia, whether civilian or military, whether semidemocratic or dictatorial, will not commit many costly blunders due to emotionalism and inexperience, or will be models of stability. The Kemalist régime in Turkey committed some appalling acts of cruelty, and by the time it handed over power in a genuinely free election it still had not created a stable foundation for democracy (as we have recently had occasion to note). The régime of the Thakins in Burma—perhaps the most tolerant and democratic of the intelligentsia régimes—at first nearly foundered in civil war, and later had to be rescued from its internal intrigues by a period of military rule. We may yet see similar crises in some of the newly-independent states of Africa. Yet looking back, the remarkable thing about both the Turkish and the Burmese cases is that they have succeeded in creating a sense of growing national unity and legitimacy which has outlasted the crises, and in the process seem to have largely immunized their peoples against totalitarian ideas.

The reason for that success seems to be that these régimes have convinced their peoples that a genuine and independent effort was being made, in however blundering a fashion, to solve their problems of survival in a rapidly changing world by planned modernization. It is in that sense that those régimes are a practicable alternative to totalitarianism. It follows that I warmly agree with Professor Seton-Watson's conclusion that the Western powers should not worry too much whether a particular régime in such a country is democratic in the sense of Western liberal democracy, but be content if it is nontotalitarian, and above all not tied to the Soviet bloc. Yet I should go farther than he does in saying that we have a positive interest in fostering modernizing régimes committed to planned development rather than régimes of tradition stagnation, and régimes working with the nationalist intelligentsia rather than those working against it, even if the former do not stick to the forms of parliamentary democracy and the latter do. And I should base this recommendation not on the Left-wing ideological grounds that economic planning is "socialism" and socialism is more important than democracy (I happen to think that there can be no socialism without democracy, and that there is none in Communist countries), but on the pragmatic grounds that such planning is urgent for freeing the people of these countries from abysmal poverty and at the same time keeping them out of the clutches of the Soviet bloc. Democracy and socialism may come later.

But, the reader may well ask, if you are prepared to compromise and cooperate with "development dictatorships," what then is your objection to totalitarianism? This question of the difference between totalitarian and other dictatorships has been treated in masterly fashion in Professor Seton-Watson's book. Here I can only pick out a few salient points.

The first is that totalitarian dictatorship recognizes no private sphere outside its grasp—that it aspires to total power as a means to achieve a total transformation of man and society. Every dictatorship ignores constitutional limitations of state power; totalitarianism ignores *all* limitations. Every dictatorship suppresses organized opposition and public criticism; totalitarian dictatorship suppresses all forms of autonomous organization and all independent sources of information, permitting only those that directly and positively serve the purposes of the ruling party. This follows from the need to make people not only submit to the government's policies, but to compel their active and enthusiastic participation in the changes planned for their lives: not only the economic and social, but the cultural revolution is to be enforced by the ruthless use of political power.

In the second place, the totalitarian dictatorship seeks to perpetuate itself indefinitely, because its ideological aim can never be fully achieved. It does not justify itself by the transitory need to overcome an acute crisis or to solve a definite task of modernization, but by the mission to usher in "the end of pre-history"—heaven on earth. It is based not simply on the downfall of traditional authority under the impact of secularization, but on its replacement by a secular religion, a political messianism that is to end all evil among men by institutional means. There is, of course, no guarantee that dictatorships that proclaim a transitory purpose will abdicate when this purpose has been fulfilled, but it is no accident that a number of them have done so after longer or shorter periods. Yet as the example of Russia and now China shows, a dictatorship that sets itself chiliastic aims can always find a new task to justify its continuation—it tends to make the revolution permanent.

Lastly, the claims of totalitarian ideology are in its nature world-wide; hence totalitarian dictatorships live in irreconcilable conflict with any state that does not recognize that claim. While that conflict need not in every phase be fought out by violent means, and need not lead to world war in any phase, it does produce a state of permanent tension with the nontotalitarian world in which all means may be used according to expediency—whether at any particular moment that state of tension may be labeled "peaceful coexistence" or "cold war." Since at present the Soviet bloc is the only totalitarian power bloc in the world, we are forced to live in such a state of permanent, world-wide conflict with the Soviet bloc—whether we like it or not.

But we are not forced to live in a similar state of permanent conflict with every national revolution or nationalist dictatorship in an under-developed country, even if its rulers begin their work of independent modernization with a strong traditional distrust of the "imperialist" West. On the contrary, it is our interest to help those countries to achieve their goals of economic development as quickly and with as little sacrifice as possible, so as to provide no cause for the distrust to harden into per-manent ideological hostility.

The tension between "North and South" is bound to diminish as the underdeveloped countries catch up, and "South" automatically comes to resemble "North" economically. The conflict between East and West can only disappear if the totalitarian, ideologically dominated régimes disappear, for only then will "East" come to resemble "West" politically.

That is the difference between the points of the compass.

NOTE

[1]   H. R. Seton-Watson, *Neither War nor Peace. The Struggle for Power in the Post-war World* (London : Methuen, 1960).

6

Marxism, West and East

George Lichtheim

. . . IT MAY be argued that an intensive militarization of public life (in China) is not in principle incompatible with the maintenance of party control, especially if the party is determined to pursue a policy of economic austerity and social egalitarianism. Such a choice could even be defended on rational grounds quite extraneous to Mao's own highly idiosyncratic version of "war communism." It can be held that in a large, poor, and overpopulated country with China's special problems, a combination of military discipline and ideological rigor is an effective means (perhaps the only effective means) of wringing an economic surplus from an unwilling population. If this be granted for argument's sake, one still has to account for the transformation of a doctrine which originally expressed the spontaneous protest of the proletariat of early capitalism. The utopian literature of modern communism, as it arose after the French Revolution, was egalitarian enough, but the aims it defined had little in common with the revolutionary nationalism of the Maoist regime. Communism in those days—broadly speaking the half-century ending with the 1848 upheaval and the *Manifesto*—defined the terms in which an elite of French and British workingmen and their intellectual leaders envisaged the distant future. That future was seen under the aspect of a stateless and classless order which would inherit the economic wealth created by the industrial revolution. It never occurred to the early pioneers of this faith, or to the authors of the *Manifesto*, that communism might become the "ideology" (in the precise sense of "false consciousness") of a movement seeking to substitute itself for what Marx called

FROM "What is Left of Communism," *Foreign Affairs*, 46 (October 1967), pp. 81–94.

the "bourgeois revolution." Yet this is what has been happening in China since 1949, following the precedent set in the U.S.S.R. since 1917.

The paradox is not lessened by the fact that the Chinese have come to stress the purity of their own system as compared to the once admired Soviet model, which is now rejected as insufficiently egalitarian and tainted by bourgeois corruption. Maoism has shown itself even more terroristic than Stalinism in trying to impose uniformity and to prevent the satisfaction of immediate material wants. This kind of terrorism, if successful (a big "if"), can only serve to channel the economic surplus into those sectors of activity to which the highest political authority has chosen to give priority. There is no secret about these priorities: they are military and technological. That is to say, they are at the furthest possible remove from the satisfaction of ordinary individual and social claims.

Once more it may be said that in a poor country on the threshold of modernization this is inevitable, and that other Asian societies (India for choice) might count themselves fortunate if they possessed the social discipline required for the aim of guaranteeing all citizens a minimum of essentials. But the more this argument is pressed, the clearer it becomes that what is being asserted is the superior effectiveness of Chinese communism in promoting the aims historically associated with the capitalist mode of production and the social order built upon it: above all, the sacrifice of immediate satisfactions for the sake of building up the wealth-creating apparatus of industrial civilization. Such an achievement, however important, is quite extraneous to the original signification of the term "communism," not to mention the historic traditions of the labor movement. It is the goal of virtually every dictatorship in a backward country, be its ideology communist, fascist, or simply nationalist. The originality of Maoism lies in the methods employed to mobilize the masses in the name of communism for the achievement of aims proper to any national-revolutionary movement: the industrialization of China and the acquisition of military means (including nuclear ones) adequate to the pursuit of great-power politics.

It is irrelevant in this context that these aims are conceived as forming part of the uprising of the world's preindustrial hinterland (which also happens to be mostly colored), and it is useless to inquire how far such motives are intermingled with more traditional ones. The power of an ideology (in the Marxist sense of the term, not in the trivial meaning assigned to it by pragmatism) is measured by the degree to which it raises men above themselves, gives them a sense of purpose, drives them to sacrifice themselves for what they conceive to be the greater good. It is not the least unnerving aspect of the current situation that the moral austerity of Chinese communism has channeled the energies of a great people into a direction potentially dangerous to itself and its neighbors.

The whole phenomenon, whatever the short-range determinants of the conflict between Moscow and Peking, is best understood as an upsurge of national sentiment within the limitations imposed by the acceptance of communism. The genuineness of this acceptance is just what renders the conflict so acute, since it is essential for the Chinese to adhere to the communist creed and simultaneously to impose their own interpretation upon it.

The problem has been solved, as usual in such cases, by a doctrinal schism. China now has its own version of the faith: much as in an earlier age the imposition of Islam upon Persia gave birth by way of the Shiite heresy to a local variant of the conquering religion. As in all such cases, the resulting pseudomorphosis—the underlying culture reasserting itself in the guise of the new universal faith—must be distinguished from the overt manifestations of the schism, which are largely accidental and secondary. Given the circumstances in which the Chinese communists won power—namely by gaining the leadership of a national-revolutionary movement whose original inspiration had run dry—an attempt to "Sinify" the Marxist-Leninist inheritance was inevitable. The particular form it has taken is another matter. It is a waste of time to examine Peking's claims to doctrinal orthodoxy. The Chinese are too remote from the origins of European socialism to be taken seriously in the role of exegetes of the classical texts. What matters is that the schism has laid bare the contradictions inherent in Lenin's view of the Russian Revolution as the link between an awakening Asia and a potentially socialist Europe. Insofar as Leninism signified such a vision, the Chinese are Leninists no longer, for they no longer believe that the industrial proletariat of the West has a privileged part to play in what is still called the "world revolution."

Marxism-Leninism is in process of disintegration. The vision of a global movement encompassing both advanced and backward countries has been abandoned by Moscow and Peking alike: by Moscow because the growing conservatism of Soviet society is incompatible with such alarming notions; by Peking because there is no longer a revolutionary workers' movement in the West which could be regarded as a reliable ally of a resurgent China. Leninism and Stalinism alike implied a commitment to the goal of a union linking East and West, the Asian peasant and the European or American city-worker. From 1920 onward, when Lenin formulated this concept at the Second Congress of the Third International, the effective political meaning of "communism" hinged upon the belief that the October Revolution had been the first act in this great drama. Leninism, both in its narrower Stalinist and in its more romantic Trotskyist understanding, was the doctrine of a world revolution. Shorn of this perspective it is no more than the theory of the *Russian* Revolution. Inasmuch as this latter interpretation is now gaining ground among communists in the U.S.S.R. and throughout Eastern Europe, the Chinese have some cause for asserting that the Russians and their allies in the communist movement are no longer serious about the conclusion Lenin set out in his last published piece of writing, when he looked forward to a great confrontation between "the counterrevolutionary imperialist West and the revolutionary and nationalist East": a confrontation in which he expected the U.S.S.R. to side with China and India against Europe and America.[1]

The tacit abandonment of this line of thought by the Soviet régime does constitute a drastic revision of Leninism (though not of Marxism, since neither Marx nor his European followers had ever dreamed of such a thing). Unfortunately for the Chinese it is not really possible for the remnant of the "revolutionary and nationalist East" to assume the role once held by the U.S.S.R. Without the latter, plus its East European satellites, Maoism is no more than an Asian phenomenon, which is another way of saying that the Leninist strategy of 1920–23 has become inapplicable. If Moscow refuses the global role assigned to it in the original scheme, and contents itself with the part of mediator between West and East (or between the United States and China), there is an end to world-revolutionary strategy. It is useless to affirm that an adequate substitute can be reconstituted on Chinese soil. Anything may be asserted on paper, but in the eyes of Asian revolutionaries "Leninism" signified primarily the willingness of the Russian Communist Party to follow the line laid down by its founder between 1920 and 1923, when he explicitly defined world communism in terms of an alliance between the Russian worker and the Asian peasant. To do the Chinese justice, Moscow's departure from this line *does* represent the abandonment of at least one significant aspect of Lenin's heritage.

If the question be raised how Lenin ever came to associate the coming triumph of what he called "socialism" with such a perspective, the answer must be that he was following out the logic of his lifelong adherence to the Populist (or Bakuninist) notion of a "dictatorship of workers and peasants," which in his theoretical scheme was to administer the tasks of the revolution during a lengthy interim period after the fall of the monarchy. As late as 1923 one finds him discussing the immediate prospects of the Soviet regime in these terms: "We . . . lack enough civilization to enable us to pass straight on to socialism, although we do have the political requisites for it. . . . We must strive to build up a state in which the workers retain the leadership of the peasants, in which they retain the confidence of the peasants. . . . If we see to it that the working class retains its leadership over the peasantry, we shall be able . . . to develop electrification . . ." etc.[2]

The naïvete of this trust in the capacity of "the workers" to exercise political leadership requires no comment. What matters is the essential coherence of the Leninist viewpoint: the Russian "worker" was to "build socialism" at home and "retain the confidence of the peasant" while doing it. In practice, the "building of socialism" devolved upon the party, which in turn became the nucleus of a new privileged stratum. For all their blinkered ignorance, the Maoists are shrewd enough to see that the jettisoning of Lenin's global strategy ("East against West") has been brought about by what they have come to describe as the degeneracy of Soviet regime—notably the formal dismantling of the "proletarian dictatorship." It is irrelevant that the latter was always a fiction, for to a communist what truly matters is that his party should *represent* the masses. What the Chinese cannot forgive is the growing identification of the Soviet regime with the aims of the privileged stratum that has grown out of the postrevolutionary society. It is quite wrong to describe this reaction as "Trotskyist," superficial resemblances notwithstanding. The Maoists are ultra-Stalinists, that is to say, believers in the efficacy of terrorism. What was valuable about Stalin's leadership in their eyes was precisely his readiness to subordinate the material interests of all classes to the aims laid down by political authority. Mao is as certain as Stalin ever was that communism can and must be built by force—even in a country possessing no industry to speak of—and that the new society must remain totally subordinate to the controlling elite until such time as all its citizens have become good communists and lost their appetite for private property. All other notions (including the Trotskyist utopia of a proletarian revolution in the West) are heretical and must be rooted out, for what matters is that the transformation must be *willed*. Given the necessary willpower, the material problems will take care of themselves.

To say that Lenin opened this Pandora's Box when he committed his party to the task of "building socialism" in Russia is not to suggest that he would have welcomed the present consequences. He was after all a Russian Social-Democrat by upbringing, and for all his heresies enough of a Marxist to believe that communism made no sense without a workers' movement. At the same time it is plain enough that between 1917 and 1923 he had traveled a good distance toward the conclusions now reached by his Chinese disciples. Nonetheless he still retained his faith in the revolutionary potential of Europe. The inherent instability of this Marxist-Leninist synthesis was masked for a while by the existence of the Third International, notably by its involvement in the mythical "German revolution"—an experiment whose outcome was the National-Socialist dictatorship, passively supported for twelve years by the bulk of the German working class. Yet if this sobering experience has made Moscow's followers more cautious, it has not shaken their doctrinal commitment to a Leninism which shall at any rate continue to bear the marks of its East European origin. It is indeed not possible for orthodox communists to accept the complete dissociation of Leninism from Marxism—something the Chinese have now brought about by setting the army and a state-controlled youth movement against the urban working class.

"Marxism-Leninism" was always a shotgun marriage, for what was original in Lenin (the notion of a world revolution centering on Russia) was not to be found in Marx. Yet for all its equivocal attempts to combine Marx and Bakunin, the Bolshevism of 1917–23 signified an unwillingness to turn one's back altogether upon the Marxian inheritance. Leninism, it was asserted in those days, was the contemporary form of Marxism, and the October Revolution, by bringing socialism to backward Russia, had bridged the gulf between Europe and Asia. One may suppose that Stalin still believed this. His successors plainly do not, and neither do the Chinese, whatever their propaganda may assert to the contrary. For the Maoists, the tradition of the old revolutionary workers' movement has ceased to possess any relevance. It is no longer a matter of asserting that socialism and communism *can* be built outside Europe; they *must* be built outside Europe, and there must be no illusions about the ability or the willingness of the European or American proletariat to take the lead in the matter, or even to render significant aid to China's struggle. What was once the faith of the European socialist movement has, after a century of eastward migration, become the ideology of an elite in charge of a national revolution in a retarded country.

This new Islam has its Koran, albeit due reverence is paid to the Old Testament, and why not? Pious Moslems respect the memory of Abraham, but their allegiance goes to the Prophet. The Chinese communists are unlikely to relinquish the claim that Mao stands in the direct succession to Marx and Lenin. To do so would be to renounce the universalism which has become their pride and which, to do them justice, sets them off from the parochialism of an earlier generation of nationalists, for whom the indigenous tradition had to suffice. But in the absence of any tradition linking the Chinese revolution with the Western labor movement, such manifestations of the will to believe must remain ideological. They translate not a shared experience—for what is there to connect the former nationalist agitator from Hunan with the heirs of the Chartists or the followers of Proudhon?—but the determination not to be excluded from what is perceived as a claim to universal import. This transformation of a Western faith into the fighting creed of a movement born and raised under very different stars is precisely what the term "ideology" signifies.

If the disintegration of Marxism-Leninism has the effect of leaving the Kremlin and its adherents in an uncomfortable position midway between East and West, it may be said that Lenin's heirs are thus belatedly paying for their master's originality. One could assemble quite a number of quotations testifying to the fact that in the final year of his political life Lenin had come to realize the perils inherent in what he himself on one occasion likened to the ascent of a high mountain. What this comparison amounted to was an implicit acknowledgment that the October coup had been an adventure into unmapped territory. In his customary fashion Lenin sought assurance by invoking the example of the earlier revolution in France (a bourgeois one). Thus one finds him writing (in February 1922): "Russia's proletariat rose to a gigantic height in its revolution, not only when it is compared with 1789 and 1793, but also when compared with 1871. We must take stock of what we have done . . . as dispassionately . . . as possible. . . ."[3]

To anyone familiar with Russian Marxism, what stands out here is the casual linking of the French Revolution (1789 and 1793) and the Paris Commune of 1871—the first a successful, if sanguinary, transformation carried through by Lenin's Jacobin ancestors; the second an abortive proletarian insurrection against the bourgeois Republic which had arisen from the subsequent turmoil. It is true that the Parisian Communards of 1871 counted a good many latter-day Jacobins in their own ranks; in particular the Blanquist faction (which more or less ran the Commune) was descended from the radical republicans of the 1840s, though Blanqui himself was fond of describing himself as a "communist." It is also true that Clemenceau, the archetypal bourgeois radical under the Third Republic, had begun his political life in the 1860s as a follower of Blanqui and in 1871 duly sympathized with the Communards, though he stood aside from the fighting. All this belongs to the inner history of French republicanism—a movement largely inspired by a Robespierrist faith in "temporary" dictatorship.

This tradition is the ultimate source of those passages in the *Communist Manifesto* (1848) and the *Class Struggles in France* (1850) where Marx paid his residual debt to Jacobinism. Marxism, in one of its aspects, has been the link between 1789 and 1917, between the French Revolution and its Russian successor. The reason is quite simply that Marx obtained his political education in the Paris of the 1840s, where the nascent communist sects were led by men like Blanqui who still thought in Jacobin terms. After 1850, Marx (and even more so Engels) abandoned these rather episodic attachments and gradually transformed themselves into democratic socialists. But this transformation became effective only in Germany and England. It was rather halfheartedly accepted in France after the disaster of the 1871 Paris Commune, and it evoked no genuine echo in Eastern Europe, where Marxism continued to signify the *Com-*

munist Manifesto rather than *Capital*. In a word, the Marx whom the Russians liked was the early Marx—the man of 1848. And they continued to admire Blanqui. The Russian radicals of the 1860s and 1870s, who transmitted the Blanquist faith in revolutionary terrorism to Lenin, were proud to style themselves "Jacobins." So far, so good. After all, even moderate Marxists like Lenin's teacher, Plekhanov, believed, for sound reason, that Russia would one day re-enact the earlier drama in France.

For all that, Lenin's casual allusion to these French examples slid over what to a Marxist is the central difficulty. The French Revolution, after all, had been led by the bourgeoisie—and been successful for this reason. The Paris Commune of 1871, on the other hand, had been bloodily suppressed after two months, and thus could hardly count as evidence that "proletarian dictatorship" was workable. Lenin's own party had launched a victorious uprising and by 1922, when he penned his *Notes of a Publicist*, had been in power for almost five years. Was Bolshevism, then, the legitimate successor of Jacobinism? And if it was, could it also claim the heritage of that luckless rebellion in 1871 which had burst the bounds of bourgeois society?

To ask such questions of course is to challenge the whole theoretical construction supporting Lenin's system of beliefs, for had he been less certain about the answer he would not have been the man he was, and neither would the Bolshevik party have become what he made of it. It was essential to his outlook, and to that of his followers, that he and they should see themselves *both* as "Jacobins" *and* as communists leading a "proletarian revolution" (and therefore also in the tradition of the 1871 Commune). The self-contradictory character of this notion was plain enough to the Mensheviks, for whom Lenin's "Jacobinism" was just what rendered his Marxism suspect. He had after all made it clear, from 1902 and *What Is to Be Done?* onward, that—unlike the mature Marx—he did *not* believe the working class could emancipate itself by its own efforts. That task, in his view, devolved upon "the party." But (as one can see from his 1922 writings) the reality of party control must on no account be allowed to weaken the faith that the October Revolution had been a "proletarian" one. In short, he was determined to have it both ways—not merely as a political leader, but as a theoretician too. When confronted with the resulting contradictions he fell back upon the notion that history was always producing unforeseen situations. Thus, although by 1922 his regime had come to terms with what he himself called "state capitalism," he was by no means willing to let his critics have the last word on the subject. Replying to one of them, the economist Preobrazhensky (who as it happened was a left-wing Bolshevik), he flatly asserted that some of the traditional Marxian distinctions were no longer applicable:

Up to now nobody could have written a book about this sort of capitalism, because this is the first time in human history that we see anything like it. . . . Now things are different, and neither Marx nor the Marxists could foresee this . . . for nobody could foresee that the proletariat would achieve power in one of the least developed countries, and would first try to organize large-scale production and distribution for the peasantry and then, finding that it could not cope with the task owing to the low standard of culture, would enlist the services of capitalism. Nobody ever foresaw this; but it is an incontrovertible fact.[4]

The "incontrovertible fact" was that the proletariat had *not* "achieved power," either in October 1917 or at any other time; but had he been able to see that his party "represented" not the proletariat but the ruling stratum of a new society, Lenin could not have made the revolution. Illusions of this sort (as Marx had pointed out in connection with the French Revolution) are a vital factor in promoting those historical changes whose true meaning discloses itself after the event.

The meaning of Lenin's revolution disclosed itself under Stalin. By now it requires a considerable act of faith for anyone to believe that the political dispossession of the working class by Lenin's party was merely a temporary affair, for Soviet society plainly is neither classless nor tending in that direction. So much must be granted to its Chinese critics. What the latter fail to perceive is that this outcome was inevitable and by no means the fault of Stalin's "revisionist" heirs. Indeed the term "revisionism" makes no sense in this context, for what is being revised is merely the vocabulary. It is true that calling the U.S.S.R. a "state of the whole people" is ludicrous if one affects to retain Marx's view of the state as an instrument of coercion. But if Lenin was prepared to argue that Bolshevik state capitalism was different from ordinary state capitalism, why should not his successors claim that the state they govern is unlike any other state—not oppressive but liberating? If it is a matter of revisionism, Lenin was the greatest revisionist of them all. After all, it was he who stood the social-democratic tradition on its head by seizing power and then claiming to hold it for "the proletariat." And there was Stalin's subsequent decision to "build socialism" in "one country"—a decision already inherent in Lenin's pronouncements, whatever Trotsky might affirm to the contrary.

Does it follow from all this that there is no longer something that can be called "world communism"? A movement may be in a state of disintegration and still have considerable staying power. Moreover, the elements that are now being set free may enter new combinations. If Peking has adopted the Leninist part of the Marxist-Leninist synthesis, the West European communist parties show signs of reviving the Marxist inheritance. In doing this they are, after all, simply reverting to a tradition older than the Russian Revolution—a tradition, moreover, which grew on European soil and does not have to be laboriously re-translated into English, German, French, Spanish, or Italian. Even the Russians can at a pinch revive the orthodox Marxism of Plekhanov, though doubtless they will continue to assert that he took the wrong line in 1914–18. *A fortiori* in Western Europe, where the communist parties are still rooted in the labor movement, it should not be too difficult for them to resurrect those elements of the Marxist tradition which they have in common with the social-democrats: above all, faith in the ability of the working class to emancipate itself by its own efforts and without the benefit of an omniscient vanguard of "professional revolutionaries." Conceivably the communist parties in these countries could even be brought to accept political democracy and to renounce, once and for all, the dream of one-party dictatorship, for which the preconditions are anyhow becoming increasingly unfavorable.

Something of the sort may indeed already be under way within the two largest and most important West European parties, the Italian and the French. Faced with the choice between permanent isolation and partial attainment of their aims, their leaders appear to have quietly opted for virtual acceptance of political democracy and toleration of other parties. The social revolution is still affirmed, but there is no longer the same insistence that it must of necessity pass through a dictatorial phase. Since this was the line Marx and Engels themselves took after 1871, when the quarrel with Bakunin obliged them to come down firmly on the democratic side, there should be no trouble about finding scriptural warrant for a position that is both Marxist and democratic.

What stands in the way of such a reorientation is not Marx but Lenin (to say nothing of Stalin, the symbol of terrorism). The communists in the West would have to admit that the Bolshevik experience does not after all provide a suitable model for the advanced societies of Western Europe and North America. If they could bring themselves to do this—and in Western Europe the time seems to be almost ripe—their tactical problems would no longer be insoluble, and in due course they might even win the confidence of their fellow citizens. What such a realignment cannot do is to reconstitute the lost unity of the world communist movement. It is bound on the contrary to hasten its demise as a *movement*, though not necessarily as a loose assemblage of like-minded parties. For communism since 1917 has defined itself in terms of fidelity to Lenin and the Bolshevik model. A "return to Marx," whatever its attraction after World War II to the pupils of Antonio Gramsci, has little meaning for communists in Asia, Africa and Latin America. To them it signifies quite plainly the renunciation of those hopes and illusions that were symbolized by the myth of the October Revolution.

And yet one does not see how the drift away from Marxist-Leninist orthodoxy can be halted, at any rate outside Eastern Europe, where the problem of gaining power has been solved. Both the rigid ultra-Stalinism of the Chinese and the traditional Marxism of Western Europe represent possible options, whereas the Leninist synthesis of 1917–23 looks more artificial with every year that passes. Too undemocratic for the West, it is still too Marxist for the East. Above all, it is too dependent upon the Marxian notion that there must be *some* concordance between the development of the productive forces and the evolution to a higher type of society, and that communism cannot simply be legislated into existence by an act of will. Lenin, after all, never quite renounced the primary assumption that socialism (let alone communism) presupposes a high degree of industrial development and a concomitant level of civilization. Indeed, he justified the adoption of the New Economic Policy in 1921–22 on the grounds that Russia was too backward for a shortcut to socialism. It has been left for Mao Tse-tung to take the final step of proclaiming communism the means of overcoming China's preindustrial backwardness. In doing so he has finally stood Marx on his head, though he can hardly be aware of it.

What is rather more important is that he has severed the link between his own brand of "communism" and the historic workers' movement from which the communist protest against exploitation and alienation originally arose. For what kept this movement going for a century was the faith that the purgatory of the industrial revolution would one day be succeeded by an age when men would find something better to do than to sacrifice themselves and their offspring for the wealth-creating apparatus of capitalist industry. If the European proletariat responded to Marxian socialism, it did so because Marx had taught the workers that "capital" was stored-up labor—their own sweat and blood which had gone to build up the great pyramid of modern industry. His followers then did not conceive that "communism" would one day come to signify an iron dictatorship dedicated to the goal of extracting the last ounce of surplus labor from the toilers, for the purpose of erecting an even more monstrous structure of totally state-owned and bureaucratically controlled capital. They did not, that is to say, foresee the advent of Stalinism, still less of Maoism, which is the application of Stalinist principles to a country far poorer and more primitive than the Russia of the first five-year plan. Whatever the pragmatic value of this gigantic experiment, it holds no promise for men and women whose ancestors in the last century passed through this particular kind of hell, though to be sure the ideology then was a different one.

Nothing can cure the Chinese of their notion that they are "building communism," though in fact they are laying the foundation of yet another state-capitalist structure. The illusion is as necessary to them as the air they breathe, for it legitimizes the drive to make their country great and self-sufficient. But just because the entire nation has been dedicated by its rulers to this back-breaking enterprise, what is officially described as communism has found expression in a riot of populist and nationalist exaltation. The appeal of Maoism is to *the people of China*—all of them (minus the celebrated "handful of plotters") and to no one besides. Here, for all the solemn tributes to Stalin's legacy, Mao and his followers have perforce abandoned even the Stalinist form of Leninism which still retained some connection with the idea of a class dictatorship exercised in the name of "the workers." Maoism is a populist ideology which equates all the toilers, and if anything prefers the peasants to the city workers. Its appeal is to "the people," not to the proletariat, and its deepest urge is to restore the primitive community of the folk, as it is supposed to have existed in a golden age before the coming of class society. In short, what we have here is the last of the great national-popular convulsions inaugurated in the France of 1793, revived in the Russia of 1917, grotesquely parodied in the Germany of 1933, and now for a change exported to Asia. Impressive enough in its own way, the phenomenon makes sense only if one dissociates it from the Marxian perspective it has inherited from a European movement of the past century. National Socialism does not acquire a different character merely because it chooses to style itself communism. But the revolution is real enough, and its ultimate direction remains to be determined.

NOTES

1   Lenin, "Better Fewer, But Better," *Pravda*, March 4, 1923 ("Collected Works," v. 33, p. 487ff). "In the last analysis, the outcome of the struggle will be determined by the fact that Russia, India, China, etc., account for the overwhelming majority of the population of the globe. . . . In this sense the complete victory of socialism is fully and absolutely assured." (*Ibid.*, p. 500.) This Eurasian perspective was already inherently Stalinist, in that it identified "the victory of socialism" with the military superiority of an Eastern bloc led by the U.S.S.R. As long as Moscow adhered to such notions, it was possible for the Chinese to tolerate Soviet pre-eminence (not to mention Stalin's personal whims). To that extent the Maoist claim to the succession is well founded.

2   *Ibid.*, p. 501: "In this and in this alone lies our hope. Only when we have done this shall we be able, speaking figuratively, to change horses, to change from the peasant, muzhik, horse of poverty . . . to the horse which the proletariat is seeking and must seek—the horse of large-scale machine industry, of electrification, of the Volkhov Power Station, etc."

3   "Notes of a Publicist," first published in *Pravda*, April 16, 1924 ("Collected Works," v. 33, p. 206).

4   Closing speech at the eleventh congress of the R.C.P. (B.), March 28, 1922 (*Collected Works*, v. 33, pp. 310–311).

Is Marxism a Social Science?

ONE of the major unresolved paradoxes of Marxism is the antinomy between Marx the revolutionary advocate and Marx the empirical social scientist and historian. Many writers have commented on the prophetic or apocalyptic nature of Marxism, with its teleological character or fixed redemptive process. Louis Halle sees Marx as a great visionary of history, an artist with a dramatic imagination; Robert Tucker views Marxism as philosophy and myth rather than as science.

But the Marxist Fathers regarded themselves as objective and dispassionate social analysts, and they attacked critics of the social order who attempted to find the solution to social problems through appeals to justice and who conjured up fantastic pictures of future society. Marx opposed what he called utopian projects for reform of the capitalist system or for conciliation between the classes. His objective was to study social relationships and the industrial system of the mid-nineteenth century in the same way as propositions were made about chemistry or physics. In his famous speech at the grave of Marx, Engels compared the work of his colleague in social science with that of Darwin in biology. Marx himself, in the Preface to the first edition of *Capital*, wrote that his ultimate aim was to lay bare the economic law of motion of modern society and to find the laws of social development.

Marx's analysis of the laws of capitalist development and his historical studies exemplify his stature as a social scientist. Yet they have not altogether answered the argument that his system is teleological. In *The Civil War in France*, Marx writes of "The higher life form toward which the existing society tends irresistibly by its own economic development." In *Ludwig Feuerbach and the End of Classical German Philosophy*,

Engels speaks of the successive historical systems "in the endless evolution of human society from the lower to the higher."

A much-debated problem in Marxism is that of determinism or free will. Is history an inevitable process proceeding according to the dialectic, or is it subject to human will? Is history rational so that what is irrational is doomed to perish? Is the proletarian revolution an automatic historical event or is there need for action and organization to produce it? Lenin was more of a voluntarist and opportunist than most Marxists in his emphasis on the need for action and his belief that "if we wait until people are ripe for socialism we shall have to wait another five hundred years."

The appearance of determinism in Marxism may be partly due to the influence of Hegelianism with its identity of the ideal and the actual. But it may also result from the mid-nineteenth-century belief in progress as well as from the Marxist anticipation that the laws of history would lead to the expected revolution.

Thus Marx talks in *Capital* of "society discovering the natural laws of its movement," of seeing "the economic formation of society as a process of natural history," and of picturing the capitalist as subject to "the immanent laws of capitalist production" which are seen as "immutable natural law." Yet the activist Marx writes, as in *The Holy Family*, that "it is not history which uses men as a means of achieving its own ends. History is nothing but the activity of men in pursuit of their ends." In his article, Donald Clark Hodges touches on this problem while assuming the greatness of Marx both as a social scientist and as a revolutionary advocate.

Two other problems may be mentioned briefly. Marxists who have captured power or aspire to it have often felt that the Marxist canon provides few concrete suggestions or prescriptions for tactical situations or for action. The Marxist concern for objective social science and distaste for speculation about the future society has led to complaints like that of Lenin when introducing his New Economic Program in 1922 that "it did not even occur to Marx to write a word about this subject."

A second problem arises for the social scientist when predictions based on the analysis go awry. Bernstein was one of the first of many to point out that Marx had misconceived the evolution of the capitalist system, that the middle class was not being eliminated, that the managerial class would become important, that the standard of living of workers was rising, and that the theory of increasing misery was being falsified. Engels had to confess about the nature of a new capitalist crisis that "history has proved us, and all who thought like us, wrong."

T. B. Bottomore discusses the significance and contribution of Marx as a sociologist, compares Marxism with recent sociological theories on conflict, class, ideologies, and revolution, and analyzes Marx as a writer concerned both with accurate empirical research and with the framing of universal generalizations.

7

Marxism as Social Science

Donald Clark Hodges

NORMATIVE Orientations of Marxian Social Science. Although science in general is subservient to human values, it is only in the social sciences that theoretical controversy is a comparatively direct expression of political differences. Marxian social science, in particular, is self-consciously and expressly conditioned by a dual political goal: (1) the abolition of exploitation; and (2) the overcoming of anarchy, inefficiency, and waste in capitalist production. Positively formulated, the ultimate purpose of knowledge in the social sciences is to bring about a classless society and a level of civilization in which all men are masters of their social and physical environments. On the one hand, Marxian social science is designed to serve the partisan morality and relative justice of a proletarian class; on the other hand, its ultimate goal is the freedom and perfection of mankind. [1] Its proximate goal is a proletarian revolution, itself a necessary condition to higher levels of productivity and the optimum in social well-being. To be successful in its first or proximate task, it is compelled to represent the class interest and relative justice of the proletariat as the common interest of all members of society, to give its partisan ideals the form of universality, to represent them as the only rational ones. At the same time, it can do this without hypocrisy because of the conviction that its partisan interest really is closest to representing the common interest of other nonruling classes, and that its fulfillment precludes the proletariat, as the bottom class in society, from constituting itself into a new ruling class oppressive like the old. Thus the Marxian ethics leads to the paradox that only a narrowly proletarian class ethic

FROM "The Dual Character of Marxian Social Science," *Philosophy of Science*, 29 (October 1962), pp. 334–339.

is capable of serving the "common good," while all attempts to serve humanity directly—in being predicated upon existing relations between social classes—turn out in fact to be a travesty upon humanist ideals. Marxian social science does not constitute an independent body of knowledge, but is an integral part of scientific socialism. Scientific socialism was the first systematic attempt to base the proletarian class struggle upon history and economics instead of upon abstract principles of justice and morality. It consists, on the one hand, of a scientific theory of history and society; on the other hand, of the strategy and tactics of the proletarian revolution. Following Engels, Lenin defined it as the theory and program of the labor movement. Its task, according to Engels, is to understand the historical and economic succession of events leading to the creation and exploitation of a proletariat and to discover in economic conditions the means of proletarian emancipation.[2] Utopian socialism had criticized the injustices of the capitalist mode of production, but it could neither explain them adequately nor obtain mastery over them. For that it was necessary to discover the historical "laws of motion" of capitalist development and to lay bare the "secret" of profit-making and surplus value. Thus Marx's two great discoveries—the materialist conception of history in application to the capitalist mode of production, and the secret of capitalistic production through surplus value—enabled socialism to become a science.

In the Marxian view, social science should subordinate theory to practice, but should not make it exclusively instrumental to the latter. The pragmatic method is regarded by Marxists as a vulgarization of the theoretical purpose of social science, or the development of an ever more complete body of knowledge about society; hence their subordination of social science to a practical goal is partly a means of advancing science from a narrow preoccupation with bourgeois interests to a broader vision of social problems based on the experience of all social classes. Knowledge is intended by them to serve the partisan interests of the proletariat, but is also regarded as an end in itself—although judged to be of only secondary importance in a class-structured society. Socialists and intellectuals in the labor movement are attracted to Marxism, according to Lenin, because it combines a strict scientific method with a revolutionary spirit and identifies the aim of social science with assisting the proletariat in its actual economic struggle. Thus the Marxian evaluation of social science is distinct from that of science for science's sake, in which the primary purpose of science is knowledge instead of practice, and from vulgar scientism, in which knowledge serves exclusively practical interests.

Scientific socialism transformed the character not only of socialism, but also of traditional philosophy. Since it has a revolutionary goal, it gives precedence to practice before theory, to class interests before intellectual ones. In the past, philosophers concerned themselves chiefly with interpreting the world; the fundamental problem of Marxist philosophy is to change it. Originally, Marxist philosophy was not a body of thought distinct from scientific socialism. As a fundamentally social philosophy, its primary subject matter was history and economics, while its socialist orientation subordinated inquiry in these fields to problems of direct and indirect revolutionary significance to the labor movement. Somewhat less accurate, as a description of Marxist philosophy, is Engels' use of the term "historical materialism"—the scientific theory of history that "seeks the ultimate cause and the great moving power of all important historic events in the economic development of society." Although Marxian philosophy is not only social but scientific—there is no distinction for it between social philosophy and social science—the term "historical materialism" has a pre-eminently theoretical connotation that fails to stress the socialist character of its philosophy.

Plekhanov noted that before Marx there were others who had recognized the predominant role of economics in history, who might also be included under the category of "historical materialists." To remedy this ambiguity he introduced the term "dialectical materialism," which had not been used by either Marx or Engels, to designate the "highest development of the materialist conception of history" and the only one that corresponded to the most recent advancements in science. Unfortunately, this term is even less accurate than "historical materialism" as a short-hand description of Marx's unique contribution to social science. It was intended to suggest and continues to suggest that philosophical materialism and dialectics constitute the heart of Marxian philosophy. Plekhanov actually identified Marxism with contemporary materialism, with the "highest stage of development of that philosophy," whose foundations were laid in ancient Greece by Democritus and by his Ionian predecessors, a Spinozism freed of its theological lumber by Feuerbach and dialectically developed by Marx and Engels.[3] Historical materialism was reduced by him to a special application or "particular case" of dialectical materialism—a thesis perpetuated by Lenin and later made into an official part of Soviet philosophy by Stalin. Thus, under the influence of Plekhanov, Lenin came to regard dialectical materialism as the "legitimate successor" of classical German philosophy; historical materialism, as a special case of the former modified by the influence of classical English political economy; and scientific socialism, as the logical culmination of French Socialism together with French revolutionary doctrine in general. This change in terminology was primarily verbal, since Lenin, and Stalin after him, continued to stress the supreme theoretical importance of historical materialism and the primacy of scientific socialism.

Marxian social scientists are constantly plagued by the problem of preserving the proletarian character of their knowledge free from contamination by bourgeois ideas, interests, and values. Since the fundamental problems and concepts of Marxian social science are subject to outside pressures that threaten to distort it, Marxian historians and economists must not only renew their sciences periodically by bringing them up to date, but must also endeavor to preserve them from disguised, alien, and frequently unconscious efforts to revise them. Considering the fine balance uniting Marxian theory and practice, there is a tendency for Marxists to be swayed toward the extremes of activism, in which theory is dwarfed by the requirements of practice, and of objectivism, in which action is primarily a means of verifying theory. Lenin argued that the defense of the purity of a proletarian-oriented social science is a necessary condition of greater objectivity within the social sciences. [4] At the same time, he believed that a serious commitment to intellectual values is necessary to free science from exclusive preoccupation with the miseries and injustices suffered by the proletariat. Thus the practical bias of Marxian social science is a means to the advancement of scientific knowledge, while a social science freed from the pressure of practical contingencies is itself a prerequisite of the successful struggle for socialism.

Epistemic Foundations of Marxian Social Science. There is a significant correlation between the two sources of socialist humanism and the distinction made by Marxian social scientists between two modes of truth. Besides the partisan truths of interest primarily to particular social classes, there are general or common truths that are shared by all. Some bodies of knowledge are designed to benefit a particular group; hence their public character is limited to experimental techniques of verification. Otherwise, and in not unfundamental respects, such knowledge is private. Far from being an abuse of language to speak of "bourgeois" social science as distinct from Marxian social science, this distinction clarifies the normative bias and, along with it, the private and exclusive character of each.

Although the ultimate goal of knowledge transcends its partisan ends, Marxian social scientists claim that the future of science itself depends upon the triumph of socialism. They argue that concentration upon the *status quo* has given bourgeois social science its static character, while disregard of the tendencies toward social disequilibrium—such as periodic economic, political, and military crises—has resulted in a new kind of obscurantism. Bourgeois social science tends to both of the extremes assiduously avoided by Marxian social scientists: to the arid rationalism of "grand theory" or pretentious system building; and to the vulgar or "abstracted empiricism" of specialized research in the service of vested interests. Criticism of bourgeois social science is modeled

chiefly upon Marx's criticism, in his preface to the second edition of
Capital, where he contrasts his own method of "genuine scientific
research" and "disinterested" inquiry with the shallow syncretism and
attempted reconciliation of irreconcilables of the grand harmonizers of
political economy, and with the vulgar pragmatism of hired intellectual
"prize-fighters" concerned not with the truth of this or that proposition
of economics, but with whether it is useful to capital or harmful, expe-
dient or inexpedient, politically dangerous or not. Thus John Stuart Mill
is upheld as perhaps the most outstanding example of sterile academicism
in economics, while Bastiat—the champion of prudent, practical
business folk—is scornfully cited as the most superficial and popular
representative of vulgar economic apologetics.

Instead of tempering the extremist tendencies of bourgeois social
science, the proliferation of philosophies in bourgeois society has helped
to reinforce them. On the one hand, philosophers proud of their professo-
rial dignity and of the noble traditions of their discipline have yet to give
up entirely the quest for universal, eternal, and absolute truths; following
in the rationalistic footsteps of Plato, Aristotle, and their modern
successors, they have helped to perpetuate a tradition of concern for
"wisdom," for general and systematic knowledge that has had a continuing influence upon the social sciences. On the other hand, these
sciences have not been immune from the influence of such irrationalistic
and anti-intellectualistic philosophies as intuitionism, vitalism, existentialism, pragmatism, and the more extreme varieties of empiricism.
Against the first of these tendencies, Marxian philosophers have en-
couraged the further decomposition of philosophy into the positive
sciences, the end of philosophical system-building, and the limitation of
philosophical inquiry to the fields of formal logic and dialectics. Against
the second, they have adopted the posture of defenders of the Goddess
Philosophical Reason in opposition to her defamers and destroyers, who
would reduce her to a mere servant either of Life or of specialized and
abstract studies in such fields as language and perception. Although
Marxian philosophers apply the term "idealism"—the philosophical
thesis of the primacy of mind over matter—to both the low and the
high roads of philosophy, they also consider philosophical materialism
to be susceptible to these two deformations. Thus the "mechanistic" and
"atomistic" materialism of Hobbes and his successors is classified as
metaphysical, whereas the type of philosophy that interprets all human
actions as motivated by egoistic or economic considerations of loss and
gain, and that is no less mechanistic and atomistic than the former, is
classified as "vulgar" materialism and rejected as a distorted and one-sided
image of reality.

Of special importance to Marxian epistemology or materialist

dialectics is the concept of "objective truth," where "truth" is synonymous with "reality," "matter," or the world as it is, independent of
human thought or perception. Measured by this criterion, the partisan
and one-sided knowledge of particular social classes and the summation
of isolated truths in a many-sided and comprehensive science of society
are at best approximations to reality. Yet, even though all knowledge in
this sense is relative, some knowledge may be regarded as "absolute" or
"eternal." There is no disputing such simple historical truths as "Napoleon I died"; similarly, the conclusion that he died on May 5, 1821, may also
be regarded as absolute or immutable in proportion as the evidence points
overwhelmingly to it. Although Lenin acknowledged that the criterion
of practice can never in principle either confirm or refute any proposition
completely, he did not espouse a thoroughgoing relativism, such as the
theory of intersubjective truth. Instead, he argued in support of Engels'
thesis that "absolute truth" is compounded from "relative truths," of
which it is the sum total, and that, howsoever relative it is to the historical
conditions of human knowledge, it comes closest to being a true image of
reality. [5] Thus Marxian dialectics, itself an instrument in the class struggle,
is forced to wage a war on two different philosophical fronts: against
metaphysics for confusing ideal models of rationality with reality; and
against positivism for reducing these models to the status of conceptual
entities and constructions.

Repeatedly, Lenin emphasized the need to master and to assimilate
the contributions of bourgeois science, without which Marxism tends to
degenerate into a barren dogmatism out of step with events and isolated
from the living realities of the class struggle. Hence intellectual partisanship is not enough: the strategy and tactics of proletarian revolution
depend for their success upon an "objective" account of the sum total of
the material relations between all the classes of a given society plus a
knowledge of the internal development of that society and its external
relations to other societies. Considering the theoretical goal of dialectics,
namely, a many-sided and all-embracing conception of the totality of
phenomena in their unity and opposition, it is abundantly evident that
the most valuable way of human knowledge, from a scientific point of
view, is the highroad of systematic philosophy and not the low road of a
unilateral class science of the proletariat. Although theory enriches
practice, and conversely, the "absolute truths" of systematic social
science incorporate within themselves the "relative truths" of bourgeois
and proletarian sciences, thereby transcending the boundaries of each.
Nonetheless, the summation of partisan truths remain partisan, albeit on
a higher level. Since Marxists believe that the proletariat is the class that
has least to gain by concealing social relations of exploitation, they are
convinced that a general social science—even more than a science

narrowly bound to serve the immediate and short-run interests of the proletariat—is also partisan to its interests.

In the works of Marxist philosophers, materialist dialectics is interpreted in at least two different senses: as a theory of the general laws of motion of nature and society, and as the science of comprehensive truth. Thus in application to social science, the dialectical method leads, on the one hand, to a search for polar oppositions, pathological elements, and agents of disequilibrium, and, on the other hand, to the formulation of a unified, interconnected, and harmonious theory of social reality in its nature and development. In this way the so-called "struggle of opposites" is balanced by their unity and interconnection; the partisan and revolutionary character of Marxian social science, with a unity of conception combining the outstanding contributions of bourgeois social science with those of scientific socialism.

NOTES

[1]   K. Marx and F. Engels, *The German Ideology*, pp. 66–69, 74–75.
[2]   F. Engels, *Anti-Dühring*, pp. 42, 393.
[3]   G. Plekhanov, *Fundamental Problems of Marxism*, pp. 1, 10–11.
[4]   V. I. Lenin, *Selected Works*, vol. XI, p. 704ff.
[5]   V. I. Lenin, *Selected Works*, vol. XI, pp. 197, 199.

8

Karl Marx: Sociologist or Marxist?

T. B. Bottomore

THE question posed in the title of this paper is not intended to exhaust all the aspects from which Marx's work may be regarded; nor is it meant to prejudge the issue as to whether a thinker—and Marx in particular— may be *both* a sociologist *and* a Marxist. But there are advantages in putting just this question. First, the consideration of Marx's thought as one of the early systems of sociology, that is, as an attempt to formulate new concepts for depicting the structure of whole societies and for explaining massive social changes, brings into prominence the most distinctive and, I would say, the most interesting of his ideas. This has become clearer with the growth of sociological studies in the past few decades and with the accompanying reassessment of the history of modern social thought. It is evident that the marked revival of interest in Marxism as a theoretical scheme (which is in contrast with its declining intellectual appeal as a political creed) owes much to the recent work of sociologists; but even at an earlier time, at the end of the nineteenth century and in the first decade of the twentieth century, the most fruitful discussions of Marx's thought seem to me to have been those which arose from sociological or philosophical concerns—in the writings of Max Weber, Croce, Sorel, and Pareto, for example—rather than those which originated in strictly economic or political criticisms.

One important reason for the present revival of interest is the fact that Marx's theory stands in direct opposition on every major point to the functionalist theory which has dominated sociology and anthropology for the past twenty or thirty years, but which has been found increasingly unsatisfactory. Where functionalism emphasizes social

FROM *Science and Society*, 30 (Winter 1966), pp. 11–17, 19–23.

harmony, Marxism emphasizes social conflict; where functionalism directs attention to the stability and persistence of social forms, Marxism is radically historical in its outlook and emphasizes the changing structure of society; where functionalism concentrates upon the regulation of social life by general values and norms, Marxism stresses the divergence of interests and values within each society and the role of force in maintaining, over a longer or shorter period of time, a given social order. The contrast between "equilibrium" and "conflict" models of society, which was stated forcefully by Dahrendorf in 1958,[1] has now become a commonplace; and Marx's theories are regularly invoked in opposition to those of Durkheim, Pareto, and Malinowski, the principal architects of the functionalist theory. . . .

In Marx's theory, the main emphasis is put upon the conflicts within society and the structural changes which result from these conflicts; and there is an underlying scheme of the progressive development of mankind. At the same time, the theory does include some partial accounts of social solidarity and of the persistence of social forms. Marx deals at length, for instance, with the conditions in which class solidarity is generated and maintained; and at the level of a total society he explains the persistence of a particular structure by the relations between classes, the position of a ruling class, and the influence of "ruling ideas." Further, Marx predicts the advent of a type of society in which social conflict will be eliminated while social solidarity and harmony will be complete. In other words, we may see in Marx's theory a juxtaposition of "conflict" and "equilibrium" models of society in two different ways: first, that conflict predominates in the social relations within the total society, while solidarity and consensus prevail in many of the subgroups (especially social classes); and secondly, that total societies may be arranged in a historical order such that in one historical period, the only one we have experienced up to now, conflict is predominant, and in another, in the future, solidarity, peaceful cooperation, and consensus will prevail.

Nevertheless, this theory does not provide an adequate reconciliation of the two models, quite apart from the errors which it may contain in the actual description and explanation of societal conflict or class solidarity. It does not, for example, allow for the possibility that conflict itself may engender or maintain social solidarity (a possibility which Simmel explored more systematically). Moreover, it eliminates conflict entirely in the hypothetical classless society of the future, and it seems also to postulate an original condition of human society, before the extension of the division of labor and the accumulation of private wealth, which was free from conflict. This view depends upon a historical conception which is at odds with the idea of a positive science which seems generally to inspire Marx's mature work. We may attribute greater or lesser importance to the Hegelianism or the positivism of Marx's theory, but it is impossible to reconcile them. Isaiah Berlin, for instance, has argued that: "The framework of [Marx's] theory is undeviatingly Hegelian. It recognizes that the history of humanity is a single, non-repetitive process, which obeys discoverable laws. These laws are different from the laws of physics or of chemistry, which being unhistorical, record unvarying conjunctions and successions of interconnected phenomena, whenever or wherever these may repeat themselves; they are similar rather to those of geology or botany, which embody the principles in accordance with which a process of continuous change takes place." [2] On the other hand, it may be claimed that many of Marx's propositions have the form at least of statements of universal laws. Thus, the famous phrase: "The history of all hitherto existing society is the history of class struggles" may be interpreted, not as a historical principle, but as a universal law of conflict in human society. Similarly, the assertion that the form of social institutions and of ideas is determined by the economic structure of society has to be regarded either as the expression of a universal law, or as a rule of method. Even where Marx says he is formulating a law of change—for example, "the law of motion of modern capitalist society"—this may be seen as a special law applicable to a particular type of society (capitalist or industrial), and in principle derivable from some more general law which refers to change in *all* societies. Thus, laws of social change do not have to be historical laws or principles; they may be universal, and applicable to all instances whenever or wherever they occur.

In Marx's own theory these two conceptions—the historical interpretation of a unique sequence of events, and the framing of universal laws covering repeatable events—coexist, and later Marxists have in the main opted for one or the other view: the positivist or scientific school being represented to some extent by Engels, and most fully by Max Adler; the Hegelianizing school by Lukács, Korsch, Marcuse, and a number of recent opponents of positivism, particularly in France. My own contention is that the general inclination of Marx's work, when it is traced from his earlier to his later writings, is clearly away from the philosophy of history and toward a scientific theory of society, in the precise sense of a body of general laws and detailed empirical statements. I recognize, of course, that it is not along this path that the main development of Marxism has occurred. Indeed, it is striking that the major contributions of Marxist research have been in the historical field, though even here they have been confined to a narrow range of problems, and that empirical investigations in the sociological domain have been rare.

A recent essay by Hobsbawm[3] restates the point about the influence of Marxism upon economic and social history with great clarity. Introducing the first English translation of Marx's only extended analysis of precapitalist societies,[4] Hobsbawm argues that Marx formulates here a theory of historical *progress* rather than a scheme of social evolution, and that it is in these terms (i.e., from the standpoint of a historian) that his distinctions between different types of society should be considered. What Marxist historians have actually done Hobsbawm examines later, and he concludes that the recent contributions are in some ways unsatisfactory inasmuch as they have neglected certain types of society— notably the "Asiatic society"—and have greatly expanded the notion of "feudal society" to fill up the gaps. The preoccupation of Marxist historians with just those questions which Marx himself examined most fully—the rise of the *bourgeoisie* within feudal society, the transition from feudalism to capitalism, and the early stages of capitalist society— does, indeed, seem excessive; and aside from the neglect of other types of social structure, it has also meant that the Marxist contribution to modern social history has been less substantial than might have been expected. In the main, it is not the Marxists who have studied closely the development of modern social classes and elites, of ideologies, or of political parties, or who have attempted to analyze revolutionary movements. This domain, which is closest to sociology, has unquestionably been much influenced, if not actually created, by Marx's ideas, but most of the important studies have been made by scholars who were not Marxists —from Sombart, Max Weber, and Michels to Geiger and Karl Mannheim, from Veblen to C. Wright Mills.

In the main line of sociological inquiry no Marxist scholar has emerged to equal the achievement of Max Weber in using Marx's very general propositions about the relation between ideologies and social structure as the starting point for a vast and fruitful investigation of the role of particular religious ideas and beliefs in social change and of their connections with various social classes. Those Marxists who, like Max Adler, wanted to present Marx's theory as a system of scientific sociology have generally confined themselves to methodological discussions, while those of the Hegelian school have either wandered into the happily imprecise and imaginative field of literary criticism (Lukács) or have, like the positivists, turned to methodological reflections (Sartre).

The contrast between the accomplishments of the more orthodox schools of Marxism and of those scholars who were simply stimulated by Marx's ideas to embark upon fresh research of their own, reflects no discredit upon Marx himself. Marx was always passionately interested in factual social inquiries—from the investigations of Quételet and Buret to the reports of the English factory inspectors and his own projected "enquête ouvrière"—and he undertook in *Capital* an empirical study of vast scope which is still unsurpassed in the literature of the social sciences. His whole work, which combines the construction of theoretical models of society with the elaboration of methods of inquiry, and with the imaginative use of these models and methods in the analysis of a type of social system and its transformations, is by any reckoning one of the great contributions to the formation of modern sociology; and when we consider how, outside the confines of the various Marxist orthodoxies, it has provoked new sociological investigations, new reflections upon problems of theory and method, and repeated reassessments (such as we are engaged upon today), then it may justifiably be regarded as the greatest single contribution—*the* decisive intellectual advance which established our subject in a recognizable form. If Marx sometimes contradicted himself, made mistakes, moved ambiguously from a Hegelian idiom to the language of modern natural science, and back again, left some of his concepts in a logically untidy form, sometimes used essentialist definitions though he was in the main a nominalist, exaggerated social conflict in his theoretical model, this seems to me excusable in a pioneer thinker whose ideas had the power to create a new branch of knowledge which, in its own development, would produce the means of correcting and refining these early formulations.

The inexcusable would be that Marx had deliberately sacrificed positive science to metaphysics, that he had sought only that evidence which supported a vision of the world and of history created by a poetic and philosophic imagination and never afterwards questioned; in short, that he was pre-eminently a Marxist, the expounder of a creed. Marx, of course, *said* that he was not a Marxist, and there is little reason to doubt that he was extremely critical of the exposition of his ideas by self-styled disciples during his lifetime. Was it that he considered these expositions inadequate, or did he object to the presentation of his ideas as a political creed? Did he see his theory chiefly as an engine of discovery, and as one which required a great deal more hard intellectual work before it would be really adequate for its purpose? We must, in any case, make a distinction between the "Marxism" of Marx and that of the Marxists. For Marx, his own system of thought could not possibly be something established or given, a simple framework for the expression of a social or political aim. It was his own creation, worked out laboriously over a long period of time, incessantly revised and admittedly incomplete. . . .

There runs unmistakably through all Marx's work (even in his youthful writings when he is still struggling out of the toils of the Hegelian philosophy) a profound commitment to the investigation of *social facts;* a commitment which again finds expression in his preface to the "enquête ouvrière," where he appeals to those who, ". . . desiring social reform, must also desire *exact* and *positive* knowledge of the conditions in which the working class, the class to which the future belongs, lives and works." The "Marxism" in Marx's own thought, and in that of his followers, has frequently been seen as the subordination of theoretical ideas and social investigations to a preconceived social ideal and a rigorously determined means of attaining it. I have already suggested that this view is mistaken with respect to Marx himself, inasmuch as it was his declared intention to make clear to his age *its own* strivings, and more particularly to display to the working class its real situation in capitalist society, the implications of its revolt against that situation, and the probable outcome of the working-class movement.

It will be profitable, however, to consider more closely the relations between theoretical judgments, judgments of fact, and judgments of value in Marx's work. The first point to note is that in Marx's life socialism and social science were closely interwoven. He became, at an early age, and probably through the influence of Saint-Simonian doctrines, a sympathizer with the working-class movement; and this commitment to socialism certainly preceded the full elaboration of his sociological theories. Nevertheless, from the beginning he was equally impressed by the new "science of society" prefigured in Saint-Simon's writings (and subsequently in Lorenz von Stein's book on the social movement in France); and his later reading of the historians of the French Revolution and of the political economists was sufficient to persuade him both that there was growing up a new field and a new method in the study of man's social life, and that the development of capitalism and the rise of the labor movement formed the essential subject matter of this study. From that time, about the middle of the 1840s, Marx's participation in the socialist movement and his efforts to advance the theoretical science of society proceeded together, and fructified each other. This, after all, is not surprising, nor uncommon. The greatest social scientists have been passionately concerned about some social problem, and usually extremely partisan (I think of Max Weber, Durkheim, and Pareto) and this may account for the significance and the intellectual excitement of their work. The question is whether this partisanship manifests itself too strongly, not simply in the selection of subjects for inquiry, but in the formation of concepts and models, which become ideal-types of too ideal a kind, and in the conduct and presentation of their investigations, which become too selective, too well insulated against the possible discovery of counterinstances.

In Marx's case (but also in some of the others, and notably in Durkheim's) there is also a more profound problem. Does the theory, or the broader scheme of thought, contain within itself a theory of knowledge which eliminates the distinction between fact and value? . . . The idea of the social determination of thought appears to destroy the autonomy of moral judgments; but in the same manner it destroys the autonomy of all judgments (including those judgments which constitute Marx's own theory, so that there is no longer any point in asking whether it is true or false). But this is not a problem in Marx's theory alone: it is a problem for any deterministic theory, and in a broad sense of any scientific theory, in psychology or sociology. It may, indeed, be argued, on the other side, that one of the virtues of Marx's social theory is that it makes a much greater allowance for the creative work of human reason in the fashioning of social institutions.[5]

A more specific problem appears in Marx's theory of ideologies, which, while it excludes science from the realm of socially determined ideas, makes moral notions wholly ideological in the sense of reflecting the interests of social classes. This makes moral ideas relative, yet Marx also expresses what appear to be absolute moral judgments. If this is, indeed, the case there is a contradiction in his thought. . . .

I do not wish to single out Marx's own scientific rectitude as the only restraint upon his ideological enthusiasms, even though it does form a striking contrast with the attitude of some of his followers. There is also the fact that in Marx's lifetime his theoretical analysis and his allegiance to the labor movement were congruent and, in a sense, mutually supporting. The labor movement developed spontaneously, and Marx could easily justify his claim to be analyzing and explaining a real process of social change. The gulf between classes was widening, class consciousness was growing, the relations between classes did form the core of the social problem, and the new doctrines of working-class organizations did foreshadow the classless society which Marx predicted. Thus, Marx's theory could find empirical confirmation, and its empirical testing provided at the same time a degree of rational and factual support for Marx's moral convictions. How closely these two aspects were associated is shown especially well in the projected "enquête ouvrière" of 1880, which is first of all in the tradition of a long series of empirical surveys of working-class conditions, but which, secondly, goes beyond these in attempting to establish the principle of an investigation of working-class conditions by the working class itself, and which does so in order to combine in a single effort of research both a factual inquiry and a heightening of class consciousness.

Here Marx's two aims are in perfect concord. We may ask whether the combination is legitimate, and I would answer with a qualified affirmative. If sociology is to have any application to actual social life, then one of its most important applications should be the wide diffusion of knowledge about the nature of social relationships in a given society in order to increase men's conscious self-regulation of their social life.

And in societies where whole classes of men are excluded from any significant part in the regulation of public affairs, it is proper to concentrate upon awakening and fostering in those particular classes a consciousness of their place in society, of their material and intellectual poverty, their lack of rights, their exclusion from power. But as the knowledge of society increases, as the position of classes changes, so must sociological thought follow these movements, revise its initial propositions, and conceive new empirical tests. . . .

NOTES

[1] Ralf Dahrendorf, "Out of Utopia: Toward a Reorientation of Sociological Analysis," *American Journal of Sociology*, vol. LXIV, no. 2 (1958).

[2] Isaiah Berlin, *Karl Marx*, third edition (London, 1963), p. 124.

[3] E. J. Hobsbawm, "Introduction" to Karl Marx, *Pre-capitalist Economic Formations* (New York, 1965).

[4] In the manuscript dating from 1857–58, which was an early draft of *Capital* and which was first published in Moscow (1939–41) under the title *Grundrisse der Kritik der politischen Ökonomie (Rohentwurf)*.

[5] Marcuse, in *Reason and Revolution* (New York, 1941), presents the case for Marx's "critical philosophy" and against Comte's sociological positivism in these terms; and more recently Sartre, in his *Question de Methode* (Paris, 1960), has argued in a similar fashion.

PART TWO

Marx: Moralist and Humanist

Marxist Ethics

THE basic problems in the Marxian ethics are those of the absolute nature or relativity of moral ideas, and the view of the nature and destiny of man. The first issue stems from the Marxian view that ideas are the outcome of social conditions and relationships. Since conditions are continually changing, ideas and values will change accordingly. Since moral ideas are said to be the reflection of the ideas of the ruling class, and history has been the story of changing classes, moral ideas are relative and no morality can claim eternal validity. Morality only condemns what has already been condemned by history. Since the proletariat is destined to capture power and create the new society, the presumption might be that its ideas should be dominant. The somewhat polemical article by R. N. Carew Hunt is a formidable attack on these and other aspects of the Marxist ethics, on the attitude that everything is desirable which contributes to the revolution, and on the alleged belief in the superiority of the proletariat.

In a more scholarly article, Eugene Kamenka traces the Marxian preoccupation with the progression of society to a "truly human society," a matter related to the nature of man. Is there an "essence" of man, or is he conditioned by history? Under what conditions can man fulfill himself?

For Marx man is not only a social animal but "an animal that can develop into an individual only in society." In his consciousness of his species, man confirmed his real social life. The Marxian ethic attempts to reconcile the individual and the social being. In *The Economic and Philosophic Manuscripts* Marx argued that the objective of the desirable society was "the definitive resolution of the antagonism between man and nature, and between man and man."

The nature of individuals depended on the material conditions of production. Therefore to change man, one must change society and social relationships. The Polish philosopher Adam Schaff has argued that the central issue for Marx was the freedom of the individual which would ensure the full development of his personality. For Marx, as for Hegel, history was the process through which man was attaining true humanity and freedom. But to free himself an individual had to aim at the emancipation of humanity as a whole, since freedom was found only in community with others. In *A Contribution to the Critique of Hegel's Philosophy of Right*, Marx argued it was necessary to overthrow all those conditions in which "man is an abased, enslaved, abandoned, contemptible being." Man would free himself and his society when the social anarchy of production was replaced by the desirable society which would be based on the social regulation of production on a definite plan according to the needs of the community and of each individual. The humanistic attitude and evocation of freedom is a fundamental part of Marx's writings, but the liberation of man and the development of man's capacities is regarded as possible only through the collective activity of men, rather than through absence of restraint as with most liberal writers. "Communism," wrote Engels, "is the positive abolition of private property, of human self-alienation and thus the real appropriation of human nature through and for man. It is the return of man himself as a social, that is human, being." In this way man will move from the realm of necessity to that of freedom.

9

The Ethics of Marxism

R. N. Carew Hunt

IT WOULD be hard to find among the writings of the mid-nineteenth century a more generous tribute to the capitalist system than is paid to it in *The Communist Manifesto*. In a short space of years it had wrought unparalleled wonders. It had established "the universal interdependence of nations." It had "drawn all, even the most barbarian, nations into civilization." By creating great cities it "had rescued a considerable part of the population from the idiocy of rural life." It had, in a word, "subjected nature's forces to man." "What earlier century," Marx asked, "had even a presentiment that such productive forces slumbered in the lap of social labor?" He did not indeed pause to inquire whether this was altogether an advantage. Yet he can scarcely be blamed, as few Victorians would have denied that production was the chief duty of man; and we may surely admit Marx to their company after the many years he lived among them.

Yet *The Communist Manifesto* is nonetheless a declaration of war against capitalist society which the workers are to overthrow by violence; and Marxists hold that any means are permissible which contribute to this end. That Moscow should proclaim this doctrine might be argued to reflect the amoralism which early manifested itself in the Russian revolutionary movement. But every Communist is taught that his first duty is to his party; and all Communist parties have shown themselves willing to adopt Lenin's doctrine that the criterion of right action is the degree to which it assists the cause of revolution. Here indeed the single exception proves the rule. In his *Left-wing Communism, an Infantile Disorder* (1920) Lenin condemned terrorism (e.g., political assassination)

FROM *The Nineteenth Century*, 145 (February 1949), pp. 108–115, 117.

because the Bolsheviks held at the time that it weakened the proletarian movement by encouraging the masses to believe that the revolution could be won for them by a few "heroic individuals" instead of carrying it out for themselves. But he was careful to point out that his objection was "of course only based on considerations of expediency"; and Marxists have long since been permitted to use such methods if they are likely to be successful. Nor indeed had Lenin himself hesitated to make use of them in his earlier years. . . .

The Marxist ethic derives logically from the general philosophic position which Marx adopted. Here three points should be noted:

First: The Hegelian dialectic denied the existence of any eternal and immutable principles upon which a system of ethics or of anything else could be founded, since ideas themselves were in a continual state of change.

Secondly: Kant had taught that while we could have no real knowledge of the external world, we do reach solid rock in the moral consciousness; and he had formulated certain principles of conduct—his famous "Categorical Imperatives"—by which morality, in the sense of private morality, should be regulated and for which he claimed a universal validity. But Hegel could not accept such an ethic as final since he was concerned with a grand historical process, directed by reason and operating through the dialectic, under which civilizations rose and fell; and to justify this process he *had* to show that there was a higher and dynamic ethic upon which the judgments of "world history" rested, since it was obvious that no nation reaches a dominant position through obedience to the precepts of private morality or by turning the other cheek.

The Norman Conquest, for example, cannot be justified by ordinary moral standards. But historians do not therefore go about condemning it as an irreparable disaster, but agree that it was of the utmost benefit to Great Britain. It could of course be argued that this only proves that in certain cases good may come out of evil. But this would not have satisfied Hegel, as it would have introduced a fortuitous element into the process which he wished to exhibit as wholly rational. He therefore held that Kant's Imperatives were vapid when they were not actually dangerous; and that many of the moral injunctions of Jesus were inapplicable to a "bourgeois society," and would speedily bring about the ruin of any state that attempted to apply them.

Thirdly: Marx agreed with Hegel in rejecting what is called abstract ethical idealism, that is, the view that there exist certain principles of right and wrong which are universal. He held that there was no such thing as "human nature" in the abstract, and that men's ideas of what is good and bad were conditioned by the economic conditions of the social organism of which they formed a part. He too was not concerned with the morality of individuals but with that of groups, though for him the group was the class and not the nation. The force behind the dialectic of history was the class struggle, and this generated its own ethic. Here, however, Marx went further than his master. Hegel had pointed out that actions which could not be justified by the moral standards of the police court might ultimately be approved by "world history" which adopted a different standard. But he never said that nations or their leaders were free to act as they pleased on the chance that their actions might be thus approved.

Marx teaches that the ethical system of any community, like its religion and laws, is simply a part of the superstructure created by the conditions of production and always reflects the interests of the dominant class. Its values are thus no more than expressions of "class morality," and as long as the class system persists no useful purpose is to be served by discussing them. When that system has been destroyed and not before, it will be possible to put ethics on a sound basis. *The Communist Manifesto* is the most powerful indictment of the capitalist order ever written, but it contains no work of "right" or "justice," and no appeal to any "moral law." Nor does Marx's use of "exploitation" in *Capital* directly imply an ethical condemnation; it is not, at least ostensibly, the expression of a moral judgment, but rather a description of social relations. His main charge against the French Utopian Socialists, and particularly Proudhon, had been precisely their obsession with "justice," whereas his object was to convince every thinking person that the capitalist system was doomed to disappear for reasons which lay within its very nature and which had nothing to do with metaphysical abstractions. [1]

Yet here we have to note a certain ambivalence between Marx the scientist and Marx the revolutionary agitator. His *Capital* purports to be a strictly scientific demonstration of the fate which must ultimately overtake the capitalist system. Yet every page reveals Marx's abhorrence of that system. Capitalists may be obliged to act as they do; but this is only because they are operating within a system which is inherently corrupt. Indeed, if Marx had held it to be otherwise, his demonstration could only have aroused an academic interest, and would not have stirred men's passions as it was intended to do. Yet his moral indignation raises an awkward question. For if the capitalist system is evil, it can only be because it is in conflict with some objective moral principle. But the existence of any such principle has been denied.

The two classical formulations of the Marxist ethic, to which all apologists invariably refer, are those of Engels and Lenin. The first is in the *Anti-Dühring*.

We therefore reject every attempt to impose on us any moral dogma whatsoever as an eternal, ultimate and for ever immutable moral law on the pretext that the moral world too has its permanent principles which transcend history and the differences between nations. We maintain on the contrary that all former moral theories are the product, in the last analysis, of the economic stage which society had reached at that particular epoch. And as society has hitherto moved in class antagonisms, morality was always a class morality; it has either justified the domination and the interests of the ruling class; or, as soon as the oppressed class has become powerful enough, it has represented the revolt against this domination and the future interests of the oppressed. That in this process there has on the whole been progress in morality, as in all other branches of human knowledge, cannot be doubted. But we have not yet passed beyond class morality. A really human morality which transcends class antagonisms and their legacies in thought becomes possible only at a stage of society which has not only overcome class contradictions but has even forgotten them in practical life.

Lenin's contribution is contained in his *Address to the 3rd Congress of the Russian Young Communist League* of October 2nd, 1920—not the most inspired of his writings:

Is there such a thing as Communist ethics? It there such a thing as Communist morality? Of course there is. It is often made to appear that we have no ethics of our own; and very often the bourgeoisie accuse us Communists of repudiating all ethics. This is a method of throwing dust in the eyes of the workers and peasants.

In what sense do we repudiate ethics and morality?

In the sense that it is preached by the bourgeoisie, who derived ethics from God's commandments. Or instead of deriving ethics from the commandments of God, they derived them from idealist or semi-idealist phrases, which always amounted to something very similar to God's commandments. We repudiate all morality derived from nonhuman and nonclass concepts. We say that it is a deception, a fraud in the interests of the landlords and capitalists. We say that our morality is entirely subordinated to the interests of the class struggle of the proletariat. Our morality is derived from the interests of the class struggle of the proletariat. . . . The class struggle is still continuing. . . . We subordinate our Communist morality to this task. We say: morality is what serves to destroy the old exploiting society and to unite all the toilers around the proletariat, which is creating a new Communist society. . . . We do not believe in an eternal morality.

It will be seen that Lenin accepts the sharp division which Marx made between the bourgeoisie and the proletariat, which are represented as two entirely different human types whose relations resemble those of a white minority exploiting a colored majority. But while this distinction is adopted by all Marxist writers and has an obvious propaganda value, it is an altogether arbitrary one and is rooted in a static conception of society as seen at a particular period of time. Marx was a great admirer of

Balzac, about whom he had intended to write a book, and it is a pity that he had not read the *Comédie Humaine* with a greater discernment, as it admirably illustrates that movement, continually operative in society, as a result of which members of the proletariat rise in the social scale for reasons often not unconnected with their superior intelligence and capacity for hard work, while members of the bourgeoisie similarly descend, possibly again for lack of such qualities. But this arbitrary class division is maintained by all Marxist writers, and is rendered even more artificial by their practice of transferring to the bourgeoisie any section of the workers with whom they may be in conflict. . . . Yet if the above passages from Engels and Lenin are read in conjunction with such glosses as Western Marxists have made during recent years, the main lines of the Marxist ethic become clear enough. [2] It is strictly materialist and natural-istic. Man is the product of Nature and is bound by Nature's laws; and it is in accordance with these laws, and not with his dreams and ideals, that society develops. A scientific study of society at once reveals that the class struggle is fundamental, and from this is born the doctrine of the social revolution which transforms Marxism from a theory into a militant activism. And, as Trotsky puts it, "the highest form of the class struggle is civil war which explodes in midair all moral ties between the hostile classes." [3]

The basis of the Marxist ethic is thus what present-day Marxists often call "the concrete human situation" in which the conditions of production are the determining factor. It is an ethic which is rooted in demands, not in intuitions, and which rejects every "transcendent" element. [4] A recent American writer on *The Communist Manifesto* observes that the workers do not seek to derive the principles which lead them to demand the abolition of the capitalist system from anything except their own interests, which, it is explained, are ultimately those of mankind in general, since those who make them represent the enslaved of all ages. Hence he declares that the Marxist ethic is simply the expression of the desires of the workers, but that these are justified because they accord with the inevitable course of social evolution. That proletarian morality is still class morality is recognized. But it is an advance on bour-geois morality because it is that of the class dialectically predestined to triumph and ultimately to create a society the ethic of which will possess an absolute value because class distinctions will have disappeared. Indeed, as Professor J. D. Bernal pointed out in an article in the *Modern Quarterly* of December, 1945, the new planned society into which we are now entering already calls for a radical change in ethical values. Some of the old virtues will remain; but virtues such as thrift, which have their roots in an outmoded individualism, will be replaced by others based on a livelier sense of social relations.

It should be noted, however, that Marxists use the term "proletarian morality" with a certain ambiguity. At times it is held to mean the morality of the proletariat during that transition period which lies between the revolution which abolishes the bourgeois state and the creation of a classless society, that is, the phase of the dictatorship of the proletariat which Lenin characterized as one of "violence unrestricted by law"; while at others it is used to denote the morality of the classless society of that "higher stage of Socialism" which lies in the future but to which the dictatorship of the proletariat will eventually give rise.

It is only possible to make a few brief comments on the foregoing.

1. We do not need Marx or Engels to tell us that standards of behavior vary from age to age and that every generation has to work out its own moral problems. If this was all they wished to say, they could only be charged with uttering a commonplace. In fact, however, as appears clearly in *The Communist Manifesto* their intention was to invalidate all ethical criticism of their teaching by denying that it could rest upon any universal principles and by representing it as no more than the expression of class interest. But this is to reject the existence of any objective standard. Every great work of literature reflects the social conditions of its age; but it also contains esthetic values which are universal. Equally, there are absolute and immutable ethical principles which have commanded assent all down the centuries. For underlying the flux of history there is a certain continuum to which all ethical judgments can be related, and which lead men to agree that Socrates was a good man and Nero a bad man, and that truth and charity are better than falsehood and malice. At all times men have agreed that it is better to assist their fellow creatures than to injure them, though the extent to which they have been prepared to render such assistance and the particular form which they have felt that it should take have depended on the moral insights of their generation.

Present-day Marxists may point out that Marx and Engels would never have contested the above, and would thus have agreed that bourgeois morality contained certain permanent elements which a classless morality would take over. But although this is doubtless what they meant, it is not what they said; and their condemnation of all ethical systems other than their own is so sweeping as to make it difficult to see what elements in them they regarded as worthy of survival or by what criterion they would be selected. Indeed it is not uncommon for Marxists to argue that such virtues as kindliness are not virtues in their own right, but only became such if and in so far as they are harnessed to the proletarian cause.

2. Marxism greatly exaggerates the power of communities in

general, and in this case of classes, to evolve genuine ethical systems. The morality of all collectivities is invariably low, if only because the sense of personal responsibility is diluted; and it is a commonplace that boards and committees will often act as none of their individual members would dream of doing. It is of course perfectly true that private morality is the outcome and product of social morality. Yet it is equally true that every advance in the moral standards of a community is the work of individuals. Lenin early formed the opinion that the proletariat, if left to itself, never develops a revolutionary ideology. But neither will it develop an ethical system worthy of the name; while it is less likely than other classes to produce the type of leader who will change what system it does evolve for a better. The ideology of Marxism itself derives from men who, like Marx and Engels, were bourgeois and not proletarians.

3. Even if we accept the Marxist thesis that all ethical systems simply reflect the interests of the dominant class, it would only follow that proletarian morality will do the same, and not that it is superior to other forms of morality. In the absence of any objective standard, bourgeois and proletarian morality are only different sets of feelings about right and wrong, and there can be no proof that one set is better than another. To prefer proletarian morality because the victory of the proletariat is guaranteed by the dialectic is incompatible with any view of ethics, since a thing is not necessarily desirable because it is unavoidable.

4. It is certainly a logical inference that if all morality is class morality, the only way to get a classless morality is to do away with classes. But it does not follow that the destruction of the bourgeoisie, or of whatever class may be regarded as in the ascendent, will create such a society; and indeed the more highly developed is the social order in which a Marxist revolution has occurred, the more inevitably will there arise a new class stratification, the upper levels of which will tend, precisely as in the past, to impose their ideas upon the lower. The new class of managers, technicians, and the like which has arisen in Russia has quickly enough revealed the same prejudices as the older class which it has replaced.

5. It is quite true that in some sense moral obligation does derive from human demands. Yet is this the end of the matter? All civilized people condemn murder. But does this condemnation spring only from the very "concrete demand" that they should not have their throats cut? Or does it not imply some perception of the sanctity of human life, a consideration which a Marxist might well dismiss as "transcendent," and which it is certainly not easy to represent as the rationalization of an economic interest? This at least appears to be the lesson of Dostoievsky's *Crime and Punishment*. . . .

6. The Marxist contention that any action is justified if it assists the cause of revolution raises the difficult question of ends and means.

Dr. John Lewis, editor of the *Modern Quarterly*, has recently quoted with approval a statement to the effect that "an end will always justify the means if the end is good and the means adapted to promote it," which is simply the old maxim (erroneously fathered upon the Jesuits) that "the end justifies the means," since it is naturally assumed that the end is good and no one has ever suggested that any end justifies any means. There are those who hold that, as we cannot define absolute standards, we are obliged to use the above principle and habitually do so. It is difficult to see the force of this contention. People of normal moral instincts do not pursue ends by means which they know to be bad, or, if they do so, they do not pretend that they are acting rightly, save insofar as they unconsciously deceive themselves. . . . Machiavelli puts the case well. If, he says, a man wishes to obtain domination over the state but then decides that he can only do so by assassinating a dangerous rival, he must renounce his designs if he objects to employing such methods, though if he persists in it, he must use all those means which are necessary to its attainment. What he must not do is to seek the end while trying to evade the means, for this is altogether contemptible. But Machiavelli does not attempt to show that this pursuit of ends by appropriate means has anything to do with moral goodness. It calls rather for that quality which he calls *virtu*, which is ethically neutral and does not concern itself with whether the end is good or bad. . . .

The central error of present-day Marxists, apart from their fundamental lack of charity toward their fellow creatures, is their attempt to set up by any and every means a planned Absolute of social justice. We do well to strive after justice. Yet in an imperfect world we can never hope to reach more than an approximation to it; and if our presumption carries us further, all we are likely to achieve is a greater injustice. *Summum jus, summa injuria.*

That our Marxist ideologist thinks otherwise is partly because the doctrine of the class struggle has taught him to regard life as an unending battle in which no quarter must be given; and partly, and perhaps even more, because he has been trained to believe that he is helping to plan society in strict accordance with scientific laws. Dialectical materialism repudiates mechanistic interpretations. Yet in practice Marxists accept them. Society, they hold, is like a machine which will only work properly if it is put together in the right (or Marxist) way. Hence our ideologist feels as little compunction in ridding himself of an opponent as does a mechanic who throws some faulty bolt upon the scrap heap when he is assembling an engine. He will point out that the dialectic shows that at the present stage of history nothing matters except the victory of the proletariat which will usher in the classless society, and that he prefers to cooperate with this inevitable historical process rather than oppose it.

And that he reasons thus is perhaps the best answer to those who contend that the dialectic is an irrelevant assertion upon the Marxist system.

NOTES

1 Vernon Venable, *Human Nature, The Marxism View* (1946), p. 205.
2 See, for example, Roger Garaudy's *Le Communisme et la Morale*. This makes the usual question-begging claim that only when the capitalist system has been abolished will men be free to develop their personalities to the full, and that Marxism is thus the true humanism.
3 *Their Morals and Ours* (New York, 1940).
4 See Sidney Hook, *From Hegel to Marx* (1936), pp. 47f.

10

The Primitive Ethic of Karl Marx

Eugene Kamenka

IN THE field of ethics, the work of Karl Marx has become largely identified with the "exposure" of moral injunctions and codes. His materialist treatment of ideologies is rightly taken to mean that historical moral codes and beliefs should not be treated as true or false, valid or invalid, but simply as "expressions" of the "material" demands of specific social classes. His own theory, Marx insisted, was not an ideology, but a "scientific" socialism based on positive discoveries in history and economics. It was not derived from any postulation of abstract, immutable moral principles or codes.

From the beginning, however, critics have been aware of a second, seemingly inconsistent, strain in the work of Marx and Engels. This is their belief that society progresses through successively higher stages to the "truly human" society and morality of communism—a belief that clearly implies objective, eternal, and immutable moral standards for appraising successive stages of social development. With this belief went a spate of denunciations of exploitation, privilege, servility, and the divided class society that leaves no doubt whatever that Marx and Engels regarded these things as positively and immutably evil.

In the consciously "scientific socialist" work of Marx and Engels after 1848 this positive ethical strain presents serious difficulties. Unlike their reductionist theory of moral codes, their positive ethical view is not put forward as a specific theory at all. It appears rather as a series of implicit valuations within a theory of history and society that amalgamates fact and value in the manner typical of Hegel. The criterion

FROM *The Australasian Journal of Philosophy*, 35 (August 1957), pp. 75–76, 81–91, 96.

behind these valuations appears at first sight not wholly coherent; sometimes it is temporal order or durability, sometimes a special but vague doctrine of freedom, sometimes an even more vague theory of the "truly human."

With a very few exceptions (such as Herbert Marcuse in his *Reason and Revolution* and H. B. Acton in parts of his *Illusion of the Epoch*), philosophical critics of Marx have done little to clear up this vagueness or to come fully to grips with his ethical theory. They have rightly emphasized the objections to any theory of "objective" values and the untenability of Marx's pretense of deriving ethical values and moral injunctions from the positive study of logic, history, or society. As a logical refutation this is indeed sufficient. But if one is attempting to understand Marx, it is a major mistake to follow many of these critics in regarding the positive ethical strain in Marx as largely unconscious, devoid of any background of ethical theory, and flagrantly inconsistent with his "exposure" of moral codes. On the contrary, Marx's conversion to Hegelianism, his *Auseinander-setzung* with the *Philosophy of Right*, his critique of capitalist society and political economy, his initial discovery of the necessity of socialism, were all the products of detailed grappling with questions which a non-Hegelian would have to call ethical. Marx, throughout those formative struggles between 1841 and 1847, was intensely conscious of his views' ethical foundation and import; he worked hard at elucidating the ethical implications of the central Hegelian concepts of freedom and rationality; he arrived at a theory which, with all its confusion and necessary vagueness, can only be called ethical and which on the face of it seemed to Marx perfectly consistent with an "exposure" of nonnatural imperativist moral beliefs and codes. . . .

Despite differences between Marx and Hegel even at the very beginning of Marx's philosophical activity, Marx's basic schema is Hegel's: To understand the world is to see its energizing principle, to grasp the form working dialectically through things toward an ultimate harmony that represents the full flowering into existence of the truly real. It is the schema that was to remain fundamental to Marx's thought for the rest of his days. It gave him, on the one hand, the framework of his dialectical conception of history; on the other, it provided him with history's temporal and moral climax, and thus with the fundamental moral assumptions of his work.

The basic ethical implications of the Marx-Hegel schema are simple, even though Hegel filled them in with the most involved and rigorously coordinated detail. The energizing principle, the concept working in things, is rational, working toward freedom and harmony. Freedom meant for Marx, as for Hegel, self-determination in accordance with one's inner constitution; it meant not being determined from without, by one's relations to other things, but by the logical principle of one's own development. Harmony meant above all freedom from inner contradiction, in the Hegelian sense of contradiction which confuses contradiction with exclusion and treats it as a character of—imperfect—existing things, not as a guarantee that such contradictories cannot both exist. Further, since contradiction provides the dialectical basis of historical change, the truly harmonious is also the stable, the ultimately durable. It represents the truly real as against the mere dependent existence, as against that which, by its dependence, is not itself. The free, harmonious whole, then, is the end of the dialectical process (although, as concept, it was there all the time). In its final unfolding what is and what ought to be are made one—they are "taken up" and reconciled in the rational which was always the truly real, but which has now also become the existing actual.

Although Marx and Hegel both reject the belief in moral standards above facts, the belief in that which "ought to be," but possibly never is, it is clear then that in their concept of the "rational" they do want to keep the notion of the moral end, the notion of "good" as something at once descriptive and commendatory. For the recognition of this good, their position implies clear moral criteria—complicated in Hegel, but exhibited in their basic simplicity in Marx. The mark of the good is freedom (self-determination, independence), harmony, unity, and stability, and above all, lack of self-contradiction (in the Hegelian sense). The mark of evil is dependence (determination from without), division, instability, and self-contradiction. Evil is also, both for Hegel and Marx, not truly *real*, but merely a negative appearance, a lack, or one-sidedness, rather than a positive quality. The conflict between good and evil is thus not eternal or irreconcilable—the evil is simply a necessary stage on the march to the good, a one-sidedness that is "taken up" and dissolved in the truly rational.

These criteria Marx used consistently in his earliest work, and he took them as establishing a positive field of morality, a positive distinction between good and evil.

Thus in his *Remarks on the Most Recent Prussian Instructions to Censors*, written in January-February, 1842, he notes that the instruction has substituted the words "decency, propriety, and external decorum" for the words "morality and the decent proprieties" in the original law. "We see," says Marx, "morality as morality, as the principle of the world, which obeys its own laws, disappears, and in place of the essence come external appearance, a decorousness imposed by the police, a conventional propriety"[1] (i,161). But for Marx it does not disappear, nor can it be explained away. After arguing that censorship is evil in all its aspects, he concludes: "That which is in general bad, remains bad, no matter which individual is the carrier of this badness, whether a private critic or an employee of the Government, only that, in the latter case, the badness is authorized and regarded from above as a necessity, in order to bring to realization the good from below" (i,165). This decidedly un-Machiavellian point is reiterated even more clearly in his *Rheinische Zeitung* discussion of the debates on freedom of the press in the sixth Rhenish diet. "We have shown," Marx writes, "that the press law is a right and the censorship law a wrong. The censorship, however, itself admits that it is not an end in itself, that it is not in itself good, that it therefore rests on the principle: 'the end makes holy the means.' But an end, which necessitates unholy means, is not a holy end . . ." (i, 211). Again, when the representative of the knights in the diet argues that all men are imperfect and need guidance and education, Marx insists that we cannot abandon objective standards merely because all things are allegedly imperfect: "If then all things human are imperfect by their very existence, shall we therefore jumble up everything together, respect everything equally, the good and the bad, the truth and the lie?" (i, 201).

Marx is not making these points merely polemically. For him, at this stage, the distinction between good and evil is an absolute one. The good, whenever he refers to it, is the positively good, bearing characters that cannot be altered by individual purposes or social rationalizations.

Above all, for Marx, the good is the free. Harmony, unity, stability, and lack of self-contradiction are logically bound up in the nature of freedom as self-determination—freedom is for Marx at once the great moral and the great historical category. Thus, in the comment on the Prussian censorship instruction, Marx contrasts positive morality with the special (spurious) morality of religion: "Morality rests on the autonomy, religion on the heteronomy of the human spirit" (i, 161). Again, in the *Rheinische Zeitung* discussion of press freedom and censorship, he says: "From the standpoint of the Idea, it is self-evident that freedom of the press has a justification quite different from that of censorship, insofar as it is itself a form of the Idea, of freedom, a positive good, whereas censorship is a form of bondage, the polemic of a *Weltanschauung* of appearance against the *Weltanschauung* of the essence, something merely negative in character" (i, 201). The identification of freedom (as self-determination) and good, however, comes out most strongly a little later in the same article: "The censored press remains bad, even if it brings forth good products, for these products are good only insofar as they represent the free press within the censored press, and insofar as it is not part of their character to be products of the censored press. The free press remains good, even if it brings forth bad products, for these products are apostates from the character of the free press. A eunuch remains a bad man, even if he has a good voice. Nature remains good, even if it brings forth abortions" (i, 205). What this view rests on is Marx's conception of freedom as self-determination, as the unhindered, undistorted working of the concept or essence of an institution or thing (seen, in all the cases he deals with specifically, as a form of the human essence, and hence of human self-determination). To be unfree is not to be one's self, to deny free play to the rules of development of one's own nature. Thus, rejecting the view that freedom of the press can be defended as a case of freedom to exercise a craft, Marx writes: "The freedom to exercise a craft is just the freedom to exercise a craft and no other freedom, because within it the nature of the craft takes form undisturbed according to its inner rules of life; freedom of the courts is freedom of the courts, if the courts follow their own rules of law and not those of some other sphere, for example of religion. Every specific sphere of freedom is the freedom of a specific sphere, just as every specific way of life is a specific nature's way of living" (i, 221).

It is this view, that things develop according to the internal rules flowing from their concept, that resulted in Marx's taking at this stage a thoroughly rationalistic view of law as being, ideally at any rate, simply natural law, the eliciting of objective inner rules, of logical implications of concepts. Thus, in his first Hegel critique, he notes the antinomy that arises for Hegel, the fact that the legislator derives his position from a constitution itself created by legislators, and solves it boldly: "The legislative power does not make the law; it only discovers and formulates it" (i, 468). Marx had already assumed this in his discussion of the press debates and his analysis of divorce. True law, he said in the press debates discussion, arises only "when the unconscious natural law of freedom has become within it the conscious law of the state" (i, 210). In an editorial footnote to a contributor's article on the divorce law he speaks disapprovingly of the "lawgiver [who] does not regard human morality but spiritual holiness as the essence of marriage, and thus puts in place of self-determination determination from above, in place of the inner natural inspiration a supernatural sanction, in place of a loyal submission to the nature of the relationship rather a passive obedience to decrees" (i, 315). In his own article on the subject Marx again proclaims his belief in natural law: "The legislator must regard himself as a scientist. He does not *make* laws, he does not invent them, he only formulates them, he enunciates the inner laws of spiritual relationships as conscious positive laws" (i, 318).

The notion of laws expressing freedom and not compulsion needs explanation, if not explaining away. Marx does his best in a passage in his discussion of the press debates. "Where the law is real law," he says, "that is, where it is the existence of freedom, it is the real existence of the freedom of man. The laws therefore cannot forestall man's actions, for they are the inner rules of life of his activity itself, the conscious mirror images of his life. Law hence retreats before man's life as a life of freedom, and only when his actual actions have shown that he has ceased to obey the natural law of freedom, does the state law force him to be free" (i, 210).

Freedom, then, is for Marx the self-determination of an institution or thing, its working in accordance with its "true" self, its concept or essence. Ultimately, however, it is only man that is truly free—it is his essence that is working in history, his freedom that is reflected in law, society, press, and marriage, for instance. "Freedom is so thoroughly the essence of man, that even its opponents bring it into actuality even while they fight against its reality. . . . No man fights freedom, at most he fights against the freedom of others." (Discussion of press debates, i, 202.) It is freedom, above all, that distinguishes man from animals—a distinction that is basic to Marx's thought in this earliest period, and that remained so throughout his life. It is a distinction made entirely in terms of freedom—man has the power to determine himself, the animal is determined by its environment. This distinction is far from original, of course, but with Marx's moral categories, it becomes not just a distinction between freedom and lack of it, but the fundamental distinction between good and evil. Thus, in his preliminary notes for his thesis, Marx discusses contemptuously Plutarch's treatment of fear of the divine as a means of bettering the unjust. "Insofar as in fear, and namely in an inner, inextinguishable fear, man is treated as animal, then in an animal it is a matter of complete indifference how it is kept in restraint. If a philosopher does not consider it the height of infamy to regard man as an animal, then he cannot be made to understand anything at all" (i, 114).

The notion that man's determination from without is a basic violation of his human essence is the notion from which Marx was soon to develop his concept of self-alienation in economic life, of man coming to be governed by his own products, especially by his own labor, which assume independent objective existence and come to dominate him. On this rests his first (predominantly ethical) indictment of political economy. In the earliest writings, this notion has not yet been strongly developed, and not at all on the economic side, but suggestions of it are there. Thus in his discussion of the wood-theft laws, Marx ends, with full rhetorical emphasis, with the point that it is a sin "against the holy spirit of peoples and of humanity . . . in making a law about wood, to think only of wood and forest, and not to solve the individual material problem *politically*, i.e., in connection with undivided civic reason and civic morality" (i, 304). The Rhinelanders, he says, are making wood into a fetish—wooden idols rise while human sacrifices fall.

The true nature of man, then, is to be free, self-determined, independent. Freedom is the self-expression of his ultimate being, of the real man as opposed to the imperfect empirical existent. "What is the kernel of empirical evil?" asks Marx in the preliminary notes for his thesis. "That the individual locks himself into his empirical nature against his eternal nature" (i, 111). This Hegelian view of freedom as the supreme moral (and historical) category receives powerful reinforcement from Marx's outstanding character trait—his almost Nietzschean concern with dignity, seen as independence and mastery over things. The strain breaks out already in his high-flown and socially idealistic school-leaving essay, *Reflections of a Youth in Choosing a Career*. "Dignity," he writes, "is that which raises man the most, which lends to his actions, to all his strivings, a higher nobility, which leaves him unimpaired, admired by the multitude and elevated above it. Dignity, however, can be afforded only by that position, in which we do not appear as servile instruments, but where we create independently within our circle" (ii, 166). It is this psychological trait, too, which accounts for the fire in passages like the following from his discussion of the debates on press freedom: "A country which, like the old Athens, treats bootlickers, parasites, toadies as exceptions from public reason, as public fools, is the country of independence and self-government. A people which, like all peoples of modern times, claims the right to think and utter the truth only for the court fool, can only be a people of dependence and selflessness" (i, 184). Nearly forty years later, one of Marx's daughters handed him one of those dreadful Victorian questionnaires which asked him, *inter alia*, to state "the vice you detest most." With palpable sincerity, he wrote the one word "Servility."

This, then, is the positive content of Marx's ethics on the individual side—to be moral is to assert one's "truly human" essence, to follow the laws of its development. It is to reject as evil all that which determines man instead of being determined by him. There are here a number of obvious difficulties—the relationship between man's universal essence and his particular being, on the one hand, and between the essence and the "laws of freedom" which he should obey, on the other. Marx *says*, as we have seen, that law and social institutions, in their rational form, are all manifestations of human freedom, forms of the human essence, but even he has to deduce the natural laws of institutions not from the concept of human freedom, but from their own specific "concepts" of law, marriage, etc. Marx gives no precise formulation of the relationship between these specific concepts and that of human freedom—it is clear, I think, that he could not do so, and that to ask for precision here, as at many other points of Marx's theory right to its fullest development, is in fact to expose that theory. Marx does not succeed in giving any precise or convincingly concrete content to natural law, or to "truly free" or "truly human" behavior, nor does he show what distinguishes the various forms of the human essence from one another. At best, in appraising individual behavior, Marx's ethical position gives him a version of Kant's universalizability principle. "No reasonable man," he says in his discussion of divorce, "would have the assurance to regard his actions as privileged actions, as actions concerning only himself; rather he will claim his actions to be lawful actions concerning all" (i, 318). Essentially, however, Marx wants to reject the need for an external code of morality to govern men. Once the human spirit is truly free, moral behavior, in individual and in social relations, flows naturally from man's essence. He needs no external standards. In the individual problems of choice and conduct in the nonrational society Marx is simply not interested—not once does he pay the least attention to possible conflicts of "duties" and "rights," except to insist that the more general interest must always have predominance (e.g., in his discussion of wood-theft laws, i, 303). It is this view, and this lack of interest, that made it easy for Marx later simply to dismiss moral codes as expressions of material class interests, without feeling that such dismissal in any way conflicted with the recognition of positive morality as something flowing out of the "truly human."

Another important point here is that morality is for Marx not a matter of individual conduct at all, but one of social organization. The human spirit that lies under the conception of human freedom is for Marx an essence, and an essence is always truly universal. The full fruition of human spirit, therefore, is seen not on the individual, but on the social, side. The spirit, precisely because it is a universal essence, expresses itself above all in the unity of men, in the overcoming of the divisions created by their empirical particularity. The rational state is "the concretization of human freedom" (i, 248), "philosophy [i.e., the critical activity of human self-consciousness] interprets the rights of man, it demands that the state shall be the state of human nature" (i, 247). . . .

To civic morality, then, and to the criticism of the state, the same moral categories apply as to the individual. In the rational state man, as individual, and as universal essence of the state, is self-determined— the state is harmonious, stable, and free from self-contradiction. "A state, which is not the concretization (Verwirklichung) of rational freedom, is a bad state" (i, 248). The imperfect or bad state is characterized by incomplete self-determination, division, instability, and self-contradiction.

Above all, for Marx the rational state is the state of a truly unified humanity. Its great enemies are special interests, privilege, and the estate or class, which elevate social divisions into a principle of society. . . .

Now in this concept of the rational state as the state of the human essence, of truly unified humanity, there are obvious difficulties. Basically, they resolve themselves into the general difficulty of determining and describing the relationship between men as individuals, as particular, empirical beings, and the state that is supposed to be a form of their essence, the concretization of their freedom. Marx himself draws attention to the way this difficulty arises in paragraph 261 of Hegel's *Philosophy of Right*, the paragraph with which Marx begins the extant portion of his first Hegel critique. In that paragraph Hegel says:

In contrast with the spheres of private rights and private welfare (the family and civil society), the state is from one point of view an external necessity and their higher authority; its nature is such that their laws and interests are subordinate to it and dependent on it. On the other hand, however, it is the end immanent within them, and its strength lies in the unity of its own universal end and aim with the particular interests of individuals, in the fact that individuals have duties to the state in proportion as they have rights against it. (T. M. Knox's translation.)

In this paragraph, says Marx, we already have a crucial antinomy, the conflict between the state as external necessity acting on men and as immanent principle within man. To speak of the state as external necessity, says Marx, is to imply collision between the state and men, to imply that in a conflict between private and public interest, private interest must give way. Admittedly, Hegel does not speak of such conflict, he portrays the situation rather as a relationship of spheres. But even so, Marx insists, Hegel's use of words like "subordinate" and "dependent" implies clearly that the character of the lower sphere is constrained from outside—we are still left with the unresolved antinomy between external necessity (for Marx, though not so simply for Hegel, normally a sign of evil) and immanent purpose. . . .

The position . . . is a curious one, and in some ways obscure, but the general tendency seems to be this: The rational state is the state of a human essence that is qualitatively, essentially, universal, and not merely numerically so. As the state of such an essence it is self-distinguishing, but absolutely precludes division or conflict. In it we find a division of functions (presumably not legislated for, but arising "naturally"), and since each function is a manifestation or activity of the human essence, each is truly representative of man's universal being, representative of men as such in their diverse but fundamentally single, united being. There is no call for an external power to apportion or harmonize their various roles, no need for a political, coercive state, outside or above the civil society that rationally arranges itself.

Popular control and relatively representative government in the ordinary sense, for which the liberal opposition fought in their practical demands, we see, have disappeared in a metaphysical construction suggestive of the theoretical eccentricities supposed to give content to the Communists' use of the phrase "true democracy." At its root lies a vague and fundamentally incoherent concept of the human essence, seen as truly and qualitatively universal, and as a dynamic form that determines man's particular being and finally takes it within itself. In his earliest period, Marx used this concept consistently, but he never examined it. It was one of his most basic assumptions, an unquestioned and, to him, unquestionable part of his philosophic heritage. In the next forty years Marx was to develop a historical materialism that strove to support his belief in the coming rational society with a mass of empirical material, but the notion of a human essence, as basic and as confused as ever, continued to underlie all his social hopes and beliefs. For Communism, as Marx saw it, is not the society of mere empirical, particular men; it is the state of a self-distinguishing humanity become metaphysically one—it is the state of the human essence. If we treat the belief in such a state as flowing merely from certain "scientific discoveries" in economics and history we shall understand neither Marx nor his vision of Communism.

NOTE

1 All of Marx's extant work up to this period, including some letters and juvenilia, has been published in the *Karl Marx/Friedrich Engels historisch-kritische Gesamtausgabe* (Marx-Engels Archiv, Germany and Marx-Engels Institute, Moscow, 1927ff.), section I, volume I, subvolumes i and ii. In this paper all bracketed roman and arabic numerals without further source reference which follow quotations from Marx indicate the first or second of these subvolumes and the relevant page. All quotations are my own translations from the German.

Alienation and Humanism

RELATED to the Marxist humanistic ethic is the concept of alienation. Alienation is a term that has been used to portray shortcomings in the human condition. Lewis Coser has suggested that the concept has been given many connotations such as powerlessness, meaninglessness, normlessness, isolation, self-estrangement, and, paradoxically, the problems caused by togetherness and overidentification.

The Marxian conception of alienation results from a number of ideas. Men are both self-divided and divided from other men by having to pursue ends other than their own in their work, and by having external ends imposed on them. Men are estranged from the products of their mental, physical, and social activity so that they are prevented from being authentic beings. Man's objects become "an alien power standing over against him instead of being ruled by him." Man is enslaved by the system of goods and commodities that he produces since the products of man become transformed into an ideal power above him, out of his control. Men reify their social relationships which, because of the production of commodities, "has assumed the fantastic form of a relation between things." The division of labor present in modern society leads to dehumanization and depersonalization, separates the interests of the individual from that of the community as a whole, and produces a "one-sided character" of man.

Alienation, for the Marxists, will end only with the revolution that changes both the conditions of production and the nature of man, with the "positive abolition of private property, and human self-alienation." Communism will overcome alienation through the creation of a community which ends the cleavage between production and consumption, intellectual and manual labor.

(129)

Marx is not specific about the nature or behavior of man when he is not alienated, but the guiding principle seems to have been that of self-activity, the key to freedom. "The whole character of a species," said Marx, "is contained in the character of its life activity, and free, conscious activity is man's species character."

Daniel Bell is one of those who regards the alienation concept as the product of the young Marx still under Hegelian influence, and sees it as a concept which the mature Marx believed was a romantic conception. Bell criticizes both what he considers to be the excessive emphasis of modern commentators on the concept of alienation, and the Marxist stress on the economic nature of alienation with the consequent neglect of problems of personality and social relationships. Bell, like other critics of Marxism, cannot accept the view that alienation would be ended if the system of property ownership were changed. Michael Harrington, believing strongly in the humanistic Marx and in the crucial importance of alienation in Marx's work, replies to Bell and other critics.

11

A Critique of Alienation

Daniel Bell

A NEW interest revolves around the theme of alienation. Marx is read not as an economist or political theorist—not for the labor theory of value or the falling rate of profit, not for the theory of the State or even of social classes, and certainly not as the founder of dialectical materialism —but as a philosopher who first laid bare the estrangement of man from an oppressive society. Alienation is taken to be the critical tool of the Marxist method, and the new canon is derived from the early, and in his lifetime unpublished, philosophical manuscripts of Marx. Even non-Marxists accept this new emphasis. Thus in Père Jean-Yves Calvez's comprehensive *La Pensée de Karl Marx*, published in 1956, 440 of a total of 640 pages are devoted to the concept of alienation and its use in social and political analysis.

All of this is rather novel. Rarely in the thirties, for example, when the first burst of Marxist scholarship occurred, did one find in the exegetical and expository writings on Marx a discussion of alienation. In Sidney Hook's pioneer account of Marx's intellectual development, *From Hegel to Marx*, published in 1936, the word "alienation" does not occur *once* in the text. It was not, of course, that Hook was unaware of the idea of alienation and the role it played in Hegelian thought. (His book, based on these early manuscripts, had traced in patient detail Marx's thought to his immediate forebears: to Feuerbach, who, in his discussion of religion, had developed the concept of alienation; to Bruno Bauer, who had emphasized the "critical method" in philosophy; to Moses Hess, who first sketched the picture of humanistic communism; and to the

FROM "The Rediscovery of Alienation," *The Journal of Philosophy*, 61 (November 19, 1959), pp. 934–950.

other young Hegelians for whom the relationship of freedom to necessity was the paramount concern.) But the intellectual problem for Hook, as it was for *all* "classical" Marxists, was, first, a defense of the idea of materialism as a viable modern philosophy—and this Hook sought to do by reading Marx uniquely as a naturalist—and, second, to resolve the "contradiction" between Marx's social determinism (i.e., that one's consciousness and knowledge are shaped by one's existence and class position), and Marx's, and Lenin's, class teleology (or the fact that socialist purpose and goal are instilled into the worker from the "outside")[1]— and this Hook sought to do by reading Marx as a pragmatist. The intellectual issue for Marxists in the thirties was the validity of historical materialism.

Different times, different *Zeitgeist*. The reason for this change is clear. In Europe today, a school of neo-Marxists, having rejected Stalinism (and, implicitly, historical materialism, which, in its projection of "higher" stages of society, had been used to justify the Bolshevik use of terror), has gone back to Marx's early writings to find a foundation for a new humanist foundation for Socialism. The revisionist philosophers in Eastern Europe do so to find doctrinal support against the official party theologues. The French post-Stalinists, such as Lucien Goldmann or Edgar Morin, see in the idea of alienation a more sophisticated radical critique of contemporary society than the simplified and stilted Marxist analysis of class. And the young English socialists, such as Charles Taylor of All Souls College, see in the concept of alienation a means of reformulating the idea of community.

While all this is a fresh, and even fruitful, way of making a criticism of contemporary society, it is *not* the "historical Marx." For, as the following analysis argues, Marx had repudiated the idea of alienation divorced from his specific economic analysis of property relations under capitalism, and, in so doing, had closed off a road which would have given us a broader and more useful analysis of society and personality than the Marxian dogmatics which did prevail. While one may be sympathetic to the idea of alienation, it is only further myth-making to read this concept back as the central theme of Marx. As a political effort by the revisionists, bound within the Marxist camp, it may have some polemical value. As a stage of the pilgrim's progress of those coming out of the Marxist forest, it is understandable. As an intellectual effort, it is false. If the concept of alienation is to have any meaning, it must stand on its own feet, without the crutch of Marx. This, then, is the burden of the paper.

For the "left-Hegelians," the teachers and colleagues of Marx, the chief task of philosophy was to specify the conditions under which

"Man" could achieve his freedom. They accepted the question which Hegel had opened up; they were dissatisfied with his formulation of the problem.

The goal of Man, Hegel had said, was freedom, a condition, he defined, in which man would be self-willed and where his "essence" would become his own possession—in which he would regain his "self." But man was "separated" from his essence and bound by two conditions which seemed inherent in the world: necessity and alienation. Necessity meant a dependence on nature and the acceptance of the limitations which nature imposed on men, both in the sense of the limitation of natural resources and the limitations of physical strength. Alienation, in its original connotation, was the radical dissociation of the "self" into both actor and thing, into a *subject* that strives to control its own fate, and an *object* which is manipulated by others. In the development of science, man could, perhaps, overcome necessity and master nature. But how was one to overcome the Orphic separateness of subject and object? Alienation was an ontological fact, in the structure of grammar as well as of life; for the self was not just an "I" seeking to shape the world according to its intentions, but also a "me," an object whose identity is built up by the pictures that others have of the "me." Thus the condition of complete freedom, in which the self seeks only to be an "I," a shaper of events in accordance with its own will, rather than being shaped by others, is a seeming impossibility. In the face of this irreducible dualism of subject-object, of "I" and "me," how does one achieve the goal of being "self-willed"?

Bruno Bauer, one of the first teachers and friends of Marx, felt that the solution lay in developing a "critical" philosophy which exposed the "mystery" of human relationships (i.e., the *real* motives behind social acts). Most human beings born into the world, said Bauer, simply accept it and are oblivious to the sources of their morals and beliefs, of their rationality and irrationality; they are "determined" by the world. By subjecting all beliefs to criticism, however, men would become self-conscious, reason would be restored to them, and therewith their self-possession. The overcoming of the dualism, therefore, was to be through the achievement of self-consciousness.

Feuerbach, to whom Marx gave credit for making the first real breach in the system of Hegelian abstractions, sought to locate the source of alienation in religious superstition and fetishism. The most radical of all the left-Hegelians, Feuerbach called himself Luther II. Where Luther had sought to demolish an institution that mediated between Man and God, the second Luther sought to destroy God himself. Man would be free, he said, if we could demythologize religion. Man was bound because he took the best of himself, his sensibility, and projected it onto some external object, or spirit, which he called divine. But the history of all thought was a history of progressive disenchantment, and if, finally, in Christianity, the image of God had been transformed from a parochial river deity to a universal abstraction, the function of criticism — using the radical tool of alienation or self-estrangement — was to replace theology by anthropology, to dethrone God and enthrone Man. The way to overcome alienation was to bring the divine back into man, to reintegrate himself through a religion of humanity, through a religion of self-love. Men's relation to each other, said Feuerbach, in first employing terms that, ironically, were adopted later by Martin Buber for religious purposes, had to be on an I-Thou basis. Philosophy was to be directed to life, man was to be liberated from the "spectre of abstractions" and released from the thongs of the supernatural. Religion was only capable of creating "false consciousness." Philosophy would reveal "true consciousness." And, by placing Man rather than God at the center of consciousness, Feuerbach sought to bring the "infinite into the finite."

This uncompromising attack on religion was equally a sharp attack on all established institutions. But beyond that, the spreading use of the concept of alienation had a more radical consequence in the minds of the left-Hegelians, because it initiated a direct break in the history of philosophy by ushering in the period of modernity. In classical philosophy, the ideal man was the contemplative one. Neither the middle ages nor the transitional period to contemporary times (the seventeenth to the mid-nineteenth century) was ever wholly able to detach itself from the ideal of the Stoa. Even Goethe, who gave us in Faust the first modern man, the man of ambition unchained, reverted, in his ethical image of the human ideal, to the Greek. In discussing freedom, however, Hegel had introduced a new principle, the principle of *action;* for man, in order to realize his self, had to strive actively to overcome the subject-object dualism that bound him. In action a man finds himself; by his choices he defines his character. For Hegel, however, the principle of action had remained abstract. In Feuerbach, while the principle of alienation is sharply defined and the source of alienation is located in religion, an abstraction remains because Feuerbach was talking of Man in general. In Marx, action was given specificity in a radical new emphasis on *work.* Man becomes man, becomes alive through work, for through work man loses his isolation and becomes a social or cooperative being, and thus learns of himself; and through work he is able to transform nature as well. [2]

In locating man's alienation in work, Marx had taken the revolutionary step of grounding philosophy in concrete human activity. The road by which he "freed" himself from the Hegelian tyranny of abstraction was a long and difficult one. [3] As a Hegelian, Marx thought first of the alienation of work in terms of idealistic dualities. Man, in working, reifies himself in objective things (i.e., in products which embody his work). This is *labor* (*Arbeit*) and is part of the "alien and hostile world standing over against him." In labor, man is "under the domination, compulsion and yoke of another man." Against this is the state of freedom where man would transform nature, and himself, by free, conscious, spontaneous, creative work. Two things stood in the way of achieving this freedom: the fact that in the alienation of work man lost control over the *process* of work, and lost control, too, of the *product* of his labor.[4] For Marx, therefore, the answer to Hegel was clear: the alienation of man lay not in some philosophical abstraction of Mind, but in the property system. In the organization of work—in labor becoming a commodity—man became an object used by others, and unable, therefore, to obtain satisfaction in his own activity. By becoming himself a commodity, he lost his sense of identity; he lost the sense of "himself."

The extraordinary thing was that Marx had taken a concept which German philosophy had seen as an ontological fact, and had given it a social content. As ontology, as an ultimate, man could only accept alienation. As a social fact, rooted in a specific system of historical relations, alienation could be overcome by changing the social system. But in narrowing the concept, Marx ran two risks: of falsely identifying the source of alienation only in the private property system; and of introducing a note of utopianism in the idea that once the private property system was abolished man would immediately be free.

The question of why men were propertyless turned Marx to economics. For a man whose name is so inextricably linked with the "dismal science," Marx was never really interested in economics. His correspondence with Engels in later years is studded with contemptuous references to the subject and he resented the fact that his detailed explorations prevented him from carrying on other studies. But he continued because, for him, economics was the practical side of philosophy—it would unveil the mystery of alienation—and because he had found in the categories of political economy the material expression of that alienation: the process of economic exploitation.

This development is seen most clearly in the *Economic-Philosophical Manuscripts*, which Marx had written in 1844 at the age of twenty-six. The *Manuscripts*, in the history of Marxist thought, is the bridge from the left-Hegelianism of the early Marx to the Marxism we have come to know. The title itself is both literal and symbolic. Beginning as an anthropology, it ends as a political economy. In it one finds the first conceptualization of alienation as rooted in work (rather than in abstract spirit, or religion), and the beginnings of the analysis of property.

And in the analysis of property, one finds the direct transmutation, which is so crucial in the development of Marx's thought, of philosophical into economic categories.

In his search for an answer to Hegel's question, Marx had sought to pin down concretely the ways in which the human being was "robbed" of his potential possibilities of realizing his "self." For Feuerbach, religion was the means whereby man was alienated from himself; for in religion man externalized his real "self." For Marx, now, the idea of the "self" had become too abstract. The key to the problem was the nature of work—the process whereby man became a social being—but the question remained as to what barred man from realizing his full nature in work. The answer, he thought, lay in the operation of the property system. But how? In the capitalist system, in the bargain made between worker and employer, the individual was formally free. What, then, was the means whereby a man, unbeknownst even to himself, was alienated and enslaved? Marx found the answer in money. Money is the most impersonal form of value. It is seemingly neutral. A man who has a direct obligation to another, as a serf does to a master, knows directly the source of power over him. But one who sells his labor power for money may feel himself to be free. The product of the laborer can thus be easily "abstracted" into money and, through the exchange system, be "abstracted" from him. [5]

Money, thus, is the concrete embodiment of the philosophical abstraction which Hegel had described airily as "spirit," and the commodity process the means whereby the laborer, by exchanging his labor power for money, is robbed of his freedom unaware. Political economy became for Marx what religion was for Feuerbach, a means whereby human values are "projected" outside of man and achieve an existence independent of him and over him. And so, alienation, conceived initially by Marx as a process whereby an individual lost his capacity to express himself in work, now became seen as exploitation, or the appropriation of a laborer's surplus product by the capitalist. Thus a philosophical expression which embodies, actually, a sociopsychological insight became transformed into an economic category.

The irony, however, was that in moving from "philosophy" to "reality," from Hegelian phenomenology to political economy, Marx moved from one kind of abstraction to another. In his system, self-alienation became transformed: man as "generic man" (i.e., Man writ large) becomes divided into classes of men. For Marx now, the only social reality is not Man, nor the individual, but economic classes. Individuals and their motives count for nought. [6] The only form of consciousness which can be translated into action—and which can explain history, past, present, and future—is class consciousness.

In *The German Ideology*, written in 1846, the idea of the "self" has disappeared from Marx's writings. Marx now mocks the left-Hegelians for talking of "human nature, of Man in general who belongs to no class, has no reality, and subsists only in the realm of philosophical fantasy." In attacking the "true Socialist," Marx writes: "It is characteristic of all these high-sounding phrases about liberation, etc., that it is always 'man' who is liberated . . . it would appear from [their] claims that 'wealth' and 'money' have ceased to exist. . . ."

In *The Communist Manifesto*, the attack is widened, and made cruelly sardonic. The German *literati*, says Marx, "wrote their philosophical nonsense beneath the French original. For instance, beneath the French criticism of the economic functions of money, they wrote 'alienation of humanity'. . . ." And mocking his erstwhile philosophical comrades, Marx speaks scornfully of "this transcendental robe in which the German Socialists wrapped their sorry 'eternal truths' . . . the robe of speculative cobwebs, embroidered with the flowers of rhetoric, steeped in the dew of sickly sentiment."

In saying that there is no human nature "inherent in each separate individual," as Marx does in his sixth thesis on Feuerbach, but only social man, and then only classes, one introduces a new *persona*. Marx makes this explicit in his preface to *Capital*, written in 1867: "Here individuals are dealt with only insofar as they are the personifications of economic categories, embodiments of particular class relations and class interests. My standpoint, from which the evolution of the economic formation of society is viewed as a process of natural history, can, less than any other, make the individual responsible for relations whose creature he socially remains, however he may subjectively raise himself above them."

Thus, individual responsibility is turned into class morality, and the variability of individual action subsumed under impersonal mechanisms. And the ground is laid for the loss of freedom in a new tyranny that finds its justifications in the narrowed view of exploitation which Marx had fashioned.

To sum up the argument thus far: In his early philosophical writings, Marx had seen, against Hegel, that alienation or the failure to realize one's potential as a self, was rooted primarily in work, rather than in the abstract development of consciousness. In the organization of work, men become "means" for the aggrandizement of others, rather than "ends" in themselves. As alienated labor, there was a twofold loss: men lost control over the *conditions* of work, and men lost the *product* of their labor. This dual conception is present, in a different form, in the later Marx: the loss of control of work is seen as *dehumanization*, occasioned by the division of labor and intensified by technology; the loss of product, as *exploitation*, because a portion of man's labor (surplus value) was appropriated by the employer.

But except for literary and illustrative references in *Capital* to the dehumanization of labor and the fragmentation of work, this first aspect, as problem, was glossed over by Marx. In common with some later (bourgeois?) sociologists, Marx felt that there was no solution to the loss of "self" in work inherent in technology. Under communism— in the "final" society—the division of labor, the cause of dehumanization, would be eliminated so that by variety in work man would be able to develop his varied aptitudes. But these fragmentary discussions take on a utopian hue.[7] In actuality one had to accept not only the division of labor, but hierarchical organization as well. In a polemic against some Italian anarchists who had argued that technology had imposed on man a "veritable despotism," Engels argued that it was utopian to question the nature of authority in a factory: "At least with regard to the hours of work one may write upon the portals of these factories: *Lasciate ogni autonomia, voi che entrate!* [leave, ye that enter in, all autonomy behind!] If man by dint of his knowledge and inventive genius has subdued the forces of nature, the latter avenge themselves upon him by subjecting him, insofar as he employs them, to a veritable despotism, independent of all social organization. Wanting to abolish authority in large-scale industry is tantamount to wanting to abolish industry itself, to destroy the power loom in order to return to the spinning wheel."[8]

What became central to *Capital* were the concrete social relationships created by private property, those of employer and employee, rather than the processes generated by manufacture. Dehumanization was a creature of technology; exploitation that of capitalism. The solution was simple, if one-sided: abolish private property, and the system of exploitation would disappear. "In contemporary capitalist society men are dominated by economic relations created by themselves, by means of production which they have produced, as if by an alien power . . . ," said Engels. "When society, by taking possession of all means of production and managing them on a planned basis, has freed itself and all of its members from the bondage in which they are at present held by means of production which they themselves have produced but which now confront them as irresistible, alien power; when consequently man no longer proposes, but also disposes—only then will the last alien power which is now reflected in religion vanish. And with it will also vanish the religious reflection itself, for the simple reason that there will be nothing left to reflect."[9]

When critics argued that technological organization might still "deform and debilitate" the worker, the Marxist called this utopian. When skeptics asserted that socialism itself might become an exploitative society, the Marxist had a ready answer: the source of exploitation, and of power, was economic, and political office was only an administrative extension of economic power; once economic power was socialized, there could no longer be classes, or a basis whereby man could exploit man. By this extension it became "clear" that the Soviet Union was a "workers' state," and no basis for exploitation existed. Thus the concept of alienation came, down one road, to a twisted end.

Having found the answer to the "mysteries" of Hegel in political economy, Marx promptly forgot all about philosophy. ("The philosophers have only *interpreted* the world differently; the point, however, is to change it," he had scrawled in his *Theses on Feuerbach*.) In 1846, Marx and Engels had completed a long criticism of post-Hegelian philosophy in two large octavo volumes and (except for some gnomic references in the *Critique of the Gotha Programme* in 1875) neither of them returned to the subject until forty years later when Engels, after the death of Marx, was, to his surprise, asked by the *Neue Zeit*, the German Socialist theoretical magazine, to review a book on Feuerbach by C. N. Starcke, a then well-known anthropologist. Engels reluctantly consented and wrote a long review which, slightly expanded, was published two years later in 1888 as a small brochure entitled *Ludwig Feuerbach and the Outcome of Classical German Philosophy*. In writing the review Engels went back to some mouldering manuscripts of Marx and found among his papers the hastily scribbled eleven theses on Feuerbach, totaling in all a few pages, which he appended to the brochure. In the Foreword, Engels alludes to the large manuscript (without mentioning even its title, *The German Ideology*), and says merely that because of the reluctance of the publishers it was not printed. "We abandoned the manuscript to the gnawings of the mice all the more willingly," wrote Engels, "as we had achieved our main purpose—to clear our own minds." (The gnawing was literal, since many pages, in fact, had been completely chewed up!)

But it is also clear that while, as young philosophy students, the debates with the other young Hegelians were necessary for the purposes of "self clarification," the absorption of both into concrete economic study and political activity had made the earlier philosophical problems increasingly unreal to them. In a letter to his American translator, Florence Kelley Wischnewetzky, in February 1886, Engels writes, apropos of his *Anti-Dühring*, "the semi-Hegelian language of a good many passages of my old book is not only untranslatable but has lost the greater part of its meaning even in German." And in 1893 a Russian visitor to Engels, Alexis Voden, found Engels incredulous when the question of publishing the early philosophical manuscripts was raised.

In a memoir, Voden recalled: "Our next conversation was on the early works of Marx and Engels. At first Engels was embarrassed when I expressed interest in these works. He mentioned that Marx had also written poetry in his student years, but it could hardly interest anybody. . . . Was not the fragment on Feuerbach which Engels considered the most meaty of the 'old works' sufficient?" Which was more important, Engels asked, "for him to spend the rest of his life publishing old manuscripts from publicistic works of the 1840s or to set to work, when Book III of *Capital* came out, on the publication of Marx's manuscripts on the history of the theories of surplus value?" And for Engels the answer was obvious. Besides, said Engels, "in order to penetrate into that 'old story' one needed to have an interest in Hegel himself, which was not the case with anybody then, or to be exact, 'neither with Kautsky nor with Bernstein.' "[10]

In fact, except for *The Holy Family*, a crazy-quilt bag of essays deriding Bruno Bauer and his two brothers, who with their friends constituted the "holy family," none of the early philosophical writings of Marx was published either in his lifetime or that of Engels. Nor is it clear whether the major exegetes, Kautsky, Plekhanov, and Lenin, were ever aware of their content. None of the questions of alienation appear in their writing. The chief concern of the post-Marxist writers, when they dealt with philosophy, was simply to defend a materialist viewpoint against idealism.

The contemporary "rediscovery" of the idea of alienation in Marxist thought is due to Georg Lukacs, the Hungarian philosopher who did have an interest in Hegel. The idea of alienation, because of its natural affinity to romanticism, had already played an important role in German sociology, particularly in the thought of Georg Simmel, who had been a teacher of Lukacs. Simmel, writing about the "anonymity" of modern man, first located the source of alienation in industrial society, which destroyed man's self-identity by "dispersing" him into a cluster of separate roles. Later Simmel widened the concept to see alienation as an inelectable outcome between man's creativity and the pressure of social institutions (much as Freud's later image of the inescapable tension between instinct and civilization).

Lukacs, coming onto Marx after World War I, was able, without knowing of the early *Manuscripts*, to "read back" from Marx into Hegel the alienation of labor as the self-alienation of Man from the Absolute Idea. The Kautsky-Lenin generation had construed Marxism as a scientific, nonmoral, analysis of society. But in Lukacs' interpretation, Marx's economic analysis of society was turned inside out and became the work, as Morris Watnick put it, "of a moral philosopher articulating the future of man's existence in the accents of a secular eschatology."

Lukacs' interpretation, which was included in a collection of essays entitled *Geschichte und Klassenbewusstsein* (History and Class Consciousness), published in 1923, smacked of idealism to the orthodox Marxists, and Lukacs quickly came under fire in Moscow. . . .

When the early philosophical works of Marx were unearthed and published, Lukacs had the satisfaction of seeing how accurately he had been able to reconstruct the thought of the young Marx. But this did not spare him from attack. The dogma, drawn from Lenin, had become fixed.

The early philosophical writings were published in 1932 in Germany. . . . There arose some small interest in the early writings of Marx, and particularly the idea of alienation. But the application of the idea was psychological and literary and soon found a louder resonance from surprisingly other sources.

The interest in the idea of alienation that unfolded rapidly in the late forties and early fifties came largely from the rediscovery of Kierkegaard and Kafka, and from the sense of despair that both epitomized.

. . . where Marx had sought to narrow the description of alienation into the exploitative social relationships created by the economic system, Kierkegaard universalized it as an ineluctable, pervasive condition of man.

There were deep reasons for this attraction to the idea of despair — and faith. The sadism of the Nazis, the ruthlessness of war, the existence of concentration camps, the use of terror, had called into question the deepest beliefs of the generation. One could argue, as did Sidney Hook, for example, that the Stalinist terror grew out of the specific historical circumstances which shaped the Russian dictatorship, and that its existence was no indictment of rationalism. But a more compelling reason — at least, psychologically speaking — seemed to come from the neo-orthodox arguments of Reinhold Niebuhr that such corruption of power was inevitable when men, in their pride, identified their own egos with the demiurge of History, and that rationalism, by encouraging utopian beliefs in man's perfectibility, had left men unarmed against the corruption which lurked in socialism.

From a second source, the "tragic vein" of German sociology, came new, intellectual support for the idea of alienation. In the influence of Karl Mannheim, and later of Max Weber, the idea of alienation merged with the idea of "bureaucratization." The two had absorbed Marx's ideas and gone beyond him. The drift of all society, said Weber, was toward the creation of large-scale organization, hierarchically organized and centrally directed, in which the individual counted for nought. Marx's emphasis ˙on the wage worker as being "separated" from the means of production became, in Weber's perspective, as Gerth and Mills succinctly put it, "merely one special case of a universal trend. The modern soldier is equally 'separated' from the means of violence, the scientist from the means of inquiry and the civil servant from the means of administration." And the irony, said Weber, is that, from one perspective, capitalism and socialism were simply two different faces of the same, inexorable trend.

Out of all this came the impact of the idea of alienation. The intellectual saw men becoming depersonalized, used as a "thing" in the operation of society as a machine; the intellectual himself felt increasingly estranged from the society. The idea of alienation, thus, was a judgment *on* society. It also reflected the self-conscious position of the intellectual *in* the society. . . .

NOTES

1 A troublesome issue that still remains unresolved in Marxist theory, for if the intellectuals create the socialist ideology, while the workers, left to themselves, achieve only trade union consciousness, as Lenin maintained, what, then, is the meaning of Marx's statement that existence determines consciousness, and that class fashions ideology?

2 The key statement of this idea in Marx is to be found, first, in the *Economic-Philosophic Manuscripts of 1844*. A more condensed version of this idea is to be found in Part One of *The German Ideology* (New York, 1939), esp. pp. 7–8.

3 A comprehensive exposition of the early views of Marx can be found in Robert C. Tucker, *Philosophy and Myth in Karl Marx* (New York, 1961).

4 For a further discussion, see Herbert Marcuse, *Reason and Revolution: Hegel and the Rise of Social Theory* (New York, 1941), pp. 276–277.

5 "Money is the alienated *ability of mankind*. That which I am unable to do as a *man*, and of which, therefore all my individual essential powers are incapable, I am able to do by means of *money*. Money thus turns each of these powers into something which in itself it is not—turns it, that is, into its *contrary*." —*Economic-Philosophic Manuscripts, op. cit.*, p. 139 (italics in the original).

It is this conception of money as the hidden mechanism whereby people became exploited (money "the common whore . . . [which] confounds all human and natural qualities") that lay behind Marx's withering analysis of the Jew, as the dealer in money, in economic society. It is this conception, too, that underlay the extraordinarily naive act of the Bolshevik regime in the first days after the October Revolution of abolishing all money in an effort to make the relationship of man to man "direct." The novel implications of this development in Marx's thought, of the *shift* in the early manuscripts from philosophy to political economy, have been explored in great detail by Professor Tucker *(op. cit.)*.

6 In *The German Ideology* Marx poses the question of how individual self-interest becomes transformed into ideology. "How does it come about," he asks, "that personal interests grow, despite the persons, into class-interests, into common interests which win an independent existence over against individual persons, in this independence take on the shape of general interests, enter as such into opposition with the real individuals, and in this opposition, according to which they are defined

as general interests, can be conceived by the consciousness as ideal, even as religious, sacred interests?"

Having posed the question so concisely, Marx, exasperatingly never goes on to answer it.

7 In *Capital*, Marx writes powerfully of the crippling effects of the detailed division of labor.

8 F. Engels, "On Authority," in *Marx & Engels: Basic Writings on Politics & Philosophy*, edited by Lewis S. Feuer (New York, 1959), p. 483.

9 Frederick Engels, *Anti-Dühring* (Chicago, 1935), pp. 332–333.

10 A. Voden, "Talks with Engels," in *Reminiscences of Marx and Engels* (Moscow, undated), pp. 330–331.

12

Marx as Humanist

Michael Harrington

. . . FOR a long time, the young Marx hardly existed at all. The *Economic and Philosophic Manuscripts of 1844* were not known at all until a few decades ago. The first English translation only appeared a year or two ago, thus raising questions of interpretation and analysis.

Marx's transition to "Marxism" began most decisively in 1843–44. It was then that his critique of Hegel brought him toward the first statement of dialectical materialism. The *Manuscripts* are, in a very real sense, the first statement of the Marxist *Weltanschauung*. They contain formulations which were to change and develop. Yet, here, the basic method and vision are outlined.

The most striking thing about the *Manuscripts* is their humanism. The indictment of capitalist society is spelled out primarily in the concept of alienation: the domination of the product over the producer, of the machine over the machine maker, of the system over the individual, of the bourgeois (that personification of the machine and system) over the worker. The stated ideal of socialism is to overcome alienation; to build a society where man will be the choosing subject of decision rather than the object.

Indeed, as Lucien Goldmann once pointed out, what separates Marx from Hegel is not so much the distinction between idealism and materialism. Hegel's idealism, after all, is objective and historical. It required only a relatively slight shift of perspective to move from this point of view to that of materialism (and entire sections of the Hegelian analysis can be brought into Marxism with little change). The real break with Hegel,

FROM "Marx versus Marx," *New Politics* (Fall 1961), pp. 112–114, 118–123.

Goldmann rightly argues, is that Marx places his emphasis on man making his history, on the power of human consciousness. The Hegelian world spirit incarnates itself in human beings, but this makes of men and their actions the charade of a mystical scheme of things. For Marx, there is no automatic, "closed" system which operates independently of man. Given all of the historical and material preconditions for socialism, there is required human choice and action—and there is the possibility of failure.

This conception of man as the measure of politics runs throughout Marx's entire life. Yet it is most clearly presented in the *Manuscripts*. Here is the definition which comes from discovery, from youthful vision.

This Marxist humanism is anathema to Communist ideology—and that is at least one factor in Russia's delay in publishing the *Manuscripts*. The idea of socialism as defined by production indices, of socialism as primarily an economics rather than a humanism, is basic to Communism. There is, for that matter, a curiously prophetic passage in the *Manuscripts*. Marx speaks of "raw" Communism which develops out of the simple negation of private property. In such a system, he writes, "the entire world of wealth . . . passes from the relationship of exclusive marriage with the owner of private property to a state of universal prostitution with the community. In negating the personality of man in every sphere, this type of communism is really nothing but the logical expression of private property. . . ."

Here, Marx is not "foretelling" the totalitarian collectivist system of contemporary Communism. He is discussing primitive panaceas which seek the simple negation of private property as the way to happiness. But, in dealing with this point of view, Marx asserts in the strongest way that personality, choice, and men are the center of his system, and not some simple rearrangement of property relationships.

If Marx did not anticipate contemporary Communism (and he did not), his method provides the basis for a Marxian critique of it. In Communist society, alienation persists; indeed, it is writ large. The totalitarian state becomes the very incarnation of all those powers which weigh upon man, which rob him of his individuality and personality. There is anticapitalism, to be sure, but an anticapitalism which is corrosive of human dignity in much the same way as its antagonist.

Clearly, then, these manuscripts are of political importance. In a time of socialist redefinition, they focus on the central humanism of the Marxian ideal. If, as some critics argue, these humanist sentiments are irrelevant to the later Marx—and to Marxism—one is here confronted by the utopian phase which preceded the totalitarian system. But if the counterposition of Marx is not a fact, then the later writings will be seen as the practical documentation and analysis of the youthful vision. And this is my point of view.

As we have already indicated, these works did not emerge in a vacuum, but in a world split between Communist totalitarianism and capitalism. Nowhere was there a strong, vital movement of democratic Marxism in the revolutionary tradition of Marx himself. Everywhere, centers of power had a vested interest in proving that the humanism of the early writings was an aberration and a sport. The Communists could not tolerate the integration of the *Manuscripts* into the Marxian canon, for that would subvert their elitist and mechanist interpretation of Marx. So they had to set Marx against Marx. And in the Western camp, the vulgarization of Marxism required that this clear statement of humanist democracy be adjudged an irrelevance of youthful enthusiasm.

In Germany, this battle took on its most sharp and political form. The German Protestants established a Commission of Marxism which, under the direction of Irving Fetscher, produced three volumes of *Marxismusstudien*. These included some of the most brilliant scholarly work on the subject in years, and they tended to see a continuity between the humanism of 1844 and the elder Marx. The East German Communists responded with a polemical fusillade. They well understand the political danger of such an interpretation of Marxism.

In Poland, the young philosophers who had participated in the October events of 1956 began their rediscovery of Marx. Party orthodoxy responded as in East Germany, though with considerably more finesse. The controversy broke out in France, where Catholic theologians found themselves quite sympathetic to the humanism of the *Manuscripts* and began a reinterpretation of Marx on this basis. (An excellent survey of the debate in France is contained in *Arguments*, January-February-March, 1959: "De Jeune Marx à Marx" by Daniel Guerin; "De Marx à nous" by Pierre Fougeyrolles.)

In this brief essay, I would like to take up two related Western interpretations of Marx, one by Merleau-Ponty, the other by Daniel Bell. Both of these writers are men of integrity, not political hacks. Their advocacy of the thesis that the young Marx is irrelevant to the crucial Marx is not an act of apology for one or the other side in the Cold War. They are, to be sure, deeply implicated in the world political crisis and this affects their judgment (as it does all of us). The important point is that, whatever their politics, they are serious and honest scholars. . . .

Daniel Bell and Merleau-Ponty . . . develop the thesis of Marx versus Marx with a certain sadness, for it is clear in each case that they have profound respect for the early Marx and a wistfulness that the mature thinker went wrong.

In his *Les Aventures de la Dialectique*, Merleau-Ponty locátes a decisive break in Marx's thought after 1848. The young Marx, he argues, was concerned with the dialectic of the relation between persons incarnated in things, and his humanism, his passion on the subject of alienation, derives from this basic world view. The mature Marx, he continues, turned to science, to the conception of history as a "second nature" ruled by inexorable but discoverable laws. Lenin, basing himself on this change, was thus able to locate the hope for socialism in a trained apparatus of professional revolutionists who were technically competent to deal with history's laws.

Interestingly enough, Merleau-Ponty's point was made some thirty years before he developed it, but this time by George Lukacs in the name of Marxian orthodoxy: Analyzing and attacking the emergence of "ethical" socialism, the tendency in the European social democracy to call upon Kantian subjectivism as a supplement to Marxist materialism, Lukacs traced an interesting relationship. Writing in *Geschichte und Klassenbewusstsein*, he derived the subjectivism of their view from the vulgar fatalism of their view of history. Once history is seen as an automatic and preordained process, Lukacs said, there are only two possible grounds for action. One was that of the technician who applies the unchanging laws in the interest of man. The other was that of the ethician who concentrates upon changing the individual since he cannot transform the unchangeable world.

In his essay, Lukacs was more concerned with the second variant, the ethical socialists, yet his dialectic of fatalism and subjectivism holds magnificently for Stalinist mechanism, its theoretical vulgarity (insofar as it is a theory at all) is the other side of its totalitarian exaltation of technique, of elitism. Once the people—or, in the terms of the early Lukacs and of Merleau-Ponty, the dialectic of history and consciousness —disappears from Marxism, the remains can be used to justify the rule of the apparatus.

It is, of course, no proof that Merleau-Ponty misreads Marx when one argues that Lukacs arrived at the same conception on the basis of a Marxian orthodoxy. The scholarly question continues: was there a disastrous break in Marxism after 1848, one which allows the totalitarians to claim a Marxian legitimacy? Before turning to the text, Daniel Bell's argument should be noted, for it raises Merleau-Ponty's problem from another, and quite interesting, angle.

Bell approaches his statement of the Marx versus Marx thesis in terms of the question of work and alienation. His proposition is that

in his early philosophical writings Marx had seen, against Hegel, that alienation, or the failure to realize one's potential as a self, was rooted primarily in work rather than in the abstract development of consciousness. In the organization of work men become "means" for the aggrandizement of others rather than "ends" in themselves. As alienated labor, there was a twofold loss: men lost control over the conditions of work, and lost the *product* of their labor. This dual conception is present even in the later Marx: the loss of control of work was seen as dehumanization occasioned by the division of labor and intensified by technology; the loss of product, as *exploitation*, because a portion of man's labor (surplus value) was appropriated by the employer. But other than literary and illustrative references in *Capital* to the dehumanization of labor and the fragmentation of work, this first aspect, as problem, was glossed over by Marx.

Clearly, Bell defines a break in Marxism quite similar to the one analyzed by Merleau-Ponty. Indeed, though the one approaches the subject as a sociologist and the other as a philosopher, their conceptions are identical. The "glossing over" of the dehumanization of the work process in Bell's version of Marx is equal to the exile of the dialectic (history as a relation between persons incarnated in things) in Merleau-Ponty's reading. The problem of both, in short, is that they cannot see a bridge between the early humanism and the later economic analysis; that they set the two in contradiction with one another. I would suggest that both are wrong, and that the mature Marx deepens the humanist categories of his early work.

There is no question that Marx shifts his language when he enters the world of *Capital*. The references to alienation decrease, the Hegelian form of the youthful insights vanish (but, as late as 1859 in the notes for the *Critique of Political Economy*, the *Grundrisse*, the vocabulary is still there). Yet this does not mark a break in the continuity of Marx's values. Take, for example, the analysis of the commodity with which Marx begins his great work. Over and over, one is told that this conception represents a theoretical key. (In 1923, Lukacs wrote, ". . . the chapter on the Fetish character of the commodity contains all of historical materialism, the entire self-knowledge of the working class as a knowledge of capitalist society. . . .") And a careful reading of these opening passages makes it clear that the very same ideas which are presented in the early writings are here worked out as the center of a close and careful economic analysis.

The first section of *Capital* defines the two aspects of the commodity: as an object of use; as an object of exchange. In this analysis, the stress is upon the fact that exchange value, the quality of the commodity as a product for the capitalist market, completely overwhelms the use value, its human significance. This opposition of use and exchange value, expressed in *Capital* as part of a technical economic theory, is the very same one which Marx defines in the early writings: the triumph of exchange value is the victory of the product over man, it is the mechanism of alienation.

Significantly enough, Marx titles one of these opening sections, "The Fetishism of Commodities and the Secret Thereof." The notion of fetishism is but another way of stating the theme of reification, of turning human relations into thing relations. Thus it is that Marx writes, "A commodity is therefore a mysterious thing, simply because in it the social character of man's labor appears to them as an objective character stamped upon the product of that labor; because the relation of the producers to the sum total of their own labor is presented to them as a social relation, existing not between themselves, but between the products of their labor. . . . A definite social relation between men, that assumes, in their eyes, the fantastic form of a relation to things."

Several points should be emphasized about this passage. First, it could be inserted into any one of the early texts in which Marx discusses alienation without violence to their spirit. Secondly, it is not a literary reference, but an essential of the most central Marxian economic category. It is not, as Bell holds, that philosophic ideas have been replaced by economic concepts, but rather that each finds its realization in the other. This was the point of view of the 1844 writings; and it appears in the *Capital* in a much more profound form. Thus it is that Lukacs, in developing a Marxist humanism in *Geschichte und Klassenbewusstsein* bases his central chapter on reification, not upon the early writings, but upon the analysis of the commodity in *Capital*. This essay was published before the appearance of the *Economic and Philosophic Manuscripts of 1844*, yet at times it sounds like a paraphrase of the early Marx.

All of this must be taken in the context of Marx's well-known contempt for economics. He detested this branch of study, yet he concerned himself with the dismal science because he was convinced very early in his life (certainly by 1843) that he must root his values in an analysis of the real world. The change in form, the dropping of the Hegelian language, is in keeping with this sense of grim obligation, but it is always a means of reaffirming the original, humanist values. In the third volume of *Capital*, for instance, Marx writes in a summary passage, ". . . we have seen previously that the social nature of labor, the combination of the labor of a certain individual laborer with that of other laborers for a common purpose, stands opposed to that laborer and his comrades as a foreign power, as the property of a stranger which he would not particularly want to save if he were not compelled to economize with it. It is entirely different in the factories owned by the laborers themselves, for instance, in Rochdale."

Still, are these but literary references? That is Bell's charge. An examination of the mature Marx does not sustain his argument. Approximately one quarter of the first volume of *Capital* is devoted to the dehumanization of work (to be precise, 203 out of 808 pages in the Kerr editions; from p. 353 to p. 556)—which is hardly a "glossing over." In this section, Marx, after carefully detailing the historical development of the division of labor under capital, speaks of "industrial pathology," and thunders that "The instrument of labor strikes down the laborer." These pages are among the most precise and documented in *Capital*, yet they fairly breathe the humanist spirit of the early writings.

Finally, Bell caps his discussion with the inevitable citation from an Engels polemic. In this quotation, Engels is telling some anarchists that authority must continue, even in the new society, that "At least with regard to the hours of work one may write upon the portals of these factories: *Lasciate ogni autonomia, voi che entrate.* (Leave behind all autonomy, you that enter here.)" In part, this extreme formulation is typical of Engels' polemical exuberance; in part, it is the effort of a literary man to catch a Dante echo. But more importantly, Bell misses the fact that the authority which Engels describes in this passage is *self-imposed*, i.e., that the rules are seen as the product of a decision of either an elected representative of the workers in the shop, or of a majority vote of the shop itself. In a sense, placing the reference in context tends to prove the exact opposite of Bell's point: that even at the intensity of an argument with anarchists, Engels *assumed* workers' control of industry. This is the case, and it is true of Marx's writing as well.

In short, the mature Marx, both in method and in explicit statement, continues the humanism of his youth. There are, to be sure, polemical exaggerations, a certain lopsidedness, but this does not justify the theory of a major break in conception. Critics like Bell and Merleau-Ponty are much more serious than the Arendt of *The Human Condition*, but even given their honesty and their sympathy, they manage to create a schizoid Marx who never existed.

The renewed interest in the early Marx is, as noted before, related to the rise of Communist totalitarianism. Since the Kremlin bases its claim to the title of "socialist" on the existence of nationalized property and economic planning in Russia, the socialist reaction to this totalitarian lie has necessarily involved an emphasis upon the humanist categories of Marx and of the socialist tradition. As soon as one realizes that socialism is not simply directed against economic irrationality, but that its deepest springs flow from a positive humanism whose task is the conquest of alienation, it becomes obvious that Russian society has nothing to do with socialism. This valid point, however, has provided a basis for the theory of Marx versus Marx: the integration of humanism and economic analysis in Marx's writings becomes, for certain radical intellectuals, through an emphasis upon the humanism, the counterposition of the two categories.

The response to Communist totalitarianism is still only one of the factors tending toward this new interpretation. It is the most obvious and, for that reason, the least important element. The other social development which makes the redefinition of Marx so plausible in this country is not located in Russia—it is the America of the fifties. During the last decade, many democratic socialist intellectuals subscribed to theories of the "massification" of American society. To a degree this was a reaction of intelligence and insight to some of the more important changes in American capitalism. But it also represented a tendency to overgeneralize a period of ten or so years which, with the exception of the Civil Rights movement, was not characterized by sharp social struggle, a time in which the unions appeared to some to have become a bureaucracy as dangerous as those of business, the state and the military. . . .

But a political humanism without an economic analysis, a political humanism without a conception of actual social forces struggling to realize values, is a contradiction at best and a nostalgic piety at worst. If the working class is seen as incapable of socialist construction, and if no historic alternative force has appeared on the scene, theology, metaphysics, cynicism, or stoicism are real options; socialist politics are not. In this sense, the original Marxian insight, the one which led him from left Hegelianism through Feuerbach to his own distinctive point of view, remains in force; secular humanism must locate itself in the actual struggles of society; it must base itself upon an analysis of society, or else it is nothing.

The theorists of Marx versus Marx shy away from the rigor of their own realism. In the process, they have created a new Marx, one who has little to do with the historical Marx. One hopes that these misreadings will be corrected, not simply by a restoration of texts, but by the living, actual men and women of our time in their fight for their own dignity.

Marxism and Religion

MARX'S attitude toward religion is closely related to his fundamental humanistic position. Marx entered into the discussion of religion by the Young or Left-Hegelians, and was particularly concerned to reply to the analysis of Ludwig Feuerbach. The latter had argued that religion was only the result of man's awareness of his essence and that God was a projection of man's imagination. In creating God and religion, man alienated himself, since God was being endowed with the qualities of man. Man would replace supernatural religion by a religion of humanity when he realizes that "the only God of man is man himself."

Like Feuerbach, Marx saw religion as fiction, as human in origin. But he did not accept Feuerbach's view that knowledge of the origin of religion would be sufficient to dispose of it and that man could then reappropriate the full potential of his human nature. It was necessary to end the conditions of man that gave rise to religion as well as to produce a change in consciousness. In fact, as Marx says in *The German Ideology*, "consciousness, like other things, can be changed by the actions of men, by the practical overturn of the real social relations. . . . Not criticism but revolution is the real driving force of history, as of religion, philosophy, and other kinds of theory."

The ending of religious belief—"the reflex of the real world"—will not affect the essential human reality, and it was essential for this reality to be changed. In his sixth *Thesis on Feuerbach*, Marx wrote that "the human essence is not an abstract, inherent in the single individual. In its reality it is the ensemble of the social conditions." Man, not God, had created the world, and the material objects made by man became his concrete embodiment.

Man is an activist and by acting can control his environment, free himself from the restrictions imposed on him, and determine his own behavior. He liberates himself by conscious control over the productive process. "The life-process of society," Marx wrote in *Capital*, "which is based on the process of material production, does not strip off its mystical veil until it is treated as production by freely associated men, and is consciously regulated by them in accordance with a settled plan." In his article, N. Lobkowicz discusses the way in which Marx's atheistic attitude was related to his desire to see a new type of human being emerge after he had given up his religious and pseudo-religious beliefs.

In spite of Marx's attack on religion as irrational, superstitious, and leading to senility, but because of his implicit humanism, some interpreters have treated Marx as a missionary and moralist of a religious kind seeking the resurrection of man. Louis Halle has compared Marx's intellectual achievement with the drama of St. Paul's vision on the road to Damascus. Max Eastman suggested that Marx had rejected utopian socialism only to find a socialist religion, with its implicit faith that the universe itself would produce a better society and that disciples needed to understand the general laws of the movement of the universe. A number of commentators, theorizing from Marx's rabbinical ancestry, have suggested that the proletariat has been given the role of the chosen people to reach the promised land. In his article Alasdair MacIntyre raises the question of whether one can be Marxist and a Christian at the same time.

13

Karl Marx's Attitude toward Religion

N. Lobkowicz

THOSE not well acquainted with Karl Marx often believe that the founder of "scientific Communism" was a militant atheist who considered the examination of religion and, in particular, of Christianity, one of his major tasks. This belief is, to say the least, inexact.

Marx, of course, was an atheist. And we may add that his atheism is neither a purely methodological one (in the sense in which modern science, for example, might be called "methodologically atheist" insofar as it disregards God as a possible explanatory factor); nor merely a skeptical one (in the sense in which some modern philosophers maintained that they would have granted God's existence if only their philosophical reflection were to force them to do so). Nor does it seem correct to say, as M. Reding did in a much-discussed book, [1] that Marx's atheism is a historical accident rather than an essential feature of the Marxian *Weltanschauung*. Marx's atheism is distinctly dogmatic, in the sense that Marx always denied decidedly and uncompromisingly the existence of a divine being; and this denial is one of the major cornerstones of Marx's outlook.

Marx, however, was far from ascribing to the antireligious fight the importance which it has, for example, in the eyes of contemporary communists. He looked on religion as a consequence of a more basic evil, the evil of a society in which man "has not yet found himself or has already lost himself again." [2] He was always somewhat surprised, indeed annoyed, by the persistent attacks on religion of such militant atheists as Feuerbach or the Bauer brothers. As he saw it, religion in general and Christianity in particular were *in extremis*, if not already dead. No

FROM *The Review of Politics*, 26 (July 1964), pp. 319–328, 350–352.

wonder, then, that the passionate atheists of the Hegelian Left reminded him of Sancho Panza who, according to Cervantes' *Don Quixote*, mercilessly beat harmless attendants at a funeral procession.[3] One does not come to blows with a dying figure, especially if such a fight cannot hasten his decease.

This last point is of some importance. After all, one might be willing to finish a dying enemy by a final deathblow. But Marx did not believe that such a direct attack against religion would ever work. Since religion is only the symptom of a more basic discrepancy, the demise of religion cannot be hastened. Any direct struggle against religion, therefore, appeared to Marx as useless and misplaced: useless, because religion simply cannot be abolished as long as the world is not put straight; misplaced, because the real enemy is the perverted social order of which, as Marx put it, religion is only the "spiritual aroma."[4] Any efficient treatment has to be radical, that is, to reach the very roots of the evil.

It is in this sense that Marx accused his onetime friend, Bruno Bauer, of treating religion as if it were an independent being: "Mr. Bauer comprehends only the *religious* essence of Judaism, not the world and thus real foundation of this religious entity."[5] To criticize religion without criticizing its secular roots amounts to persisting in a standpoint which is not less "theological" than the religious standpoint itself. Aristotle and, more recently, Hegel, used to say that contraries belong to the same genus. Atheism which takes itself to be an end in itself, when it is only the negation of, and the antithesis to, religion, cannot radically succeed in transcending the "religious level":

The question about an *alien* being, about a being above nature and man—a question which implies the admission of the inessentiality of nature and man—has become virtually impossible. *Atheism*, as the disavowal of this inessentiality, has no longer any meaning, for atheism is a *negation of God* and postulates the *existence* of man through this negation; but socialism *qua* socialism no longer stands in any need of such a mediation.[6]

Later it will be noted that this passage, though implicitly aimed at Ludwig Feuerbach, is modeled on Feuerbach's own conceptual scheme. Here it may suffice to state that, whereas Feuerbach and the Left-Hegelians viewed religion simply as a wrong ideology, that is, as a competing *Weltanschauung* which misinterprets the nature of man, Marx considered it as the reflection of a wrong world. In *Theses on Feuerbach* Marx stated that Feuerbach saw religion as a sort of division of the world "into a religious, imaginary world, and a real one" and then proceeded to the "dissolution of the religious world into its secular basis." In short, he unmasked religion as a self-illusion and opposed to it what he considered to be the true facts. But what he overlooked, as Marx pointed out, is the fact "that after completing this work, the chief thing still remains to be done. For the fact that the secular foundation detaches itself from itself and establishes itself in the clouds as an independent empire can only be explained by the self-cleavage and self-contradictoriness of this secular basis."[7]

There is even a sense in which Marx would seem to be prepared to admit that religion is "true." For though it is objectively false and thus cannot be defended against a scientific *Weltanschauung*, it adequately reflects a world which itself is wrong.[8] Religion is true in the sense of "true" intended in the possible reply to someone who, having lost himself to material pleasures, maintains that man does not differ from animals: "Of course, you made it true."

Feuerbach had shown that God is nothing more than a fictitious agglomerate of everything which is admirable, good, and beautiful in man; because he has yielded them to an "alien being," the religious believer views himself as stripped of all perfections. Marx, for his part, proceeds to show that the image which the believer has of himself is correct. Though God, of course, does not exist and all religion is simply nonsense, man is right in believing that he has no perfection of his own; indeed, this is the sole reason why he invents religion—to compensate for and to sublimate his real wretchedness. Just as the absolute monarch who despises his subjects and treats them as if they were not human beings is right, since there actually are no true men where the "monarchic principle" is not queried,[9] so too, the religious believer with his "perverted world consciousness" is right, since he is the product of a perverted world of which religion is merely a reflection.[10]

Accordingly, Marx's criticism of religion moves on two levels. There is, first, the unmasking of religion which, according to Marx, has been in the main completed by his predecessors, especially by Feuerbach. But as this unmasking of religion reveals that religion is "true" in the sense just described, a second kind of criticism has to follow: religion has to be *made false*, that is, the secular world has to be changed in order to cease producing this pathological secretion. Once the secular world is discovered to be the source of religious ideas, it must be "annihilated in theory and in practice."[11] As Marx put it in his famous introduction to the never-completed *Critique of the Hegelian Philosophy of Right*, the criticism of heaven has to turn into a criticism of earth.[12] *This* kind of criticism cannot be limited to words. Feuerbach's analysis of religion resulted in no more than the correction of an error; Marx's more radical analysis inevitably leads to revolutionary action.

This idea that religion is merely an epiphenomenon which, if properly analyzed, reveals the nature of a fundamentally wrong world, explains Marx's reserve with respect to all doctrinal and aggressive atheism, not to speak of any violent coming to grips with the churches. The atheism of Feuerbach and of all the Left-Hegelians looked almost like a "last stage of theism, a negative recognition of God"[13]; they simply ascribed "much too great an importance" to the fight against religious illusions.[14] The French Revolution itself showed that terrorism, instead of exterminating religion, only succeeds in converting it from a public into a private affair.[15]

The few references to religion made by Marx in his later years indicate that, in spite of his lack of interest in this kind of problem, his view on religion and atheism did not change as the years passed. Thus, for instance, in his critique of the so-called Gotha Program of 1875, though stressing that bourgeois "freedom of conscience" is nothing but the toleration of all possible kinds of religious freedom of conscience, Marx argues that "everyone should be able to relieve religious and bodily nature without the police sticking their noses in."[16] In 1874, Engels even went so far as to claim that "the only service which one can still render to God is to declare atheism a compulsory article of faith."[17]

How, then, did it come about that advocates of communism have been among the most violent persecutors of religion? E. Weil recently provided an answer which, as is the case with most good answers, is so obvious that it is easily overlooked.[18] As the proletarian revolution did not take place, Marx's pupils sought to explain the apparent failure of the master's predictions. These explanations thus enabled the believers to continue their adherence to the Marxist creed in spite of the inadequacy of its predictions. The explanations also provided prerequisites for future revolutionary actions.

At this point the Marxists discovered the power of ideas which to Marx had been only afterthoughts to real events. They discovered that religion, being basically antirevolutionary, for it invites men to accept this vale of tears, was a powerful brake restraining history from taking the course predicted by Marx. Thus Christianity and Christian Churches again become a true enemy as the representatives of competing social and political doctrines. They were also powerful supranational organizations which opposed the interest of the proletarian class in general and the proletarian revolution in particular. As Weil put it, Marx believed that only a transformation of the circumstances could succeed in making religion superfluous; his followers, in an odd but quite understandable return to Feuerbach, reached the conclusion that the fight against religion is a precondition of the transformation of circumstances.

Marx's original attitude toward religion, however, is far more shocking than that of his followers. Religion, especially Christianity, always had its enemies and almost every religion has been criticized, attacked, or persecuted at one time or another. But seldom if ever has

Christianity been so radically "taken unseriously" as in Marx. What could be more humiliating to a Christian than to be told that he is not an enemy worth fighting, since he is done for anyway?[19]

In the *Communist Manifesto* Marx and Engels defended themselves against "bourgeois objections to Communism." This defense follows a peculiar pattern: whenever accused of wanting to abolish this or to establish that, the authors of the *Manifesto*, instead of clearly stating that they do or do not want to do it, reply: "There is no need to do it. History already has done it for us." Thus, for instance, when accused of trying to introduce community of women, they reply: "The Communists have no need to introduce it; it has existed almost from time immemorial." The authors then proceed to show how and why. Similarly, when accused of trying to abolish Christianity and to establish atheism, they reply (after having duly emphasized that such charges do not deserve serious examination): "When the ancient world was in its last throes, the ancient religions were overcome by Christianity. When in the eighteenth century Christian ideas succumbed to the ideas of the enlightenment, feudal society fought its death battle with the then revolutionary bourgeoisie." That is to say, Christianity gave up the ghost on the eve of the French Revolution, just when the class now to be replaced by the proletariat was coming into power.

In a book review written about two years after the *Manifesto*, Marx explained that all conceptions and ideas are transformed with each great transformation of social circumstances. Different social circumstances generate different religions. In his time, people have at last discovered the secret of this historical process and are no longer willing to deify this process in the exuberant form of a new religion. They simply "strip off all religion."[20]

In the presence of such an almost flippant attitude toward religion it would seem proper to ask: what made Marx think that Christianity is dead and that all religion is in its last agonies? Indeed, to maintain that "all religion is nothing but the fantastic reflection of the exterior powers which dominate man's everyday life"[21] is one thing; to say that all religion has been played out as a historical phenomenon is quite another thing. Yet it is, let us repeat this, precisely this last point which permits Marx to desist from all pugnacious attitudes toward religion.

If I am not mistaken, neither Marx nor Engels ever stated why they believed Christianity to be dead; indeed, they never put it literally this way. But they occasionally speak of an eventual "withering away" of religion; and as to why religion sooner or later will disappear, they seem to offer two kinds of answer.

The first type of answer is found mainly in Engels. It amounts to saying that, as religion is only a "fantastic reflection" of those powers of

nature and society which man does not understand and thus is unable to
master, religion will disappear with the progress of science, somewhat as
alchemy and other "occult sciences" disappeared with the advent of
modern science. A passage from Engels' drafts for *Anti-Dühring* illustrates this argument:

> To primitive man, the forces of nature were something alien, mysterious,
> superior. At a definite stage through which *all* civilizations pass he assimilates
> such forces by personifying them. This inclination to personify produced
> gods everywhere—and the *consensus gentium* which is used to prove God's
> existence proves nothing more than the universality of this inclination, and
> thus also of religion, as a necessary, but transitory stage of civilization. It is
> not till the forces of nature are really understood that the gods and God are
> expelled from their positions one by one. At present, this development has
> reached a point which permits one to say that it is virtually completed.[22]

This argument, of course, is not peculiar to Marxism. It is common
to all rationalism with an atheist tinge. Accordingly, whenever developing this argument, Engels tends to deviate from the original Marxian
conception according to which all "theoretical products and forms of
consciousness such as religion, philosophy, morals, and the like" have
to be explained exclusively in terms of the "material process of production." Thus, for example, after having emphasized that religion is
based upon what today we would call nonsense, Engels admits that
religion and similar wrong conceptions of nature and of the human
condition "in most cases, have only a negative economic foundation."[23]

Apart from this rationalist argument, there is a specifically Marxist
argument for the withering away of religion. It is an argument that
cannot really be separated from the first argument, and that has not been
explicitly stated. It amounts to saying that, as religion is the pus of a sick
world, it will disappear as soon as the world is restored to health again.
Whereas the former argument assumed that religion originates from
man's impotence in the presence of "blind forces," the latter is based
upon the assumption that religion is both an expression of, and a protest
against, "economic alienation." In religion, man's own activities as
though they were operating independently of the individual, "operate
on man as an alien, divine, or diabolic activity," just as, and because, in his
material life man has lost himself to another. Consequently, the abolition
of the ultimate roots of this self-alienation (which, in 1844, Marx saw as
involved in the very act of labor) in restoring man's true nature, also
destroys religious alienation. "The positive transcendence of *private
property* as the appropriation of *human* life *is, therefore,* the positive
transcendence of all alienation—that is to say, the return of man from
religion, family, state, etc., to his *human*, i.e., *social* mode of existence."[24]

In short, once man has found his way back to himself in the "material" order, he has no need to delude himself. Religion as an expression of his distress will disappear exactly as morbid delusions vanish with the body's restoration to health. Insofar as it is a protest against this distress, the sigh of an oppressed nature, it will become superfluous. The illusory happiness which the religious opiate offers will be replaced by "real happiness."

Although this argument cannot truly be separated from the one mentioned earlier, the difference between the two arguments may be stated. The first does seem to allow for the abolition of religion independently of the social revolution, simply in terms of the progress of science; the second, on the contrary, considers the final restoration of man, that is, the social revolution, a necessary condition of the ultimate downfall of religion.

As the progress of man's mastery over nature and the social world finally enables man to destroy the coercion of social circumstances, it might be argued that science will overcome religion exactly when the progress we make in the means of production effectuates man's final shedding of everything asocial. The two processes are perfectly parallel, as it were. The progress of man's mastery over nature is the ultimate principle of history; Marx's claim that man is living in a state of alienation, in the end, amounts to saying that he is governed by physical, biological, economical, in short, preconscious and thus subhuman, powers instead of governing them. But the progress of man's mastery over nature finds its adequate expression in science, and is in turn furthered by science, the history of which is the history of the gradual clearing away of all ideological nonsense, "or rather the history of its replacement by fresh, but always less absurd nonsense."[25]

Whereas Engels' more rationalist argument views the withering away of religion mainly as the gradual destruction of an ideology by science, the second argument, mainly found in Marx's early writings, is based upon the assumption that the economic and social restoration of man entails a dissolution of all ideological superstructures into spontaneous and, as it were, "earth-based" attitudes of man.

Yet it is precisely at this point that the second argument cannot do without the first one. Indeed, Marx has to explain why, for example, morals, philosophy, and arts are not simply liquidated but rather freed from a false "ideological" consciousness, that is, integrated in man's real life, whereas religion just disappears. This, it seems, can be done only by showing that religion, contrary to all other ideological forms, has no proper foundation at all in man's material life. To this end, then, scientific research must solve the pseudoproblems of religion. Even the state, though it, like religion, will wither away, has a real foundation; in future society, the state will die by losing its legitimate function, whereas religion will wither away by losing its entirely illegitimate function. . . .

It is obvious that someone who wants to create a "new man," and who believes that this "new man" will emerge in terms of man's effort alone, cannot tolerate religion. Even if religion were only a symptom of a more basic evil, it is also the most radical expression of an attitude which has up to now prevented man from prevailing against this evil. As long as man has the possibility of feeding himself with hopes of a better future *beyond* life and history, he never will be able to summon up the energy and determination required by Promethean deeds.

Accordingly, for Marx, the criticism of religion has the function of forcing man to give up all illusions. To some extent, this is true of Feuerbach's antireligious critique as well. For example, Feuerbach explicitly commented upon the connection between a vigorous interest in politics, on the one hand, and the emancipation from religion, on the other hand. Man, as Feuerbach viewed him, immediately upon recovering from religious and philosophic alienation, would relax in the serene light of his own Divinity. Thus, there would be almost no need to set man's Promethean energies free. Accordingly, Feuerbach hardly had to urge the renunciation of *all* illusion. Man, as Feuerbach viewed him, has to give up only his faith in a *transcendent* God and in a *beyond*, not his faith in the existence of an eternally present divinity.

Marx's man, on the contrary, is never less God than at the moment when he abandons his religious and pseudoreligious beliefs. Instead of being able to revel in his Divinity, he is forced to realize how wretched a being he is—and consequently to revolt and to act with the force of a desperate man who has nothing to lose and everything to win. As Marx puts it: "The criticism of religion disillusions man, to make him think and act and shape his reality like a man who has lost his hope and come to reason."[26]

Earlier in this essay, I distinguished three causes of Marx's peculiar atheism: the complete lack of religious experience; the influence of Hegel and his pupils; and Marx's secular messianism. The first two features largely explain why Marx never became a militant atheist; the last feature, on the contrary, seems to explain why Marxist atheism always remained *latently* militant and, more generally, why atheism is an integral element of Marx's *Weltanschauung*. Perhaps, it may be put this way: an eschatological philosophy such as that of Marx which, on the one hand, predicts with quasiscientific certainty an ultimate salvation, and, on the other hand, makes the predicted salvation completely dependent upon man's action, is bound to be atheist. For only a man who gave up all his daydreams and illusions, who forgot once for all the hopes of a beyond, who knows that no divine intervention is possible, who considers all laws of nature, history, and society, as perfectly knowable and therefore as manipulable—only such a man is determined enough to bring about the ultimate salvation, the "Communist revolution." In a word, a philosophy in action such as Marxism is in need of atheism as much as it needs materialist scientism: it has to exclude everything which would permit man to elude reality or to be resigned; it has to predict the *eschaton* as an event of secular history; and it has to rule out *a priori* everything beyond man which may hinder or help history's predicted and carefully planned course.

It is easy to see why an atheism based upon these premises became militant[27] as soon as its advocates discovered that religion was slower in dying than expected. Curiously enough, however, Marx seems to have been opposed to militant atheism on the ground of the very same premises: to fight against the Divine entailed taking it seriously. And it entailed, too, the danger that atheism would become a pseudoreligion; Feuerbach and all Left-Hegelians were here a warning example.

NOTES

[1]   M. Reding, *Der politische Atheismus* (Graz, 1958).
[2]   K. Marx-F. Engels, *Werke* (East Berlin, 1961), I, 378. Hereafter cited as *MEW* followed by volume and page. As far as possible, I have used this recent edition. As it does not contain some of Marx's early writings, I have also used the *Historisch-kritische Gesamtausgabe*, ed. by D. Rjazanov and, since 1931, by V. Adoratskij (Berlin, 1929). Hereafter cited as *MEGA* followed by division, volume, part if applicable, page.
[3]   *MEW*, III, 216f.
[4]   *MEW*, I, 378.
[5]   *MEW*, II, 115.
[6]   *MEGA*, I, 3, 125.
[7]   *MEW*, III.
[8]   As I. Fetscher has pointed out in *Marximusstudien* (Tübingen, 1957), II, 33, Marx always described "ideologies" as false reflections of a false world; the same applies to religion. But precisely because they are *reflections*, both ideologies and religion are "true" in the sense described above.
[9]   *MEW*, I, 340.
[10]   *MEW*, I, 378.
[11]   *MEW*, III, 6. In Engels' edition of the *Theses on Feuerbach*, the passage runs: "criticized in theory and revolutionized in practice." Cf. *ibidem*, 534.
[12]   *MEW*, I, 379.
[13]   *MEW*, II, 116.
[14]   *MEW*, III, 218.
[15]   *MEW*, II, 118, cf. I, 357.
[16]   *MEW*, XIX, 31.
[17]   *MEW*, XVIII, 532.
[18]   E. Weil, *Marxismusstudien* (Tubingen, 1962), IV, 159.

19 This has been well emphasized by H. Gollwitzer in *Marxismusstudien* IV. See my review in *Natural Law Forum* (1963), pp. 137ff.

20 *MEW*, VII, 201. The passage is translated in the selection: Marx-Engels, *On Religion* (2d ed.: Moscow, 1963), pp. 90ff.

21 *MEW*, XX, 294.

22 *MEW*, XX, 582ff.

23 Engels to C. Schmidt, October 27, 1890, *On Religion*, p. 284. Engels says that religion "stands furthest away from material life, and seems to be most alien to it," *MEW*, XXI, 303.

24 *MEGA*, I, 3, 115. There is a certain ambiguity here. In the *Manuscripts of 1844*, Marx stated that though private property *appears* to be the cause of alienation, it is really its consequence, "just as the gods are *in the beginning* not the cause but the effect of man's intellectual confusion." *MEGA*, I, 3, 91f. But if private property is a consequence of alienated labor, how can its *Aufhebung* abolish all alienation? The only possible answer seems to be that the expression "positive transcendence of private property" means more than simple expropriation; private property is "transcended" by a development which permits man to govern both nature and the social world, by a development in the course of which private property disappears.

25 Engels to C. Schmidt, *On Religion*, p. 284.

26 *MEW*, I, 379.

27 In order to avoid misunderstandings, I have to add that even contemporary Marxism-Leninism clings to the Marxian theory of a nonmilitant atheism; yet it is significant enough that, *in practice*, Communists often felt obliged to act contrary to this theory. As far as theory goes, Lenin, for example, is in perfect agreement with Marx.

14

Marxists and Christians

Alasdair MacIntyre

IT IS an interesting paradox that large statements of doctrine are more usually aimed at heresies among one's own adherents than at those who hold other doctrines. This is true not only of Christians. The recent papal encyclical on politics was aimed at easing and accommodating Christian Socialists rather than at setting out a polemic against Marxists. Similarly, the recent Soviet encyclical on Communism addressed itself only to those who already accepted the basic premises of Soviet orthodoxy. More than this, the tendency to official peaceful coexistence is present in both documents. The papal document affirms its own positions rather than denies those of what the English translation of an earlier encyclical called "Atheistic Communism." And there have been Marxists who would have stressed in their description of the coming state of Communism the withering away of religion. The Soviet document notably does not.

Yet if the discussion appears lifeless at the level of official exchanges between the not always Christian bureaucracy of the Vatican and the much more dubiously Marxist bureaucracy of the Kremlin, it is even more difficult to arouse interest in this debate at what one may call local level. What makes it difficult to discuss Christianity and Marxism in the British 1960s is that the one has become more respectable than ever, the other more disreputable. To be a Marxist in our society is to be a member of a tiny isolated minority; to be a Christian is to be part of the at present rising wave of bourgeois piety. Where in the 1930s and 1940s Christian students in British universities would have been pushed by circumstance into confrontation with Marxism, today pietism and ecclesiasticism

FROM *The Twentieth Century*, 170 (Autumn 1961), pp. 28–37.

absorb them more and more. The Communist Party exerts an attraction on few people of any kind, and where Christians encounter it today it is likely to be in the guise of a public relations firm in the service of Khrushchev Enterprises Inc. Other Marxist groupings are usually numerically insignificant. When Marx is discussed in universities or schools it is normally a subject for academic refutation. The Christianity of the 1960s has a quality of complacent self-sufficiency that does not seem to destine it for painful encounters and the Marxism of the 1960s is unlikely to make an immediate impact on anybody, at least in Britain.

This framework of deep pessimism about the whole enterprise is a necessary starting point. Otherwise anything more positive that I have to say will appear out of proportion. What I want to do is first to characterize the kind of dialogue that might go on between Christians and Marxists in the 1960s at occasional moments in odd places. I then want to look at the problems for Christianity that *might* be created by this dialogue. But I have to say *might*. And insofar as this discussion is important it is not just for people who wear the official labels, who think of themselves as Christians or Marxists. The Christianity of Pasternak (so different from that of the bishops) and the Marxism of Brecht (so different from that of his bishops) infect the consciousness of many people who will think themselves quite alien to this dialogue. But it will cast its shadows in their minds.

Can one be both Christian and Marxist? The first cynical, but historically vindicated answer, is that one can be Christian and anything. In the cold war, as in almost all hot wars, Christians were on both sides. So rephrase the question. Can one be both consistently Christian and consistently Marxist? Here the answer that I want to suggest is that Marxism and Christianity are most obviously incompatible when Christianity is given an explicit political interpretation and most notably akin in areas that are at one remove from political action.

The first fact that Marxists have to face about Christianity is that it is politically ambiguous. Ever since in England the sufferings of King Charles I were likened to those of Christ the King at the same time as the Levellers were preparing to institute Christ's kingdom understood in a very different sense, it has been clear that Christianity admitted both of radical and of conservative interpretations. Marxism is at odds with both. The radical utopian strain in Christian politics is suspect for Marxists just because it is utopian. By utopian Christians I mean those who believe that the Kingdom of Heaven can be domesticated upon the earth forthwith. For such Christians politics is a matter of an immediate and radical break with the existing order. Individuals or communities attempt to sell all they have and live without material possessions; they refuse military service and espouse nonviolence. With varying degrees of eccentricity they establish new forms of community, or new political movements. The essence of this type of politics is the belief that Christianity can be incarnated in a program which can be applied forthwith to the solution of political problems.

Marxists may often sympathize with such movements, especially when they belong to the past. And Marxists do not usually fail to applaud genuine radical charity of a kind which does not attempt to be a substitute for political change. Consider the very high regard in which Danilo Dolci's work is held by them (as it certainly ought to be). What they castigate in Christian utopianism is what this has in common with other forms of utopianism, its escapism and its lack of insight into the means of social change. Utopianism is escapist because in societies where large-scale transformation is in fact impossible it contents itself with creating small pockets of change, which cannot in any case hope to survive. Because it concentrates on this it fails to accept responsibility for the slow, patient tasks of large-scale transformation.

This is not why most Christians reject Christian utopianism. They have done so because they have seen Christianity as scarcely politics at all. The powers that be are ordained of God; one must make one's peace with them except when they persecute the church or force it into obviously un-Christian acts. Otherwise the Christian is indistinguishable from the good citizen. This is the starting point for a much more influential doctrine than Christian utopianism, Christian conservatism. On the conservative view, the Kingdom of God belongs not to history, but to the end of history. In history the dominant fact is that of original sin. Politics is the negative job of preventing the effects of sin from overwhelming us; as Luther put it, the state is a bulwark against sin. Because of this, all utopianism, indeed all revolutionary transformation, is dangerous. Man cannot progress very far; he is condemned to trudge around in a necessarily imperfect world.

Of course in the detail of their thought Christian utopians and Christian conservatives both rise to greatness. What I have said only touches the hem of a Thomas Münzer or an Edmund Burke. But the detail, the greatness, and the nuances are not what are transmitted to most ordinary Christians. What comes over to them is something much more like the caricatures I have drawn. And what comes over most dangerously is just the ambiguity in Christian politics. The slide from utopianism is there waiting ready to provide a path of political disillusionment for young Christians. The generosity of impulse which they derive both from their youth and their Christianity is easily betrayed in the first instance into a utopianism as extreme as it is ineffective. Gradually they discover the ineffectiveness and they do so just at that period in their lives when getting a job and building a home make it easy to compromise with the existing social order. Christian conservatism is at hand to rationalize this compromise. From having believed in a too easy perfectibility of human nature, they come to believe that human nature cannot be transformed at all.

It is significant that Christian theologies customarily attack Marxists for believing in the perfectibility of human nature. But Marxists believe neither in original sin nor in original virtue. On the one hand they take a more pessimistic view of human nature than do Christian utopians. Engels quotes with approval Hegel's remark that "One believes one is saying something great if one says that 'man is naturally good.' But one forgets that one says something far greater when one says that 'man is naturally evil.' " One says something greater because it is the role of evil in the world, of "the negative" in the Hegelian sense, to present precisely those limits, dangers, and barriers which have to be overcome and transcended in human history. The utopian sees evil as peripheral and accidental, not as central to human life. But the conservative sees evil as not merely central but necessary; as setting a task only in the sense in which Sisyphus was set a task. From a Marxist standpoint, the conservative vision of human nature seems unhistorical, static, with neither insight into nor trust in human potentiality. It defines human beings in terms of their past. "We are what the past has made us." No. We are whatever we can make of ourselves out of what the past has given us.

At the political level, then, there are deep antagonisms. There is more likelihood of sympathy in attitude to the social values of the liberalism of the affluent society. Christians ought to be as unhappy about a society in which money reigns as Marxists are. There is, of course, a deep rift between the Gospels and later Christianity on the subject of money. By and large, modern Christians treat money as morally neutral. You can use it for good or for evil. The Gospels, by contrast, are pretty unequivocal in condemnation of money (not entirely, of course), and Christian spirituality ought to sit down with Mammon fairly uneasily. When it fails to do so it is often heretical in other ways, as MRA is. More than this, the types of character which are predominant in the affluent society are likely to be equally alien to Christians and to Marxists. The society of the status-ridden career, of the expense account, of the large bureaucratic corporation, tends to produce a majority of conformists and a minority of eccentric, anarchic rebels. The stereotype of the organization man has as its counterpart the stereotype of the Beat generation. The facile happiness of the well-adjusted and the facile unhappiness of the maladjusted become typical moods. Above all, in a consumer society the values of competitive acquisition and the rejection of those values become a focal point of concern. Even if Christians do not reject the society which produces these things, classical Christianity can scarcely be squared with the irresponsibility either of conformism or individualist rebellion. And because of all this, sensitive Christians will be driven to ask questions about society of the kind to which Marxist Socialism gives answers.

Very few of them will accept the Marxist answers, most because they will absorb the anti-Marxist ideology of the age, a few instead or also because they see Marxism as tainted with atheism. But even in its atheism Marxism has some things in common with Christianity which both of them find lacking in liberal rationalism. For Marxist atheism is not merely negative: It has the scale of a world view and it claims the importance of a world view. Marxists resemble Christians in refusing to see belief in God or disbelief in God as a mere intellectual mistake. For Marxists belief in God is a characteristic "mystification" functioning to conceal the realities of nature and society. Just as Christians do not see belief in God as a belief in just one more being additional to other beings, so Marxists see belief in God as a distortion of our total vision. In having an over-all view of the world, both Marxists and Christians find themselves at odds with liberal empiricists. Again, for liberal empiricism, fact is one thing and value is another. Discovering what sort of place the world is and deciding how to act in it are two quite distinct and separate tasks. Here again there is an insistence on the unity of theory and practice by Christians and Marxists (even if in different senses of those much abused terms) which does violence to the most fundamental categories of the liberal mind. More than this, both Christianity and Marxism insist upon trying to make people aware of their cosmic and social situation, on trying to make people transcend the horizons of private life. Adolescents are always more open than others to this insistence; the adult life of our society is built on the premise that most people cannot hope to understand, far less to change, the social universe.

I have suggested that the trouble for Christianity in the 1960s (from a Marxist point of view) is likely to derive from the fact that Christians inherit from their past values which cannot be realized within the structure of capitalism. Some of these values are ascetic ones which are purely religious and are also alien to Marxism. Others are akin to values of Socialism. "The history of early Christianity," wrote Engels, "has many characteristic points of contact with the present labor movement. Like the latter, Christianity was at first a movement of the oppressed; it began as a religion of the slaves and the freed, the poor and outlawed, of the peoples defeated and crushed by the force of Rome. Both Christianity and Proletarian Socialism preach the coming deliverance from slavery and poverty. . . ." Engels saw the key difference in the otherworldliness of Christianity. But Kautsky, rightly or wrongly, saw Christianity as itself originally concerned with an earthly deliverance. "The liberation from poverty which Christianity declared was at first thought of quite realistically. It was to take place in the world and not in Heaven." Only later was Christianity perverted by other worldliness. This strain of political radicalism is usually evoked to some degree by unjust social orders and is likely to be evoked in the 1960s. But the strain for Christians, especially younger Christians, will arise when they find Christianity once again blessing the established social forms. Although the affluent society can afford other and more expensive opiates, it will contrive to find Christianity indispensable.

One reason for this is that our social structure will generate in individuals deep anxiety about status. Another more important one is that to celebrate the great movements of birth and death and marriage there are no rituals but those of religion. Only religion seems to give meaning to those occasions which are felt to be important. In Christianity there are cases of symbolism imperfectly comprehended in which the undernourished imagination can find refreshment. Moreover, Christianity provides some release from the sense of helplessness which is so widespread. Every few months the world seems liable to nuclear destruction; the social units are so large as to be clearly out of control; all the conquests of space by science often deepen the individual's sense of insignificance. The very simple need to believe in a loving father outside whose care not a sparrow, not a fundamental particle, perishes is unlikely to die. But because the rift between the symbolism of Christianity and the social structure is now so great the individual's helplessness will in fact be increased. His resort to religion will console him at the cost of leaving him understanding still less. For so long as he believes he is helpless he grasps something important about himself, a small first step toward ending his helplessness. Whereas a religious belief that he is helpless only in an earthly sense deprives him of the stimulus to look further.

At the same time the assimilation of the church to the social order means that churchmen for the most part passively reflect the dominant values. Where one does find social protest, it is always neatly balanced by the presence in the church of defenders of the *status quo*. The vast mass of church members are unradical middle-class people. Thus the church milieu in which the Christian lives and the motives which lead people to the church will be socially conservative. This will intensify the strain upon those Christians whose values do lead them into conflict with the existing order, especially young Christians. What sort of question will confront them?

From time to time issues arise such as that of apartheid or those raised by the Campaign for Nuclear Disarmament. Christians find themselves working side by side with Marxists and other non-Christians on a basis of deep agreement. On the same issues they find themselves divided from many of their fellow Christians in the profoundest way. This is bound to raise for them the question of how and why different people in the community take up different attitudes. They are bound, if they are serious, to become aware of the psychological and sociological roots of such attitudes. If they look back to the struggle of the seventeenth century, they will find religious motivations omnipresent and extremely powerful. If they look at the twentieth again they will find religious motivations restricted to a minority anyway and not always very strong there. They will be forced to enquire about the nature of the change from one society to another and the nature of the society in which the contemporary church lives. Above all, they will begin to provide sociological explanations of facts which they have been brought up to hear theologically explained.

Someone is bound to say at this point that to give sociological (or biological or physical) explanations is in no way incompatible with giving theological explanations. Divine creation is not a rival explanation to natural selection, and divine vocation is not an alternative which excludes social role. But this is a dangerous defense for religion, if applied too generally. Upon the matter of the possible use of the H-bomb, as to whether it would ever be permissible to use it or not, one would expect a divinely inspired morality to be clear. And if it is not clear, is it sin that clouds the minds of Christians or what? Or does sin cloud the minds of those who take one view but not of those who take the other? Or what? I think asking these questions reveals very clearly that the moral situation and the motivation of Christians is the same as that of everybody else. And then what of grace and guidance?

What I am arguing is that participation in those political and social movements into which their Christianity will help to push some more radical members of the church will raise for these people just the questions which may lead them out of the church in a Marxist direction.

One additional reason for thinking that this might happen is that something not too unlike this path was taken by the founders of Marxism. Engels had a pietist Evangelical background; Marx's school essays on religion still survive. They are warmly eulogistic of what Marx took to be Christianity. The secularized Christianity of Feuerbach was a bridge for both of them to their later positions. The category of "alienation" was precisely that by which the young Marx passed from quasitheological to quasisociological explanations. Its original Hegelian use in which it stands for the rupture between finite and Absolute Spirit makes it almost a pseudonym for "original sin." Its later Marxist use makes it descriptive of certain types of economic activity.

The religious dimension in Marxism survived to Marxism's detriment and helped to shape the forms of its corruption. Bukharin noted that: "One of the most widespread forms of ideological class struggle against Marxism is its treatment as an eschatological doctrine, with all its accompaniments of chiliasm, of soteriology, of myth." In fact, of course, in its attitude to heresy and orthodoxy, in its ecclesiology of the party, and in its apotheosis of Stalin, Soviet Marxism revealed the recurrence of religious patterns. (I do not mean this to be taken as an *explanation* of Stalinism.) And those Marxists who broke with Stalinism have been divided into those who retained the religious element in their Stalinism but merely changed their religion, and those who had to embark on a new criticism of a religion of which they had long thought themselves free.

It will be objected to this whole discussion that I have talked about the possible effect of Marxism on Christians but not *vice versa*. There is a good reason for this over and above my own standpoint. The history of Marxism over the past years is so defaced by crimes and betrayals that anyone who is not yet disillusioned with Marxism is unlikely to be so in the near future. Marxists will remain few in number. Christians are much more numerous and this fact alone makes it probable that the very small traffic between the two doctrines will be largely one way.

PART THREE

Classic Marxist Themes:

Philosophy, History,

and Economics

The Dialectical Process

FOR the Greeks, the word *dialectic* meant an exchange of ideas; in Plato, it was used to mean a dialogue in which opposing positions interacted so that truth emerged to the greatest possible degree. Hegel, who was interested in the formulation of a philosophy of history, used the dialectic to explain the historical process as the unfolding and coming to self-consciousness of the Idea of Freedom.

Marx shared with Hegel the view that history is a logical process, a process in which freedom is progressively increased. But he criticized Hegel for being more concerned with logic than with reality, and for committing the error of conceptual reification. "Hegel," wrote Marx, "gives us the constitution of the concept instead of the concept of the constitution." To the philosophic idealism of Hegel, which was concerned with the development of thought, Marx propounded his opposite, materialistic approach. "The whole of what is called world history," Marx wrote in the *Economic and Philosophic Manuscripts*, "is nothing but the creation of man by human labor."

But Marx differentiated his philosophical position from that of the "mechanical materialists" or "vulgar empiricists," those who held that matter was the basis of mental phenomena or that ideas stemmed from chemical processes. Mere empirical generalization was inadequate without some informing principle or concept through which understanding of the essential or historical development could be reached. The dialectic would provide such an understanding. Unlike the mechanical materialists, who saw things in isolation and at rest, Marxists see everything as in a process of change.

In the Preface to the second German edition of *Capital*, Marx refers to the dialectic as meaning "every historically developed social form as in fluid movement, and therefore takes into account its transient nature not less than its momentary existence." But it was Engels rather than Marx who provided an explanation of dialectics, though, as Sidney Hook has suggested, he used the term in at least seven different meanings.

The Marxist theory holds that dialectics is a science of history that seeks to discover the laws of motion applicable to all social development and that it proceeds through the struggle of opposites. All phenomena contain internal opposites and contradictions. "Movement itself," said Engels, "is a contradiction," for the struggle of opposites is an immanent law of movement. This contradiction applies between form and content as well as internally; the principle of the unity and the conflict of opposites is the central thesis of dialectics. Although dialectic, or dialectical materialism, as it has been termed in the Soviet Union, has been regarded by Marxist exponents as a fundamental part of the doctrine, it has always been something of a mystery. In his explanation of the dialectic, Engels spoke of certain laws, such as the negation of the negation, the change from quantity into quality, and the law of the unity of opposites or identity of contradictions, and he provided some simple examples of these laws. But it is never clear if these laws are always as applicable to society and history as they are to nature. Nor, even if one agrees that dialectics implies development, is it obvious why the dialectical process should lead to or seemingly end in a socialist society or "the closing chapter of the prehistoric stage of human society." There seems no reason why the dialectical process should operate in a progressive direction, nor why there should be any logical relationship between the working of the dialectic and the economic and social doctrines of Marxism or the actions of Communism. In the Soviet Union, not surprisingly, the concept of the dialectic has taken on a petrified air, and it now bears, as Gustav Wetter has written, "a far greater resemblance to Scholasticism than to that of Hegelian dialectics." In the following articles, Max Eastman and Herman Simpson provide an attack and a defense of the dialectical concept.

15

Against the Marxian Dialectic

Max Eastman

Religious Frame of Scientific Socialism

. . . IN ORDER to understand the renewed apotheosis of the word *dialectic*, we must remember that while matter-of-fact men—or men in their matter-of-fact moods—have been building science and trying to clarify its principles, other men or moods of men, less based in matter and less bent on fact, have been inventing a variety of complicated intellectual machinery for keeping up the old wish-fulfilling views of the world as a whole, in spite of the disillusioning discoveries of science about each particular part of it. This wish-fulfilling machinery constitutes about half, I suppose, of what is called modern philosophy. And it constitutes far more than half of what is called German idealistic philosophy. That may be described, almost wholesale, as a "disguised theology." It was so described by Marx himself. And the most ingenious of all these disguised theologians—the "master wizard," as Marx called him—was George Wilhelm Friedrich Hegel, who dominated German intellectual life when Marx was young.

Hegel's wish-fulfilling machinery has two legs upon which it stands, and without which it is nothing. One is an absolute conviction as to the notion, put forward somewhat tentatively, I think, by Plato, that the veritable realities of this world are ideas and not things. The other was the brilliant device of conceiving these ideas, not as static entities, but as in a state of fluid, logical development. Plato had said that these real ideas, conceived as changeless, are to be studied and arrived at by a debating, or dialectic, process, a process of affirmation, contradic-

FROM *The New Republic*, 78 (February 21, 1934), pp. 36–39.

tion, and reconciliation of the opposing views. Hegel declared that these ideas are themselves going through this process. This autodebating, or dialectic unfolding of an idea, is what every reality in this world, he said, consists of. And not only every particular reality, but the world as a whole, is a Mind engaged in defining its content by affirmation, self-contradiction, and reconciliation of the opposites in a higher unity. It is a Divine Mind, evolving with logical necessity and with intense, creative emotion, like a deadly serious, soulfully important and noble and inexorable parlor game of dialectic toward the goal of "self-realization."

It is easy, when you do not believe in any of it at all, to smile at such a colossal enterprise of self-deception. But if you enter into it, and see with what staggering sweeps and intricate ingenuities it is bewilderingly constructed, and if you remember, too, that it flourished a hundred and more years ago, when our own grandparents were believing in the literal licks of hell's flames up the pants-legs of the sinner, you will not smile too scornfully. Remember, too, that Hegel did not wait for modern science to confront the godhead with this world of flux and universal evolution so well known to us. He got the jump on science. He foresaw this world, and had his mighty and obscure machinery of cosmic casuistics ready for the job of reinstating soulfulness, before the scientists themselves quite knew what they were coming to.

Marx learned this system in his youth, and fervently believed it all. He was twenty-five years old before he threw aside Hegel's scheme for reading soul into the universe, and particularly into the bloody pages of human history, and began talking about life's problems as ordinary, practical-minded people talk. It was then that he denounced Hegel as the "master wizard," denounced his whole system as "drunken speculation," and endorsed the opinion of the German "materialist," Ludwig Feuerbach, that all speculative philosophers are "priests in disguise." Indeed, Marx went further than Feuerbach, who himself softened the hard facts of science with a sort of "anthropological philosophy," or philosophy of human love. Marx renounced all kinds of wish-fulfilling speculation whatsoever, declaring that if you adopt the attitude of a scientific investigator, no philosophy of any kind, except a mere "summary" of your findings, is either possible or necessary.

We recognize but one science, the science of history . . . a history of nature and a history of men. . . . With the presentation of reality, an independent philosophy loses its existence-medium. In its place can appear, at the most, a summary of the general results abstracted from an investigation of the historical development of men.

Nevertheless, when he came to formulate his own view of what science is—a thing which he did very sketchily, and that is why there is so much argument about the nature of "Marxism"—it appeared that he had really got rid of but one-half of Hegel's machinery of wish-fulfillment—the notion, namely, that reality is made out of ideas. The notion that reality is "dialectic," which was the very kingpin in the whole soulful-consolatory apparatus of the master wizard, he never did get rid of. Reality is material, he said emphatically, and even human history can be explained in its grand outlines as an evolution of material things. Nevertheless, this evolution is proceeding toward humanly ideal ends. "All successive historic conditions are only places of pilgrimage in the endless evolutionary progress of human society from the lower to the higher," as Engels put it. And this mysteriously "upward" movement, moreover, is taking place in the very manner proper to an apotheosis of the parlor game of dialectic. It first asserts something, and then this something passes over into its opposite, and then by its own "self-active motion," or in other words, by a *logical* necessity, it reconciles or "sublates" these opposites in a higher—that is, a more desirable—unity.

Dialectic in Marx and Lenin

Modern Marxists will hasten to assure you that the "triadic" character of this movement is not essential. And they are quite right; the essential thing is its going "from the lower to the higher," and its doing this by way of conflict with a self-contradictory "totality." Nevertheless I will take a triadic example from Marx. Wealth, or private property, he said, is "the positive side of an antithesis"; "proletariat and wealth are opposites"; it lies in the very nature of a dialectic reality that the conflict between these two "opposites" should resolve itself in a successful proletarian revolution, in which "the proletariat itself disappears, no less than its conditioning opposite, private property."

To declare that "proletariat and wealth are opposites" is such loose thinking that to us it seems obvious the purpose must be other than the definition of fact with a view to verified knowledge. And yet this loose thinking forms the framework into which the wealth of empirical information in *Capital* is forced, in order to make plausible the "historic necessity" of a successful social revolution. This loose thinking is essential to the belief that reality is dialectic. It will be found *whenever and wherever* a downright attempt is made to explain what that belief is. Even Benedetto Croce, who wants to save all that he possibly can of Hegel's philosophy because he likes it, is compelled to remark this. Hegel made an "essential error," he says, in failing clearly to conceive what he meant by "opposite"—failing, indeed, to distinguish things which are opposite from things which are merely "distinct"! And Croce explains:

Who could ever persuade himself that religion is the not-being of art, and that art and religion are two abstractions which possess truth only in philosophy, the synthesis of both; or that the practical spirit is the negation of the theoretical, that representation is the negation of intuition, civil society the negation of the family, and morality the negation of rights; and that all these concepts are unthinkable outside their synthesis—free spirit, thought, state, ethicity—in the same way as being and not being, which are true only in becoming?

Obviously, nobody could persuade himself of these fantastic propositions unless he had some reason to do so other than the desire to understand the world. Hegel's reason was that he wished to keep up, in spite of scientific understanding, a certain attitude of feeling toward the world. It was an attitude of action, rather than of feeling, that Marx and Lenin wished to keep up, but the thinking by which they did so was just as loose, and the lists of "opposites" which they composed just as fantastic, as those of Hegel. In fact, they merely added the class struggle, the opposition of "wealth," or bourgeoisie, and proletariat to the old lists.

Here, for instance, is Lenin's conception of dialectic, written in his notebook, after reading Hegel's *Science of Logic*:

Dialectic is the study of how there can be and are [how there can become] identical opposites—under what circumstances they are identical, converting themselves one into the other—why the mind of man ought not to take these opposites for dead, stagnant, but for living, conditional, moving things, converting themselves one into another. . . .

The doubleness of the single and the understanding of its contradictory parts . . . is the *essence* . . . of the dialectic. . . .

In mathematics: + and—. Differential and integral.

In mechanics: action and reaction.

In physics: positive and negative electricity.

In chemistry: the combining and dissociation of atoms.

In social science: the class struggle. . . .

To this list, he adds, in some later notes, the distinction in logic between the particular and the general: "A leaf of a tree is green; Ivan is a man; Zhuchka is a dog, etc. Here already (as Hegel's genius observed) is the dialectic; the particular is the general." And, in another place, he calls the progress of the mind "from living contemplation to abstract thought, and from this to practice" a "dialectic path."

The science of psychology, with all its failings, has done enough for us so that when a man makes, in dead earnest, such preposterous assertions as that + and—, action and reaction, wealth and proletariat, particular and general, bear the same relation to each other—still more, that wealth and proletariat resolve their opposition in the social revolution with the same "self-active motion" with which a mind resolves in practice the "opposition" between contemplation and abstract thought—we know that he is driven, whether consciously or not, by some motive other than a desire to understand the world. He is not engaged in scientific investigation, but in wish-fulfillment thinking. Just what the wish was, moreover, whose satisfaction gave a color of solid and solemn truth to this loose mixture of remarks, appears in almost every page of Lenin's notes. This, for instance, from the paragraph next following:

Development is a "struggle" of opposites. . . . Only [this conception] affords a key to the "self-movement" of every existent thing; it, alone, offers a key to "leaps," to "interruptions of continuity," to "transformations into the opposite," to the destruction of the old and the arising of the new.

It is the "leaps," the "interruptions of continuity," the "destruction of the old and the arising of the new"—in short, the social revolution—that Lenin is interested in. And an underlying, always unspoken, assumption that the new is going to be what he wants it to be—that the real is in harmony with the human ideal, provided it is *our* ideal—is just as essential to his philosophy as it was to Hegel's. As a philosopher of "dialectic materialism," he is using his mind, not in order to promote the success of his action but in order to assure himself that his action will succeed.

This is made clear in his very first published work, his declaration of faith in Marxism, where he discusses the relation of the idea of historic necessity to personal action. (The italics are mine.)

The idea of historic necessity does not in the least undermine the role of personalities in history; history is all composed of the activities of persons, who are indubitable agents. The real question arising in an appraisal of the social activities of persons is: In what condition are these actions *guaranteed success?* Where is the *guarantee* that this action will not remain a solitary deed, drowned in a sea of contrary actions?

Marx—to sum it up—rejected Hegel's divine spiritualization of the world and the historic process; he declared the essential thing to be solid, stubborn, unconscious, and unconsoling matter. And then he proceeded to read into that matter the very essence of the Divine Spirit as it had been conceived in Hegel's consoling system, its self-active motion by an inherent logical necessity, the necessity with which, in a debating mind, the conclusion follows from the premise, toward an ideal end. The end was different, and so were the actions and emotions of one who participated in its evolution toward them, but the conception of the universe was essentially the same.

It must be understood, of course, that the human mind and will are directly involved in this process, that "men make their own history." They make their own history, but they are also capable, in the person of the Marxist, of knowing the inevitable outcome of that making. And this is because the general course of history is determined not by the nature of man, but by the nature of things. Says Marx:

Man makes his own history, but he does not make it out of conditions chosen by himself, but out of such things as he finds at hand. . . .

It is unnecessary to add that man is not free to choose the forces of production which serve as the foundation of his entire history, for every force of production is an acquired force, the product of former activity. . . . By virtue of the simple fact that every generation finds at hand the forces of production acquired by an earlier generation . . . there arises a connection in human history, and the history of mankind takes form and shape.

I have added as a new contribution the following propositions: (1) that the existence of classes is bound up in certain phases of material production, (2) that the class struggle leads necessarily to the dictatorship of the proletariat, (3) that this dictatorship is but a transition to the abolition of all classes and the creation of a society of the free and equal.

In a preface to the second edition of *Capital*, Marx makes it even more clear that his material world is doing the same thing that Hegel's ideal world did—fulfilling the wishes of the philosopher. He quotes with approval a critic who describes his method as follows:

Marx only troubles himself about one thing: to show, by rigid scientific investigation, the necessity of successive determinate orders of social conditions, and to establish, as impartially as possible, the facts that serve him for fundamental starting points. For this is quite enough if he proves, at the same time, both the necessity of the present order of things, and the necessity of another order into which the first must inevitably pass over; and this is all the same, whether men believe or do not believe it, whether they are conscious or unconscious of it.

It is thus that Marx endowed his material world with the faculty of traveling with reliable, if not divine, necessity toward ideal ends. Far from abandoning all philosophy for science, he did not even really abandon Hegel's philosophy. He merely replaced Hegel's World Spirit with a World Robot who performs to a different purpose—and without demanding social attentions—all the work which the World Spirit was employed to perform.

"Scientific socialism," then, *in its intellectual form*, is anything but scientific. It is "philosophy" in the very sense that Marx himself denounced philosophy. A revolutionary science would study the material world with a view to changing it according to some practical plan. Marx studied the world with a view to making himself believe that it is in process of change according to his plan. Since his plan *is* practical, a revolutionary science is contained in his writings—tangled up in, and somewhat distorted by, an optimistic system of belief. But the belief is superscientific, metaphysical—religious in the truest sense of the term. It is a scheme for reading the ideal purpose of the communists and their plan for achieving it into the objective facts, so that their account of the changing world and their plans for changing it become one and the same thing. "It is not a question of putting through some utopian system," they cry, "but of taking a conscious part in the process of social transformation which is going on before our very eyes"—and therefore— "All our theories are programs of action." Or, as we find it in the words of Lenin, the dialectic philosophy is "deeper and richer" than "objectivism," because it "includes in itself, so to speak, partisanship, obliging a man in every appraisal of events directly, frankly, and openly to take his stand with a definite social group."

Utilities of the Dialectic Faith

To identify theoretic knowledge-of-fact with the program-of-action of a special social group—to regard partisanship as "deeper" than objective investigation—is so exactly *not* the attitude in which science approaches the world, whether it be pure science or applied, that you would hardly expect to find this thought still living in the minds of educated, modern men like Lenin and Trotsky. To hold your wish or purpose in suspense, while you define existing facts, may be said almost to be the essence of what science is. For a practical revolutionist, however, this complicated mental trick has, or at least has had, advantages entirely apart from its wish-fulfillment function. It has inculcated a flexibility of mind, a freedom from fixed concepts, in dealing with social phenomena, a habit of constantly recurring to the facts for new starting points, new slogans, which—foreshadowed in Marx—became in Lenin the basis for the most brilliant political leadership, perhaps, that this world has seen. It inculcated this free and fluid, and nevertheless inflexibly purposive manner of thinking, before it could have been learned from the evolutionary science of social formations and of the human mind.

It is not true, as Marxians assert, that Marx brought into the social theories of the eighteenth-century rationalists the idea of development, and taught them to regard society as a totality and not just a dog-pile of individuals. Both the study of society as an organic whole, and the study of that whole as in a state of evolution, grew up out of the views as in a state of evolution, grew up out of the views of the eighteenth-century rationalists, pushed on by the general development of evolutionary science, without the slightest influence from Marx's working-class philosophy of dialectic materialism. It is true, however, that with his metaphysical conception of society and the mind as cooperatively evolving on a dialectic pattern *toward the goal of communism,* Marx anticipated a social-engineering attitude, and invented a technique of engineering with class forces, which might have been a very late result of that more purely scientific development. Just as Hegel forestalled the scientists with his conservative metaphysic, so Marx, with his revolutionary metaphysic, was far ahead of them in the technique of social action. That is, of course, no reason for clinging to a system that is unscientific.

There are two other facts, however, which make it hard to escape from Marx's wish-fulfillment system, and yet retain his scientific contribution and hold to his technique of revolution. One is that social science, when it is applied in action on a grand scale, does differ from physical or mechanical or any other kind of engineering, in that the scientists themselves are a part of the material they work with, and *what they think about the experiment may affect its result.* That gives to the dialectic myth bound up in scientific socialism a value similar to that sometimes possessed by the Christian Science myth in the eyes of a neuropathologist. True and resolutely practical science does not hesitate on that account, of course, to explode the myth and face the problem that results. It merely finds an obstacle of genuine, though limited, utility to overcome.

A similar, though still more limited, utility is the emotional ease with which this metaphysical objectification of their plans enables the scientific intellectuals, the "professional revolutionists," as Lenin called them, to identify themselves with the spontaneous movement of the working class. The idea that the socialist thinker—who comes almost inevitably from other classes—is merely "bringing the proletariat a consciousness of its own destiny," enables him to avoid a certain appearance of patronizing, or "putting something over on" the proletariat. His theory-program is a mere "mental reflection" of the proletariat's own evolutionary position; his own class origin is incidental; the proletariat would, moreover, in the long run evolve its own consciousness and reach its goal without him. This nicety of the dialectic conception inculcates a mood of humble cooperativeness in the intelligentsia that can hardly be denied a value on occasions. Nevertheless, it is just this nicety that Lenin overstepped so rudely in his book *What Is to Be Done?* which laid the foundations for the Bolshevik triumph.

These subtleties of emotional equilibrium are worth nothing, in the long run, compared to a clear vision of the facts. And the fact is that Marx's dialectic philosophy, with all its wish to be "scientific," and even to outscience the scientists, is a survival of the intellectual machinery with which oversoulful people have kept up, in the face of science, wish-fulfillment thoughts about the world. It is an elaborate device for reading the plans of the communists into their description of the developing conditions. The world is on our side, it teaches them. The real and the motion toward our ideal are the same thing. In order to perceive with accuracy, we must conceive with class bias. Which is only a last refined disguisement of the saying: God is on our side.

16

In Support of the Marxian Dialectic

Herman Simpson

Historical Determinism

EASTMAN rejects not only Marx's theory of *economic* determinism. He also rejects the very conception of *historical* determinism. He imagines that he is thus rejecting Marxism, or the dialectic. He is grossly mistaken. He is rejecting a most important element in the intellectual progress of the past two centuries. The idea that history is subject to natural law did not originate with Marx, or even with Hegel. Let me cite some contemporaries of Marx, not one of whom can be charged with leanings toward communism.

The cautious John Stuart Mill writes in his *Logic:*

The longer our species lasts, and the more civilized it becomes, the more, as Comte remarks, does the influence of past generations over the present, and of mankind *en masse* over every individual in it, predominate over other forces; and though the course of affairs never ceases to be susceptible of alternation both by accidents and by personal qualities, the increasing preponderance of the collective agency of the species over all minor causes, is constantly bringing the general evolution of the race into something *which deviates less from a certain and preappointed track.*

Henry Thomas Buckle, in his *History of Civilization in England,* goes further than Mill; he seeks for the natural laws governing human action:

FROM "The Marxian Dialectic: A Reply," *The New Republic*, 78 (February 28, 1934), pp. 64–67.

Rejecting the metaphysical dogma of free will, and the theological dogma of predestined events, we are driven to the conclusion that the actions of men, being determined solely by their antecedents, must have a character of uniformity, that is to say, must, under precisely the same circumstances, always issue in precisely the same results. . . . We have man modifying nature, and nature modifying man; while out of this reciprocal modification all events must necessarily spring. The problem immediately before us is *to ascertain the method of discovering the laws of this double modification.*

Mill and Buckle were primarily social scientists. John William Draper was primarily a natural scientist: physicist, chemist, physiologist. But he was also a student of society. His *Intellectual Development of Europe* gained him international fame. He opens that book with the queries:

Does the procession of nations in time, like the erratic phantasm of a dream, go forward without reason or order? Or is there a predetermined, a solemn march, in which all must join, ever moving, ever resistlessly advancing, encountering and enduring an inevitable succession of events? . . .

It is of law that I am to speak in this book. In a world composed of vanishing forms I am to vindicate the imperishability, the majesty of law, and to show how man proceeds, in his social march, in obedience to it.

The search for law, necessity, uniformity, in human events can be traced throughout the eighteenth century, in such men as Herder, Montesquieu, Vico, possibly even back to Spinoza. And of course, ever since the seventeenth century, the economists of France and England were engaged in establishing a theoretical system of uniformities, coexistent and sequent, in one special department of human affairs.

The conception of a social-historical determinism is no peculiar possession of Marxism; it is the basic conception of all social science. It includes not only explanation of the past, but also prediction of the future. And Eastman rejects it in the name of science!

Errors of Marx and Engels

Readers of *Penguin Island* will recall that the chief of the general staff did not relish the idea of piling up evidence against Captain Dreyfus. No proofs are the best proofs, he said; no proofs cannot be disproved. Eastman has taken this advice to heart. In repudiating Marxism as a whole, he presents no argument, which is the strongest of all arguments, since it cannot be refuted. When he assures us that the framework— meaning the theory—of *Capital* consists of loose thinking, one may indeed marvel at the assurance, but how can one answer it? But he is careless enough to point out two specific errors on the part of Marx and one on the part of Engels, and unfortunately for him these can be looked into.

First error: Marx says that proletariat and wealth (private property) are opposites, and that in course of the conflict between these opposites, the proletariat itself disappears no less than its conditioning opposite, private property. Eastman is outraged: "To declare that proletariat and wealth are opposites is such loose thinking"... that its purpose can be no other than "to make possible the 'historic necessity' of a social revolution."

Anyone familiar with the evolution of Marx's ideas will note at a glance that the above quotation is from one of his early works: capital is not yet differentiated from wealth. In *The Communist Manifesto* the opposition is formulated, sociologically, as between bourgeoisie and proletariat, and economically, as between capital and wage labor. In fact, the quotation is from *The Holy Family* (not a book of devotion, if you please), written in 1844, while Marx's ideas were still in process of fermentation. (The years 1842–46 were for Marx an era of intellectual transition, from philosophy to science.) Marx is writing under the influence of Feuerbach's humanism. Private property, he says, cannot exist without a dehumanized proletariat; but the proletariat, conscious of its degraded condition, cannot abolish that condition without abolishing private property. The terminology is certainly un-Marxian, but the essential idea is Marxian: To emancipate itself, to cease to be a proletariat, the proletariat must abolish capital. What loose thinking there is in opposing proletariat and wealth, is another of Eastman's secrets. Those who own wealth are not proletarians, and proletarians have no wealth. What "wealth" some proletarians may have saved before 1929 has by this time completely vanished. Isn't that plain?

Second error: Eastman quoted Marx: "Man makes his own history, but he does not make it out of conditions chosen by himself, but out of such things as he finds at hand...."

In this context, "things" can only signify: the physical environment external to man. And Eastman, tilting against historical determinism, comments as follows: "Men make their own history, but they are also capable, in the person of the Marxist, of knowing the inevitable outcome of that making. And this is because the general course of history is determined not by the nature of man, but by the nature of things." A cruder misquotation and misinterpretation I have rarely come across.

Marx says in *The Eighteenth Brumaire*:

Men make their own history, but they do not make it of their free will, under conditions chosen by themselves, but under such conditions as they find at hand, given and handed down. The tradition of all dead generations weighs like a nightmare upon the brain of the living.

And he goes on to illustrate this idea out of the revolutionary history of France. Marx is concerned here not with the force of things external to man, the natural environment, but with the force of tradition, itself the work of man. Certainly, history is made by men in accord with their own nature—it certainly cannot be made by them in accord with the nature of some other being—but under conditions not of their choice. (And that is why Eastman's great plan of social engineering is a wild, utopian chimera.) In his complete lack of understanding of Marxism, Eastman finds himself caught in the antediluvian contradiction: nature of man—nature of things, as though there were a nature of man beyond space and time, independent of the physical and social environment.

Third error, Eastman quotes Engels as follows: "All successive historic conditions are only places of pilgrimage in the endless evolutionary progress of human society from the lower to the higher." This sounds optimistically evolutionary, and Eastman rises in righteous indignation. This time I cannot guess the source of the quotation, but I am willing to accept it as it stands, for I know how this matter of human evolution appeared to the author of the *Anti-Dühring* and *The Evolution of the Family, the State, and Private Property.*—Looking back over the human past, Engels saw an evolution—with many long interruptions and even regressions—from the formless horde to the organized tribe, feudalism, city-state, nation-state, empire; from self-sufficient small communities to world-commerce; from primitive agriculture and petty handicraft to the capitalistic great industry, which breaks through the barriers of nations and states, renders class division and class exploitation superfluous, and leads ultimately to the world community—communism. The driving force in the successive transformations he saw in the evolution of the instruments of production and exchange, which at one stage led to the coalescence of hordes into the tribe, at another stage broke up the tribe and gave rise to classes and class conflicts, states, and wars. At one stage it did away with communal property in the land, at another stage it renders private property in land and instruments of production a barrier to the further development of the productive forces.—This transparently simple, realistic conception appears to Eastman so "mysterious" that he can account for it only by Engels' addiction to an ancient Greek "parlor game." His suspicion is thoroughly aroused: Does not this evolution proceed "toward humanly ideal ends," and is it not therefore a "soulful-consolatory apparatus"? By no means. To landlords and capitalists, communism is an abomination, to be avoided even at the cost of fascism. Yet landlords and capitalists are human, and are attached to their ideals, which are lordly and capitalistic.

The Marx-Engels Dialectic

If we leave Eastman's blind guidance and go to Marx and Engels themselves, we may learn something concerning the dialectic as they conceived it.

In his early writings, during his intellectual transition period mentioned above, Marx criticized the mystifying side of the Hegelian dialectic; but to the best of my recollection he nowhere describes or defines his own conception of it. He comes nearest to doing this in the preface to the second German edition of *Capital*. He quotes at length from an article in a Russian review, dealing exclusively with the method of that work. I give here a few characteristic sentences in condensed form:

The one thing which is of moment to Marx is to find the law of the phenomena he is investigating. And not only . . . within a given historical period. Of still greater moment to him is the law of their variation, of their development, of the transition from one form into another, from one series of connections into a different one. This law once discovered, he investigates in detail its effects. . . . These laws are independent of human consciousness, will and intelligence. . . . When a society passes from one stage into another, it becomes subject to other laws, and the same phenomenon (for instance, population) falls under different laws in different social orders.

Marx's comment is: This is the dialectic method. And he adds: "My dialectic method is not only different from the Hegelian, but is its direct opposite."

Marx also refers directly to the dialectic in the chapter on the rate and mass of surplus value, in the same work. He first shows that money (generally exchange value) cannot be transformed into capital unless it has attained a certain minimum, which differs for various periods, countries, and industries. He then remarks: "Here, as in natural science, is shown the correctness of the law discovered by Hegel, that merely quantitative differences beyond a certain point pass into qualitative changes." And in a footnote he shows how this law holds in chemistry. We must note this, however: Marx does not say that the required minimum for the conversion of money into capital follows from Hegel's law. No. He first establishes the fact, and then says that it is in agreement with Hegel's law. The dialectic is no magic key.

Engels has written rather extensively on the dialectic. In *Socialism, Utopian and Scientific*, he describes it generally. It consists in viewing nature and man as in constant change and flux, and in constant interaction. To Newton, the celestial bodies were stable and eternal; to Linnaeus, the species were immutable; nowadays we know that these are transient forms of being. The same holds true of society.

In the *Anti-Dühring*, Engels goes into considerable detail. He shows the principle of contradiction in mechanical motion, in the higher mathematics. Life itself consists in a continual solution of contradictions; it is identity in change. He illustrates the conversion of quantitative into qualitative changes with examples from chemistry, economics, military history. Men thought dialectically, he says, long before Hegel formulated the laws of the dialectic.

In the essay on Feuerbach, Engels again takes up the dialectic, which he defines as follows:

The science of the general laws of motion, whether of the external world or of human thought—two series of laws, which, identical in substance, differ in form, since the human mind can consciously apply them, while in nature, and until now largely also in history, they assert themselves unconsciously, in the form of external necessity, through an endless series of apparent fortuities.

He next tells us what "the great fundamental thought" of the dialectic is:

The World is not to be comprehended as an aggregate of completed things, but as a complex of processes, in which the apparently stable things, no less than their mental reflections (concepts), go through a ceaseless transformation of birth and death, in which a progressive evolution asserts itself, notwithstanding all apparent fortuitousness and temporary regressions. *But it is one thing to admit this in phrase, another to apply it in detailed concreteness* in each sphere of investigation. But when we make this the starting point in investigation, then we no longer demand final solutions and eternal truths; we become aware of the necessary limitations of all knowledge, of its being conditioned by the circumstances in which it has been acquired. Nor can we be impressed by the old metaphysical and still current contradictions of true and false, good and evil, identical and different, necessary and accidental. We know that these opposites have only relative validity, that that which is now recognized as true has its hidden false side, and also that that which is now recognized as false has a true side, by virtue of which it was once regarded as true; that that which is regarded as necessary is made up entirely of fortuities, and that that which is supposed to be accidental is the form under which necessity hides itself.

We are, of course, interested above all in the application of the dialectic to history and society. This is Engels' general statement of it:

The course of history is governed by general inner laws. Taken as a whole, and in spite of the consciously willed aims of the individuals, chance rules on the surface of things. The conflicts of countless individual wills and acts bring about in history a condition analogous to that which prevails in nature. . . . But wherever chance seems to prevail, there are always hidden inner laws, which have to be discovered. . . . History is the resultant of the conflicts of wills and acts, which are determined by passion or by reflection. . . . We must discover the motives back of the acts, and the determining forces—the historical causes—back of the motives. . . . Thus we arrive at the class struggles, the conditions and the relations of classes, the modes of production, and in the last analysis, the productive powers and the exchange relations.

This highly condensed presentation of Engels' exposition should give us a pretty clear idea of the dialectic. It is no open sesame, which only needs to be uttered in order to open before us the gates of knowledge. It is no original invention of Marx: Engels mentions Descartes and Spinoza, Diderot and Rousseau, as having applied it with success. Marx divested it of all idealistic elements; but every natural scientist is a materialist within his own laboratory and his own specialty; it is only when they leave their laboratory and specialty that so many scientists become idealists, spiritualists, deists. And it is this materialistic dialectic which, in the hands of Marx and Engels and a few—very few indeed—of their most gifted followers, became a mighty instrument of investigation, of appraising the course of events, and hence of action.

A Tool for Giants

I would call the reader's special attention to one sentence of Engels: "It is one thing to admit the dialectic and all it implies in phrase, it is another thing to apply it in detailed concreteness." For it seems to me that there is more to the dialectic than Marx and Engels have told us, more perhaps than many of their disciples would admit. It seems to me that one may learn all the laws of this higher logic, yet never become a dialectician, just as one may learn everything about poetry, its history and its technique, yet never really become a poet. Exceptionally great analytical power, coupled with the ability to see things whole, in their ramifications and concatenations, in action and interaction, in their causes and their effects—this power seems to be as rare as the highest poetical gifts. A few illustrations from Marx will perhaps make this clear.

Proudhon arrived at the conclusion: *La propriété c'est le vol.* And Marx replied: Theft is a violation of property, it presupposes property, therefore it cannot be an explanation of property.

The ordinary economist explains so many things by the abstract phrase: demand and supply. Marx points out that demand is conditioned by the relations of various classes and their respective economic position; by the proportion of the total wages to the total surplus value; and by the proportion of the various parts into which surplus value is split (profit, interest, ground rent, taxes, etc.). Supply, again, is conditioned by the most diverse factors in various industries, classes, and countries. For example, a large corporation closes its plants when products must be sold at a loss, but a small farmer must produce the more the lower prices fall.

It is not given to everybody to see that, while capital seeks to obtain the greatest possible amount of surplus value, the methods which it necessarily employs tend to reduce the number of laborers employable by a given capital, so that the same factors which permit the raising of the degree of exploitation of labor, also reduce the number of laborers exploited. Or that the same laws which cause a growing mass of profit for the entire social capital also cause a fall in the rate of profit. Or that the mere sinking of the rate of profit includes the fact that "constant capital," and therewith the entire capital, is increasing.

Turning from economics to politics, it required an extraordinary intellect to see in 1870, as Marx saw and proclaimed, that the annexation of Alsace-Lorraine by Germany would lead to an alliance of France with Tsarism and would end in a world war. (It took more than twenty years for the alliance to be consummated, and more than forty years for the war to come.) Or to see in 1870, and again in 1882, that the next impulse to social revolution in Europe would come from Russia.

And because the dialectical faculty can achieve such marvelous insight into phenomena, it sometimes appears to me that perhaps Marx and Engels overrated the importance of the dialectic as it came to them formulated by Hegel, and that even without Hegel their theoretical and practical achievements might have been just as great. Be that as it may, in their hands the dialectic became a scientific method of highest potency. By its means they revolutionized the social sciences, where experimentation is impossible and the sheer force of thought must take its place.

The Materialist Conception
of History

A CRUCIAL, and perhaps the most influential, feature of Marx's writings is his conception of history, usually referred to as historical materialism or the materialist conception of history. The concept, applicable to development in all societies, underlies all the Marxist work in some fashion, though stated in slightly different ways. For Marx and Engels, "the fundamental form of activity is, of course, material on which depends all other forms, mental, political, and religious." Men distinguish themselves from animals as soon as they begin to produce their means of subsistence, their material life itself. The nature of individuals depends on the material conditions of their production. Production, and exchange of products, is the base of every social order. The distribution of products, and the division of society into classes or estates, "is determined by what is produced and how it is produced and how the product is exchanged." Marx differentiated societies in history according to this criterion. The ultimate causes of all social changes and political revolutions are to be sought not in the minds of men but in changes in the mode of production and exchange.

The economic structure of society constitutes the real foundation on which a legal and political superstructure arises and to which forms of social consciousness correspond. But it is not always clear, although the ultimate significance of the economic factor is always stressed, whether the superstructure automatically reflects the economic structure at a particular time or whether it can have an independent existence of its own. The Marxists themselves were aware of this problem at the end of their lives. In a letter to Mehring on July 14, 1893, Engels confessed that he and Marx had "laid the main emphasis at first on the derivation of political, juridical, and other ideological notions, and of the actions arising through the medium of these notions, from basic economic facts. But in doing so we neglected the formal side—the way in which these notions come about—for the sake of the content."

Many critics of Marxism have equated the materialist conception with historicism—the conviction that the laws of historical development are known and that future developments can be predicted—or with determinism, the belief that the process of history takes an inevitable direction. Karl Popper has even referred to Marxism as "the purest, the most developed, and the most dangerous form of historicism." Even those not wholly unsympathetic to the Marxist approach, like C. Wright Mills, argue that Marxism tends to understate the significance of political forms, which may drastically modify or even determine the economics of a society, the impact of political and military forces, the role of government in controlling economic behavior, and the importance of nationalism.

Commentators will differ on the question of the determinism of the Marxian theory. But the practice of Communists has been to neglect or ignore any deterministic aspects of Marxism. At its most extreme, the voluntarist attitude was shown by Stalin in his Report to the Seventeenth Congress of the Communist Party in 1934 that "the part played by so-called objective conditions has been reduced to a minimum; whereas the part played by our organizations and their leaders has become decisive, exceptional."

How useful is the materialist conception of history for the analysis of specific historical events? J. H. Hexter casts some doubt on its utility and suggests a more useful alternative approach for the particular problem which concerns him. A more general attack on the Marxist historical approach is mounted by H. B. Mayo, who discusses, among other things, the deterministic problem.

17

Marxism as a Philosophy of History

H. B. Mayo

MARX'S economic interpretion of history may be judged in two ways. One way is to subject it to detailed scrutiny and relate it to the evidence of historical and statistical research. This has been done a number of times and it is not my purpose to repeat the examination here. Let it suffice to say that when historical materialism is judged by such scientific tests as are applicable (prediction, ability to explain and fit the facts, and practical success) the theory emerges pretty badly damaged. Its substantial thesis, that is to say, is untenable, although a residue of insights and partial truths doubtless remains: a residue which affects the work of every historian and social scientist and has already been incorporated into the main stream of Western thought.

Marx's theory may also be judged on more broadly philosophical grounds, as an instance of the species known as "philosophy of history." This fashionable phrase does not refer to a method of writing or studying history (methodology), but to something much wider, which may be called the "meaning" of history, or the attempt to give "significance" to the course of events.

The search for a meaning in history is an ancient pastime. From Plato onwards, and even from earlier days, men have tried to agree on the "fable of history." The plain man clearly holds a philosophy of history, even if it is only the lessons in patriotism which he absorbs from his school books and his environment. Never more than now were men frantically examining the records of the past to find the laws upon which they could base a faith to live by. Many people make this

FROM *Canadian Historical Review*, University of Toronto Press, 34 (March 1953), pp. 1–12.

search, like Marx, with their faith already cut and dried, and it is not surprising that they then emerge from the archives with a set of selected or even manufactured "facts" to guarantee the truth of their interpretations of history. Even so, it is a search which has often employed the most sensitive and subtle minds, and it is with some diffidence that I add to the sea of ink which has been spilled on philosophies of history in general.

One great stumbling block faces us at the outset: can *any* philosophy of history be tested by an appeal to the evidence of historical occurrences? The answer is not easy to give, but on the whole it appears that the record of events is not such as to establish the truth of any philosophy. Most basic philosophic and theological questions are of the type that neutral and scientific inquiry cannot answer. Such questions as: what is the purpose of life? is there a meaning behind history? are not answerable by the natural or social sciences. This warning must be kept in mind in any rational or scientific analysis of Marx's laws of history.

The idea that the course of history, like that of the physical universe, is subject to laws lying behind the seemingly fortuitous events, is one which has fascinated many learned people in all ages. Marx never doubted that such laws exist, and that they are knowable. He claimed indeed to have discovered them, to have laid bare the pattern of law that actually exists beneath the surface, to have "made the processes of history conscious." The question of historical laws is inseparable from the Marxist meaning of history, for to Marx the laws were the guarantee that history would bring the revolution and afterwards the classless society.

We may now put the question to Marx. Has he, by calling attention to economic influences, done more than give us a useful clue to understanding how social change often occurs? Has he in fact revealed any law by which history ineluctably develops? The facts of industrial development since Marx's day do not conform to Marx's expectations, since neither the sharpening class struggle nor the increasing impoverishment have come about. This does not noticeably worry the Marxist because he rests his case upon an ultimate act of faith which, like most faiths, is elastic enough to cover all contingencies. The dialectic of history, like all ambitious historical interpretations, can thus hardly be refuted by experience; on the contrary, experience must be adjusted to the theory, which is always an easy task for an ingenious believer. Marx himself believed, and as a Hegelian could not help but believe, that there was a pattern of logical and dialectical necessity in history. The Marxist construction is not so much, as it is often taken to be, a series of deductions from a few fixed premises as a kind of *Gestalt* or pattern imposed upon society and history. To assume such a fixed and necessary pattern in history is metaphysical in the worst sense of that word, and puts the shaping of events forever beyond the reach of man, even collectively, and even in the classless society.[1]

There are several weighty reasons why Marx the dialectician was wrong, some of them telling with equal force against all ambitious "laws" of history. The first great error, underlying the assumption of any laws of history, is to assume that there is only one history revealed to us. History is not just something that has happened once and for all, a series of limited and publicly available facts. To begin with, there are many gaps in our records, so that it is always easier to derive so-called laws where the historical record is scanty. Perhaps for that reason it has been said that "ignorance is the first requisite of the historian," and for the same reason too the so-called scientific historians such as Vico, Montesquieu, Machiavelli, and Marx have been led astray by the limited historical evidence available to them. Many civilizations have come and gone of which we possess only the most fragmentary knowledge. There is little doubt that only Marx's ignorance of the ancient and mediaeval worlds enabled him to make his simple generalizations about them.

Then again, such information of the past as we do possess is heavily weighted in certain directions. Only some types of material were put on record—for instance, legal codes and the chronicles of kings—and even this documentary evidence is often meager and written to prove a point. The records of archaeology too are of a certain durable kind, so that in reconstructing an early civilization, reliance is put on evidence weighted in favor of the material and practical. But a civilization is much more than its artifacts.

Finally and even more important is the fact that the only history we can be aware of is history as we read or select it. At times the information is absent, at others the facts are often too numerous for all to be taken into account. Selection is always personal, and "facts" are not the same to all. Since all historical events are unique, so far as we know, choosing those which are significant or relevant is always difficult, and is invariably carried out in the light of a prior theory or principle of selection.

Yet such a view is not that of sheer skepticism, and is not to say that history is whatever we say it is. The evidence must be scrutinized with care, and above all assessed with intellectual integrity. There is both good and bad written history (aside altogether from literary style) and even though it may be written from different viewpoints it is not all merely agreeable fiction. We are entitled to demand of the historian that he should state his bias and make plain what question he puts to the historical record. If different questions are put, different answers will be obtained, and so there is often a gulf between an agreed account of what happened and its interpretation. In short, the only answers we can get from history are those which our questions are designed to elicit; the only meaning we shall find is the meaning we ourselves put into history. Our question, or meaning, then becomes the principle of selection which determines what things "matter," and how they are interpreted. Marx, like all interpreters of history, was incurably teleological (although he did not think so) when he wrote the story of history and gave it a plot and a climax. . . .

There are, in short, as many histories, as many "red threads," as there are interests or beliefs or philosophies. Since there is and can be no one exclusive meaning, the search for a simple formula, a single pattern of law, is futile. That is why the cyclical theories of the Greeks, the organic analogies of Spengler, the challengers and responses of Toynbee, are not publicly verifiable interpretations of all history, but merely suggestive abstractions reflecting the tastes of their inventors or of their times. That is why Marx too, seeking to justify his pattern of the historic class struggle ending in the classless society, is engaged in a metaphysical and nonrational quest. Man is responsible for what happens, not destiny or chance or any economic or social forces, or any other factor external to man himself. The future therefore also depends on ourselves and is not written in the stars or the dialectic.

Marx may retort that his law of history is merely a probability, a generalization based upon a large number of cases. Treated in this way Marxism becomes a working hypothesis which may be tested by the evidence. But it is not a tenable reply for Marx, for two reasons. First, Marx used only three cases—slavery, feudalism, capitalism—of which the first two were examined with so little care they hardly serve to support any kind of generalization. The foundation of the whole law is in fact the one case of capitalism, and hence there is no induction about it; and even this one case, as the evidence plainly shows, has not conformed to the law. Second, Marx was not setting out a cautious statement of probability, a working hypothesis, an extrapolation of social trends prefaced by *ceteris paribus*. He cast the horoscope of capitalism, making no allowance for other trends, and admitting no possibility that the future could take a course other than that which he outlined. The major error behind Marx's dialectic law of history may be summed up by saying that he was merely universalizing his private plans for capitalism.

An essential part of Marx's theory, it will be recalled, is that ideologies are a "reflection" of the economic foundation; that they are merely part of an economically determined superstructure. If this is true, then the second great objection which may be raised is that what Marx had to say was relevant only to nineteenth-century conditions, especially those prevailing at the time he lived and wrote, but is not applicable either to past economic systems or to the future. Marx saw the economic roots of ideology clearly enough in the case of the *bourgeoisie* of his day, and Engels too noted the same thing when he blamed the *bourgeoisie* for identifying generalizations from their own class viewpoint with the eternal laws of nature. Yet what is said about the *bourgeoisie* is equally true of Marxists. Plekhanov came near to admitting this when he said that Marxist theory could only have come into being when determined by the evolution of capitalist methods of production. Max Beer wrote: "Marxism is quite a natural growth of the revolutionary soil of the first half of the nineteenth century"; and J.B.S. Haldane writes today: "Marxism is the best and truest philosophy that could have been provided under the social conditions of the mid-nineteenth century."[2]

The essential truth of this common criticism of Marxism still holds: the theory itself, that is to say, is economically determined and it is an open question whether another theory will not be thrown up out of another foundation. This objection does not altogether dispose of the broad generalization at the basis of Marx's system, i.e., that economic forces are immensely important in history—a truism which can hardly be denied—but it is a fatal objection to the more specific parts of Marxism and to any determinate predictions. Like all determinist theories, Marxism is trapped in its own logic, although Marxists appear to think they themselves are exempt from determinism. The conclusion is inescapable: that Marxism is only true as an abstraction of one of the tendencies at work in the capitalism of the mid-nineteenth century. Or as Marx himself put it, the theory expresses "in general terms, actual relations springing from an existing class struggle, from a historical movement going on under our very eyes."[3] That was in 1848. When generalized, it becomes a good rationalization of what Marx wanted for the proletariat in the future, and may be a useful guide to the historian or sociologist, but it is a long way from this to a massive interpretation of all history.

The third great objection to Marx's conception of history is his explanation of the course of history by reference to a single factor, the basic proposition of which, as Engels emphasized in his speech at Marx's graveside, is that mankind must eat before it can do anything else.[4] Now this stand is vulnerable on two counts: first, one can explain history just as well by reference to any other single desire of man, such as his sexual instinct, or his will to power. We have even been offered a "syphilitic interpretation" of history. Second, all single-factor explanations of history are open to suspicion, whether the factor is found is man or in nature. If it is found in nature there is the insuperable difficulty of explaining away the different cultures which have flourished in the same geographical environment. If the factor is found in man, the obstacle is no less. From the dawn of recorded history man has had the same biological nature as now, but reference to this constant factor will not explain why the same basic "urges" have taken such different forms in the many civilizations. No doubt it is true that the economic foundation has conditioned, or influenced, other social changes; but it is equally true that other changes and factors have conditioned the economic. The rise of industrialism, for example, has taken interestingly different forms in England, the United States, and Japan. Marx and Engels are both on record as noting that the results may differ because of differing circumstances, and the action of man himself. As a student of economic history, Marx wrote: "Thus events strikingly analogous but taking place in different historic surroundings led to totally different results"; and Engels: "Everything which sets men in motion must go through their minds; but what form it will take in the mind will depend very much upon the circumstances." [5] But this modest and sensible attitude is rarely found in Marxist literature, and is quite out of keeping with Marx's implacable laws of history.

There is even serious doubt whether it is possible to isolate the influence of one factor throughout all history. Are not historical causes so complex and interacting that it is in fact impossible to say that most great historical events had a single cause? This seems particularly true when we are trying to analyze the rise and fall of a civilization, and especially when we bear in mind the shortages of historical information on earlier civilizations. Many things contributed to the rise and fall of the Roman Empire, and a long series of steps up to capitalism, some of them peaceful and some of them not. To take one alleged overriding influence, and to use it to impose order upon the complexities of historical change with all their contingencies and imponderables, is only to achieve simplicity by violating the facts. The truth is we simply do not know how some factors, even relatively simple factors such as the physical environment, or the role of leadership, have affected history at different times. An imposed simplification may often be useful, even necessary, but which order is chosen and imposed on the facts will depend on the purpose in hand, and so will have only a special or particular validity. That is one of the reasons why history is always rewritten. What Marx has done is to give his personal order a universal, almost an absolute, validity.

The fourth objection is closely allied, and arises from Marx's assumption that history has moved "upward," whether in a straight line or, as the Marxist would prefer to put it, in a spiral by a series of dialectical "leaps." One trouble with this is in the bland assumption that there is something called universal history of which it is possible to trace the direct lineage. Toynbee avoided this mistake neatly enough in his catalogue of civilizations, although even Toynbee's classification is ambiguous, since he was unable to decide exactly how many civilizations he should count, i.e., he deals with specimens which he is unable to identify when he sees them. Marx, like Hegel before him, was concerned only with European history, and his references to other civilizations, whether in the contemporary East or in the ancient world, were seldom more than perfunctory. These civilizations were not, and cannot be, brought into one stream, the flow of which may be traced from its source through all its meanderings, until it ends in European industrialism.

The other difficulty is in the idea of progress. Before a discussion of historical progress can be carried on intelligently, some criterion must be laid down. Although hardly any standard which we choose to take would be beyond dispute, nevertheless a plausible case can be made out for progress as measured in certain terms commonly accepted in the Western world. If we could agree on some *objective* standard, such as productivity per capita, then progress could be measured with fair ease. Indeed, Marx's standard of progress, as well as the standard by which he evaluated different cultures, was just that: efficiency in producing goods and services.[6] Not every one, however, would agree that the society with the highest material standard of living is necessarily the best. . . .

Our knowledge of nature and of man's social behavior has enabled us more and more to take our personal and collective destiny in hand, and consciously to plan it in many piecemeal directions. This enlargement of our freedom, by enabling us to substitute intelligence and will for drift, seems to be a step forward, since it enables us to build nearer to our heart's desire. All this, however, is clearly a liberal view of progress, which was on the whole common to Hegel, Marx, and a great majority of nineteenth-century writers. . . .

The course of history (if we must use that ambiguous phrase) has been influenced by many factors, among which the economic have doubtless had their part and an important one. Climate, geography, natural disasters, diseases, great leaders, ideas, and even chance or the length of Cleopatra's nose— all these and many more influences have made events what they have been. The appearance of Marx himself or of Hitler, or the decision of the German general staff to allow Lenin to cross Germany to Russia in 1917, may in a sense all be regarded as accidents. Yet it seems foolish to assert that the course of events in Europe and Russia would have been precisely the same had these men not lived. Engels took the view that when the time was ripe for it the idea *had* to be discovered, and the related view that the great man miraculously appears whenever the circumstances demand him. "That if a Napoleon had been lacking, another would have filled the place, is proved by the fact that the man has always been found as soon as he became necessary."[7] This is clearly untenable, for all that circumstances can create is the opportunity for someone to come to the fore. And what of the times when the idea and the man did not appear? And who is to judge when the man has been necessary? Where, one may ask, was the genius to unite the Greek city-states, to save the Roman Empire from collapse, to forestall the rise of Hitler, Mussolini, or Franco, to prevent Stalin's travesty of Marx's more humane dreams, to lead Britain out of the depression of the 1930s, or to bring together in accord the squabbling victors of 1945?

Marx had a part of the truth in stressing the play of technology and economic forces in history. It is an important part of the truth, and in our personal lives we all readily see there is an economic aspect to almost everything we do. Certainly there have been conflicts of many kinds in history, among them class conflicts; some of them fruitful, some not; and doubtless at any one time, there were and are economic limits within which man's choice must operate. But it will always remain that the most important element in man's history is man himself, when allowance has been made for the economic and all other factors. It was partly because he overemphasized the limits and underestimated the extent of choice that Marx proved less accurate at prediction than he thought he would be. It was because he read his own presumed meaning into history, and then borrowed Hegel's dialectical law to support it, that he was able to view history as a single track upward. But it nonetheless was a pure assumption, a hope, not a proven thesis.

The fifth error in the Marxist theory of history is a great confusion of laws or uniformities of nature with "laws" or trends in society. Over and over again the identity of the two are asserted in Marx's writings. "The forces operating in society work exactly like the forces operating in nature: blindly, violently, destructively, so long as we do not understand them and fail to take them into account." "For what each individual wills is obstructed by everyone else, and what emerges is something that no one willed. Thus past history proceeds in the manner of a natural process and is also essentially subject to the same laws of movement."[8] Regardless of man's will and behavior, there is the same necessity in history as in nature. All we can do, he said, is to choose sides, and by choosing we merely shorten or lengthen to a trifling extent the birth pangs of the coming society. Although this gives us more choice and influence than Marx thought, it still leaves us at the mercy of the modes of production: we are still in the mass mere instruments of fate, carried along by the "blind forces of society."

A full treatment of this subject—the difference between natural science and social "laws"—cannot be attempted here. What Marx and Engels did was to draw (like Bagehot) a misleading and dangerous analogy between physical nature and society. It comes very close to a social Darwinist outlook, although Marx himself usually avoided that absurd extreme.

We must note the implication of Marx's views, that it rules out all possibility of piecemeal social planning, and still more the total planning which Marx himself seems to have had in mind. Yet clearly, we *are* able to form and carry out many public policies: in town planning, taxation, foreign exchange control, etc. Nor is this falsified if we freely admit that in planning parts of society we cannot normally predict all the consequences, and that some of these consequences may be of a kind we did not bargain for. The results merely compel us to take thought, and formulate other plans and further coordination. We decide, for example, that in the public interest the school leaving age shall be raised, and as a result of the policy there are unforeseen repercussions upon industry and public finance. We can either deliberately allow these to take their course, or institute further action to take care of the repercussions. To say there is no master plan for everything is not the same thing as saying some things are not planned, when there is agreement on what should be done. Every piece of collective action freely arrived at, whether by private organizations or by the state, enlarges the area of conscious and voluntary decision and by that very fact reduces the sphere to which autonomy and necessity apply. The difference here between Marx and the democrat is that Marx would allow no possibility of substantial reform or social planning until after the revolution. We had better, by God, accept the universe, as Carlyle forcibly put it—although even so we may adapt parts of it to our will— but we are not, within very wide limits, obliged to accept the sway of social forces, and it is what we do within these limits that makes our history.

In the Marxist view, mankind is borne along as on a tide, and until Marx came on the scene man could not even see the direction in which he was drifting. In the happy classless society, when the change has been made from private to public ownership, mankind will be absolved from the rule of economic necessity. The magic of the dialectic is summoned to account for the discontinuity, not to say illogicality, of the famous "leap" into *freedom*. . . .[9]

NOTES

1 Marx himself, when he was not thinking in dialectical terms but was behaving like an economic historian, protested in his life against an "historico-philosophical

theory of the *marche générale* imposed by fate upon every people." But this did not alter his conviction of the truth of *his own* inevitable law of history. *Selected Correspondence of Marx and Engels, 1846–1895* (London, 1934), p. 354.

2   G. V. Plekhanov, *Fundamental Problems of Marxism* (London, 1941), p. 95; M. Beer, *The Life and Teaching of Karl Marx* (London, 1929), p. 25; J. B. S. Haldane, *Marxist Philosophy and the Sciences* (London, 1938), p. 17.

3   *Communist Manifesto.*

4   *Karl Marx: Selected Works* (2 vols., London, 1942), I, p. 16.

5   *Selected Works*, I, p. 459.

6   Sometimes the Marxist standard has been described as freedom for mankind, which in turn involves three factors: (1) increased productivity, (2) collective action, and (3) human development. The first two may be measured, but the third is of course subject to a number of interpretations. Marx once gave a more humorous definition of progress: "Social progress can be measured exactly by the social position of the fair sex (the ugly ones included)." *Selected Correspondence*, p. 255.

7   *Selected Correspondence*, p. 518.

8   *Selected Works*, I, pp. 180, 382.

9   There is a special difficulty about the Hegelian and the Marxist dialectic of history. In both, a point is reached when the dialectic ceases operation, when the laws of past history no longer apply, the Moving Finger having writ, stops writing. It has been suggested that this apocalyptic note is a heritage from Christianity, which has always emphasized a final judgment or an "ultimate" end to man's history on earth.

18

A New Framework for Social History

J. H. Hexter

BY SOCIAL history, I mean that sort of history writing that makes social groupings and especially socioeconomic classes the focus of its attention. At present scholars concerned with this kind of history seem to make one of two choices, neither altogether happy. They try to operate without a framework, or they operate within a stultifying framework— the Marxist interpretation of history. To choose the former is to choose inaccuracy and incoherence in describing chaos. To choose the latter is to choose intelligibility and coherence in describing a myth, and then to baptize the myth as history. The curious and brute fact is that a good number of historians *say* they choose the first horn of the dilemma; and then firmly impale themselves on the second horn. More historians than I should like to number, much less name, are in their historical practice bad and incompetent Marxists, incompetent because unconscious; Marxist in spite of themselves. They say they have no framework for social history, yet they write the social history of Western civilization for every century up to the nineteenth in terms of the rise of the middle class and the decline of the aristocracy, in those strictly Marxist terms and in no other.

Now why do so many historians in fact write history from a point of view that in theory they sincerely reject? The explanation of this paradox, I believe, might go something like this. With the power of genius Marx drove home the importance for history of the conflict of economic interests organized through social classes aiming at the attainment, retention, and extention of power. But Marx did not merely *raise* the problem of classes. To his own satisfaction he solved it. This

FROM *Reappraisals in History*, Northwestern University Press, Evanston, and Longmans Green, London (1961), pp. 14–21.

solution, based on the observed fact of class conflict, is a complete and coherent theory of social change. It is called dialectical materialism. It conceives of the social process as a regular succession of stages of socio-economic development emerging from one another as antitheses and syntheses. Historians were rightly impressed by Marx's insight into the conflict of classes. It gave them a whole new set of exciting insights into the way things happened. But when they picked up the notion of class conflict, they quite unconsciously picked up with it Marx's theory of social change. They bought themselves a package deal. The trouble is that the concept of class interest and class conflict is sound, one of the consistent patterns of history; but the Marxian theory of social change, dialectical materialism, is only the brilliant product of an over-heated, overspeculative, nineteenth-century German imagination. Since any new framework for social history ought to seek to avoid the confusion into which an unwary absorption of the Marxist scheme has hitherto led historians, we had better have clearly in mind the bare essentials of that scheme as it applies to the Western world.

The Marxist scheme derives its explanation of almost a millennium of the history of Western civilization from three indisputable observations of fact and one somewhat gratuitous assumption. The first fact is that before the year 1000 the dominant social class in the Western world was composed of men who derived both their income and their power from the possession of large amounts of land and of enforceable claims on the labor and income of the men who worked the land. The second fact is that between A.D. 1000 and Marx's own day the Western world underwent vast changes, economic, social, political, religious, intellectual. The third fact is that in Marx's own time in the countries most advanced economically the dominant social class was composed of men who derived income and power not from land but from the ownership or control of industrial and trading capital. The gratuitous assumption is that the total history of all the major processes of change —economic, social, political, religious, intellectual—for the whole millennium can be explained in terms of the ceaseless conflict of the two classes, the landed class and the business class, a conflict marked by the gradual, irregular, but uninterrupted decline of the former, and the contrapuntal uninterrupted, irregular, but gradual rise of the latter. For about fifty years these facts and this one gratuitous assumption have served as the effective framework of social history. They have been the stickum with which the specialists have held together whatever particular bits of social history they have happened to be dealing in. Historians who have not used that stickum have simply sold their wares loose, as if to say to the consumer of history, "Here it is. Put it together if you can. We can't."

What is wrong with the Marxist theory is fairly clear. The trouble lies with the gratuitous assumption, which is in fact Marx's theory of social change. To the exigencies of Marx's gratuitous assumption the multiplicity and variety of change in a millennium of Western civilization simply cannot be fitted. The course of history from the ninth century to the nineteenth was just not as Marx described it. Indeed, the fruitful part of Marx's vision—the sense of the historical role of economically based social groupings, their inner structure, their interplay and conflicts, has been utterly blasted by its barren aspects, a pitifully narrow and provincial theory of historical change; and the whole Marxist operation has degenerated into sterile pedantry. That historians, by no means Marxist, have joined in the dreary game of "Button, button, where is the bourgeoisie?" has made that game no more edifying or less dreary.

What can we learn from this sad misadventure? First, that any new framework for social history must not be a prefabricated theory of social change for which historians will forever thereafter be called upon to supply proofs. Second, that it must be a tentative sort of scaffolding, easily extended or torn down and reconstructed to help us in handling our materials, as we learn more about what we can do with those materials. Third, that on the fundamental principle that "History is what happened to happen," it must take social and economic groupings as it finds them. It must not therefore prostrate itself in unholy worship before the altar of the materialist mystical three—feudal, bourgeois, proletarian.

Now the caveats just entered considerably simplify the task of this essay. They absolve me from attempting to draw up a substitute for Marx's over-all theory of social change. The way social change in fact took place is something we may find out about by *using* our framework; it is not and *ought not be* something to be found *in* the framework. Moreover, with no commitment to an over-all theory of social change, it becomes possible to propose a framework for a particular time span and for a particular area without feeling bound to warrant its utility at all other times and in all other places. The place my framework for social history is built for is England, the time for which the framework is built is from around 1000 to 1750.

The period of English history we are considering is about a century short of the time span for which the Marxist dialectic was primarily constructed. Moreover, we are going to start with a solid fact as Marx did. Indeed, we are going to start with the very same fact that Marx started with: around the year 1000 the dominant social class in the Western world was composed of men who derived their income and indirectly their power from the possession of land and of enforceable claims on the labor and income of the men who worked the land. The second fact is very like Marx's second fact: from the year 1000 up to within a hundred years of Marx's prime, the Western world underwent vast changes—economic, political, social, religious, intellectual. Our third fact, however, is rather different from Marx's: one century before Marx's time, in the country most advanced economically, England, the dominant social class still derived most of its income and power from the possession of large amounts of land.

This third fact is the one most likely to arouse controversy, and within the compass of this essay adequate evidence to establish it cannot be offered. Indeed, it is not easy to state precisely the conditions of proof of the statement that one class or another is dominant. For the case in point I will mention only one special index, the game laws. In the eighteenth century the operation of these laws provided the landed gentry with a charter of hunting privilege that effectively excluded all other classes. This privilege differed from others enjoyed by other groups in that it did not derive its justification from any benefit, real or imagined, that the grant or exercise of the privilege might confer on the country. It was a privilege conferred by a ruling class on itself merely as a perquisite of ruling. It is not without significance that by Marx's day, middle-class action in England had radically altered the structure of the eighteenth-century game laws along with the rule of the landed of which those laws were a symbol.

Of course, if one accepts this third fact as accurate, the whole perspective of social history shifts away from the customary Marxist pattern. That pattern, you will recall, is bound up with the thesis that the vast transformations of seven or eight centuries are wholly intelligible only if viewed as consequences of the rise of the bourgeoisie and the decline of the landed aristocracy. If in fact the aristocracy did continually decline during the period in question, then the hypothesis would merit consideration; if not, not.

But if we take the work *decline* in any common sense, then the landed aristocracy of England did *not* continually decline between 950 and 1750. After the Norman conquest in the eleventh century, England acquired a fully systematic feudal organization with the landed aristocracy, of course, at the top. The foundations of feudalism—its basis in tenure of land, conditional upon the rendering of military service— crumbled in the next two centuries, destroyed by the increased circulation of money and its own inadequacies as a means of raising an army. Commercial farming began to play a significant part in the rural economy. Alongside the rural economy a reasonably consequential urban economy appeared. The local laws under which English communities had hitherto been ruled were shunted toward obsolescence by the law of the king's courts, the common law of England. The waves of the renaissance of the twelfth century lapped against England's shores, and systematic learning acquired a measure of economic, political, and social value for him who possessed it. Still the landed aristocracy sat at the top of the heap. The secular boom of the thirteenth century gave way to the secular bust of the fourteenth. English trade shrank and so did commercial farming. After the 1350s the big operator, whether in agriculture or finance, was up against it. The efficient, hard-headed, high-handed central administration that England had known from the days of Henry II to those of Edward I gradually fell into decay. England's assembly of estates grew out of its infancy and became Parliament. By the scheme of commissions of array, indenture, and livery the power of the feudal group was replaced by that of "goodlordship," a new kind of clientage that has been described as "bastard feudalism." In any case, at the top of the illegitimate heap there was still a more or less legitimate landed aristocracy.

The Tudors put an end to the violence of the waning Middle Ages, and private armies were no longer *de rigueur* in the best circles. The Tudors also broke with the Roman Church and threw rich nourishing packets of monastic land onto the market. The vogue of humanism put an unheard-of premium on book learning. The House of Lords no longer dominated the House of Commons. But as lord lieutenants, deputy lieutenants, justices of the peace, and outrageously enough after all, as representatives of the very towns of the "rising bourgeoisie" in the House of Commons, the landed aristocracy still stood at the summit, the ruling class of England. I will not pursue the ponderous progress of the aristocracy any further down the corridor of the centuries. What we are dealing with is not a continuously declining class, but a class that rather successfully maintained its power during all the vicissitudes of three quarters of a millennium during which almost everything else changed quite, quite drastically. Of course the landed class itself changed drastically too. If it had not done so it could not have maintained its power. It is a far cry from Geoffrey de Mandeville's adulterine castles in the reign of King Stephen to the pleasant country mansions of the Whig oligarchs in the reign of George II. Nevertheless a continuity is there and it is substantial. In the history of the English aristocracy from 1066 on, there are bends; but there is no break in the continuity of its existence. Moreover, the roots of the power of Stephen's bad barons and of George's arrogant oligarchs were the same; they lay in the main in the extensive possession of land. But while the roots stood fast, that which grew from them underwent not one but several metamorphoses, fitting itself into societies such as Geoffrey and Stephen never dreamed of. The problem then is one of adaptation. Through seven-odd centuries the English aristocracy deployed their landed wealth in such a way as to retain power in their hands; but the way they deployed that wealth changed as the world they lived in changed around them. How then did they do it?

It seems to me that if historians were systematically to pursue that question down through the centuries they might learn a good deal about the social history of England. But specifically how should historians go about exploring the problem of aristocratic domination and its metamorphoses? To the question of technique there is obviously no one answer. So I will only propose one possible approach, the value of which could be tested only by trying it in practice.

I believe some biologists suggest that the key to the understanding of the nature of health is the study of disease, that the examination of the abnormal provides the clue to the normal. Now the different modes of organizing society seem to be subject each to its own peculiar disease. The characteristic malaise of aristocratic supremacy in English society was what English social diagnosticians were to recognize and describe as "the overmighty subject." . . . As a rough approximation, over-mighty subjects were men who in one way or another had acquired enough power in one form or another to be, or to be regarded as, a threat to the official custodians of public authority. . . .

When we seek what underlay the excessive power wielded by these overmighty subjects, we discover that it was in all cases similar: all of them used their lands as a base from which to move to a position of command or control over men. Ultimately it is only by means of such a transformation that wealth can become the basis and instrument of domination, since men, not money or land, are the source of power. Precisely what kind of men, precisely how they were organized, how the "boss" built his "machine," how he used it, to what collective sentiments (if any) he appealed to gain support and to vindicate his conduct, all these questions and many more would be the object of investigation. As such investigation proceeded we might learn some-thing of the condition of society during the career of each overmighty subject, for in each instance it is the general organization, the habits, the institutions, the state and development of the natural and human resources of the society in which they operate that condition the ac-tivities, limit the success, and determine the failure of the overmighty subjects. That Geoffrey de Mandeville supported his position on a string of strategically situated Essex castles, that the puritan connections aimed at and won initiative in the House of Commons, that the Duke of Newcastle made himself the almost indispensable man by the busy and judicious management of a tidy cache of rotten and pocket boroughs —this tells us something about Geoffrey, the Puritan connection, and the Duke; but it also tells us something about the nature of the societies in which these particular courses of action provided the lines of access to power. . . .

The Contribution

of Marxism to Economics

THE Marxist analysis treats as fundamental the ultimately determining role of the economic factor in history and social development. This factor is sometimes referred to as the "production and reproduction of real life," but usually as the "mode of production" or "the forces of production and the relations of production." Though the general meaning is clear, some critics have been puzzled about which particular content, such as the state of technical knowledge, should be regarded as belonging in these abstract concepts. A severe critic like John Plamenatz even argues that the term "relations of production" is nonsensical.

Marx spent most of his mature life in the British Museum formulating the laws according to which the productive and distributive process of the capitalist system took place. Unfortunately, *Capital*, the book on which Marx labored so long, remained unfinished at his death, most of it being subsequently published by Engels. Most commentators agree that the work is not only forbiddingly difficult, but also internally inconsistent between the different volumes so that it does not form a coherent whole.

But commentators differ both on the elucidation of the major economic ideas of Marx and on the value of his contribution to economic theory. The analysis of value, and the argument that exchange ratios in capitalism are ultimately determined by the labor theory of value, is a fundamental part of the Marxian economic theory, yet the relationship between value and price is ambiguous. The Marxist view of the inevitability of the decline of capitalism is sometimes attributed to the fall in the rate of profit, which results in consequent crises, and sometimes to the inherent tendency of the system to conditions of overproduction and underconsumption. In *Capital*, Marx wrote that production will come to a "standstill at a point determined by the production and realization of profit, not by the satisfaction of social needs," and that "the last cause of all real crises is the poverty and restricted consumption of the masses." Yet Marx also wrote that "crises are always preceded by a period in which wages rise generally, and the working class actually gets a larger share of the annual product intended for consumption."

Whatever the ultimate cause of the crises of capitalism, the system had to be replaced. The lack of social regulation of production led to price fluctuations, interruptions, even catastrophes, in the process of reproduction. In capitalism, internal order is established by means of the competition of individual capitalists, by their mutual pressure on each other. The law of value exerts its influence and maintains the social equilibrium of production as a blind law. This blind law would be replaced by a socialist system in which social production was controlled by social foresight and rational planning.

Many critics have indicated the falsity of some of Marx's economic predictions, especially his view of increasing misery in capitalist societies. Others have held that Marx said little of value about savings, interest, or rent, in which he closely followed the English economist Ricardo, and little original about entrepreneurial initiative. Yet Marx is acknowledged to have made important contributions to business cycle theories and to the study of capitalist crises. Some have regarded his theory of economic equilibrium as precursory to Keynes in its view that equilibrium can be established at a level in which resources are underemployed. The articles by Oscar Lange, Wassily Leontief, and Paul A. Samuelson constitute a continuing discussion over a thirty-year period about the quality of Marx's work and an assessment of his contribution to economic analysis.

19

Marxian Economics

and Modern Economic Theory

Oscar Lange

1. IN THE *Kyoto University Economic Review*,[1] Professor Shibata brought up the question of the relative merits of Marxian economics and the modern theory of economic equilibrium. He contends that the theory of general economic equilibrium which has its most precise and complete formulation in the works of the School of Lausanne, "is ineffectual in making clear systematically either the organization of present-day capitalistic society or the laws of its development," while the Marxian political economy, "though it is now shown to contain many defects, sets forth theories which are either intended to enunciate systematically the organization of present-day capitalistic society and the laws governing its development, or have inseparable and necessary bearings on them." And Professor Shibata asks what it is that makes Marxian economics so powerful a tool for understanding the basic phenomena of capitalism while the mathematical theory of economic equilibrium is quite powerless.

This superiority of Marxian economics seems strange, indeed, in view of the fact that it works with concepts which are long since outdated and which ignore the whole development of economic theory since the time of Ricardo. Professor Shibata thinks that the sterility of the theory of general economic equilibrium is due to its complexity and the high degree of abstraction which make its application to actual problems impossible. Marxian economics instead, being concerned rather with aggregates and averages than with the mental structure of the individuals taking part in the organization of capitalist production, is more amenable to direct practical application. Professor Shibata

FROM *The Review of Economic Studies*, 2 (1935), pp. 189-201.

tries, therefore, to restate and simplify the Lausanne system of equations so as to make it possible to apply them practically. In this Professor Shibata has performed an exceedingly fine piece of analysis for which any serious economist should be grateful. It seems to me, however, that Professor Shibata has not touched the very essential point which accounts for the (real or alleged) superiority of Marxian over "bourgeois" economics. It is, therefore, my purpose to discuss: (1) in what the real or alleged superiority of Marxian economics consists, and (2) whether this superiority is due to the economic concepts used by Marx, or to an exact specification of the institutional (or, if the reader prefers the expression, sociological) data which form the framework in which the economic process works in capitalist society.[2]

2. The Marxist's claim to superiority for his economics is that "bourgeois" economics has utterly failed to explain the fundamental tendencies of the development of the capitalist system. These tendencies are: the constant increase of the scale of production which by substituting large-scale for small-scale production has led to the transition from the free-competitive capitalism of the nineteenth century to the present monopolistic (or rather oligopolistic) capitalism; substitution of interventionism and "planning" for *laissez-faire;* the transition from free trade to high protectionism and economic nationalism in international relations; the constant expansion of the capitalist method of production in noncapitalist countries, which as long as competition was free led to a relatively peaceful permeation of capitalist economy and Western civilization through the whole world, but which with oligopolistic and interventionist capitalism leads to imperialist rivalry among the principal capitalist powers; the increase of economic instability in the capitalist system, which by destroying the economic and social security of the population of capitalist countries, causes them to rebel against the existing economic system, whatever the ideology and program underlying this rebellion (socialism or fascism).

The claim that "bourgeois" economists have failed to explain these tendencies in the development of capitalism, and to formulate them into a theory of economic evolution, seems to be justified indeed. How utterly they failed to do so is conspicuous from the fact that many of them denied this development until the phenomena apparently became so overwhelming as to be familiar to anybody but the professional economist who was always the last to recognize their existence. Thus the tendency toward the concentration of production was denied, or, if admitted, was regarded as of minor significance for the nature of the economic system, until the monopolistic (or oligopolistic) character of the basic industries became so obvious that a special theory of limited competition had to be developed to supplement orthodox economic theory. The transition from free trade to protectionism was mainly interpreted as an act of economic folly; its close connection with the transition from free competition to monopolistic control has as yet scarcely been realized by "bourgeois" economists. The imperialist rivalry of capitalist powers has mainly been explained in purely political terms, the connection between imperialist rivalry and the fight for monopolistic control scarcely being realized. It was very generally held among "bourgeois" economists both at the beginning of the twentieth century and in the years preceding 1929, that the economic stability of capitalism was increasing and that business fluctuations were becoming less and less intense. Thus the Marxian claim that "bourgeois" economists failed to grasp the fundamental tendencies of the evolution of the capitalist system proves to be true. They either denied the existence of these tendencies or, if they took account of them, they never succeeded in explaining them by a consistent theory of economic evolution, but effectively offered no more than a historical description. On the other hand, Marxian economics must be admitted to have anticipated these tendencies correctly, and to have developed a theory which investigates the causal mechanism of this evolution and thus shows its inevitability. . . .

But this superiority of Marxian economics is only a partial one. There are some problems before which Marxian economics is quite powerless, while "bourgeois" economics solves them easily. What can Marxian economics say about monopoly prices? What has it to say on the fundamental problems of monetary and credit theory? What apparatus has it to offer for analyzing the incidence of a tax, or the effect of a certain technical innovation on wages? And (irony of Fate!) what can Marxian economics contribute to the problem of the optimum distribution of productive resources in a socialist economy?

Clearly the relative merits of Marxian economics and of modern "bourgeois" economic theory belong to different "ranges." Marxian economics can work the economic evolution of capitalist society into a consistent theory from which its necessity is deduced, while "bourgeois" economists get no further than mere historical description. On the other hand, "bourgeois" economics is able to grasp the phenomena of the everyday life of a capitalist economy in a manner that is far superior to anything the Marxists can produce.[3] Further, the anticipations which can be deduced from the two types of economic theory refer to a different range of time. If people want to anticipate the development of capitalism over a long period, a knowledge of Marx is a much more effective starting point than a knowledge of Wieser, Boehm-Bawerk, Pareto, or even Marshall (though the last-named is in this respect much superior). But Marxian economics would be a poor basis for running a central bank or anticipating the effects of a change in the rate of discount.

3. The difference between the explanatory value of Marxian and "bourgeois" economics respectively is easily accounted for if the essential features of modern economic theory are recalled. Economic theory as developed by the Austrian, Marshallian, and Lausanne schools is essentially a *static* theory of economic equilibrium analyzing the economic process under a system of constant *data* and the mechanism by which prices and quantities produced adjust themselves to changes in these data. The data themselves, which are psychological (the preference scales of the consumers), technical (the production functions), and institutional (the forms and distribution of property of the factors of production, the monetary and banking system, etc.) are regarded as outside the scope of economic theory. The study of the data is a matter of descriptive and statistical investigation, the study of changes in the data is the province of economic history. If there are any "laws" discoverable in the change of data, their study is outside the range of economic theory. Further, the institutional data of the theory are not specified. Insofar as the theory of economic equilibrium is merely theory of distribution of scarce resources between different uses, it does not need any institutional data at all, for the relevant considerations can be deduced from the example of Robinson Crusoe. Insofar economics is not even a social science. When economic theory is concerned with the pricing process, the specification of institutional data is very general. All that is assumed is the existence of the institutions necessary for the functioning of an exchange economy. But the consequences of the additional institutional datum which distinguishes capitalism from other forms of exchange economy, i.e., the existence of a class of people who do not possess any means of production, is scarcely examined.

Now, Marxian economics is distinguished by making the specification of this additional institutional datum the very cornerstone of its analysis, thus discovering the clue to the peculiarity of the capitalist system by which it differs from other forms of exchange economy. Another characteristic feature of Marxian economics (which will be shown to be closely connected with the former one), is that it provides not only a theory of economic equilibrium, but also a theory of economic evolution. For modern "bourgeois" economics, the problem of economic evolution belongs not to economic theory but to economic history. The study of changes in the data of the economic system is regarded as being beyond the scope of economic theory: for these changes are considered to be from the economists' point of view accidental, not results of the economic process. In opposition to this point of view, Marxian economics provides further a *theory* of economic evolution.[4]

The Marxian theory of economic evolution is based on the contention that it is possible, in certain circumstances, to deduce the necessity for, and also the direction of, a certain change of economic data, and that such a change follows, in a particular sense, from the very mechanism of the economic process in capitalist society. What this mechanism is and what the term *necessity* means in this connection will be seen later; here it is sufficient to mention that the fundamental change in data occurs in production (a change of the production function) and that the "necessity" of such change can be deduced only under the institutional setup specific to capitalism. Thus, a "law of development" of the capitalist system is established. Hence the anticipation of the future course of events deduced from the Marxian theory is not a mechanical extrapolation of a purely empirical trend, but an anticipation based on the recognition of a law of development and is, with certain reservations, not less stringent than an anticipation based on the static theory of economic equilibrium such as, for instance, the anticipation that a rise in price leads, under certain circumstances, to a decline of the amount of a commodity demanded.

4. The economist whose horizon does not extend beyond the limits of a purely static theory of equilibrium usually denies the possibility of a theory of economic evolution. He is too much accustomed to see in the evolution of what he regards as the pure data of his science a certain kind of "accident" which may be described by the historian and statistician but which cannot be accounted for causally, at any rate not by economic theory. His argument is in general that the phenomena are too complicated to be capable of theoretical formulation, i.e., to be accounted for by one single principle (or a few principles). He contends that in the study of economic evolution so many factors must be taken into account that economic evolution can virtually only be described historically and cannot be forced into the pattern of an oversimplified (and therefore wrong) theory. However, this argument is scarcely convincing, it is too much like that put forward by the historical school against the possibility of even static economic theory. The pricing problem, so the historical and purely institutionalist economist argues, is much too complicated to be explained by one single principle (marginal utility), but should rather be described historically and statistically so as to take due account of all the factors influencing the price of a commodity. And such factors are, besides utility, the cost of production, relative scarcity, the cost of transportation, the extent to which the commodity is imported or exported, its quality, the climate if the commodity is an article of clothing, etc. How crazy, one might conclude

on this type of argument, to explain the complicated result of so many causes by one single principle such as marginal utility.

Another argument is that even if a theory of economic evolution is in principle possible, it does not belong to the field of economics. If by this it is meant that the theory of economic evolution requires *additional* assumptions beyond those contained in the theory of economic equilibrium, this is obvious, for if the theory of economic equilibrium already contained these assumptions it would deduce a process of evolution instead of a state of equilibrium. Whether, however, the deduction of the necessity for a change of certain data from certain principles is called *economic* theory or not is merely a matter of terminology. It should be noted, however, that in Marxian theory this change of data is deduced from the principle of profit maximization which is at the basis of the theory of economic equilibrium and that the phenomena connected with it were regarded by the classical economists as belonging to the traditionally established body of economic theory. Hence a theory of economic evolution explaining certain changes of data as resulting from "within" the economic process in capitalist society may duly be included in the science of economics.

5. I have pointed out that the real source of the superiority of Marxian economics is in the field of explaining and anticipating a process of economic evolution. It is not the specific economic concepts used by Marx, but the definite specification of the institutional framework in which the economic process goes on in capitalist society that makes it possible to establish a theory of economic evolution different from mere historical description. Most orthodox Marxists, however, believe that their superiority in understanding the evolution of capitalism is due to the economic concepts with which Marx worked, i.e., to his using the labor theory of value. They think that the abandonment of the classical labor theory of value in favor of the theory of marginal utility is responsible for the failure of "bourgeois" economics to explain the fundamental phenomena of capitalist evolution. That they are wrong can be easily shown by considering the economic meaning of the labor theory of value. It is nothing but a static theory of general economic equilibrium. In an individualistic exchange economy, based on division of labor, in which there is no central authority to direct which commodities, and in what quantities, are to be produced, the problem is solved automatically by the fact that competition enforces such a distribution of productive resources between the various industries that prices are proportional to the amount of labor necessary for producing the respective commodities (these being the "natural prices" of classical economics). In essence this is as static as the modern theory of economic equilibrium, for it explains price and production equilib-

rium only under the assumption of certain data (i.e., a given amount of labor such as is necessary to produce a commodity—an amount determined by the technique of production). Nor is this theory based on more specialized institutional assumptions than the modern theory of economic equilibrium; it holds not only in a capitalist economy, but in any exchange economy in which there is free competition. To be exact, however, it really holds precisely only in a noncapitalistic exchange economy of small producers, each of whom owns his own means of production (an exchange economy composed of small self-working artisans and peasant farmers, for instance; Marx calls it "einfache Warenproduktion").[5] In a capitalist economy it requires, as Marx has shown himself in the third volume of *Capital*, certain modifications due to differences in the organic composition of capital (i.e., the ratio of the capital invested in capital *goods* to the capital invested in payment of wages) in different industries. Thus the labor theory of value has no qualities which would make it, from the Marxist point of view, superior to the modern more elaborate theory of economic equilibrium.[6] It is only a more primitive form of the latter, restricted to the narrow field of pure competition and even not without its limitations in this field. Further, its most relevant statement (i.e., the equality of price to average cost plus "normal" profit) is included in the modern theory of economic equilibrium. Thus the labor theory of value cannot possibly be the source of the superiority of Marxian over "bourgeois" economics in explaining the phenomena of economic *evolution*. In fact, the adherence to an antiquated form of the theory of economic equilibrium is the cause of the inferiority of Marxian economics in many fields. The superiority of Marxian economics on the problem of the evolution of capitalism is due to the exact specification of the institutional datum which distinguishes capitalism from "einfache Warenproduktion." It was thus that Marx was able to discover the peculiarities of the capitalist system and to establish a theory of economic evolution.

6. The shortcomings of Marxian economics due to its antiquated theory of economic equilibrium, and its merits due to its possession of a theory of economic evolution, both become conspicuous if the contribution of Marxian and of "bourgeois" economics to the theory of the business cycle are considered. Neither of them can give a complete solution to the problem.

That Marxian economics fails is due to the labor theory of value, which can explain prices only as equilibrium prices (i.e., "natural prices," in the terminology of Ricardo). Deviations of actual from "natural prices" are more or less accidental and the labor theory has nothing definite to say about them. But the central problem of business cycle theory is one of deviation from equilibrium—of the causes, the course, and the effect of such deviation. Here the labor theory of value inevitably fails. The inability of Marxian economics to solve the problem of the business cycle is demonstrated by the considerable Marxist literature concerned with the famous reproduction schemes of the second volume of *Capital*. This whole literature tries to solve the fundamental problems of economic equilibrium and disequilibrium without even attempting to make use of the mathematical concept of functional relationship.

But on the other hand, "bourgeois" economics has also failed to establish a consistent theory of business cycles. It has done an exceedingly good job in working out a number of details of the greatest importance for a theory of business cycles, such as studying the effects of the different elasticities of the legamina in our economic system. And it has elucidated in a manner hitherto unprecedented the role of money and credit in the business cycle. But it has not been able to formulate a complete theory of business cycles. This inability is a direct consequence of its being only a static theory of equilibrium and of adjustment processes. Such a theory can analyze why, if a disturbance of equilibrium has occurred, certain adjustment processes necessarily follow. It can also analyze the nature of the adjustment processes following a given change of data. But it cannot explain why such disturbances recur regularly, for this is only possible with a theory of economic evolution. Thus the modern theory of economic equilibrium can show that a boom started by an inflationary credit expansion must lead to a breakdown and a process of liquidation. But the real problem is to explain why such credit inflations occur again and again, being inherent in the very nature of the capitalist system. Similarly with the case of technical innovations as a cause of the business cycle. In a theory of economic evolution the business cycle would prove to be the form in which economic evolution takes place in capitalist society.[7]

Only by a theory of economic evolution can the "necessary" recurrence of a constellation of data leading to a constantly recurring business cycle be explained. A mere theory of economic equilibrium which considers the problem of change of data to be outside its scope can tackle the problem of the business cycle only in two ways: either (1) by seeking the regularity of the recurrence of business cycles in a regularity of changes of data resulting from forces outside the economic process as, for instance, meteorological cycles or successive waves of optimism or pessimism, or (2) by denying the existence of a regularly recurrent business cycle and regarding business fluctuations as due to changes of data which are, from the economic theorist's point of view, "accidental" and hence the concern rather of the economic historian. In the latter case the scope of economic theory would be limited to explaining each business fluctuation separately, as a unique historical phenomenon, by applying the principles of the theory of economic equilibrium to the factual material collected by the economic historian.

7. I have stressed the point that the distinguishing feature of Marxian economics is the precise specification of an institutional datum by which Marx defines capitalism as opposed to an "einfache Warenproduktion," i.e., an exchange economy consisting of small independent producers each of whom possesses his own means of production. The institutional datum, which is the cornerstone of the Marxian analysis of capitalism, is the division of the population into two parts, one of which owns the means of production while the other owns only labor power. It is obvious that only through this institutional datum can profit and interest appear as a form of income separate from wages. I believe that nobody denies the important sociological bearing of this institutional datum. However, the question arises whether this institutional datum, which is the basis of the Marxian definition of capitalism, has any bearing on economic theory. Most of modern economic theory is based on the tacit assumption or even flat denial that any such bearing exists. It is generally assumed that, however important the concept of capitalism (as distinct from a mere exchange economy) may be for sociology and economic history, it is unnecessary for economic theory, because the nature of the economic process in the capitalist system is not substantially different from the nature of the economic process in any type of exchange economy.

This argument is perfectly right insofar as the theory of economic equilibrium is concerned. The formal principles of the theory of economic equilibrium are the same for any type of exchange economy. The system of equilibrium equations is applicable indiscriminately to a capitalist economy or to an "einfache Warenproduktion." Whether the persons who own the productive services of labor and capital (labor power and the means of production, in the Marxian terminology) are the same or not affects, of course, the concrete results of the economic equilibrium process, but not its formal theoretical aspect. But the same is true of the formulation of the theory of economic equilibrium which was used by Marx, i.e., of the labor theory of value. This theory, too, applies indiscriminately to any type of exchange economy, provided only that there is pure competition. It was argued repeatedly by Marx himself that the "law of value" by which equilibrium asserts itself in an exchange economy based on the division of labor holds for any type of exchange economy, whether capitalistic or an "einfache Warenproduktion." Even more, Marx develops his theory of value first for an "einfache Warenproduktion" later showing the (unessential from his point of view) slight modification it must undergo if applied to a capitalist economy. Thus the institutional basis of capitalist society has no essential significance for the general theory of economic equilibrium. Insofar, the prevailing opinion of economists is right. The whole significance of this datum is in terms of a sociological interpretation of the economic equilibrium process.

However, the institutional datum underlying the Marxian analysis of capitalism becomes of fundamental significance where the theory of economic evolution is concerned. A theory of economic evolution can be established only on very definite assumptions concerning the institutional framework in which the economic process goes on. The instability of the technique of production which is the basis of the theory of economic evolution can be shown to be inevitable only under very specific institutional data. It is clear that it could not be shown to exist in a feudal society, or even in an "einfache Warenproduktion." Of course, a certain amount of technical progress exists in any type of human society, but only under capitalism can it be shown to be the necessary condition for the maintenance of the system.

8. The necessity of technical progress for the maintenance of the capitalist system is deduced in Marxian economics by showing that only in a progressive economy can capitalist profit and interest exist.

The profit of the capitalist entrepreneur, from which also interest on capital is derived, is explained by Marx to be due to the difference between the value of the worker's labor power and the value of the product created by the worker. Now, according to the labor theory of value, the value of labor power is determined by its cost of reproduction. As in any civilized society, a worker is able to produce more than he needs for his subsistence he creates a surplus which is the basis of his employer's profit. However, the crucial point in the Marxian theory is the application of the labor theory of value to the determination of wages. If the market price of cotton cloth exceeds its "natural price," capital and labor flow into the cotton cloth industry until, through increase of the supply of cotton cloth, its market price conforms to the "natural price." But this equilibrating mechanism, which is the foundation of labor theory of value, cannot be applied to the labor market. If wages rise above the "natural price" of labor power so as to threaten to annihilate the employers' profits, there is no possibility of transferring capital and labor from other industries to the production of a larger supply of labor power. In this respect labor power differs fundamentally from other commodities. Therefore, in order to show that wages cannot exceed a certain maximum and thus annihilate profits, a principle different from the ordinary mechanism making market prices tend toward "natural prices" must be introduced.

The classical economists found such a principle in the theory of population. They taught that the pressure of the reproductive instincts of the population on the means of subsistence reacts on any increase of wages above the "natural price" of labor power to such an extent as to counteract effectively the increase of wages. Ricardo says explicitly[8]: "However much the market price of labor may deviate from its natural price, it has, like commodities, a tendency to conform to it. . . . When the market price of labor exceeds its natural price. . . by the encouragement which high wages give to the increase of population, the number of laborers is increased, wages again fall to their natural price." Thus the working class is assumed to be in a vicious circle which it cannot transcend. Marx rejected the Malthusian theory of population,[9] contending that even without such reproductive facilities wages could not rise so as to annihilate profit. For capitalism creates, according to Marx, its own surplus population (industrial reserve army) through technical progress, replacing workers by machines. The existence of the surplus population created by technical progress prevents wages from rising so as to swallow profits. Thus technical progress is necessary to maintain the capitalist system[10] and the dynamic nature of the capitalist system, which explains the constant increase of the organic composition of capital, is established.

That the labor theory of value is not necessary for this argument is easily seen, for its application to the labor market is a purely formal one, since the equilibrating mechanism which is at the basis of this theory does not work on the labor market. It is technical progress (or the "law of population" in the case of the classical economists) which prevents wages from swallowing profits.

We can now see in what sense Marxian economics deduces from theoretical considerations the "necessity" of economic evolution. Of course, the necessity of the fact that labor-saving technical innovations are always available at the right moment cannot be deduced by economic theory and in this sense the "necessity" of economic evolution cannot be proved. But Marxian economics does not attempt to prove this. All it establishes is that the capitalist system cannot maintain itself without such innovations. And this proof is given by an economic theory which shows that profit and interest on capital can exist only on account of the instability of a certain datum, i.e., the technique of production, and that it would necessarily disappear the moment further technical progress proved impossible. The economic theory presented here is, of course, but a mere sketch of how Marx explains the evolution of capitalism and a suggestion as to how his theory can be completed so as to bridge over the gaps he left. The modern development of economic theory, however, makes it possible to construct a far more satisfactory theory of economic evolution.

It is obvious that the necessity of economic evolution under capitalism is entirely due to the institutional datum distinguishing capitalism from an "einfache Warenproduktion" and that it would not exist in the latter form of exchange economy. Therefore, "bourgeois" economics, omitting to specify exactly the institutional datum of capitalism, is unable to establish a theory of economic evolution, for such a theory cannot be evolved from the very broad assumptions of exchange economy in general. From our account of the Marxian theory of economic evolution, it becomes evident that the necessity of economic evolution does not result from the exchange and pricing process as such, but from the special institutional setup under which this process goes on in a capitalist system. The specification of institutional data by "bourgeois" economic theory is too broad, since it gives no more than the institutional data common to any type of exchange economy. But since this very broad specification gives results which are too general to be applicable to special problems, it usually superimposes a very narrow specification of institutional data concerning the monetary and banking system (e.g., the existence or nonexistence of the gold standard, whether the banking system makes an inflationary credit expansion possible or not, etc.). But between the first specification of institutional data, which is very broad, and the second specification, which is very narrow, there is a gap: the institutional datum distinguishing capitalism from an "einfache Warenproduktion." And this is precisely the datum which is of fundamental significance for the theory of economic evolution.

9. Through the exact specification of the institutional framework of capitalist economy, Marxian economics is able to establish a theory of economic evolution in which certain data evolve "from within" the economic system. But not all changes of data are explained in this way by the Marxian theory. The evolution of certain data resulting from the very mechanism of the economic system influences certain extra-economic factors such as the policy of the state, political and social ideas, etc., which, reacting back on the economic system, change other of its data. This consideration supplies the explanation of the transition from *laissez-faire* to state interventionism and from free trade to protectionism and economic nationalism, the emergence of imperialist rivalries, etc. The causal chain through which the evolution of certain economic data influences certain extra-economic factors and the reaction of these factors back on the data of the economic system is, however, not within the subject matter of economics. It belongs to the theory of historical materialism, the object of which is to elucidate the causal chains connecting economic evolution with social evolution as a whole. Therefore, the full evolution of capitalism in all its concreteness cannot be explained by a theory of economic evolution alone. It can be explained only by

a joint use of both economic theory and the theory of historical materialism. The latter is an inseparable part of the Marxian analysis of capitalism.

10. Our results may be summarized as follows: (a) The superiority of Marxian economics in analyzing capitalism is not due to the economic concepts used by Marx (the labor theory of value), but to the exact specification of the institutional datum distinguishing capitalism from the concept of an exchange economy in general. (b) The specification of this institutional datum allows of the establishment of a theory of economic evolution from which a "necessary" trend of certain data in the capitalist system can be deduced. (c) Jointly with the theory of historical materialism, this theory of economic evolution accounts for the actual changes occurring in the capitalist system and forms a basis for anticipating the future.

NOTES

[1]   Kei Shibata, "Marx's Analysis of Capitalism and the General Equilibrium Theory of the Lausanne School," *The Kyoto University Economic Review*, July 1933.

[2]   As the word *capitalism* is used frequently very ambiguously, it should be mentioned here that it is used in this paper in its Marxian sense, i.e., capitalism means an exchange economy with private ownership of the means of production, to which the further sociological datum is added that the population is divided into two parts, one of which owns the means of production while the other part, owning no means of production, is compelled to work as wage earners with the means of production belonging to the other part. Only because of this sociological datum do profit and interest appear as personal income separate from wages.

[3]   This difference is connected, of course, with the respective social functions of "bourgeois" and Marxian economics. The first has to provide a scientific basis for rational measures to be taken in the current administration of the capitalist economy (monetary and credit policy, tariffs, localization, monopoly prices, etc.), the social function of the latter has been to provide a scientific basis for long-range anticipations guiding the rational activity of a revolutionary movement directed against the very institutional foundations of the capitalist system. But in providing a scientific basis for the current administration of the capitalist economy, "bourgeois" economics has developed a theory of equilibrium which can also serve as a basis for the current administration of a socialist economy. It is obvious that Marshallian economics offers more for the current administration of the economic system of Soviet Russia than Marxian economics does, though the latter is surely the more effective basis for anticipating the future of capitalism. In so far, modern economic theory, in spite of its undoubted "bourgeois" origin, has a universal significance.

[4]   The difference between a *theory* of economic evolution and a mere historical account of it is excellently explained in Chapter II of Schumpeter's *Theory of Economic Development* (English translation. Cambridge, Mass., 1934). Schumpeter is the only economist outside the Marxist camp who has formulated a theory of economic evolution. However, the close connection of his theory with Marxian ideas is obvious.

[5]   Cf. *Capital*, vol. III, 1, p. 154 *seq.* (4th ed. Hamburg, Meissner, 1919).

6   In the Marxian system the labor theory of values serves also to demonstrate the
    exploitation of the working class under capitalism, i.e., the difference between
    the personal distribution of income in a capitalist economy and in an "einfache
    Warenproduktion." It is this deduction from the labor theory of value which makes
    the orthodox Marxist stick to it. But the same fact of exploitation can also be deduced
    without the help of the labor theory of value. Also without it, it is obvious that
    the personal distribution of income in a capitalist economy is different from that
    in an "einfache Warenproduktion" (or in a socialist economy based on equalitarian
    principles, in which the distribution of income would be substantially the same as
    in an "einfache Warenproduktion"), for profit, interest, and rent can obviously be
    the personal income of a separate class of people only in a capitalist economy.
    If interest is explained by the marginal productivity of capital, it is only because
    the workers do not own the capital they work with that interest is the personal
    income of a separate class of people. If interest is regarded as due to a higher valuation
    of present than future goods, it is only because the workers do not possess the sub-
    sistence fund enabling them to wait until the commodities they produce are ready
    that the capitalist advancing it to the workers gets the interest as his personal income.
    Just as in Marx's case it is because the workers do not possess the means of produc-
    tion that the surplus value is pocketed by the capitalist. To make the Marxian
    concept of exploitation clearer by contrast it may be noticed that Pigou (*The
    Economics of Welfare*, 3rd ed., 1929, p. 556) and Mrs. Robinson (*The Economics
    of Imperfect Competition*, p. 281 *seq.*) define exploitation of the worker as occurring
    when he gets less than the value of the marginal physical product of his labor. This
    means that exploitation is defined by contrasting the distribution of income in
    monopolistic capitalism and in competitive capitalism. The middle-class character
    of this idea of social justice is obvious. For the socialist, the worker is exploited
    even if he gets the full value of the marginal product of his labor, for from the fact
    that interest or rent is determined by the marginal productivity of capital or land
    it does not follow, from the socialist point of view, that the capital- or land-owner
    ought to get it as his personal income. The Marxian definition of exploitation is
    derived from contrasting the personal distribution of income in a capitalist economy
    (irrespective of whether monopolistic or competitive) with that in an "einfache
    Warenproduktion" in which the worker owns his means of production.

7   This character of the business cycle as the specific form of economic development
    under capitalism has been stated very clearly by Schumpeter.

8   *Principles*, Chapter V, p. 71 (of Gonner's ed., 1929).

9   *Capital*, I, chap. XXIII.

10 Marx himself did not see clearly that in his theoretical system the virtual existence
    of a surplus population created by technical progress is necessary for the maintenance
    of the capitalist system. He applied the labor theory of value to the labor market
    without being aware that the equilibrating mechanism at the basis of this theory
    does not work in respect to labor power. But his theory of surplus population which
    he opposed to the Malthusian theory allows us to complete Marx's argument so as
    to bridge the gap in his system. It may be mentioned that a proletarian surplus
    population can also be created through driving out of small independent producers
    (for instance, artisans and peasants) from the market through the competition of
    capitalist industry. This source of surplus population was very important in the
    early history of capitalism. So long as such a source of surplus population exists,
    the capitalist system might exist, in theory, even without technical progress other
    than the dynamic process inherent in the destruction of precapitalist systems.

20

The Significance of Marxian Economics

for Present-day Economic Theory

Wassily Leontief

UNLIKE the modern theory of prices, the present-day business cycle analysis is clearly indebted to Marxian economics. Without raising the question of priority, it would hardly be an exaggeration to say that the three volumes of *Capital* helped more than any other single work to bring the whole problem into the forefront of economic discussion.

It is rather difficult to say how much Marx actually contributed to the solution of the problem. After years of intensive controversy, there is still no solution. I expect that this statement will not elicit any open contradiction, although I do not remember having read or heard a business cycle theorist admit that he was unable to solve this or that problem; the nearest he comes to such an admission is when he declares that the particular problem is insolvable, which implies that not only he but also no one else will be able to solve it.

The two principal variants of the Marxian explanation of business cycles, or rather "economic crises," are well known. One is the theory of underinvestment based on the famous law of the falling rate of profits; the other is the theory of underconsumption. Both might contain some grain of truth. Which business cycle theory does not?

Scanning the pages of Marxian writings, it is easy to find numerous hints and suggestions which can be interpreted as anticipating any and every of the modern theoretical constructions. . . .

Toward the end of his life Marx actually anticipated the statistical, mathematical approach to the business cycle analysis. An approach which, incidentally, only recently was declared by an authoritative Soviet Russian textbook on mathematical statistics to be nothing else

FROM *American Economic Review*, 28 (March 1938), pp. 3, 5–9.

but an insidious invention of the Intelligence Division of the French General Staff.

The significance of Marxian economics for the modern business cycle theory lies, however, not in such indecisive direct attempts toward the final solution of the problem but rather in the preparatory work contained mainly in the second and partly in the third volume of *Capital*. I have in mind the famous Marxian schemes of capital reproduction. . . .

However important the technical contributions to the progress of economic theory, in the present-day appraisal of Marxian achievements they are overshadowed by his brilliant analysis of the long-run tendencies of the capitalistic system. The record is indeed impressive: increasing concentration of wealth, rapid elimination of small- and medium-sized enterprise, progressive limitation of competition, incessant technological progress accompanied by the ever-growing importance of fixed capital, and, last but not least, undiminishing amplitude of recurrent business cycles—an unsurpassed series of prognostications fulfilled, against which modern economic theory with all its refinements has little to show indeed.

What significance has this list of successful anticipations for modern economic theory? Those who believe that Marx has said the last word on the subject invite us to quit. The attitude of other somewhat less optimistic—or should I say pessimistic—critics is well expressed by Professor Heimann: "Marx's work remains by far the most comprehensive and impressive model of what we have to do." The whole issue of the significance of Marxian economics for modern theory is thus transformed into a methodological question.

I enter this higher plane of discussion with feelings of considerable reluctance and serious apprehension. Not that Marx and his followers were sparse in their contributions to controversial methodological questions; on the contrary, it is rather the overabundance of contradictory and, at the same time, not very specific advice that makes it so difficult to find our way through the maze of divergent interpretations and explanations. It was in the same spirit of despair that Marx himself, in one of his lighter moods, exclaimed, "I am not a Marxist."

Roughly, all these methodological prescriptions can be divided into two groups. On the one side are the general considerations, which, although highly interesting from the point of view of philosophy and the sociology of knowledge, are entirely nonoperational from the point of view of practical scientific work. It might be true, for example, that a bourgeois economist, by the very virtue of his social and economic position, is essentially unable to recognize the driving forces and to discern the fundamental relations which govern the rise and fall of capitalist society. But what can he do about it? Give up teaching and investigating and join the proletarian ranks? This might render him a more useful member of society, but will anybody seriously maintain that such a change could improve his economic theory?

Into the same group of essentially nonoperational prescriptions I would also place all references to the efficiency of the dialectical method. It might be true that the concept of unity of opposites inspired Newton in his invention of infinitesimal calculus and helped Marx in his analysis of capital accumulation—at least it would be rather difficult to disprove such contentions—but it is very doubtful whether even a most careful reading of Engels' exposition of this principle could help Mr. Keynes, for example, with his solution of the unemployment problem.

On the other hand, Marxian methodology seems to contain some more concrete principles and concepts which deserve serious and detailed consideration. It is this aspect of the problem which was so ably brought to light by Dr. Lange in his brilliant article, "Marxian Economics and Modern Economic Theory."[1] Translating the Marxian slang into the vernacular of modern economics, he defines the issue at stake as the problem of data and variables in economic theory.

Admitting the superiority of the modern equilibrium theory, Dr. Lange tries to explain the marked success of Marxian prognostications by the particular attention which the author of *Capital* gave to the treatment of his data. It is an interesting thesis and it deserves a closer, critical scrutiny.

Data comprise all those elements of a theory which are used in the explanation of the variables but are not explained themselves within the system of the same theory, i.e., they are simply considered as being "given."

Among these there are first of all those general propositions which indicate whether we are going to talk about cabbages or kings and thus describe the general "universe of discourse," as the logician calls it. These data are predominately qualitative in character. The so-called institutional assumptions of economic theory belong to this first category.

Marx persistently derided contemporary classical economists for their failure to specify explicitly the institutional background of their theories. He was doubtless right and the same criticism applies equally well to some of the modern theorists. Fortunately enough in the process of their actual work, the bourgeois economists implicitly and maybe even unconsciously framed their theories in complete accordance with the fundamental, relevant facts of the institutional background of capitalist society. Thus the subjective methodological shortcomings did not impair the objective validity of their theoretical deductions.

The second type of data comprises statements of basic interrelations which constitute the immediate point of departure for derivation and formulation of specific propositions of our theoretical system. Technical production functions, shapes of the demand curves describing the consumers' choice, schedules of liquidity preferences—all these are examples of this second type of data. They are predominately quantitative in character.

It is this category of data which was meant by Clapham in his famous reference to the "empty boxes of economic theory." The boxes are not much fuller now than they were twenty years ago, but the Marxian theory hardly contains the stuff which could be used to fill the vacuum.

Dr. Lange seems to be of a different opinion. He points out in this connection the concept of technological progress as the mainstay of the Marxian theory of economic evolution of the capitalist society. This progress is being made responsible for the formation of a permanent army of unemployed which in its turn is supposed to prevent the otherwise unavoidable absorption of all profit by an ever-increasing national wage bill. Dr. Lange's statement of the problem suffers, however, from serious ambiguity.

As indicated before, substitution of machinery for labor can easily take place without new inventions, simply through movement from one point of a given production function to another. Reduced interest rate due to ever-increasing supply of accumulated capital might easily lead to such a result. The technical datum—the technical horizon of the entrepreneur—will remain in this case as stable as for example the cost curve of a monopolist might remain stable while he is changing his position by sliding along his curve in response to some demand variations.

A quite different phenomenon takes place when an entrepreneur reduces his demand for labor not in response to changing interest or wage rates but because a previously unknown new invention makes it profitable to use less labor and more machinery, even if interest as well as wage rates were to remain the same as before. Here we are facing a genuine change in primary technological data.

Both types of adjustment mark the evolution of capitalist economics. Dr. Lange does not seem to make a clear-cut distinction between the two, but the general drift of his argument points toward the second rather than first type of labor displacement. Neither is the position of Marx himself particularly clear. The great stress put upon the process of progressive accumulation, which the author of *Capital* considers to be a necessary condition of the very existence of the present economic system, indicates that it is rather the first type of substitution which he has in mind.

Anyway, the fact that the Marxian theory lends itself on this point to so many different interpretations, shows that insofar as the careful specifications and analysis of basic data are concerned, it is rather the Marxist who can learn from modern economists than vice versa.

Finally, we come to the third and last aspect of this methodological conflict. Modern economic theory limits itself to a much narrower set of problems than that which is included in the scope of Marxian economics. Many items treated as data in the first system are considered to be in the group of dependent variables in the second. Insofar as the general methodological principle is concerned, any effective extension of a theoretical system beyond its old frontier represents a real scientific progress.

To avoid a misunderstanding, it must be kept in mind that such extension cannot possibly result in a complete liquidation of independent data. It simply replaces one set of data by another. So, for example, if we were to include governmental action as a dependent variable within the system of economic theory, the amount of public expenditure of the height of import tariffs had to be considered as a function of some other economic variables in the same way as the output of a firm in competition is considered to be a function of the prevailing market price. It is perfectly obvious, however, that the first type of relationship is much less definite in its character than the second. This, I think, is the reason why the modern economist is reluctant to discuss both types of interrelations on the same plane. And he is right because neither part can profit from such artificial connection, which does not mean that the result of the two types of investigation could not and should not be fruitfully combined in attempts toward some kind of a wider synthesis. Occasional alliances and frequent cooperation are, however, something quite different from radical unification accompanied by complete obliteration of existing border lines.

Neither his analytical accomplishments nor the purported methodological superiority can explain the Marxian record of correct prognostications. His strength lies in realistic, empirical knowledge of the capitalist system.

Repeated experiments have shown that in their attempts to prognosticate individual behavior, professional psychologists systematically fall behind experienced laymen with a knack for "character reading." Marx was the great character reader of the capitalist system. Like many individuals of this type, Marx had also his rational theories, but these theories in general do not hold water. Their inherent weakness shows up as soon as other economists not endowed with the exceptionally realistic sense of the master try to proceed on the basis of his blueprints.

The significance of Marx for modern economic theory is that of an inexhaustible source of direct observation. Much of the present-day theorizing is purely derivative, secondhand theorizing. We often theorize not about business enterprises, wages, or business cycles but about other people's theories of profits, other people's theories of wages, and other people's theories of business cycles. If, before attempting any explanation, one wants to learn what profits and wages and capitalist enterprises actually are, he can obtain in the three volumes of *Capital* more realistic and relevant firsthand information than he could possibly hope to find in ten successive issues of the *United States Census*, a dozen textbooks on contemporary economic institutions, and even, may I dare to say, the collected essays of Thorstein Veblen.

NOTE

1 *Review of Economic Studies*, June 1935. (See this volume, pp. 215ff.).

21

Marxian Economics as Economics

Paul A. Samuelson

THE "contradictions of capitalism," which Karl Marx saw everywhere, are as nothing compared to the contradictions of Marx himself. Marx was a gentle father and husband; he was also a prickly, brusque, egotistical boor. . . . Although Marx was a learned man, he shows all the signs of a self-taught amateur: overelaboration of trivial points, errors in logic and inference, and a megalomaniac's belief in the superiority of his own innovations. He introduced into scholarly literature manners not seen since the polemics of the renaissance. . . .

Evaluations of Marx show the same pattern of contradictions. Professor Bronfenbrenner . . . deems Karl Marx "the greatest social scientist of all times." Keynes consistently refers to the "turbid rubbish of the Red bookstores" and dismisses the book we commemorate today as a "bible, above and beyond criticism, an obsolete textbook which I know to be not only scientifically erroneous but without interest or application for the modern world." This attitude Joan Robinson regards as rather a pity, saying: "Keynes could never make head or tail of Marx. . . . But starting from Marx would have saved him a lot of trouble [as it did Kalecki]." In my Presidential Address, I find Marx referred to as "from the viewpoint of pure economic theory, . . . a minor post-Ricardian . . . a not-uninteresting precursor of Leontief's input-output." . . .

FROM *American Economic Review*, 62 (May 1967), pp. 616, 619–623.

The Labor Theory of Value

As every encyclopedia reader knows, Marx believed in the labor theory of value. . . . Let me therefore be dogmatically terse.

Proposition 1. Adam Smith held a labor theory of value for about as long as it takes a grown man to turn two pages of his book. David Ricardo never shook himself free of this incubus, but no reader of Sraffa's edition can fail to be persuaded that only some of the simplified numerical examples in the Ricardian system need have any reliance on such a theory.

Proposition 2. From the standpoint of science, the labor theory of value breaks down even before complications of capital enter into the model. With land scarce and different goods varying in their labor-land intensity, already goods will exchange at relative prices that are not proportional to socially necessary labor content. Ricardo nodded and thought that by going out to the external margin of no-rent land, he could "get rid of the complication" of land costing. Why should we, or the Soviet planners, nod with him? (This point is obvious and appears in the first pages of the new edition of my *Economics;* yet when I searched the literature of the labor theory of value for it years ago, I could turn up only one reference to Lionel Robbins.)

Proposition 3. If Marx had intended to use the labor theory of value to lay bare the laws of motion of capitalism and if he had been barking up the right tree, then the inadequacies of the labor theory of value as exposited in Volume I of *Capital* would not really have mattered.

Let me explain what I mean. Most of Volume I would stand up if Marx stipulated, purely for expository simplicity, that the organic composition of capital (or as we would say, labor's fractional share of value added) were the same in all industries. By fiat the contradiction between equal rates of surplus value and equal rates of profit would disappear. (And make no mistake about it, Böhm-Bawerk is perfectly right in insisting that Volume III of *Capital* never does make good the promise to reconcile the fabricated contradictions. When Paul Sweezy says that Rudolf Hilferding, in refuting Böhm's specific critiques of Marx, "gives a good account of himself and shows that even at the age of twenty-five he could stand up and trade punches with so experienced and inveterate a polemicist as Böhm-Bawerk," I have to pinch myself to remember that relative prices of goods do really change as demand changes even when their socially necessary labor contents do not change —which is all the dispute is really about.)

In 1865, when Marx was at the height of his powers and had to boil down the message of his masterwork for a workers' audience, he introduced into the pamphlet, *Value, Price, and Profit*, the simplifying notion that prices are proportionate to labor values—saying "apart from the effect of monopolies and some other modifications I now pass over." I suggest that much ink and blood would have been spared if he had done likewise in *Capital*. When a modern theorist assumes equal factor intensities in a two-sector Ramsey-Solow model, he does not defend the oversimplification: he is content to know that anything interesting turned up in it is likely to be of relevance for a more complicated model.

In summary, if labor-theory-of-value reasoning, as applied to an impeccable model of equal factor intensities, turned up new light on exploitation in an existing system or if it turned up new light on the laws of development of capitalism, it would be an invaluable tool even though not defensible as a general theory of markets.

If, and if. Let us see whether Marx was at all barking up the right tree.

Laws of Motion of Capitalism?

The usual claim for superiority of Marx's system is not that he beats the vulgar economists at their own game of describing equilibrium pricing, but that their game is not worth the playing: whereas Wicksell, Walras, and Chamberlin give a good enough description of the economic system as it is, we must turn to the Marxian system for insight into the laws of development of the capitalistic system. Its inferior statics can be forgiven, considering its much superior dynamics. Such a claim, if it can be sustained, is indeed a weighty one.

Leontief, in his 1937 address, makes heavy weather of finding much to praise in Marx besides his anticipations of input-output. . . .

You will notice that Leontief credits Marx with great prophetic powers but is noncommittal as to whether Marx's economic theories helped him to arrive at these (possibly merely lucky) guesses. Lange attempts to make stronger claims for Marxian theories. He says they deduce that "the fundamental change occurs in production and that the 'necessity' of such a change can be deduced only under the institutional setup specific to *capitalism*. Thus a 'law of development' of the capitalist system is established . . . not a mechanical extrapolation of a purely empirical trend. . . ."

So much for the claims. But is it so? Let us be honest children and ask whether the Emperor is really wearing clothes, and whether those clothes really do follow some grand theoretical pattern.

Specifically, was Marx right as a prophet of the future of Victorian capitalism? The immiserization of the working class, which he thought to reduce from the labor theory of value and his innovational concept of surplus value, simply never took place. As a prophet Marx was colossally unlucky and his system colossally useless when it comes to this key matter. This is not to deny Joan Robinson's view that such a prophecy had a certain propagandistic value. She says, "This error, like Jesus' belief that the world was shortly coming to an end, is so central to the whole doctrine that it is hard to see how it could have been put afloat without it. . . . 'You have nothing to lose but the prospect of a suburban home and a motor car' would not have been much of a slogan [for *The Communist Manifesto*]." With friends like this, who has need for an enemy?

Let's now move on to the growing monopolization under capitalism. For thirty years Marx seemed to have been right in this prophecy, even though for the next seventy years he does not seem to be borne out by the most careful of researches on industrial concentration. But suppose he (and numerous non-Marxian socialists) had been right in this view. Would such an extrapolation be deducible in any way from the surplus value ratios, $S/(V+C)$, of any of the volumes of *Capital*? No one has yet shown how, and I have to agree with the recent book of Paul Sweezy and Paul Barran which seeks to identify as an important explanation of the stagnation of Marxian social science the fact that "the Marxian analysis of capitalism still rests in the final analysis on the assumption of a competitive economy" *(Monopoly Capital*, 1966, p. 4).

Since time is short let us rush on to consider whether it is an inevitable law of capitalist development that the business cycle should be getting worse and worse. Shibata and Lange, writing in the 1930s, might be forgiven for thinking so, just as writers in 1929 can have been expected to celebrate the demise of economic fluctuations. Who can blame someone for not having predicted in 1867 the successful development of the Mixed Economy, in view of the fact that so astute a philosopher as Joseph Schumpeter managed to miss foreseeing it as late as 1947? I throw no stone at Marx, because I have never believed in the big-picture theories of anyone—Toynbee, Spengler, Schumpeter, Veblen, Marx, or even Rostow and Galbraith. But those who have been bewitched by a belief in the timetable of history, as deduced by theoretical laws of motion of capitalism, should taste the bitter bread of disillusionment.

Had Lange been writing in 1937, after Keynes, he might have added to the 1935 sentence "Marxian economics would be a poor basis for running a central bank or anticipating the effects of a change in the rate of discount" the sentence, "and it would be a poor basis for understanding the role of fiscal policy in maintaining high employment."

What admissions! This is equivalent to saying, "Marxian economics is powerless to explain the 1937–67 developments of European and American economies."

The cash value of a doctrine is in its vulgarization. To understand the pragmatic content of Marshall, you must read Fairchild, Furniss, and Buck. To prove the Marxian pudding, only read the Soviet textbooks dealing with American and Western economic systems. Esthetics aside, their predictive powers have been unbelievably erratic and perhaps only to be understood in terms of the dictum: Marxism has been the opiate of the Marxians.

PART FOUR

Class Conflict, Revolution, and Political Power

Class and Class Conflict

ALTHOUGH the concept of class is crucial in Marxist theory, no single comprehensive exposition of the subject exists in Marx's writings. To everyone's disappointment a chapter in the manuscript of *Capital* which promised to deal with the subject ended after one paragraph.

In *The Eighteenth Brumaire of Louis Bonaparte*, Marx, writing of French peasants, tried to define a class "insofar as millions of families live under economic conditions of existence that divide their mode of life, their interests, and their culture from those of other classes, and put them in hostile contrast to the latter." But the references of Marx and Engels to class, especially in their historical studies, were often more elaborate than this, as S. Ossowski shows in the closely reasoned chapter of his book included here.

The account of class relationships in historical works such as *The Class Struggles in France* and *The Eighteenth Brumaire* involves analysis of day-to-day activities and the operation of political institutions rather than deduction from the movement of history on dialectical lines about the fate of the different classes. For the Marxists there is always some irreconcilability between the objective laws of history and the subjective actions of individuals which may run counter to those laws. The empirical facts of French politics were not easily incorporated into the general theory of class.

Nor was understanding of specific historical events a simple process, as was shown by Marx's differing and contradictory interpretations of Louis Bonaparte and his relations to the classes in France. Nevertheless, the Marxist aim, as Engels wrote in *Germany: Revolution and Counter-Revolution*, was to find "rational causes based on undeniable facts to explain the chief events, the principal vicissitudes of the movement."

Inherent in the Marxist analysis of class are the theses that the class structure results from the relations of production, that the most significant relationships are between those who own and those who do not own the means of production, that there is inevitable antagonism between the classes, and that class conflict has been the way in which social change has occurred. In the excerpts from his book presented here, Ralf Dahrendorf modifies the Marxist analysis and suggests that social conflict may take forms other than class conflict, and that social changes may occur for a variety of reasons.

In a letter to Weydemeyer on March 5, 1852, Marx denied that he had originated the idea of class conflict, and pointed out that "long before me the bourgeois historians had described the historical development of this struggle of the classes." But the concept has become associated with Marx, if not attributable to him, and so have the criticisms of this kind of analysis. Critics have often pointed out that contrary to the analysis of Marx there is evidence of class collaboration, the nonpolarization of classes as the economy develops, the weakening rather than heightening of antagonism between classes in highly developed industrial states, the reluctance of the working class to become politically conscious in any revolutionary way or to be aware of its supposed destiny, the basing of revolutionary movements on racial and national rather than class factors, and the prominent role of the despised peasantry. As the oracle of the New Left, Herbert Marcuse pessimistically wrote in his book *Reason and Revolution*, "those social groups which dialectical theory identified as the forces of negation are either defeated or reconciled with the established system."

22

The Concept of Social Class

S. Ossowski

THE concept of social class is something more than one of the fundamental concepts of Marxian doctrine. It has in a certain sense become the symbol of his whole doctrine and of the political program that is derived from it. This concept is expressed in the terms "class standpoint" and "class point of view," which in Marxist circles used until recently to be synonymous with "Marxist standpoint" or "Marxist point of view." In this sense "class standpoint" simply meant the opposite of "bourgeois standpoint."

According to Engels,[1] Marx effected a revolutionary change in the whole conception of world history. For Marx, so Engels maintained, had proved that "the whole of previous history is a history of class struggles, that in all the simple and complicated political struggles the only thing at issue has been the social and political rule of social classes."

The concept of social class is also linked with what Engels in the same article calls the second great discovery of Marx, to which he attaches so much importance in the history of science—the clarification of the relationship that prevails between capital and labor. Finally, it may be said that the concept of social class is bound up with the entire Marxian conception of culture as the superstructure of class interests.

The role of the class concept in Marxian doctrine is so immense that is is astonishing not to find a definition of this concept, which they use so constantly, anywhere in the works of either Marx or Engels. One might regard it as an undefined concept of which the meaning is explained contextually, But in fact one has only to compare the various

FROM *Class Structure in the Social Consciousness*, Macmillan, New York, and Routledge, London (1963), pp. 71–78, 80, 84–88. © Stanislaw Ossowski, 1963.

passages in which the concept of social class is used by either writer
to realize that the term *class* has for them a variable denotation: that is,
that it refers to groups differentiated in various ways within a more
inclusive category, such as the category of social groups with common
economic interests, or the category of groups whose members share
economic conditions that are identical in a certain respect. The sharing
of permanent economic interests is a particularly important characteristic
of social classes in Marxian doctrine, and for this reason it has been easy
to overlook the fact that although it is, in the Marxian view, *a necessary
condition* it does not constitute a *sufficient condition* for a valid definition
of social class.

Marx left the problem of producing a definition of the concept
of social class until much later. The manuscript of the third volume
of his *magnum opus*, *Capital*, breaks off dramatically at the moment when
Marx was about to answer the question: "What constitutes a class?"
We do not know what answer he would have given if death had not
interrupted his work. Nor do we know whether he would have attempted to explain the discrepancies in his earlier statements. . . .

In using the concept of class based on economic criteria, Marx
sometimes restricts the scope of this concept by introducing psychological
criteria. An aggregate of people which satisfies the economic criteria
of a social class becomes a class in the full meaning of this term only when
its members are linked by the tie of class consciousness, by the consciousness of common interests, and by the psychological bond that arises out of
common class antagonisms.[2] Marx is aware of the ambiguity and
makes a terminological distinction between *Klasse an sich* and *Klasse
für sich*, but he does not in general make much further use of these more
narrowly defined concepts.

Marx sometimes uses a different term to denote a class which is
not a class in the fullest sense because it lacks psychological bonds. For
instance, he sometimes uses the term *stratum;* on other occasions he
avoids using a more general term and confines himself to the name of
a specified group such as the "small peasantry." At times he may even
call certain classes which are conscious of their class interests "fractions"
of a more inclusive class. In the case of capitalists and landowners, for
instance, Marx sometimes sees them as two separate classes, at others as
two fractions of a single class, the bourgeoisie.

All these discrepant uses of the term *class* were probably the less
important for Marx because, according to his theory, further social
development would render them obsolete. This was to result from the
growth of the social consciousness and from the predicted disappearance
of the difference between the *Klasse an sich* and the *Klasse für sich* as well

as from the progressive process of class polarization in the social structure.

The matter can, however, be put in a different way. We may take it that Marx, instead of providing a definition of social class which would make it possible to fix the scope of this concept, is giving the model of a social class, the ideal type which is to be fully realized in the future, in the last stage of the development of the capitalist system. In the period in which Marx wrote, the industrial proletariat of Western Europe was approximating to the ideal type of a social class. Other social groups separated on the basis of economic criteria could be called classes only to a greater or lesser extent, and could approximate to the ideal type only in some respects. Hence, endeavors to apprehend them by means of conceptual categories with sharply drawn boundaries of application must lead to confusion.

However that may be, one should, when considering the Marxian conception of class structure, remember that the component elements of this structure are confined to those groups which Marx calls "classes" when contrasting them with "strata," in which "the identity of their interests (those of the members of a 'stratum') begets no unity, no national union and no political organization." . . .

The Basic Dichotomy

Marx and Engels are above all the inheritors of the dichotomic perceptions found in folklore and of the militant ideology of popular revolutions. Reading their works, one never loses sight of the age-old conflict between the oppressing classes and the oppressed classes. . . , the manifold polar division of the various oppressor and oppressed classes in earlier societies gives way to a single, all-inclusive dichotomy. According to the forecast of *The Communist Manifesto*, the capitalist society was to achieve this dichotomy in full in the penultimate act of the drama, in the period that precedes the catastrophe. In approximating to such a dichotomy, the social structure of the capitalist world would then be nearing its end. . . .

Marx discerned "the inevitable destruction of the middle bourgeois classes and of the so-called peasant estate."[3] In Engels' version, the era marked the accomplishment of "the division of society into a small, excessively rich class and a large, propertyless class of wage workers."[4] The workers' rising in Paris on June 22, 1848, was regarded by Marx as "the first great battle . . . between the two classes that split modern society . . . the war of labor and capital."[5]

Two Conceptions of the Intermediate Classes

Marx the revolutionary and Marx the dramatist of history developed a dichotomic conception of a class society. Marx the sociologist was compelled in his analysis of contemporary societies to infringe the sharpness of the dichotomic division by introducing intermediate classes. He could not overlook the "mass of the nation . . . standing between the proletariat and the bourgeoisie." These intermediate classes were a very important element in the pictures of his own era given us by Marx in his historical studies. Sometimes he speaks of "intermediate strata" when giving a narrower definition of a social class. Elsewhere the term *middle estate* appears, although in this context it does not denote an institutionalized group such as the French *tiers état*.

There is such a variety of social statuses and economic positions in these intermediate classes that it is difficult to confine them within a uniform scheme. The term *intermediate classes* suggests a scheme of gradation. And in fact one sometimes finds in Marx's writings the conception of the intermediate classes as groupings of individuals occupying an intermediate position in the economic gradation in respect of their relation to the means of production, or to the variety of their social roles and sources of income. For instance, in the *Address of the Central Community to the Communist League*, written by Marx and Engels in 1850, the petit bourgeoisie includes the small capitalists, whose interests conflict with those of the industrialists. And again, in his *The Civil War in France*, Marx refers to the "liberal German middle class, with its professors, its capitalists, its aldermen and its penmen." Here he conceives of the middle class in the sense in which the term is used in England or the United States. A capitalist—that is to say, an owner of the means of production—may belong to one class or another depending on the amount of capital he owns. One should, however, bear in mind that Marx is not thinking here of "high society" nor of rows and columns in statistical tables. For him the amount of capital owned by an individual is associated with separate class interests.

It was not, however, this conception of an intermediate class that was incorporated in the set of basic concepts in the Marxian analysis of the capitalist society. In constructing his theoretical system, Marx set up the foundation for another conception of the class which occupies the intermediate position between the class of capitalists and the proletariat. This conception was not in fact formulated in its final form by either Marx or his pupils. It is nevertheless related to the scheme of class structure of the capitalist society that is characteristic for Marx and Marxism, a scheme in which three social classes correspond to three kinds of relations to the means of production.

In this scheme the intermediate class, which Marx usually calls the "petit bourgeoisie" regardless of whether reference is being made to urban or rural dwellers, is determined by the simultaneous application of two criteria. Each of these criteria, taken separately, forms the basis for a dichotomic division of social classes, although in a different way. One criterion is the ownership of the means of production. This is a criterion which, in a dichotomic scheme, divides society into propertied and propertyless classes. The second criterion is work, which, however, in contradistinction to Saint-Simon's conception, does not include the higher managerial functions in capitalist enterprises. We have also come across this second criterion in the dichotomic scheme. It divides society into working classes and idle classes. In this conception, the intermediate class consists of those who belong to both the overlapping categories; those who possess their own means of production and themselves make use of them.

Marxism applies still another version of this trichotomous division, a version which is usually not differentiated from the former one. In it the first criterion of division (the ownership of the means of production) remains the same. On the other hand, the second criterion is not work but the fact of not employing hired labor. In this version, the intermediate class is more narrowly defined than in the earlier one. It does not include all those working people who possess their own means of production but only those who work on their own account without employing hired labor. According to this version, a wealthy farmer who employs two or three regular hired laborers, or who has small holders working for him in exchange for an advance in cash or kind, is included in the class of rural capitalists. In the first version the petit bourgeoisie includes two strata; those who work in their own workshops and employ hired labor, and those who do not employ such labor. Sociologically speaking, the first version is more suited to describe some conditions, the second more suited to others; thus it depends on various circumstances which need not be discussed here. The combination of the two versions gives two functionally differentiated intermediate classes.

From the viewpoint of the Marxian assumptions concerned with the tendencies of development in capitalism, the position of the petit bourgeoisie, which is intermediate between the two basic classes, is sometimes interpreted in yet another way. The petit bourgeoisie is said to belong to the propertied class so far as present conditions are concerned, to the proletariat with regard to its future prospects. Thus not only the craftsman but also the small holder are potential proletarians.[6]

There is also an economic gradation that corresponds to this trichotomous scheme. The capitalist class is that class which owns large-scale means of production or at least sufficient to make possible the employment of hired labor; the petit bourgeoisie consists of those who dispose of the means of production on a modest scale; while the proletariat is in principle the class that owns no means of production whatsoever. In this functional scheme, however, it is not the degree of wealth that determines the boundaries between classes but the social roles, namely their relation to the means of production, work and their relation to the hiring of labor. . . . With Marx the revolutionary, the dichotomic conception of social structure is dominant. With Marx the theorist, we sometimes have to deal not only with the trichotomous scheme with a middle class between the two opposing classes, but also with a scheme which is inherited from bourgeois economics. This is the trichotomous functional scheme of Adam Smith. This scheme appears rarely in the works of Marx and Engels, but its importance is increased by the fact that it is the starting point of the last chapter of the third volume of *Capital*, the chapter which is devoted exclusively to an analysis of classes in modern society. This uncompleted chapter, entitled "Classes," opens with the words:

The owners merely of labor power, owners of capital, and landowners, whose respective sources of income are wages, profit, and ground rent, in other words, wage laborers, capitalists, and landowners, constitute then three big classes of modern society based upon the capitalist mode of production.

Two Categories of the Class Struggle

It must not be forgotten that the use of the same terms in describing reality in its different aspects and in formulating generalizations made from different viewpoints can lead to misunderstandings. It is easy to overlook the fact that the concept of the class struggle, the basic concept for Marxian doctrine, comprises two different categories of historical process. The first includes liberation struggles within the framework of the perennial conflict between the oppressing classes and the oppressed classes; the second includes struggles between classes competing for power in a society with a multidivisional structure. It is not often perceived that the class struggles referred to in the first chapter of *The Communist Manifesto* are social conflicts of a kind different from those mentioned by Engels in his introduction to a new posthumous edition of Màrx's *Class Struggles in France*.

In *The Communist Manifesto* we read:

The history of all hitherto-existing society is the history of class struggles. Freeman and slave, patrician and plebeian, lord and serf, guildmaster and journeyman, in a word, oppressor and oppressed, stood in constant opposition to one another, carried on an uninterrupted, now hidden, now open fight.

In Engels' introduction, on the other hand, we find quite another picture of the class struggle:

All revolutions up to the present day have resulted in the displacement of the definite class rule by another; but all ruling classes up to now have been only small minorities in relation to the ruled mass of the people . . . the common form of all these revolutions was that they were minority revolutions. Even when the majority took part, it did so—whether willingly or ont—only in the service of a minority.[7]

I have cited these two well-known passages to show that both those who, while regarding the class struggle as the driving force of history, treat the history of class struggles at times as if it consisted exclusively of the conflict between an oppressed majority and a minority of exploiters, and at other times as if it consisted exclusively of conflicts between minority classes competing for power could appeal to the example of the classics of Marxism.

It is as well to realize this point, for this duality is linked with tendencies to still greater simplification in presenting historical events. An instance of this may be found in the tendency to regard the so-called "premature liberation movements," such as the peasants' or workers' insurrections in the periods preceding the full triumph of the bourgeoisie, as if they had no other significance in history than that conferred on them by their participation in the struggles between classes occupying superior positions in the social structure and competing for power. One of the leading Marxists of contemporary France, Garaudy, ascribes a reactionary role to the French Communists of the eighteenth century, on the grounds that their activities weakened the offensive strength of the bourgeoisie in its struggle with the feudal lords. Writing forty years earlier, Jaurès would appear to have given a similar evaluation of the conspiracy of Babeuf.

The Sharpness of Class Divisions and the Class Interpretation of Cultural Phenomena

It would seem that in the very assumption that class struggles are the driving force of history, two different views concerning causal relationships are intertwined.

The first of these views holds that the driving force of history consists of struggles between an oppressed class and an oppressor class. The second maintains that it comes from struggles between classes with different interests. Among Marx's predecessors, the first view recalls Babeuf, the second Madison or Ricardo. In the first case, the basic phenomenon adduced in causal explanations is the appropriation of the "surplus value" and the oppression of man by man. In the second it is the antagonisms of class interests, antagonisms which are not confined to situations in which the appropriation of the "surplus value" is involved.

It is true that in his conception of history Marx undoubtedly assumes that the necessary condition for the existence of all class division is the existence of an exploited class and that the dichotomic division of society into exploited and exploiters is the source of all class divisions. And this additional assumption, which emerges even more clearly in Engels' writings, gives precedence to the first of the two views mentioned above. On the other hand, in the concrete historical studies of both Marx and Engels, the second view takes precedence and class struggles are interpreted more broadly.

This elasticity in the interpretation of basic concepts is not unconnected with the practical significance of Marxian doctrine as a weapon of revolution. It is no accident that one can single out several different ways of conceiving social structure in the writings of Marx and Engels. Nor is it accidental that such varied trends of thought have intermingled in the Marxian theory of social class, including trends flowing from the dichotomic view of society, the heritage of folklore and the revolutionary movements on the one side, and on the other side from the scheme of Adam Smith. For the concept of social class to perform the role which it did in the history of Marxism and during the social changes of the last century, it had to satisfy seemingly contradictory requirements. A synthesis of the different aspects of the class structure was necessary for this doctrine, which sees in the class struggle the driving force of history and the justification for its political program, which seeks the explanation of all historical processes in class antagonisms, and gives a class interpretation to all cultural phenomena.

Because of its militant program, this doctrine must emphasize in the strongest possible way the sharpness of class divisions and the asymmetry of relations in the social structure. The scheme of gradation and the dichotomic scheme are constructed in terms of asymmetrical relations. The sharpest class division is achieved by this dichotomic conception, in which the division of two classes is the only division. In the scheme of gradation this sharpness is weakened by the introduction of intermediate classes; and the clarity of class contours is still further blurred as the number of classes in the social structure increases. This is particularly so when the number of social classes is not clearly fixed, and when it is possible to distinguish five or at other times six or eight classes.

The dichotomic view is the most convenient for the tasks which the Marxian doctrine was to carry out, because of the sharpness of the asymmetrical divisions. On the other hand, a large number of social classes is an assumption which is needed for the "class interpretation" of the complicated processes of history and the whole variety of cultural phenomena. This interpretation, which ascribes a many-sided significance to class divisions and draws all spheres of spiritual life into the orbit of the class struggle, cannot be confined within a dichotomic structure. If all political or religious struggles are to be interpreted as class struggles, if we are to correlate the various literary and artistic trends with underlying class relations, if we are to look for a reflection of class interests and class prejudices in moral norms, then we must make use of a greater number of classes than the two basic ones in *The Communist Manifesto*.

NOTES

1   ME, vol. II, p. 149; the quotation comes from F. Engels, *Karl Marx*.
2   Cf. the following passages: "The separate individuals form a class insofar as they have to carry on a common battle against another class." (K. Marx and F. Engels, *The German Ideology*, The Marxist-Leninist Library, volume XVII, London, 1940, pp. 48–49.) "The organization of the proletarians into a class, and consequently into a political party." ("Manifesto of the Communist Party," *ME*, vol. I, p. 41.)
3   ME, vol. I, p. 75; quotation from K. Marx, *Wage, Labor, and Capital*.
4   ME, vol. I, p. 73; quotation from F. Engels' Introduction to Marx's *Wage, Labor, and Capital*.
5   ME, vol. I, pp. 147–148; quotations from K. Marx, *The Class Struggles in France, 1848–1850*.
6   Cf. Engels: *The Peasant Question in France and Germany, ME*, vol. I, pp. 384, 395.
7   *ME*, Vol. I, pp. 113–14; the quotation comes from F. Engels' Introduction to Karl Marx's *The Class Struggles in France, 1848–1850*.

23

A Sociological Critique of Marx

Ralf Dahrendorf

ACCORDING to Marx, capitalist society is a class society. There is in this society a category of persons who possess effective private property, and another category of those who have no such property. The former is called capital or bourgeoisie, the latter wage labor or proletariat. The typical private property of capitalist society consists of the means of industrial production, i.e., factories, machines, and the like, or capital. The owners or capitalists directly control their means of production; the nonowners or wage laborers are dependent, by the labor contract, on the means of production and their owners. Property and power and the exclusion from both go together; they "correlate." There is also a correlation between these factors on the one hand, and socioeconomic position on the other hand: the capitalists are wealthy, secure, and have high status; the wage laborers are lacking a subsistence minimum. This difference in position makes for conflicting interests and conflicting groupings—classes—which fight each other at first on the local level of the individual enterprise, eventually on the political level.

There are, of course, persons in capitalist society—such as landlords, independent craftsmen and small businessmen, peasants, and intellectuals—who stand outside this tension and whose interests are not directly affected by it. These groups, however, not only decrease in numerical importance but increasingly lose their influence on the conflicts determining the structure of society. The capitalist bourgeoisie and its counterpart, the industrial proletariat, move more and more

FROM *Class and Class Conflict in Industrial Society*, Routledge, London, and Stanford University Press, Stanford (1959), pp. 34–35, 124–129. © 1959 by the Board of Trustees of the Leland Stanford Junior University.

into the center of the social process. Their conflicts dominate the scene of capitalist class society and draw all other groups into their orbit or condemn them to complete insignificance. Society is dominated by the antagonism between the interests of those who defend their possession of effective private property and those who elevate their nonpossession into a demand for a complete change of the property relations.

This sketch of Marx's view of capitalist society is incomplete in one important point. It describes a structure, and not its process of development, whereas it is on the latter count that Marx made his sociologically important contribution to social analysis. Marx tried, at times retrospectively, more often predictively, to determine the tendencies of change that can be derived from this structure. With respect to the development of class structure he emphasized in particular the following four processes:

1. Inherent in capitalist society, there is a tendency for the classes to polarize increasingly. "The whole society breaks up more and more into two great hostile camps, two great, directly antagonistic classes: bourgeoisie and proletariat." Here, the model of two dominant classes is no longer merely a heuristic postulate, but describes a factual condition. "The earlier petty bourgeoisie, the small industrialists, the merchants and rentiers, the craftsmen and peasants, all these classes sink down into the proletariat." It is really misleading to speak of two "great" classes, since social development, according to Marx, produces a polarized class society with a relatively small ruling class of capitalists and an extraordinarily large oppressed class of wage laborers.

2. As the classes polarize, their class situations become increasingly extreme. On the one hand, the wealth of the bourgeoisie is swelled by larger profits based on increasing productivity as well as by the progressive concentration of capital in the hands of a few individuals. "One capitalist kills many others." On the other hand, "with the continuously decreasing number of capital magnates who usurp and monopolize all advantages of this process of change . . . [comes an increase in] the mass of poverty, of pressure, of slavery, of perversion, of exploitation, but also of revolt on the part of a working class permanently increasing in size which is skilled, united, and organized by the mechanism of the capitalist mode of production itself."[1] Here, the so-called theory of pauperization has its place, according to which the poverty of the proletariat grows with the expansion of production by virtue of a law postulated as inherent in a capitalist economy.

3. At the same time, the two classes become more and more homogeneous internally. In the beginning of this process, the classes are

clearly delimited from the outside, but rather heterogeneous within. Marx says of the bourgeoisie that its members "have identical interests insofar as they form a class in opposition to another class," but "contradictory and conflicting interests as soon as they are confronted with themselves."[2] Analogously, the proletariat is not, in the beginning, a "class for itself." However, a number of processes mold the different constituents of the classes into uniform groups without significant internal differences or conflicts. "More and more the collisions between individual workers and bourgeois assume the character of collisions of two classes." This is partly due to pressure from without, such as the growing intensity of the class struggle. Partly it is the effect of social and even technical factors. In the case of the proletariat Marx refers on the one hand to the growing extent of class organization as a unifying factor, on the other hand to the "tendency of equalizing and leveling in work processes" within industry itself,[3] i.e., the reduction of all workers to unskilled laborers by the technical development of production. Similarly, a combination of economic, and in the narrow sense social, factors unites the bourgeoisie as a class.

4. Once history has carried these tendencies of development to their extremes, the point is reached at which the fabric of the existing social structure breaks and a revolution terminates capitalist society. The hitherto oppressed proletariat assumes power; effective private property is socialized; classes cease to exist; the state is withering away. The proletarian revolution inaugurates the communist, classless society.

Marx's image of capitalist society is the image of a society undergoing a process of radical change. This change culminates in a revolutionary act, into which all earlier developments converge and from which all later developments depart. The executors of this process are structurally generated, organized human interest groups—the classes. One of these—the bourgeoisie—defends with sinking chances of success the existing distribution of property, and with it the whole social status quo. The other one—the proletariat—attacks this status quo with growing success until the day on which its interests become reality, the values of a new society. The capitalist form of economic and social structure is doomed, and the classes are its gravediggers. . . .

Marx's theory of class provides the background of subsequent argument, his analysis of capitalist class society that of later analyses. If we succeed in refuting the sociological theories of Marx or the hypotheses derived from them, we have good reason to rejoice. For science grows by the refutation of accepted propositions and theories, and not by their stubborn retention.

Social Change and Class Conflict (I): Marx Sustained

Many aspects of Marx's theory of class have to be rejected in the light of sociological knowledge. These do not include, however, the heuristic purpose of Marx's sociological work and its immediate consequences. It is without doubt important to develop categories to describe social changes. Concepts like "role differentiation," "transference of functions," "leveling of statuses," and the like serve this purpose. But it is clearly more important to find ways and means to explain change. It is, of course, most unlikely that any one hypotheses will be capable of accounting for all types of change that can be observed in the course of history, and insofar as Marx advances an absolutist claim for his own theory we shall have to depart from him radically. At the same time, Marx has explored one of the most interesting, and perhaps the most significant, relationship between social structure and social change by postulating conflict groups and their clashes as forces that make for change. Obvious as it may seem that social conflicts often result in the modification of accepted patterns of organization and behavior, it has neither been seen by all nor been explored as systematically by anybody as by Marx.

Throughout his life, Marx was clearly influenced by the memory of two events which overshadowed the consciousness of the nineteenth century, although they were its heritage rather than its product: the French Revolution and the Industrial Revolution. There were obvious explanations for both of them, and these were widely held. One might summarize them by the phrases that "men make history" and that "inventions make history." Even today, historians find it hard to free themselves from the conception that at the turning points of history there stood outstanding and powerful individuals or important and consequential inventions. Indeed, it would be nonsensical to try and deny the effect of these forces. But, as Marx well knew, in the French Revolution and the Industrial Revolution another kind of force had also become apparent. Apart from powerful individuals and revolutionary inventions, larger and more anonymous aggregations of men had played a visible part in bringing about these events. Nor had they been unanimous in purpose and action. It was, rather, the conflict between aggregates of differing (but considerable) size, and the changing fortunes of this conflict, that had effected a restructuring of society so far-reaching that it could only be called revolutionary. As we shall see, the revolutionary tradition of the eighteenth century not only inspired Marx but misled him as well. He tended to believe that the only way is which social conflicts could produce structural changes was by revolutionary upheavals. But despite such errors, he did discover the formative force of conflicting social groups or classes. This "discovery" is accompanied, in the work of Marx, by two steps of analysis which, although rather formal, are nevertheless worth mentioning and sustaining.

Firstly, Marx succeeded in tracing conflicts that effect change back to patterns of social structure. For him, social conflicts were not random occurrences which forbid explanation and therefore prediction. Rather, he believed these conflicts to be necessary outgrowths of the structure of any given society and, in particular, of capitalist society. It is doubtful whether Marx, by assuming property relations to be the structural origin of conflict, was right in the substance of his analysis. But this does not diminish the analytical achievement of tracing in the structure of a given society the seeds of its supersedure. The idea of a society which produces in its structure the antagonisms that lead to its modification appears an appropriate model for the analysis of change in general.

Secondly, Marx properly assumed the dominance of one particular conflict in any given situation. Whatever criticism may be required of the Marxian theory, any theory of conflict has to operate with something like a two-class model. There are but two contending parties—this is implied in the very concept of conflict. There may be coalitions, of course, as there may be conflicts internal to either of the contenders, and there may be groups that are not drawn into a given dispute; but from the point of view of a given clash of interests, there are never more than two positions that struggle for domination. We can follow Marx in this argument (which, for him, is often more implicit than explicit) even further. If social conflicts effect change, and if they are generated by social structure, then it is reasonable to assume that of the two interests involved in any one conflict, one will be pressing for change, the other one for the status quo. This assumption, again, is based on logic as much as on empirical observation. In every conflict, one party attacks and another defends. The defending party wants to retain and secure its position, while the attacking party has to fight it in order to improve its own condition. Once again, it is clear that these statements remain on a high level of formality. They imply no reference to the substance or the origin of conflicting interests. But, again, it will prove useful to have articulated the formal prerequisites of Marx's and, indeed, of any theory of conflict. With these formal points, our agreement with Marx ends. Although the heuristic purpose and general approach of his theory of class can and must be sustained, this is not the case with respect to most other features of this theory. Only by rejecting these can we hope to clear the way for a more useful theory of class conflict in industrial societies.

Social Change and Class Conflict (II): Marx Rejected

Since Talcott Parsons wrote his *Structure of Social Action*, the neglect of a systematic analysis of the dynamics of social action by sociologists has become increasingly conspicuous. Only very recently have a number of scholars set out to explore and map this white spot in the atlas of sociological knowledge. If only for this reason it is of some importance to determine the logical status and limits of dynamic analysis rather more precisely than is necessary today with respect to problems of, say, social stratification. We have tried to reduce the spongy concept of social change to that of structural change. This constitutes a gain, but it is not in itself sufficient. At a later point we shall have to return to the dangerous question "When does a structure begin to change or, conversely, up to what point does it remain unchanged?"—a dangerous question because it implies an essentially static concept of structure. So far we have merely touched upon the two cardinal requirements of a theory of change, i.e., the construction of the model of a functionally integrated structure, and the discovery of certain factors or forces the effect of which leads to a modification of this structural model. As to the first of these requirements we have, in the structural-functional approach, a considerable instrumentarium at our disposal today. But with respect to the codification of forces that effect structural change everything is still to be done. *Ad hoc* and at random factors are introduced wherever necessary, and all too often these factors are afterward generalized in an impermissible manner. Thus we get so-called theories of the primacy of the economy, of race, of elites, of cultural diffusion— or of classes. . . .

Among the forces that are capable of changing elements of social structure, two large groups must evidently be distinguished—those that originate outside a given structure and those that are generated by the structure itself. We shall use for the former the concept of exogenous structure change, or exogenous factors, and for the latter that of endogenous structure change, or endogenous factors. . . .

Within each of these fields of factors, further distinctions are required. Thus, exogenous change can result from military conquest and deliberate intervention with existing structures; but it can also result from the diffusion of culture patterns unaccompanied by political or military force. In past decades, many efforts have been made, above all by social anthropologists, to bring the different forms of exogenous change into an ordered context introducing such concepts as "diffusion," later "acculturation," "culture contact," and "culture change." Empirical instances of some of these forms have been studied in great detail. But despite Malinowski's attempt to systematize such approaches, [4] this effort has not yet advanced beyond a loose catalogue of possible factors. The sociology of war and of contacts between advanced societies (until now an utterly neglected field of study) could also contribute to closing this gap in theory.

However, we are not only no further, but possibly less advanced, with respect to the classification of forces operative in endogenous structure change, although many seem to think that this is the proper subject matter of sociological inquiry. Although the number of such factors proposed by sociologists to fulfill requirements of research (and sometimes demands of philosophical or political convictions) grows steadily, a systematic examination of these factors and their interrelations has not even been attempted. The matter is further complicated by the fact that is some cases, such as the differentiation of roles or functions and of technological processes, we can hardly venture a guess as to which factors contribute to their emergence, to say nothing of certain knowledge about them. Marx's attempt to connect the development of productive forces with that of classes marks one of the weakest points in his sociology. It appears most improbable that the complication of the social division of labor, or technological processes that have social consequences, can be explained in terms of group conflicts. In any case, structure changes resulting from social conflicts between organized groups or between the representatives of unorganized masses constitute but one form of endogenous change.

Even within this considerably restricted sphere of social conflicts affecting structure change, it is not only possible but necessary to distinguish a plurality of different forms. It obliterates the precision of analysis if, with one and the same set of categories, we try to analyze conflicts between slaves and freemen in ancient Rome, Negroes and whites in the United States, Catholics and Protestants in contemporary Holland, capital and labor in capitalist society—to mention only a few possibilities. All these conflicts can result in structure changes; they are in this sense factors of endogenous change. Moreover, several of these types of conflict may be superimposed on each other, and may thus constitute a single conflict front in a given country and situation. For purposes of analysis, however, it is necessary to introduce distinctions if one wants to master reality with the tools of science. Endogenous change is but ono kind of social structure change; social conflict is but one of the causes of endogenous change; and class conflict is but one type of social conflict. Endogenous change may be of great, even dominant, significance in a given society; but that is a matter for empirical research. In principle a theory of class illuminates only a small segment of the wide field which can be described by the vague concept of structure change. We can neither expect nor, above all, assume that a theory of class will cast a glimmer of its light on other aspects of structure change as well.

It is apparent that from this point of view Marx is in a sense guilty of the same mistake of which, in a different context, we have accused those who have endeavored to supersede the theory of class with a theory of stratification. They, too, have illegitimately transposed a theory from its legitimate place to other areas of inquiry. The assertion that the history of all past society is the history of class struggles is either meaningless or false. It is meaningless if it is merely intended to say that, *inter alia*, there were also class conflicts in every society. But Marx did not mean this. He believed that the dominant conflicts of every society were class conflicts, and indeed that all social conflicts and all structure changes can be explained in terms of antagonisms of class. This generalization is as impermissible as it is untenable. . . .

NOTES

[1] *Capital*, I, p. 803.
[2] *The Poverty of Philosophy*, p. 140.
[3] *Capital*, I, p. 441.
[4] *The Dynamics of Cultural Change* (New Haven, 1945).

Revolution or Peaceful Change?

MARX believed that the class struggles in the capitalist system would lead to a proletarian revolution. In his early work, *The Poverty of Philosophy*, Marx wrote that "the emancipation of the oppressed class implies necessarily the creation of a new society." Emancipation would stem from the proletariat becoming conscious of itself and making a revolution, thus becoming the bearer of social change and the creator of social humanity. "Only the proletariat of the present day," wrote Marx in *The German Ideology*, "who are completely shut off from all self-activity, are in a position to achieve a complete and no longer restricted self-activity, which consists in the appropriation of a totality of productive forces and in the thus postulated development of a totality of capacities."

Though the need for revolution and its inevitability is inherent in Marxism, interpretations differ about whether the revolution is to occur by violence or by peaceful change, and about whether the proletariat is adequately prepared or is willing to undertake the task.

Marx often used military and obstetrical metaphors in his writings, including those about force. He always spoke of class struggle, not the striving for humanity and justice. But there are also a number of times in his work when the need for force is not stressed, as in the 1872 speech at Amsterdam when Marx admitted that in "certain countries such as the United States and England, the workers may hope to secure their ends by peaceful means." If Engels in *Anti-Dühring* said that "to reject violence was the parson's mode of thought, lifeless, insipid, and impotent," and spoke of the worthlessness of Parliamentary cretinism, he also, at the end of his life in 1895, talked of universal suffrage as a "new weapon and one of the sharpest" for the workers of Germany. It was a bitter irony for Engels to confess that "we the 'revolutionaries' are thriving far better on legal than on illegal methods of revolt." In the excerpts from their writings presented here, S. M. Lipset and Robert Tucker take different positions on the role of violence or gradualism in the Marxist theory.

A related problem is that of whether the revolution, once made, would be confined to one country or extended to other countries, and become "permanent." At one time the Russian Communists all thought the revolution had to be expanded. But the subject became one of the major issues of contention between Stalin and Trotsky, the contenders for the succession to Lenin. For Stalin, the conquest of power would be the final act in the revolution, after which the task was to create a self-sufficient socialist society. For Trotsky, a proletarian revolution in one country can be regarded only as provisional, and socialist construction in one country was possible only on the foundations of class struggle on an international scale. Factors such as the uneven development of industrial capitalism, the rivalries of great powers, the differing strengths of revolutionary movements, the role of the peasantry—all would affect the manner in which revolution was made and how it might be extended.

Moreover, factors such as these have modified for later Marxists the view of Marx in *The Holy Family* that "the aim of the historical action of the proletariat is laid down in advance. . . in its own situation in life, and in the whole organization of contemporary bourgeois society." In his article, Harold Rosenberg discusses the drama of history and the fate of the proletariat, reluctant to undertake what Marx thought was its manifest destiny.

24

The Proletariat and Revolution

Harold Rosenberg

FOR [Marx] the revolution is an historical certainty. From this translation of the dramatic into the "scientific" arise the essential ambiguities
of Marxism. Accepting the revolutionary proletariat as an hypothesis,
we should look for the emergence of this heroic image in the finite
struggles of the working class, in its poetry. Each such struggle would
then appear as laden with suspense and pathos. Of more practical importance, we could be aware whether the values attached to this image
were in the way of being realized. But with Marx all finite efforts of
the workers are subsumed under the *concept* of the class-conscious
proletariat. Thus, though he thinks of the revolution as a tragedy, he
does not behold its incidents as tragic, and his work lacks the pathetic
tonality appropriate to its notion of the workers transforming themselves through constant risk of their lives. . . .

Marx attempts to guarantee the appearance of the proletariat as
actor in two ways. The first is through metaphysics: In his Introduction
to *The Living Thoughts of Karl Marx*, Trotsky summarizes this position:

The productive forces need a new organizer and a new master, and, *since
existence determines consciousness*, Marx had no doubt that the working class,
at the cost of errors and defeats, will come to understand the actual situation,
and, sooner or later, will draw the imperative practical conclusions. (My italics.)

Assuming that the proposition, existence determines consciousness,
is correct, can it be relied upon to produce the *particular* kind of consciousness (revolutionary) anticipated by Marx? If Marx could be

FROM "The Pathos of the Proletariat," *Kenyon Review*, 11 (Autumn 1949), pp.
616–629.

aware in advance of the situation and of its necessary effect on the mind of the workers, the consciousness of Marx would have preceded existence, which is in violation of the proposition. It might be answered that the capitalist situation already existed in Marx's time and that it is the development of that situation, first understood by him, that the workers will come to grasp. But this would be to detach the situation from the human beings in it and to conceive it as unaffected by changes in mankind. Within the movement of capitalism Marx might predict the general direction of certain processes—concentration of capital, accelerated crises, etc.—but he cannot predict the total historical situation of the masses, which includes the history of their consciousness of themselves in their situation, or their lack of it. Yet nothing less than this total situation can be meant by "existence" in its determination of consciousness.

Marxism must therefore admit that it can predict nothing concerning the consciousness of the proletariat and hence of its action, in which case the proletariat remains an hypothesis and not a certainty; or it must reduce the situation to a given number of external elements, definable in advance, and thus become identical with what is known as "vulgar materialism" or "mechanical Marxism."

The failure of the situation to give rise to revolutionary consciousness leads Marx and Marxists to a second type of effort to guarantee the revolution: through politics and propaganda. . . . Engels recognized the failure of "the basic economic facts" to explain "the way in which these [political, juridical, ideological] notions come about." In the same year (1893) he exhibits more concretely the consequences of this failure for Marxism. In the revolution of 1848, he recalls in his Introduction to *The Class Struggles in France*, Marx relied upon the masses' understanding of their situation to sustain their revolutionary spirit:

The proletarian masses themselves, even in Paris, after the victory, were still absolutely in the dark as to the path to be taken. And yet the movement was there, instinctive, spontaneous, irrepressible. Was not this just the situation in which a revolution had to succeed? . . . If, in all the longer revolutionary periods, it was so easy to win the great masses of the people by the merely plausible and delusive views of the minorities thrusting themselves forward, how could they be less susceptible to *ideas which were the truest reflex of their economic position, which were nothing but the clear, comprehensible expression of their needs, of needs not yet understood by themselves, but only vaguely felt.* To be sure, this revolutionary mood of the masses had almost always, and usually very speedily, given way to lassitude or even to a revulsion to its opposite, as soon as illusion evaporated and disappointment set in. But here it was not a question of delusive views. . . . (My italics.)

His social-economic analysis had convinced Marx that the proletariat was objectively powerful enough to overcome the government. Since existence determines consciousness, the workers had already "vaguely" grasped the truth of their position. All that was needed was to clarify this awareness with ideas which were nothing else than what they already knew. The "instinctive movement" would thereupon be sustained against a collapse into disillusioned apathy; and "the proletariat grown wise by experience must become the decisive factor."

The "ideas which were the truest reflex" failed, however, to produce this steadying effect. "History," Engels goes on to say, "has proved us, and all who thought like us, wrong." Not wrong in relying on the truth, but wrong, he explains, in estimating the situation—it was not ripe for proletarian revolution. This mistake raises numerous questions regarding the determination of consciousness which Engels ignores. Does the diminishing of the fervor of the masses in 1850 signify that they were more conscious than Marx of their situation, instinctively aware of its unripeness? So it would seem, since their abandonment of revolution conformed to the real position rather than to Marx's erroneous notion of it. But if the masses acted correctly without the Marxian "reflex," and even in opposition to it, what is the function of the reflex? Also, should it not be admitted that the mood of the masses is a better measure of the situation than the Marxian analysis? Another question: Had Marx correctly estimated the "unripe" situation of 1848, would his truth then have had the effect of maintaining revolutionary fervor? We know that in such a situation Marx counsels wary support of a bourgeois revolution for the sake of progress and warns the proletariat that the fruit of their struggle will be taken from them. He strives to check fervor by criticism rather than to heighten and maintain it. Must not this dispelling of illusion have the same effect as the bitter awakening described by Engels, depleting the masses' revolutionary energy?

At any rate, Engels' confession of error would have been more magnanimous if, giving full weight to the fatal consequences of misleading the workers even on one occasion, he had inquired into the dangers of Marxian certainty and of its tendency in political practice to convert its philosophy into its opposite and to ascribe to its own program the finality of existence itself. Instead, Engels proceeds with a demonstration that in 1893 history has corrected its earlier deficiencies and that the situation is now prepared for proletarian revolution. Evidence of this is the triumph among the workers of "the theory of Marx, sharply formulating the final aims of the struggle." Apparently, existence and consciousness have been firmly welded together:

At that time the masses, sundered and differing according to locality and nationality, linked only by the feeling of common suffering, undeveloped, tossed to and fro in their perplexity from enthusiasm to despair; today a great international army of Socialists, marching irresistibly on and daily growing in number, organization, discipline, insight, and assurance of victory.

The collective "I" of the proletariat has finally defined itself—it has become the Party. Proletarian unity and action, conceived as an anguished response to the real conditions and "having no ideals to realize," has become a disciplined, self-assured "march" toward defined aims. Proletarian consciousness, once consisting of "the content and material of its revolutionary activity," has become Marxist theory. [1]

Engels seems unaware that what he is describing as an historical development is to an equal degree a decisive shift in Marxist philosophy, that its reliance upon existence to supply the proletariat with a self and an intelligence is being quietly abandoned in favor of party ideology and discipline. His contention that the rise of a marching party is a reflection of the changed position of the proletariat cannot eliminate the qualitative difference between the kind of concrete intelligence that arises out of a spontaneous movement and the stratagems which the Marxist brain will deduce from its outline of the situation and its place in the scenario of history.

For Engels in 1893 the continuity of the revolutionary movement no longer depends upon the reflexes of a proletariat that has been forced into revolt; it is no longer subject to the intermittences of the heart and mind of the working class:

In order that the masses may understand what is to be done, long, persistent work is required, and it is just this work which we are now pursuing, and with a success which drives the enemy to despair.

Instead of learning in action, the working class is put to school by the Party; it marches with its will in the secure custody of the leadership. Marching has indeed replaced revolutionary action, the movement which was to have been the source itself of the "alteration" of the workers. [2] The "decisive shock force of the international proletarian army" has become, says Engels, the two million voters of the German Social Democracy and their allies. "We, the 'revolutionaries,' the 'rebels,'" he observes complacently—noting that "the irony of world history turns everything upside down"—"we are thriving far better on legal methods than on illegal methods and revolt." With the military language—"shock troops," "army," and "revolutionaries" in quotes —what has become of the shrewd spirit and the notion that the working class makes itself human only through revolt?

Was Engels' conversion of Marx's drama of history from an order assumed to be inherent in events into a didactic fable of socialist politics a betrayal of the master's thought a decade after his death? In no respect. Marx, too, had attempted to overcome by political means the laggardness of existence in production revolutionary consciousness:

> If this country [England] is the classic seat of landlordism and capitalism, by virtue of that fact it is also here that the material conditions of their destruction are most highly developed. The General Council [dominated by Marx] being at present placed in the happy position of having its hand directly on this great lever of the proletarian revolution . . . it would be sheer folly, we would almost say it would be an outright crime, to allow that hold to fall into purely English hands!
>
> The English have all the material requisites necessary for the social revolution. What they lack is the spirit of generalization and revolutionary ardor. *It is only the General Council which can supply this deficiency,* which can thus accelerate the truly revolutionary movement in this country and consequently everywhere. . . . As the General Council we can initiate measures which later, in the public execution of their tasks, appear as spontaneous movements of the English working class. (My italics; Resolution of the General Council of the International Workingmen's Association, Jan. 1, 1870.)

Somehow the material conditions have failed in England to transform themselves into intellect and ardor, and Marx holds it to be criminal folly to depend upon them to do so. Nor will a true reflex "suffice." He proposes to substitute himself for the mass "I" of the British proletariat by originating its acts. Yet he has no intention of formally rejecting his doctrine of immanence and self-emancipation. He wished his acts to "appear as spontaneous movements of the English working class." And if accused of Machiavellianism, he has already replied that he is but "accelerating the truly revolutionary movement" called for by his script of history.

Marx's passage from philosophy to instigation seems rather a vacillation following the course of events than a final step. Actual upheavals, like the Commune or the American Civil War, restore his perspective of spectator and prompter of an historical drama developing through the concrete consciousness and actions of class actors inspired by their situation. The laws of history then appear to assert themselves ironically against *all* political programs. Engels, too, confronted by revolutionary action, but without the "greater level" to tempt him, rests his expectations on dramatic irony; in 1885 he writes to Zasulich concerning Russia, where no Marxist organization existed:

People who boasted that they had *made* a revolution have always seen the next day that they had no idea what they were doing, that the revolution they *made* did not in the least resemble the one they would have liked to make. That is what Hegel calls the irony of history, an irony that few historic personalities escape.

When the drama is being physically enacted, Hegel re-enters "materialism."

What proves unendurable to the philosopher of class conflict is the apparent discontinuity of the drama, the long intermissions in which the proletarian protagonist fails to appear on the stage. Theoretically, the revolution is always in progress, with an ever-present proletariat growing more class-conscious and more active. In actuality, Marx is painfully aware, the action on the stage is not continuous and the "contradictory" process of development fails to translate itself into human conflict. Revolts are far apart and when they do occur prove to be but moments lacking in extension. Even worse than the discontinuity of the action is the discontinuity of the hero. Social peace, dissolving the working class into individuals with nonclass identifications, causes the proletariat to fade again into the metaphor on which it was founded and to become an historical nothing. This makes normal political activity extremely difficult for the working class as Marx conceived it.

To establish the proletarian hypothesis as a fact Marx originates, at least in embryo, a new kind of politics, which goes beyond support of the working class and development of socialist theory, as in *The Communist Manifesto* and *Capital*. In response to the prolonged quiescence of the proletariat, he assigns to his theory the function of the material conditions as the source of proletarian consciousness and action—he seeks *to create* the proletariat as a revolutionary class. Out of this effort arises Marxist politics, in which union and intelligence are born not from the total pathetic experience of those who endure the situation but from the detached brain that has analyzed it.

As philosopher and historian Marx attacks the utopians and "Marxists" for their dogmatism and their dreams of making history according to their plans; as a politician he himself is a Marxist. The intuition of history as a tragedy which, with the elimination of myth, may come to its close through a saving catastrophe is submerged under a programmatic optimism. Its existence and its action centered in the Marxist organization, the proletariat seems to lose its hypothetical character. The semblance of moving toward the goal appears to relieve the workers of the pathos of choosing between permanent revolution and nothingness. In time the human "recoil" before the "indefinite prodigiousness" of socialist revolution ceases to play any part in the writings of the movement (except with Georges Sorel and Rosa Luxemburg), or is used as a justification for techniques of discipline.

But having translated class consciousness from tragic self-recognition into political tutoring, Marxism is haunted by its philosophical premises. If its analysis is the consciousness of the socialist revolution, whose existence determines this consciousness? The class's? Or the Party's? Or is it undermined by both? So long as Marx could say, "The great social measure of the Commune [which was not a Marxist creation] was its own working existence," it was clear that theory was subordinate to the concrete action of the class and that communism was in truth attempting to be the intelligence of "the real movement that abolishes the present state of things." Once, however, class spontaneity has yielded to steady marching at the heels of the Party, the latter must look to itself as the source of historical consciousness, since it is it that experiences while the masses are undergoing the "long, persistent work" of learning. But if its own existence guides it, the Marxist Party is "an independent being" and its theory a mere ideology.[3] In that case the high claims of socialism for the release of human individuals into unlimited creativity through the "self-activity" of the proletariat are no longer legitimate. Those hopes rested upon the origin of the collective act in history itself, in the reflex of the individuals of the class to their concrete situation, rather than, as formerly, in a separated community or ideal; but no socialism has produced its own illusory community and independently existing creation of the mind.

Thus in the heart of Marxism a conflict prevails between metaphysics (existence determines consciousness and defeats all preconceptions) and politics ("we can initiate measures"). The "dialectical" overcoming of this conflict through combining its messianism of total liberation with guidance of the masses as an "army" results logically in a politics of hallucination. In Marx's "we can initiate measures which will later appear as spontaneous movements"—this sentence shows the actual content of the synthesis of spontaneity and control—a new principle is making its appearance, though dimly. It is neither the materialist principle of the primacy of existence nor the idealist one that action has its source in thought. It suggests that action can release a revealed destiny which both dominates existence and precedes thought. With the affirmation of this power we stand at the verge of twentieth-century political irrationalism.

Primarily, destiny-politics consists of a demonic displacement of the ego of the historical collectivity (class, nation, race) by the party of action, so that the party motivates the community and lays claim to identity with its fate and to its privileges as a creature of history. In *What Is To Be Done?*, Lenin begins by denying that the proletariat can be an independent historical actor; for him it is a collective character with a role but without the revolutionary ego and consciousness necessary to play its part. Its struggles are but reflexes of economic contradictions which can never of themselves result in revolution. The giant figure of the proletariat is doomed to remain a personification of exploitation and misery until it is possessed by an alien subject that will send it hurtling along its predestined path. This conscious and active ego is the Bolshevik Party of "scientific" (destiny-knowing) professional revolutionaries. In the most literal sense the Party's relation to the class is demoniacal; after a series of paroxysms the collective body of the class is inhabited and violently moved by a separate will which is that of another group or even of one man. Lenin uses the word "subjectivity" to mean precisely the Party and its decisions.

If the revolutionary violence of the proletariat resulted from its historical situation, the class would bear no moral responsibility—it will be recalled that Marx accorded to the capitalists, too, immunity from class guilt. The class exists "outside" the individual and compels him, while its own acts are necessary in the sense that necessity exists in the physical world. Besides, even if the class were responsible, who could judge it? Only history itself, whose creature and "agent" it is. "History is the judge," says Marx, "the proletariat its executioner." Hence so long as its hero is actually the revolutionary working class of Europe, Marxism need not concern itself with the morality of its means —the truth itself and its revelation, through which the instinctive movement of the victim-hero is transformed into a conscious act, is its sole and exclusive means.

Political Marxism demands for itself the metaphysical privileges of class action. The violence of the "vanguard," having become "dialectically" the act of the proletariat, justifies itself by the existence of the workers as victims of the wage system. Any attack upon that system by Marxist intellectuals and wielders of power becomes a liberating movement on the part of the class. Thus the Party need not account for the means it employs—all the more so since its program is taken to be identical with the reality which is the ground of all future values. It even denies that the form of its organization is a "principled question"—to be totally authoritarian does not prevent its being totally democratic, since its acts are the acts of the proletariat and the proletariat is, by definition, the demos.

As it attributes to the class the subjectivity of the Party, without regard to the actual will or consciousness of the workingman, it also attributes subjectivity to the "embodiments of particular class interests."

Capitalists and members of other classes are held automatically guilty of historical crimes, despite the unwillingness of Marx to "make the individual responsible for relations whose creature he socially remains." Thus dictatorship and terror exercised by the proletarian *alter ego* go hand in hand with bringing the social categories artificially to life.

Morally bewildered by assuming for itself the role of the class, Marxism destroys by the same means the basis for the historical insight that was the genius of its author. The Party wishes to analyze events in class terms; standing in the place of the proletariat it can see only itself. Traditional parties are aware that they represent specific configurations of interests and desires. The party of action does not feel itself *in the presence of* any social body. The featureless mass of laborers exists historically only in that the Party creates it; the Party program is the true expression of the workers' interests and their own demands are but errors to be eliminated or exploited. The Party is an absolute with regard to the class, and through it an absolute with regard to history. Referring to the "lag" of workers behind the Party of the most advanced, Engels asserts:

and this alone explains why it is that actually the "solidarity of the proletariat" is everywhere realized in different party groupings which carry on life and death feuds with one another, as the christian sects in the Roman Empire did amidst the worst persecutions. (Letter to Bebel, 1873.)

As a liberating program, Marxism founders on the subjectivity of the proletariat. So soon as it declares itself, rather than their common situation, to be the inspiration of men's revolutionary unity and ardor —how else can it offer itself simultaneously to the French working class and to nonindustrial French colonials?—Marxism becomes an ideology competing with others. When fascism asserted the revolutionary working class to be an invention of Marxism, it was but echoing the Marxist parties themselves. If the class as actor is a physical extension of the Party, fascism was justified in claiming that a magical contest in creating mass-egos could decide which collectivities are to exist and dominate history. Moreover, it proved that heroic pantomime, symbolism, ritual, bribes, appeals to the past, could overwhelm Marxist class consciousness. What choice was there for the workers between the fascist costume drama and a socialism that urges them to regard their own working clothes as a costume? In Germany and Italy the working class was driven off the stage of history by the defeat of the Party— in Russia it was driven off by its victory.

The elimination of the illusory community has proved to be far more difficult than Marx imagined. Though released from the sacred, the consciousness of the workingmen has not become an infallible reflection of their bare material condition. Their past-less barbarism has failed to immunize them to heroes and ideals. In moments of crisis the newfangled men seem as susceptible to self-surrender as their tradition-bound predecessors. They have neither chosen nor been compelled to change themselves into the inhuman "character assigned to them by the process of production."

Yet the proletarian personification remains. A single external character imposes itself upon the human mass of wage workers. And the presence of the mask continues to *imply* action on its part, no matter how many times it shows itself to be in fact incapable of it. Neither theory nor events can refute the hypothesis of the revolutionary working class. So long as the category exists, the possibility cannot be excluded that it will recognize itself as a separate human community and revolutionize everything by affirming itself and its traditionless interests.

In this proletarian category the twentieth century has concentrated a unique power. No modern government can survive against the expressed will of its workers—decades ago Sorel pointed out that trading on the chances of that expression is the main feature of contemporary politics. Whatever be concluded about history as an epic of class struggle, the potent effects in our time of the *likelihood* of class struggle cannot be denied. On the one hand, the present social order is permanently menaced by the workers' tremendous potential power; on the other, the fact that this power rests with an anonymous category, an historical "nothing," tempts all modern mythmakers to seize upon the class as raw material for new collectivities by which society can be subjugated. Cannot the history-less proletariat be converted into *anything* as readily as into itself? Keeping the drama in suspense between revolution by the working class on its own behalf and revolution as a tool for others, the pathos of the proletariat dominates modern history.

NOTES

1   Contrast Engels' *Introduction* to the following passage in Marx's text of four decades earlier: "A class in which the revolutionary interests of society are concentrated, so soon as it has risen up, finds directly in its own situation the content and material of its revolutionary activity: foes to be laid low, measures, dictated by the needs of the struggle, to be taken; the consequences of its own deeds drive it on. It makes no theoretical inquires into its own task."

2   "Both for the production on a mass scale of this communist consciousness, and for the success of the cause itself, the alteration of men on a mass scale is necessary, an alteration which can only take place in a practical movement, a revolution." (*The German Ideology.*)

3   The mark of an "ideologist," says Engels, is that "every act, since it is transmitted by thought, also seems to him in the last analysis to be *founded* on thought." Is not the act of the proletarian who is undergoing Party instruction *founded* on Marxism?

25

Is Gradual Change Possible?

S. M. Lipset

SINCE the bulk of the writings of Marx and Engels occurred during the period of slowly emerging legal labor movements, they themselves tended increasingly to accept the logic of gradual change, of the need to build workers' organizations of all varieties, parties, unions, and cooperatives. It was wrong to try to speed up the pace of revolution. Socialism's triumph would follow from the inevitable growth of such movements to a position of power as capitalist industrialization created a majority of proletarians employed under conditions of large-scale industry, who would develop class consciousness as a result of the inherent conflicts with the owning class. . . .

The two founding figures of the doctrine, like later parties that claimed to be their orthodox successors, modified their beliefs in line with changing circumstances of capitalist society. Perhaps the most ironic example of how little effect explicit formulations have on the way in which later generations of Marxists perceive what earlier ones wrote may be found in an official Communist edition of the *Correspondence of Marx and Engels* in which the following is printed on the *same* page. Engels wrote in his critique of the draft program of the Erfurt Congress of the German Social-Democratic Party in 1891: "If one thing is certain it is that our Party and the working class can only come to power under the form of the democratic republic. This is even the *specific* form for the dictatorship of the proletariat. . . ."

The Communist editors then state: "On these statements of Engels, Lenin comments in *State and Revolution:* 'Engels repeats here in a par-

FROM "The Sociology of Marxism," *Dissent*, 10 (Winter 1963), pp. 60–63.

ticularly emphatic form the fundamental idea which runs like a red letter throughout Marx's work, namely, that the democratic republic is the *nearest* approach to the dictatorship of the proletariat.'"[1] Apparently Lenin and the editors were unable to distinguish any difference between the words "specific form" and "nearest approach."

Influence of French Revolutionary Thinking

While most of the analyses of the origins of Marx's philosophical ideas have properly stressed the transition from Hegelianism, much more important for an understanding of his politics and sociology is the extent to which Marx's thought before 1848 was dominated by French revolutionary thinking, by an idealization of the role of the Jacobins, of the possibility of total revolution. As Lichtheim states, "the *Manifesto* spells out the implications of a world-view which owed more to reminiscences of 1789-94 than its authors would have been willing to admit." The chiliastic views expressed in this founding political document were appropriate for a tiny sect anticipating revolution in absolutist Europe.

A concern with French politics remained the source point from which much of Marxian ideas about class and politics were drawn. After the *Manifesto*, the *Class Struggles in France*, *The Eighteenth Brumaire*, and *The Civil War in France* became the basic texts of concrete class analysis. Yet, ironically, as Lichtheim points out, France, though the country of the great bourgeois political revolution, was relatively much less advanced in economic terms. Britain and the United States, the most developed countries economically, should have been the prime examples of capitalist class relations and politics, but each deviated from the assumptions of growing class tensions. Britain retained stable aristocratic institutions, and the American working class was a model of moderation. (Lichtheim pays little attention to the extent that Marx tried to draw socialist lessons from America. Thus, as Lewis Feuer has pointed out, Marx saw in the early American Workingmen's Parties of the 1820s and 1830s evidence that strong socialistically inclined labor parties were endemic outgrowths in a bourgeois republic, and even urged that the American experience proved that the working class would come to power.)

The general question of why France was economically backward as contrasted to the English-speaking nations did not concern Marx directly, although he was aware of the fact. Marx tried to explain the increasing political conservatism of the French and other continental bourgeoisie on the ground that they were frightened by the emergence of the proletariat as a distinct class which threatened private property; but he ignored the fact that this phenomenon did not explain why the French businessmen were much more reluctant than the English to take advantage of identical economic opportunities.[2] Explanations that would account for variations in class behavior by reference to the differing value systems of national societies were absent, except on an *ad hoc* basis, from Marx's work. It is ironic that Marxists have taken as the classic model of bourgeois polities and societies precisely the one nation, France, which later-day social scientists were to treat as the classic case of a society whose business class least reflected the capitalist ethos.

The French experiences reinforced the revolutionary and Blanquist aspects of Marxism which came to fruition in Leninism. Marx pointed to the Paris Commune as conclusive proof that the proletariat could come to power in its own right, that it could destroy the old state apparatus, and Marx's propagandistic pamphlet on this subject was subsequently to serve Lenin in good stead in his polemics. Yet the fact was, as Marx himself acknowledged in a private letter in 1881, the Commune "was merely the rising of a city under exceptional conditions, the majority of the Commune was in no way socialist, nor could it be." He went on to criticize the Communards for not having shown a "modicum of common sense" in reaching a compromise with their opponents in Versailles. But though Marx's final judgment of the Commune was that it had exaggerated the potential of the situation, that it had not been socialist and had been foolishly unwilling to compromise, his published *The Civil War in France* was to instruct generations of Marxists that the Commune "was essentially a working-class government, the political form at last discovered under which to work out the economic emancipation of labor."[3]

Effects of the Commune

Although the Paris Commune deserves a special place in the annals of socialism, since it gave rise to the one major example of socialist internationalism (the German Social-Democratic leaders faced jail to defend it), its ultimate impact on the Marxist movements can only be regarded as tragic. The tragedy was not its failure—that, as Marx argued, was inevitable—but the fact, as Lichtheim suggests, that it introduced "a political myth" which sharply contradicted the political concepts which had been emerging with the formation of the First International in 1864. By that time, Marx has lived in England for fifteen years, and the *Inaugural Address* which he wrote for the International reflected British experience. Unlike the 1848 *Manifesto*, which stressed revolution, the *Address* as Lichtheim notes emphasized "the aims of organized labor, working through legislatures. . . ." It praised British labor for having pushed the Ten-Hours Bill through Parliament, and saw in the growth of the cooperative movement promise for even greater advances. As Marx wrote: "The value of these great social experiments cannot be overrated." The Paris Commune had led Marx temporarily to return to the youthful rhetoric of chiliastic revolution contained in the *Manifesto*, and his even more violent "Jacobin-Blanquist aberration in 1850," the *Address of the Central Committee of the Communist League*. But basically, except for his pamphlet on the *Commune*, Marx had abandoned an insurrectionist image of the revolution and had formed, as Lichtheim points out, "a political outlook which fitted the requirements of the modern age. In this mature conception, labor's conquest of power represents an aspect of the struggle for democracy."

The words written by Marx in the heat of internationalist ardor seeking to glorify the deeds of the Communards in a propaganda document were to plague the Marxist movement in the twentieth century. They enabled Lenin both to ignore the conclusions of the mature Marx and Engels in favor of democracy, and to distort the reality of the Commune itself. For as Julian Martov and many other Mensheviks pointed out, they, rather than the Leninists, advocated policies which corresponded to the activities of the Commune which Marx had approved. The Commune had been the legally elected government of the municipality of Paris, and it had been controlled by a coalition of left parties; no effort had been made to exclude anyone from it. If the Commune presented a political model for a socialist state, it was a model of a completely free democracy with competing parties, not a society led by a "vanguard" party.

But while Marx and Engels did change their ideas in the direction of what later was to be known as reformism, the fact remains that a total working-class conquest of power remained the ultimate goal. Their analysis of class struggle always posited a continuing basic conflict between the workers and their parties with the dominant class. This image of a continuing class struggle did not find much support in the politically more democratic western countries. Britain was to remain the great disappointment. In Latin Europe, the workers' movement divided between reformist, largely non-Marxist socialist parties, and anarchist or syndicalist movements. Political democracy produced political reformism, while small-scale industry and the absence of centralization sustained "libertarian" doctrines. . . .

NOTES

1 Karl Marx and Friedrich Engels, *Correspondence 1846–1895* (New York: International Publishers, 1936), p. 486 (emphasis mine). But if Lenin was unable to acknowledge he was a "revisionist," that he had rejected Marx and Engels' belief in democratic institutions, Stalin could and did.

2 For a detailed account of situations in which French capital demonstrated its unwillingness to take advantage of economic opportunities which were seized by their British equivalents, see David Landes, *Bankers and Pashas* (London, 1958).

3 In Lewis S. Feuer (ed.), *Karl Marx and Friedrich Engels. Basic Writings on Politics and Philosophy* (Garden City, 1959), p. 369. For a detailed study of the Paris Commune which demonstrates the nonsocialist character of the uprising, see Edward Mason, *The Paris Commune* (New York, 1930).

26

Ambivalence about Gradual Change

Robert Tucker

THE attitude of Marx and Engels toward the political institutions of liberal parliamentary democracy was ambivalent. On the one hand, they saw the democratic republic in bourgeois society as being, like all previous forms of the state, a class dictatorship. The liberal democratic state was a camouflaged "bourgeois dictatorship."[1] Its representative government and universal suffrage meant no more than the opportunity of "deciding once in three or six years which member of the ruling class was to misrepresent the people in parliament."[2] Yet Marx and Engels were not inclined to dismiss democratic political institutions as useless or unimportant. Rather they saw in them a school of political training for the working class in bourgeois society, a stimulus to the growth of revolutionary class consciousness in the proletariat. For the debate by which parliamentary democracy lived necessarily had to spread to the larger society outside: "The parliamentary regime leaves everything to the decision of majorities; how shall the great majorities outside parliament not want to decide? When you play the fiddle at the top of the state, what else is to be expected but that those down below dance?"[3]

But was it possible, as later Social Democratic Marxists came to believe, for an anticapitalist revolution and socialist transformation of bourgeois society to take place in a peaceful and orderly way through the electoral process in a parliamentary democracy? Could the workers achieve political power by democratic means and proceed by those means to change the mode of production? On one or two occasions

FROM "Marx as a Political Theorist," in N. Lobkowicz (ed.), *Marx and the Western World*, University of Notre Dame Press (Notre Dame, 1967), pp. 114–116.

Marx alluded to such a possibility, most notably when he allowed in a speech about the Congress at the Hague in 1872 that in England and America, and possibly in Holland as well, the workers might conceivably attain their revolutionary aim by peaceful means. [4] However, it is uncertain how seriously he or Engels actually entertained such a belief, which was at variance with a fundamental tendency of their thought over the years. Addressing himself in 1874 to believers in a nonauthoritarian revolution, Engels inquired: "Have these gentlemen ever seen revolution?" And he went on: "A revolution is certainly the most authoritarian thing there is; it is the act whereby one part of the population imposes its will upon the other part by means of rifles, bayonets, and cannon-authoritarian means, if such there be at all. . . ." [5] It is true that later in his 1895 introduction to a new edition of Marx's *Class Struggles in France*, Engels found the Social Democratic movement to be thriving on universal suffrage and the ballot box; but even there he did not assert that the working class could actually come to power by these means. He said nothing to suggest that he had altered the view, expressed some years earlier, that universal suffrage was not, and could not be, anything more than a "gauge of the maturity of the working class." Its mission was to herald the revolutionary *dénouement:* "On the day the thermometer of universal suffrage registers boiling point among the workers, both they and the capitalists will know what to do." [6]

Marx and Engels saw in the class state not only organized coercion but also an element of deception. In each of its historical incarnations, the state had been the dictatorship of a minority class of owners of the means of production, but its class character had been camouflaged. In Europe, for example, monarchy had been "the normal incumbrance and indispensable *cloak* of class-rule." [7] In addition, the modern democratic republic claimed to be a state ruled by the people as a whole through their elected representatives in parliament; the control of this state by the capitalist class, and their use of it for class purposes, was concealed. This theme of the manipulation of political forms to cover up minority-class rule is a minor one in Marx and Engels but merits special attention because it influenced later elitist theories of the state. In the elitist theories of Mosca, Pareto, and others, the ruling class is no longer defined in Marx's manner, and the possibility of a future society without a ruling class is explicitly or implicitly denied. But notwithstanding the fact that the elitists were anti-Marxists and offered their view of the state in part as a rebuttal of Marx's, their thinking showed the impact of classical Marxist political theory. Pareto admitted as much when he praised the "sociological part" of Marx's teaching, the idea that societies are divided into classes of rulers and ruled. This basic notion, along with the tendency to see minority-class rule as something concealed behind external political forms, is something for which the elitist theory is largely indebted to Marx. And it may be through this channel that Marx has had his most enduring influence upon political thought in the contemporary West.

NOTES

1 *MEW*, VII, 33; cf. *Selected Works*, vol. I, p. 163.
2 *MEW*, XVII, 340; cf. *Selected Works*, vol. I, p. 520.
3 *MEW*, VIII, 154; cf. *Selected Works*, vol. I, p. 288.
4 *MEW*, XVIII, 160; cf. K. Kautsky, *The Dictatorship of the Proletariat* (Ann Arbor, 1964), p. 10. See also Marx's article "The Chartists," *New York Daily Tribune* (August 25, 1852), *MEW*, VIII, pp. 342ff., suggesting that in England universal suffrage must inevitably result in the political supremacy of the working class.
5 *MEW*, XVIII, 308; cf. *Selected Works*, vol. I, p. 638.
6 *MEW*, XXI, 168; cf. *Selected Works*, vol. II, p. 322.
7 *MEW*, XVII, 341ff.; cf. *Selected Works*, vol. I, p. 522. Italics added.

Is Dictatorship Necessary?

MARX dismissed as utopian all speculation about the way in which the future society would be organized. The ultimate aim—the abolition of political power—was declared, but the means by which this desired objective was to be attained was left unknown.

In a few of his writings Marx mentioned the need for a dictatorship of the proletariat as a transitional organ from the stage of capitalism to that of socialism. Hal Draper provides in his article an exhaustive analysis of the original Marxist references to the concept. Other commentators, however, have refused to accept the concept as meaningful for Marx, or to agree that the ill-fated Paris Commune of 1871 was the prototype for future communist societies.

But Lenin and other Russian disciples of Marx began emphasizing the concept, more appropriate to Russian traditions and conditions than to Western Europe, both before and after the 1917 Revolution. Lenin and, in particular, Stalin, used the concept to defend Soviet dictatorship. The dictatorship of the proletariat is held to be the weapon of the proletarian revolution, and is necessary to guide the revolution toward its completion and to the socialist society. It therefore had a positive role, as well as the negative role of crushing the resistance of the former exploiters and bourgeoisie.

In practice, however, the dictatorship of the proletariat would be wielded by the single party, cohesive and disciplined. The original Marxist argument was that the logical development of capitalism would produce a politically conscious proletariat which would make the revolution. The writings of Marx and Engels contain many criticisms of Blanquism, the view that power could be captured in a revolutionary coup made by a small group. In his introduction to Marx's *Class Struggles in France*, Engels wrote that "the time of surprise attacks, of revolutions carried through by small conscious minorities, is past." Implicit in his argument is the idea that the level of revolutionary working-class consciousness would rise as the industrial system developed, conditions were ripe, and the proletariat mature.

But many of Marx's disciples in effect rejected this view. Lenin argued that the working-class movement by itself would not produce a revolutionary ideology. A party of professional revolutionaries was necessary "to divert the working-class movement from the spontaneous trade unionist striving to come under the wing of the bourgeoisie." The party and its leader would speak and act in the interests of the proletariat.

Both Rosa Luxemburg and Trotsky, in his early years, thought that this Leninist distortion of the original Marxist thesis on the role of the proletariat would lead to the enslavement of the working-class movement to an intellectual elite hungry for power, and that power would become concentrated in the hands of a small number or even a single party leader. The experience of Bolshevism, and of the Stalinist years in particular, provide a sad illustration of the truth of this criticism. Robert Tucker discusses the validity of the analyses made by Lenin and by Social Democratic Marxists of the original Marxist thesis.

27

The Dictatorship of the Proletariat

Hal Draper

WE NOW come to the loci in which Marx and Engels used the term "dictatorship of the proletariat." There are eleven in all (counting a work with more than one such passage as only one). They cluster in three periods: (1) 1850-52, i.e., after the revolution of 1848; (2) 1872-75, i.e., after the Paris Commune; and (3) 1890-91, this last period being, we shall see, a sort of echo from 1875.

In both the first and second periods, and most clearly in the very first locus, Marx used the term particularly in *connection with* the Blanquists.[1] What exactly was the nature of this connection? Marx's attitude toward Blanqui and his movement remained essentially the same from 1844, when Marx first became a socialist, to the end. This attitude combined complete rejection of the Blanquist putsch, to be made by a conspiratorial group with great admiration for Blanqui as a devoted and honest revolutionist; it combined great respect for Blanqui as a socialist militant with no respect for his ideas on how to make a revolution. In revolutionary periods Marx sought joint *action* with the Blanquists and other revolutionary currents — a "united front"—in spite of political disagreement. Such united-front contact took place especially in 1850 and again after the Paris Commune. In both cases these were "united fronts" or joint action in London, between Marx and Engels and Blanquist *refugees* from the fighting in France.

In these contacts, Marx and Engels, rejecting the Blanquist concept of dictatorship, *counterposed to it* their own formulation of the "dictatorship of the proletariat."

FROM "Marx and the Dictatorship of the Proletariat," *New Politics*, 1: 4 (Summer 1962), pp. 95–104.

This is what Engels explained in retrospect when, in 1874, he set down explicitly the difference between the Blanquist and the Marxist idea:

From Blanqui's assumption, that any revolution may be made by the outbreak of a small revolutionary minority, follows of itself the necessity of a dictatorship after the success of the venture. This is, of course, a dictatorship, not of the entire revolutionary class, the proletariat, but of the small minority that has made the revolution, and who are themselves previously organized under the dictatorship of one or several individuals. [This passage is referred to below as Locus 7.]

One can hardly demand a clearer line of demarcation between the Blanquist dictatorship of the active revolutionary minority and a *class dictatorship* or domination, the rule "of the entire revolutionary class." This emphasis on *class* dictatorship is what we find in the first locus.

The first use of "dictatorship of the proletariat" is in Marx's articles, later assembled under the title *The Class Struggles in France 1848–1850*, in his new London magazine *Neue Rheinische Zeitung, Politisch-Ökonomische Revue*. The first article (in the first issue) was written in January and published in early March.

After the defeat of the June 1848 workers' uprising, says Marx, "there appeared the bold slogan of revolutionary struggle: *Overthrow of the bourgeoisie! Dictatorship of the working class!*" [Let us call this Locus 1a.]

There is a problem here. Marx writes that "the bold slogan" appeared: "Overthrow of the bourgeoisie!" But then there immediately follows the slogan of the "dictatorship of the working class." Is Marx intending to say that this slogan "appeared" among the revolutionary workers too? But it is quite certain that it did not. I suggest he is not literally claiming that this hitherto-unknown slogan "appeared," but rather he is explaining, in apposition, what the "bold slogan" of overthrow of the bourgeoisie means — in the first place, what it means to him, Marx. In reality he is launching the slogan himself, putting words to the inchoate working-class aspiration expressed in the revolution.

In the second article (written at the beginning and published toward the end of March) Marx comments that the proletariat was "not yet enabled through the development of the remaining classes to seize the revolutionary dictatorship" and therefore "had to throw itself into the arms" of the social-democrats. [This qualifies as Locus 1b.] He is here not only excluding the idea of establishing the "revolutionary dictatorship" by a band of conspirators, but also even by the proletariat as long as it does not yet have the support of other classes. As elsewhere in the same work, as previously in the *Manifesto*, the "rule" or "dictatorship of the proletariat" is firmly linked to the idea of majority support.

The third article (written March 5-15 and published in mid-April) said:

the proletariat rallies more and more round *revolutionary socialism*, round *communism*, for which the bourgeoisie has itself invented the name of *Blanqui*. This socialism is the *declaration of the permanence of the revolution*, the *class dictatorship* of the proletariat as the necessary transit point to the *abolition of class distinctions generally*, to the abolition of all the relations of production on which they rest, to the abolition of all the social relations that correspond to these relations of production, to the revolutionizing of all the ideas that result from these social relations. [Locus 1c.]

It is ironic that this, by Marx himself, is the only contemporary passage on record which links Blanqui's name with "dictatorship of the proletariat"! It is *Marx* who does the linking. Of course, he is not saying it is Blanqui's slogan; he is saying that the bourgeoisie has attached Blanqui's name to this revolutionary socialism, emphasizing the *class* character of the revolutionary regime.

We can now suggest why the term "dictatorship of the proletariat" makes its appearance *in connection with* the Blanquists but not *by* the Blanquists. Ordinarily Marx's expression for this idea was "rule of the proletariat," "political power of the working class," etc., as in the *Manifesto*. When, however, it is a question of counterposing this class concept to the Blanquist-type dictatorship, it is dressed in the formula "class dictatorship." Class dictatorship is then counterposed to Blanquist dictatorship.

In united fronts with the Blanquists, it was only such a class formula that could be acceptable to Marx. Such a united front was formed in early 1850 when Marx still considered a new revolutionary upsurge to be imminent. He set about developing a framework for joint action by revolutionary groups from various countries, an embryonic International, through representatives in London, including the left-wing Chartists around Harney, the Communist League of the German émigrés, and the French revolutionary refugees "who wanted to differentiate themselves from the bourgeois democrats [and therefore] usually called themselves Blanquist" (as Arthur Rosenberg puts it in *Democracy and Socialism*).

In April there was formed a Société Universelle des Communistes Révolutionnaires on the basis of a brief Programmatic Agreement signed by Marx, Engels, and August Willich for the Communist League, Harney, and two Blanquist émigrés. The constituent organizations retained their independence while joined in practical collaboration. Article 1 of the Agreement read:

The aim of the association is the downfall of all the privileged classes, to subject these classes to the dictatorship of the proletarians by maintaining the revolution in permanence until the achievement of communism, which is to be the last organizational from of the human family. [Locus 2.]

This is in Willich's handwriting, and perhaps the exact formulation is his too.

At the very same time that this agreement was made, Marx and Engels published in *NRZ-Revue* an open criticism of the Blanquist conspiratorial illusions which their French allies held, characterizing them as "forestalling the process of revolutionary development, pushing it artificially into crises, making a revolution on the spur of the moment without the conditions for a revolution. . . . They are the alchemists of the revolution," etc. This educational critique of Blanqu*ism*, at the very moment after they had entered into a united-front agreement with Blanqu*ists*, was a deliberate effort by Marx and Engels to utilize the new relationship to "straighten out" their allies, to influence their views.

While it is doubtful if the SUCR ever really got off paper in the first place, in any case it died for good after September, when Marx concluded that the revolutionary wave was spent and that reorientation toward a new period was necessary.

Marx's *Class Struggles in France* next evoked an echo within Germany. In Frankfurt, the *Neue Deutsche Zeitung* was coedited by Joseph Weydemeyer and Otto Lüning (who were also brothers-in-law). Weydemeyer had been a supporter and personal friend of Marx since 1845 and was anxious to publicize Marx's writings; Lüning was a sympathizer of the so-called "True Socialists." The *NDZ* in June carried a long review in four installments summarizing Marx's work, written by Lüning. In addition, in one critical passage Lüning put the spotlight on Marx's idea of "the revolutionary rule, the dictatorship of the working class" (Lüning's words). A transitional dictatorship was necessary, he agreed, yet "class rule is always an immoral and irrational state of affairs," and the aim should be "not the transference of rule from one class to the other but the abolition of class differences."

It should be noted that he did not direct any objection to the *Diktatur;* he was speaking of any *Klassenherrschaft*, any class rule. In the July 4 issue Marx had a brief letter to the editor *(Erklärung)*. [Locus 3.]

you reproached me with advocating the *rule and the dictatorship of the* working classes, while as against me you urge the *abolition of class differences generally*. I do not understand this correction.

You knew very well that *The Communist Manifesto* . . . says: [Here Marx quotes the same passage we referred to earlier.]

You know that I advocated the same view in *The Poverty of Philosophy* against Proudhon . . . [This refers to the last page or two of the book.]

Finally, the very same article which you criticize . . . says: [Here Marx quotes our Locus 1c.]

One of the interesting features of this communication is that Marx (like Lüning himself) is not aware of any special point, to be explained or defended, in the use of *Diktatur*. It does not seem to be a problem. The passage in the *Class Struggles* with its "dictatorship of the proletariat" is assimilated in his own mind with his formulations in *The Communist Manifesto* and elsewhere, confirming the oft-expressed view that the term "dictatorship of the proletariat" is to be equated with the *Manifesto's* formulation "rule of the proletariat."

That this exchange with Lüning centers not around "dictatorship" but the basic idea of working-class rule emerges clearly from Lüning's subjoined note on Marx's reply. He agrees that Marx's correction is "well-based." But he still complains that

Herr Marx himself, but even more his supporters, constantly put the accent on the *rule* of the class, the *abolition* of which they let peep out only reluctantly as a later concession. In contrast I wished to place the abolition in the foreground, as the goal and aim of the movement.

As far as Marx's passages are concerned, most particularly the one Lüning picked up, it is easy to dispose of his complaint, but more interesting is his side-blow against the "supporters" of Marx who put too great stress on the "rule." It is true that Lüning's petty-bourgeois socialism was naturally uneasy at any idea of working-class rule, whether in the foreground or background, but it is still interesting to see in his words a reference to that one of Marx's "supporters" who was his own coeditor and brother-in-law and with whom he had no doubt often discussed—namely, Weydemeyer.

Weydemeyer now becomes the link with the next locus, which is one of the two most often cited: Marx's letter to Weydemeyer of March 5, 1852. This is the one and only time that the term crops up in Marx's private correspondence. Why does it make its appearance at this time? There is an episode to be filled in.

After escaping from Germany and finally deciding to emigrate to America, Weydemeyer arrived in New York on November 7, 1851. The first article of his published in the U.S. (written in December) appeared in the January 1, 1852 issue of the New York *Turn-Zeitung*. Its title was "The Dictatorship of the Proletariat."

This is probably the only article with such a title until at least 1918. It is all the more interesting since the article is not really about the dictatorship of the proletariat for the most part. Most of it is a condensation of a good part of *The Communist Manifesto*. There is a reference to *die Diktatur des in den grossen Städten konzentrierten Proletariats* only in the last paragraph.

For present purposes the most important thing about Weydemeyer's article is simply its existence. Indications are that when Marx penned his famous letter of March 5 to Weydemeyer, he had just recently received the latter's own article on "The Dictatorship of the Proletariat."

This letter, moreover, is devoted to giving his friend suggestions for material for subsequent articles, in the course of which he advises on the treatment of certain American opponents. The reference to "dictatorship of the proletariat" comes in here. The next paragraph says: "From the foregoing notes take whatever you consider suitable." In other words, Marx has been jotting down notes to be used by Weydemeyer for his, Weydemeyer's, own articles.

What Marx wrote was that he did not claim credit for discovery of classes or the class struggle:

What I did that was new was to prove: 1) that the *existence of classes* is only bound up with *particular historical phases in the development of production*, 2) that the class struggle necessarily leads to the *dictatorship of the proletariat*, 3) that this dictatorship itself only constitutes the transition to the *abolition of all classes* and to a *classless society*. [Locus 4.]

In using "dictatorship of the proletariat" here, instead of his usual "rule of the proletariat," etc., Marx was echoing Weydemeyer, who himself was echoing Marx in 1850. Marx was throwing in a phrase that had special connotations and associations for his correspondent. His use of it in a private letter in passing depended on a certain amount of "understood" background. In this sense Weydemeyer was not just the recipient of the famous letter but its begetter.

For the next twenty years, no sign of the term appears in any writing, public or private, by Marx or Engels. (Or by anyone else, including Blanquists.)

During these decades there was little contact between Marx and the Blanquists; it is no accident that during these same two decades the term "dictatorship of the proletariat" does not show up. The Blanquists talked as usual about the revolutionary dictatorship of their band or of "Paris," and the Marxists talked as usual about the "rule of the proletariat" or "political power of the working class." What we have seen is that the term "dictatorship of the proletariat" as used by Marx is the reformulation of the latter when counterposed to the former.

When Marx wrote his great defense and analysis of the Paris Commune, *The Civil War in France*, he still had no contact with the Blanquists. The term "dictatorship of the proletariat" does not appear in his work. There are three features of it important for the rest of our story:

(1) Marx presents the Commune as "a working-class government . . . the political form at last discovered under which to work out the economical emancipation of labor." This and other formulations are so sweeping that a government so described must be, for Marx, that which he elsewhere called "dictatorship of the proletariat."

(2) What determined the character of the Commune, for Marx, was the *hegemony of the proletariat* in the revolution, that is, the fact that all the other class elements in the revolution looked to it as the vanguard and leader.

(3) At the same time, lengthy sections of *The Civil War in France* are devoted to painting in glowing colors the thoroughgoing *democratic* character of the Commune: universal suffrage, all officials and judges elective and revocable, abolition of the standing army, end of all "hierarchic investiture," depoliticalization of the police, communal democracy from below replacing the shattered centralized state, etc. All this Marx summed up by saying that the Commune "supplied the Republic with the basis of really democratic institutions . . . its special measures could but betoken the tendency of a government of the people by the people." (In contrast, the Blanquists regarded the Commune's democratic measures as a weakness and a mistake. The contrast between these two diametrically opposed analyses of Commune democracy was contained in *ovo* in the two different formulations on the "dictatorship.")

With the defeat of the Commune, the influx of Communards to London included many Blanquists and their leaders. Here for the first time many of them came into prolonged contact with Marx, his circle, and the General Council of the International. There was considerable impact on them for several reasons: the role of Marx's *Civil War in France* as a champion of the Commune in the eyes of the scandalized official world; Marx's massive relief work for the refugees; the addition of a number of Blanquists, especially Vaillant, to the General Council, working with Marx; the Blanquists' joint fight with Marx against the Bakunin faction; friendship with Marx's two French sons-in-law, Longuet and Lafargue.

For these reasons, and perhaps also because the experience of the Commune reinforced the same direction, the ideas of the London

Blanquists underwent a degree of "Marxification." Their political formulations were largely affected, if not their essential putschism. This was displayed especially in two programmatic statements they issued, in 1872 and in 1874, both of these containing references to "dictatorship of the proletariat."

Publicly as well as privately, Engels stated more than once during this period, rather exultingly, that the new Blanquist program had dressed itself in Marxist ideas. Once was in his *The Housing Question* (1872):

when the so-called Blanquists made an attempt to transform themselves from mere political revolutionists into a socialist workers' faction with a definite program—as was done by the Blanquist fugitives in London in their manifesto, *Internationale et Révolution* [1872]—they . . . adopted, and almost literally at that, the views of German scientific socialism on the necessity of political action by the proletariat and of its dictatorship as the transition to the abolition of classes and with them of the state—views such as had already been expressed in *The Communist Manifesto* and since then on innumerable occasions. [Locus 5a.]

Here we have Engels stating categorically and publicly that when the Blanquists (in London anyway) *did* use "dictatorship of the proletariat" for the first time in 1872, they took it from Marx, not the other way round as Postgate believed. Twice more in this period Engels described the "Marxification" of the London Blanquist program. Furthermore, the passage on "dictatorship of the proletariat" in the 1872 program *Internationale et Révolution* of the Blanquists virtually says itself that this is a new view for them "axiomatic since the 18th March," i.e., since the Paris Commune.

As for Marx and Engels: first use of the term *dictatorship of the proletariat* in this period is by Engels in his book *The Housing Question* (1872), originally three newspaper articles. The term occurs twice; we have already given Locus 5a. In the second passage Engels polemicizes against a Proudhonist as follows:

Friend Mülberger thus makes the following points here:

1. "We" do not pursue any "class policy" and do not strive for "class domination." But the German Social-Democratic Workers' Party, just *because* it is a *workers' party*, necessarily pursues a "class policy," the policy of the working class. Since each political party sets out to establish its rule in the state, so the German Social-Democratic Workers' Party is necessarily striving to establish *its* rule, the rule of the working class, hence "class domination." Moreover, *every* real proletarian party, from the English Chartists onward, has put forward a class policy, the organization of the proletariat as an independent political party, as the primary condition of its struggle, and the dictatorship

Here "dictatorship of the proletariat" is tossed in with the utmost casualness as a mere synonym for the conquest of political power.

Why did the term recur to Engels now, after a fifteen-year gap? Perhaps because he was already looking back at Marx's *Critique of the Gotha Program* in anticipation of the coming Erfurt party program discussion. For not long after, Engels proceeded to get Marx's 1875 critique published for the first time, with results leading to our next two (and last) loci.

Engels knew that its publication would be "a bomb" because of its attack on Lassalle, whose legend had grown. The target was also the rapidly developing opportunist trends in the party. On both scores there was indeed a violent reaction. One of the things that was seized on was the fact that the newly published document used the term *revolutionary dictatorship of the proletariat*. In the Reichstag itself, the social-democratic deputy Karl Grillenberger arose to repudiate Marx and say for the party that

the Social-Democratic party rejected the suggestion which Marx had made for its program. Marx was annoyed by the fact that the German Social-Democratic party has worked out its program as it thought fit in view of conditions in Germany, and that therefore for us any revolutionary dictatorship of the proletariat is out of the question.

The veneer of "Marxism" which lay over the top strata of the party had broken through. It is doubtful whether the good Reichstag deputy shuddered more over the word "dictatorship" or the word before it.

Eighteen days after, Engels finished his introduction to a new edition of Marx's *The Civil War in France*, the last words being "the dictatorship of the proletariat." This line of thought takes off from another attack (similar to Locus 7) on the Blanquist concept of "the strictest dictatorship, and centralization of all power in the hands of the new revolutionary government." In contrast Engels offers the Paris Commune, reviewing (as did Marx) its great expansion of democracy and control from below. Then follows a criticism of "the superstitious belief in the state" typical of Germany, and the need "to throw the entire lumber of the state on the scrap heap." Then the last paragraph:

Of late, the Social-Democratic philistine has once more been filled with wholesome terror at the words: Dictatorship of the proletariat. Well and good, gentlemen, do you want to know what this dictatorship looks like? Look at the Paris Commune. That was the dictatorship of the proletariat. [Locus 10.]

Three months later he had another "bomb" ready for the "Social-

Democratic philistines": a critique of the new draft program (Erfurt program). In this, as he wrote Kautsky, he "found an opportunity to let fly at the conciliatory opportunism of the Vorwärts [party organ] and at the *frisch-fromm-fröhlich-freie* 'growth' of the filthy old mess 'into socialist society.'"

Here Engels raises very sharply the question of the demand for the democratic republic, which had been omitted from the program. In the course of this he remarks:

One thing that is absolutely certain is that our party and the working class cannot achieve rule except under the form of the democratic republic. This latter is even the specific form of the dictatorship of the proletariat, as the Great French Revolution already showed. [Locus 11.]

True, he agrees, the program cannot openly come out for the democratic republic in so many words, but ways must be found to say as much:

... what in my opinion can and should go into the program is the demand for the *concentration of all political power in the hands of the representation of the people*. And that would be enough in the meantime, if one cannot go any further.

So "concentration of all power in the hands of the representation of the people" stands for the forbidden "democratic republic," and this in turn is "the specific form of the dictatorship of the proletariat." The advocate of that revolutionary dictatorship which perturbed the "Social-Democratic philistines" is arguing with them that they should hint at their goal of a democratic republic instead of adapting themselves to the kaiser regime's legality.

With this episode of 1891, prefiguring the future, comes to a close the story of the term *dictatorship of the proletariat*, as far as Marx and Engels are concerned. But of course, as we know, this is only the first chapter in the history of that phrase.

NOTE

[1] Of the 11 Marx-Engels loci on "dictatorship of the proletariat," Lenin's *State and Revolution* gave the ones here numbered 5a, 6, 8, 11, adding no. 4 in its second edition. Kautsky's reply pretended there was only one in Marx. Ernst Drahn, *Karl Marx und Fr. Engels über die Diktatur des Proletariats* (1920) knows only of loci 4, 8, 10. Max Beer's "An Inquiry into Dictatorship" *(Labour Monthly*, August 1922) mentions only 1a, 1c, 4, 6, 8, Sherman H. M. Chang's *Marxian Theory of the State* (1931) quotes 1a, 1c, 4, 5a, 6, 8—exactly one half the available passages, the most to date. The opposite record is held by Stanley W. Moore, *The Critique of Capitalist Democracy: Introduction to the Theory of the State in Marx, Engels, and Lenin* (1957), which never reveals that the term is to be found in Marx or Engels at all.

28

The Proletarian State

Robert Tucker

MARX and Engels thought the state would disappear in the higher phase of the communist society, but in the transitional lower phase of communist society—society as it would exist in the aftermath of proletarian revolution—the state would survive as a dictatorship of the working class. *The Communist Manifesto* thus speaks of the proletariat constituting itself as the ruling class. In *The Class Struggles in France*, written in 1850, Marx proclaimed "the class dictatorship of the revolution, the class dictatorship of the proletariat as the inevitable transit point to the abolition of class differences generally, to the abolition of all the productive relations on which they rest, to the abolition of all the social relations that correspond to these relations of production, to the revolutionizing of all the ideas that result from these social connections."[1] Returning to the theme in a letter of 1852 to Joseph Weydemeyer, Marx declared that "the class struggle necessarily leads to the dictatorship of the proletariat" and that "this dictatorship itself constitutes only the transition to the *abolition* of all classes and to a *classless society*."[2] Finally in his unpublished notes of 1875 on the Gotha Program, Marx wrote: "Between capitalist and communist society lies the period of the revolutionary transformation of the one into the other. There corresponds to this also a political transition period in which the state can be nothing but *the revolutionary dictatorship of the proletariat*."[3]

The doctrine of proletarian dictatorship is undoubtedly an integral part of classical Marxism and its political theory. On the other hand, Marx and Engels were not inclined to go into detail on this theme and left

FROM "Marx as a Political Theorist," in N. Lobkowicz (ed.), *Marx and the Western World*, University of Notre Dame Press (Notre Dame, 1967), pp. 338–343.

it somewhat unclear how they concretely envisaged the future proletarian dictatorship. This paved the way for later Marxist controversy over the question. Although diverse schools of Marxist thought have recognized the doctrine of the proletarian dictatorship as an inalienable part of Marxism, they have differed, at times very deeply and bitterly, over the amount of importance to be attached to it and the proper interpretation to be placed upon it. Indeed, the theoretical and practical question of what the proletarian dictatorship would and should look like in practice, and the related question of what the founders believed on the point, directly underlay the great schism of 1917 and after between orthodox Social Democratic Marxism and the Communist Marxism of Lenin and his followers. The issue was whether or not the latter were acting as good Marxists in setting up the Soviet one-party state and calling it a Marxist "dictatorship of the proletariat." In an effort to prove in advance that this would be a valid Marxist action, Lenin in the summer of 1917 wrote *The State and Revolution*, his principal contribution to Marxist political theory. The doctrinal conflict was joined when the German Social Democratic leader Karl Kautsky published a Marxist criticism of the Bolshevik Revolution in his pamphlet of August, 1918, *The Dictatorship of the Proletariat*, to which Lenin later responded with *The Proletarian Revolution and the Renegade Kautsky*.

In attacking the Russian Bolsheviks on Marxist grounds for setting up a dictatorial regime and ruling by force and violence in the name of the proletariat, Kautsky contended that democracy and Marxist socialism were inseparable. A Marxist dictatorship of the proletariat would not be a dictatorship in the "literal sense" of suspension of democracy and rule by a single person. Rather it would be class rule by the proletariat and, as such, it would be majority rule according to the generally accepted democratic procedures and with full protection of minorities. In the proletarian context, therefore, the term "dictatorship" was to be understood in a Pickwickian sense as referring *not* to a form of government but rather to "a condition which must everywhere arise when the proletariat has conquered political power," namely, the condition of proletarian "sovereignty" in a society composed of the majority of proletarians. Moreover to prove that this was the Marx-Engels' viewpoint as well as his own, Kautsky cited Marx's description in *The Civil War in France* of the Paris Commune as a polity that abolished a standing army and state officialdom and operated on the basis of general suffrage and citizen rotation in elective public office. Had not Marx himself called the Commune an essentially working-class government? And had not Engels, in his preface to a twentieth-anniversary edition of Marx's famous pamphlet, expressly held up the Commune as the first example of dictatorship of the proletariat?[4]

Testimony could thus be found for a Social Democratic interpretation of the founders' views on the proletarian dictatorship. Marx did portray the Commune as a libertarian new order and hailed it as "the political form at last discovered under which to work out the economic emancipation of labor."[5] Nor was this the only evidence in support of the Kautskyan case. *The Communist Manifesto* had, after all, described the predicted future establishment for proletarian class rule as the "winning of democracy" *(Erkämpfung der Demokratie)*. Much later in his criticism of the draft of the Erfurt Program of the German Social Democratic Party, Engels wrote that the working class could only come to power under the form of the democratic republic and added: "this is even the specific form for the dictatorship of the proletariat, as the great French revolution has already shown."[6]

Yet the Kautskyan interpretation of the founders' position was ultimately shaky and unconvincing, for it ignored important conflicting evidence. The very words of Engels just quoted show the untenability of Kautsky's view that Marx and Engels conceived the proletarian dictatorship not as a form of government but as a "condition" only. They saw it as the final form that the state was destined to take in history. And Engels' reference to the French revolution in this context is only one of many indications that the political *content* of the proletarian dictatorship, even within the frame of a democratic republic, was envisaged in a very different manner from Kautsky's as described above. There is adequate evidence to show that when Marx and Engels spoke of the future proletarian dictatorship, they were not using the term "dictatorship" in a merely Pickwickian sense but literally. It is true that they offered no such general definition of the term as Lenin's according to which "Dictatorship is rule based directly upon force and unrestricted by any laws." Nor were they as explicit on the applicability of the general formula to the case of the proletarian state as Lenin was when he added: "The revolutionary dictatorship of the proletariat is rule won and maintained by the use of violence by the proletariat against the bourgeoisie, rule that is unrestricted by any laws."[7] Yet this appears to have been the direction of their thinking.

One of the indications of it is their critical reaction to the draft Gotha Program's call for a "free people's state." They objected to the idea that a "free state" should be a stated goal of the workers' party in Germany and did so on the explicit ground that a proletarian state could no more be a free one than any other form of state could. "As, therefore, the state is only a transitional institution which is used in the struggle, in the revolution, in order to hold down one's adversaries by force," declared Engels in his letter of March 18-28, 1875, to Bebel about the draft Program, so "it is pure nonsense to talk of a free people's state: so long as the proletariat still *uses* the state, it does not use it in the interests of freedom but in order to hold down its adversaries, and as soon as it becomes possible to speak of freedom the state as such ceases to exist."[8] Like all previous historical forms of the state, the proletarian state was looked upon by the founders of Marxism as an instrumentality of class struggle, a means of "holding down" a class in society, a repressive force. Nor did they shrink, even in their mature years, from the corollary that the revolutionary dictatorship of the proletariat would have to resort to the weapon of terror. Engels insisted on the need for a revolution to maintain itself in power by means of terror and criticized the Communards of 1871 for not having done so resolutely enough. Could the Commune have lasted a single day, he inquired, without resorting to the "authority of the armed people" against the bourgeoisie? And: "Should we not, on the contrary, reproach it for not having used it freely enough?"[9] Marx, stating in a letter of 1881 that the majority of the Commune was in no sense socialist, made clear what, in his view, a genuinely socialist government should be prepared to do on assuming power: "One thing you can at any rate be sure of: a socialist government does not come into power in a country unless conditions are so developed that it can above all take the necessary measures for intimidating the mass of the bourgeoisie sufficiently to gain time—the first *desideratum*—for lasting action."[10]

All this speaks against one further argument that has been adduced in favor of the Social Democratic exegesis of classical Marxism on the proletarian dictatorship. The argument holds that the thinking of Marx and Engels underwent a democratic evolution over the years, that they moved from a youthful Blanquist tendency or Jacobinism in 1848 and its aftermath to a mature outlook that was sober, moderate, and genuinely democratic. According to the Russian Menshevik leader Martov, for example, Marx and Engels originally conceived the idea of proletarian dictatorship in the late 1840s under the influence of the Jacobin tradition of 1793, with its minority political dictatorship and the Terror. But later, as Marx and Engels became convinced that conscious support of the majority of the population was required for a socialist revolution, their conception of the proletarian dictatorship lost its Jacobin content and they envisaged proletarian class rule "only in the forms of a total democracy."[11]

The weakness of this line of argument is clear from testimony already cited above. Although the mature Marx and Engels were not the flaming revolutionists that they had been in their youth, they remained faithful to the Marxian revolutionary idea and vision. It is true that they envisaged proletarian rule as a majoritarian dictatorship, but also, as we have just had occasion to observe, that democratic protection of the rights of the class minority was no part of their image of it. In their later as well as their earlier years, they saw the class rule of the proletariat as essentially a regime of revolution (a "class dictatorship of the revolution," as Marx had called it). They took it for granted that as such it would have bourgeois class enemies whom the government of the proletarian majority would have to deal with—and in their view ought to deal with—by forcible means, not excluding terror. The proletarian government, like every other, would be repressive in nature.

Lenin was on strong textual ground in emphasizing this point in the controversy with Social Democratic Marxism, but that is not to say that his exegesis of the doctrine of proletarian dictatorship was correct in all details or even in all essentials. If Kautsky unduly deprecated the significance of this doctrine in classical Marxism, Lenin unquestionably exaggerated it. Not content with saying in *The State and Revolution* that to be a genuine Marxist one had to accept not only the class struggle but also the proletarian dictatorship as its outcome, he subsequently asserted that the conception of proletarian dictatorship was "the essence of Marx's doctrine" and "sums up the whole of his revolutionary teaching."[12] This was to blow up one important part of Marx's thought out of all true proportion. Furthermore if Kautsky overly "democratized" Marx's notion of the proletarian dictatorship, Lenin too construed it in a manner that Marx had not foreseen. There is nothing, for example, to indicate that Marx conceived the proletarian state as party-state, a dictatorship of a single party ruling, or claiming to rule, *on behalf* of the proletariat. Nor did he picture it in Leninist fashion as a form of polity destined to endure through an entire historical epoch of transition to communism, for the transition itself was understood in different terms. Precisely because the proletarian state would be a regime of the immense majority in an advanced society, a majority in the process of abolishing private property and therewith the division of labor in production, it would soon lose its repressive *raison d'être* and wither away. As a "dictatorship of the revolution," it would have a short life at the close of man's prehistory. Such, at any rate, is the belief that Marx and Engels seem to have entertained.

NOTES

1 *MEW*, VII, 88; cf. *Selected Works*, vol. I, p. 223.
2 *Selected Works*, vol. II, p. 452.
3 *MEW*, XIX, 28; cf. *Selected Works*, vol. II, p. 32ff.
4 *The Dictatorship of the Proletariat*, pp. 30, 43-44, 46.
5 *MEW*, XVII, 342; cf. *Selected Works*, vol. I, p. 522.
6 Marx and Engels, *Selected Correspondence 1846–1895* (New York, 1942), p. 486.

[7]   Lenin, *Selected Works*, vol. II, p. 365.

[8]   *Selected Works*, vol. II, p. 42.

[9]   *MEW*, XVIII, 308; cf. *Selected Works*, vol. I, p. 638.

[10] Marx to Domela Nieuwenhuis, February 22, 1881, *Selected Correspondence*, p. 386.

[11] J. Martov, *The State and the Socialist Revolution* (New York, 1939), pp. 57, 63. The lingering influence of this line of argument in present-day Marx scholarship in the West is to be seen in George Lichtheim, *Marxism: An Historical and Critical Survey* (New York, 1961).

[12] Lenin, *Selected Works*, vol. II, p. 362. For the passage referred to in *The State and Revolution*, see *ibid.*, p. 163.

The Future of the State

WHETHER or not the transitional stage from capitalism to socialism was to be the dictatorship of the proletariat, the ultimate need, according to Marxist theory, was the elimination of the state, an aim which Marx and Engels shared with the anarchists they so frequently criticized. In Marxism, forms of the state, like legal relationships, are rooted in the material conditions of life. The state in a capitalist system was not an abstract entity but an organ attending to the life of bourgeois society. It was defined as "the total of the functions protecting bourgeois society and its foundation in private property." As in all other previous systems, the state was the instrument of class domination; in capitalism, it was the agent of the bourgeoisie.

But in the future classless society there would be no need for a special organ which was the means of coercion by which the ruling class oppressed the other classes. "Even the radical and revolutionary politicians," wrote Marx, "look for the source of the evil, not in the nature of the State, but in a particular form of the state which they want to replace by another form." Marx and Engels held that oppressive political power and coercion, embodied by the state, would no longer be needed in the socialist society. After the proletarian revolution the state could wither away because the proletariat would be mature and capitalism would have developed all the productive forces for which there was room.

As late as the spring of 1917, Lenin in *The State and Revolution* thought of administration in a future regime as a relatively simple matter, and looked forward to the withering away of the state. But since capture of power by the Bolsheviks in 1917 the role of the state has been increased and its power enhanced. The problem for the Soviet

(303)

Union has always been to explain this heightened power; the reasons have included exterminating the bourgeois opponents, liquidating internal dissenters and would-be wreckers of the Communist state, developing industry and agriculture, and defense against the encirclement of the Soviet Union by the capitalist countries.

The ultimate paradox of the attempt to maintain the original doctrine while exerting strong power was illustrated by the formulation of Stalin in his 1930 Report to the Sixteenth Congress of the Communist Party: "We stand for the withering away of the state. At the same time we stand for the strengthening of the dictatorship of the proletariat, which is the mightiest and strongest state power that has ever existed. . . . Is this contradictory? Yes . . . but this contradiction is bound up with life, and it fully reflects Marx's dialectics."

The article by Calvin Hoover illustrates this theoretical problem in Marxism. George Brinkley assesses the attempt made by Khrushchev while in power to reformulate the concept of the withering away of the state, to reduce some of the Stalinist rigidity, and to take some steps to decentralize power.

29

The Soviet State Fails to Wither

Calvin B. Hoover

ONE could hardly imagine a less sensational headline than the title of this article. . . . In Russia is a state whose ruler has greater and more un-limited power than has the premier, president, or monarch of any other modern country. The state controls a greater range of human activity than any before in history. It has none of the traditional safeguards for control of the government by the people. No parliamentary opposition to the regime has ever existed. There is no protection for the individual in the courts against the arbitrary power of the state. There is an immense police force to insure internal control. The government has one of the greatest and most powerful armies of all time at its disposal. Surely it must be pure insanity to contemplate the possibility of the withering away of the Soviet state!

In the face of the complete contradiction between doctrine and reality, however, the orthodox Marxist dogma of the disappearance of the state under Communism has never been abandoned by the Communist Party. On the contrary, after a lull during the war and the immediate postwar period, the doctrine is once more the occasion of discussion and official statements of policy. . . .

One must ask why these articles appear at all, and why they appear at this time? Why is there interest in a subject which seems to have so little to do with actuality? Indeed, why do the rulers of the Soviet state allow this subject to be mentioned, since it would seem to be so em-barrassing to them? The answer must be found, in the first instance, in the impossibility of divorcing a system of political power completely

FROM *Foreign Affairs*, 31 (October 1952), pp. 114–127.

from its ideological foundations, however fully the government controls the instruments of coercion and propaganda. . . .

That the Soviet state should have its ideological origins in Marx's and Engels' doctrine that any and all states are instruments of class domination and that when a truly Communist society had been attained the state would have wholly "withered away" is one of the most fantastic contradictions in the history of human institutions. . . .

It is easy to understand why the doctrine that there can be a society which has none of the coercive powers of the state was essential to the Marxian concept of Communism. It seemed perfectly obvious to Marx that the existence of the capitalistic system depended upon the police power of the state, which protected the property rights of capitalists and guaranteed the functioning of a system of exchange which enabled the capitalist to extract his "surplus value" from the labor of the proletariat. Marxian Communists have been at one with the Anarchists in their designation of the capitalistic state as an instrument of exploitation which must be destroyed. It is not so generally understood, however, that their agreement with the Anarchists about the fundamentally undesirable nature of the state did not stop here. It is still orthodox Marxism, Leninism, and even Stalinism that any form of the state is to be tolerated only temporarily, and that when Communism has been attained there is to be no state.

This doctrine of a society without a state has served Marxists as a device to avoid a fundamental answer to the question of who is to run the state after capitalism has been destroyed. Why should it be reasonable to expect that the rulers of a collectivist society would operate a state more in the interests of the whole population, and less in their own interests, than have the rulers of bourgeois states? Through their theory of the withering away of the state Marxists can deny that the question has reality, for they blandly assert that under Communism there is to be no state at all.

Of course, they say, a purely temporary caretaker's state has to be set up by the proletariat. For would not the capitalists, even if once overthrown, re-establish the bourgeois state if there were no counter force to prevent this? Lenin claims that Marx and Engels foresaw precisely this difficulty. Consequently, he explains, in his *State and Revolution*, "the particular power of suppression of the proletariat by the capitalist class . . . must be replaced by a particular power of suppression of the capitalist class by the proletariat (the dictatorship of the proletariat)."

How long was this new state, embodying the dictatorship of the proletariat, to last? On the eve of the October Revolution, Lenin maintained that "the particular power of suppression of the capitalist class by the proletariat (the dictatorship of the proletariat)" was to begin to wither away on the morrow of victory; "the proletariat, according to Marx, needs only a withering away State—a State, that is, so constituted that it begins to wither away immediately and cannot but wither away. . . ." He goes on to say in another passage, "How can we otherwise pass on to the discharge of all the functions of Government by the majority of the population and by every individual of the population?" And still further along he says, "the great majority of the functions of 'the old State' have become enormously simplified and reduced, in practice, to very simple operations such as registration, filing, and checking. Hence they will be quite within the reach of every literate person, and it will be possible to perform them for the usual 'working man's wage.'"

By this device of the "temporariness" of the Soviet state, by the use of the amorphous phrase "dictatorship of the proletariat," and by a grotesque underestimate of the complexities and difficulties of administering a collectivist type of economy, Lenin evaded answering the problem crucial to all organized forms of human society—"How is the minority of men from a given society which is to rule the majority of the population to be selected, and how can this minority be prevented from developing into a tyranny?" Lenin simply took as axiomatic the right of the Central Committee of the Bolsheviks under his leadership to wield unlimited power in the name of the dictatorship of the proletariat. Neither Lenin nor Stalin felt the necessity of testing the validity of their mandate to wield this power by submitting to an election, the freedom of which could be guaranteed by any of the standard devices developed in democratic societies of the West.

The thoroughness and ruthlessness with which the Bolsheviks destroyed the organization of industry, the civil government, and the armed forces of their Tsarist predecessors—by definition the instruments of the bourgeois exploiters—embarrassed Lenin, Trotsky, and their colleagues and successors not at all in their task of erecting a new state power. The death penalty for infractions of discipline was reinstituted and used more freely in the Red Army than it had been in the Tsarist Army. It had to be, since the bulk of its soldiers had to be reclaimed from the dissolved masses of the old army. No one has ever expressed more succinctly the final basis upon which the discipline of armies rests than did Trotsky, in his reference in *My Life* to the task of creating discipline in the Red Army during this period: "So long as those malicious tailless apes . . . the animals that we call men—will build armies and wage wars, the command will always be obliged to place the soldiers between possible death at the front and the inevitable one in the rear."

The restoration of industrial discipline was not so simple. The application of the principle of "single responsibility and authority of the manager" was limited, so long as the managing personnel was still largely inherited from the old regime. As Soviet-trained personnel gradually took over industry, however, and the former managing personnel retired, or were otherwise liquidated, respect for authority was enforced with the same ruthlessness in this sphere of state power as in the armed forces. . . .

The coercive powers of the Soviet state are not and never were reserved for use against the former ruling class, as Marxian doctrine forecast. The Soviet state may determine the kind of work an individual has to do and the place where it must be done. Organs of the state determine wage rates, piece-work rates, and working conditions without benefit of collective bargaining by labor unions. Labor discipline is sternly enforced with the aid of the labor unions, themselves organs of the state. The state and not the workers in any plant appoints the plant management. All this is well known. In large part it is entirely logical, and perhaps indeed inevitable, in the organization and operation of a fully collectivist economy. It well illustrates the fallacy of the claim of Marxist theorists that the operation of the economy involves the administration "not of men but of things."

From the earliest times the Soviet state has never hesitated to employ extreme violence against any individuals or groups, regardless of class origin, whom it decided at the moment to designate as "enemies of the people." There are few more pathetic documents than the appeals issued by the Kronstadt sailors, in 1921, when they had set up their own Soviet. Trotsky had earlier referred to the Kronstadt sailors as "the pride and glory of the Revolution," but now he put them down with heavy slaughter, using the armed forces of the Soviet Government.

When the masses of the peasant population resisted collectivization in 1929–30 with desperate determination, their leaders, and even ordinary peasants, were treated with no greater tenderness than the *kulaki* themselves. They were often dispossessed and exiled en masse to the northern territories or to the steppes of Central Asia. Hundreds certainly, thousands probably, were shot on various charges of resistance to the state. Later, when the peasants in 1932 tried to sabotage collectivization by a kind of passive resistance, hundreds of thousands in the Ukraine and elsewhere were allowed to die of famine by an administrative decision of the Soviet Government. Almost every conceivable semantic device has been employed at various times to represent the current victims of the coercive powers of the state as class enemies. When peasants who resisted collectivization could not possibly be called *kulaki,* they were referred to as *podkulachestvo,* "group under *kulak* influence."

In the great purge which began in 1935 following the assassination of Kirov and continuing through 1938, proletarian or peasant origin or record of service during the Revolution or Civil War offered no protection to Soviet citizens against the executioner. Not only were scores of well-known Bolshevik leaders like Kamenev, Zinoviev, and Bukharin liquidated. So also died Dibenko, a sailor who had played a great role in the revolutionary seizure of the Baltic fleet during the October Revolution and had been the leader in quelling the revolt of the sailors of Kronstadt against the Bolsheviks. So died Antonov-Ovseenko, who had planned and led the attack against the Winter Palace which was the final act in the overthrow of the Kerensky Government. So perished countless "Old Bolsheviks," some of whom had fought at the barricades in the Revolution of 1905 and many more of whom had played heroic roles in the Civil War. The record is clear and the evidence overwhelming. The "temporary" dictatorship of the proletariat has produced the most totalitarian state of modern times. As Stalin stated in the Political Report of the Central Committee to the Sixteenth Congress, 1930:

We are for the withering away of the state, while at the same time we stand for strengthening the dictatorship of the proletariat which represents the most potent and mighty of all the state authorities that have existed down to this time. The highest development of state authority to the end of making ready the conditions for the withering away of state authority: there you have the Marxist formula!

How has it been possible thus to put off, decade after decade, any application of the doctrine which was so fundamental to the thinking of Marx and Engels, which Lenin himself embraced and to which Stalin finds it necessary now and again to pay homage? How has it been possible to reconcile this failure of the state to wither at all both with current Communist doctrine and with actual events?

The concept of the withering away of the state is only one phase of the theory of the mature Communist society. The doctrine of the withering away of the state consequently has had to be integrated with the whole theory of the way the present Soviet system relates to the future ideal Communist society. According to the official doctrine, the present Soviet system already represents a fully Socialistic economic and social system. Private ownership of the means of production has ceased to exist and the exploiting classes have "long ago" been liquidated. There exists only one class, divided, it is true, into those who work with their hands and the intelligentsia who work with their brains. If it were not for the continued existence of capitalistic countries with which war is a constant likelihood, so the theory goes, the full realization of the Communist society would await, at most, only a few more decades of increase in the production of consumption goods; then the present system of distribution according to productivity would become distribution according to need.

The need to rationalize the extraordinary contradiction between the doctrine of the withering away of the state and the actuality of the Soviet apparatus of government—"the most potent and mighty authority of all the state authorities that have existed down to this time" —thus gives official Soviet theorists no rest. Lenin, even though he continues to maintain that the state would begin immediately to wither away after the seizure of power in the name of the proletariat, confronted in August 1917 by the actual tasks of seizing and holding power, began in his *State and Revolution* the process of rationalizing the contradictions between the Soviet state as he visualized it after the triumph of the dictatorship of the proletariat and the ideal Communistic society. This he did by formulating the concept of two stages of Communism. According to Lenin, it was only in the second stage that the ideal Communist society would come into existence.

During the first stage, which Lenin called Socialism in contrast to the Communism of the second stage, the state was to continue to exist as the instrument of the dictatorship of the proletariat even though it would begin to wither away. Distribution would be according to productivity, instead of according to need, as it was to be under Communism. The population during this first stage would have to undergo the process of cultural re-education essential to entrance into the ideal Communist society.

Stalin still further developed the concept of stages. In his report to the Eighteenth Party Congress in 1939, he described the stages which he considered finished.

Since the time of the October Revolution our Socialist state has passed through two principal phases in its development: (a) the first phase is the period from the October Revolution down to the liquidation of the exploiter classes, and (b) the second phase is the period from the liquidation of the capitalist elements, urban and rural, down to the complete triumph of the Socialist system of economy and the adoption of the new Constitution.

He went on to speak of the then current stage:

Accordingly, the functions of our Socialist state have changed as well. The function of military suppression within the country has subsided and died out, for the reason that exploitation has been annihilated and exploiters have ceased to exist and there is no one to suppress. In place of the function of suppression, the state has come to possess the function of safeguarding Socialist property from thieves and pillagers of the property of the people.

The function of the military defense of the country against attacks from without has been preserved in its entirety. . . . The function of economic coordination and cultural education by state organs also has remained and received full development. . . .

Development cannot, however, pause at this point . . . we are advancing further: to Communism. Will the state be preserved among us likewise during the period of Communism as well? Yes, it will be preserved unless capitalist encirclement shall have been liquidated and the danger of military attacks from without eliminated; of course the forms of our state will change once again with a change of the internal and external setting. No, it will not be preserved and will wither away if capitalist encirclement shall have been liquidated and replaced by Socialist encirclement.

This statement made by Stalin in 1939 outlines the two major elements in the party line which are reiterated in the Glaeserman article in *Izvestia* and in all the recent pronouncements which deal with aspects of the withering away of the state or the attainment of the ideal Communist society. On the one hand, the failure of the state to disappear is explained on the ground that the essential preconditions to the establishment of a Communist society—first in the necessity for the liquidation of the domestic exploiting class, then the necessity for going through the stage of Socialism, and finally the necessity for the replacement of capitalist encirclement by Socialist encirclement—must all be gone through. On the other hand, a complicated system of semantics is relied upon to demonstrate that the Soviet system is steadily developing into the ideal Communist society. Glaeserman says:

In the second phase of development of the Socialist state, after the liquidation of the capitalist elements of town and countryside, the function of military suppression within the country withered away. It was replaced, as Comrade Stalin points out, by a new function, the function of protecting Socialist property from thieves and embezzlers of the public wealth. . . . The function of the economic organizational and cultural educational work of the state agencies was fully developed and became the basic activity of the state inside the country. . . . The transition was made from restricted suffrage to unrestricted suffrage, from not quite equal suffrage to absolutely equal suffrage, from indirect to direct elections, from open to secret balloting, all of which marked a further development of the Socialist democracy. . . . This also meant a further strengthening of the Socialist state as a mighty instrument in the hands of the working people in their struggle for the victory of Communism.

Thus Soviet theorists endeavor to resolve the paradox of the steady growth in the power of the state at a time when it should be withering away by the representation, totally contrary to reality, of a diminutior in the coercive character of the state, and an equally unreal representation of an increase in the control over the state by the people.

One of the attributes of state power through the ages has been the perquisites which its wielders have claimed as compensation for their pains. Power itself is, of course, the most valued of all perquisites. The more absolute the role of coercion in the operation of the state apparatus the more welcome is the possession of authority. Yet it is rare when power is accepted by the ruling class as the sole coin of payment. During the first decade of Soviet rule, nevertheless, efforts were made to limit the financial compensations of members of the Communist Party. As late as 1930, for example, a Party member could not retain for himself more than 500 rubles per month. It is true that compensation in kind for state and Party officials, such as better living quarters, the right to a car and a chauffeur, and the like rendered this limitation illusory even then. It has long ago been dispensed with; the ethics of austerity are no longer honored. The principle of higher pay for higher productivity, and for responsibility and position in the hierarchy, is accepted as fully as in capitalistic countries. It has been extended to members of the Party as well as to the whole of the "intelligentsia"—the term now used whenever the Soviet rulers feel the necessity of explaining and defending the privileges of their class.

While the Communist doctrine of "from each according to his ability, to each according to need" has never been repudiated as a goal, what is known, quaintly enough, by the contemptuous phrase of "bourgeois leveling" is often savagely attacked. It is assiduously argued that those who produce more, and who occupy more responsible posts, have greater needs; thus it does not conflict with Marxian doctrine that they should have greater rewards. As Stepanyan quotes Stalin: "Marxism proceeds from the fact that people's tastes and needs are not and cannot be identical and equal either in the period of Socialism or Communism. There you have the Marxist understanding of equality. Marxism has not recognized and does not recognize any other kind of equality. It is time to learn that Marxism is the enemy of wage leveling." In other words, it is very possible that if the Soviet rulers some day announce that the Soviet Union has become a fully Communist society, the present great inequalities in compensation will continue.

It is interesting to note that in the *Izvestia* article Glaeserman also elaborates Stalin's declaration that the state must be retained even under Communism if the threat of capitalist encirclement still exists. He says:

The Soviet Union is no longer isolated today; both to East and West its neighbors are countries that have been freed from the yoke of imperialism. However, it does not follow that the political concept of capitalist encirclement has lost its meaning. Comrade Stalin teaches that "capitalist encirclement cannot be viewed as a mere geographical concept." *The frontiers of the capitalist world have been pushed further away from the Soviet Union, but this world still exists and consequently the threat of a military attack on the U.S.S.R. still exists.* (Italics supplied by the writer.)

Stalin had put it even more flatly when he said that the Soviet state would not wither away until "capitalist encirclement shall have been eliminated and replaced by Socialist encirclement." Glaeserman also dutifully weaves in the needed counterpoint by reciting the educational and cultural achievements of the Soviet state, which are supposedly laying the foundations for the ideal Communist society. But he returns to the main theme at the end: "The works of the great theoretician of Marxian-Leninism, Comrade Stalin, light the road to Communism, arm the people ideologically and teach us to look constantly to further strengthening of the Socialist state—mighty weapon in the struggle for Communism."

All the current writers follow Stalin in developing the position staked out by Lenin that all the functions of planning and administering the whole economy may be carried on by a bureaucracy, however large, without there being any state at all. It is further claimed that neither the administration of the criminal law by the present Soviet state nor its administration in a fully Communist society, by which men are punished for crimes of violence, theft, and the like, really represents the functioning of the state.

Even Pashukanis, one of the principal authors of the Soviet Constitution of 1936, who believed that law as well as the state itself would have withered away when a Communist society had been attained, admitted that "certain crimes against personality and so forth will not disappear." He maintained that such crimes should be regarded "*per se* as a task of medical pedagogy." In 1937 Pashukanis was denounced as an "enemy of the people" and disappeared. One wonders whether the type of "crime" for which he presumably forfeited his life would be prevalent in an ideal Communist society and whether its treatment would in such a case be considered a "task of medical pedagogy" rather than as a task for the secret police.

The argument is hardly compatible with the doctrine that crime is the product of capitalism but it does illustrate the incredible convenience of Marxian terminology in solving political, economic, and social problems. By definition the state is an instrument of class oppression. By definition class oppression has disappeared. Hence the state disappears as well, even though the functions carried on by the bourgeois state and other enormously important added functions are still to be carried on. The contradictions between the present Soviet system and the ideal Marxian Communist society are in essence the same as those between the present Soviet system and anything which non-Marxian Socialist philosophers of the nineteenth century would have considered a Socialist society. There is nothing in Marxian doctrine, any more than there is in any other socialistic philosophy, which would justify the personal dictatorship of Stalin, accompanied as it is by truly oriental adulation. There is nothing which would foreshadow the current Red Army, with its measures to maintain discipline far more severe than those of any army of a modern capitalist country, with privileges and authority of the officer class over common soldiers proportionately great, paralleled by a corresponding system of privileges for the whole ruling class, civil as well as military. There is nothing which could justify or explain the employment of extremes of violence by the Soviet state against masses of the population who could by no stretch of the imagination be considered members of the former exploiting classes. . . .

The power of the Soviet state, reflected in a government not of law but of men, has, of course, continued to grow. There have been periods of some relaxation in the repressive power of the state over men. After the wholesale deportation of the *kulaki* in the very early thirties, accompanied by some of the early public spectacle trials, there was a relaxation of perhaps a year until the assassination of Kirov in late 1934. Then the terror was resumed and was continued into 1938 with a ferocity not shown since the days of the Cheka during the Civil War. When Russia entered the Second World War, the coercive powers of the state were still further extended. . . .

It is profoundly significant that the one considerable period of relaxation of the terror and of the powers of the state in general was during the time of the New Economic Policy. It is wholly logical that this time of temporary retreat toward capitalism, from 1921 to 1928, should have been such a period, for the minimization of state power is fundamental to capitalism. By contrast, the immense mass of evidence in the Soviet experience supports the conclusion that any fully collectivist society which is the product of revolution is certain to expand the power of the state over men almost without limit. Once this power has been established, it is unlikely to contract unless by another revolution.

30

The "Withering" of the State
Under Khrushchev

George A. Brinkley

The Theoretical Background

. . . IN THE classics of Marxism the state was viewed as a super-structural by-product of an economic base geared to exploitation, to be destroyed as a result of the outcome of the class struggle in the victory of the revolutionary proletariat. This was so because the state, it was held, was the instrument of coercion in the hands of the ruling class, designed, with all its accoutrements in the form of police, armed forces, courts, laws, etc., to keep that class in power and to exploit the un-propertied working masses. While the revolutionary overthrow of capitalism by the latter would immediately take the form of a dictatorship of the proletariat for purposes of destroying the opposition and facil-itating the transition to socialism (or communism), the direct aim of the temporary dictatorship was to be the abolition of coercion and exploitation and therefore the abolition of the instrument which made such possible, the state. As the *Manifesto* declared, "Political power, properly so called, is merely the organized power of one class for op-pressing another." Therefore:

When, in the course of development, class distinctions have disappeared, and all production has been concentrated in the hands of a vast association of the whole nation, the public power will lose its political character. [1]

This view of the fate of the state machinery after the revolution envisaged the assumption of all of the necessary functions of public organization by the people themselves, by society. Since man was

FROM *The Review of Politics*, 23 (January 1961), pp. 37–51.

conceived of as a good creature enslaved and corrupted by bad social organization, chiefly an unjust economic order, the reforming of the social order would mean the liberation of man not only from exploitation but from evil itself. The establishment of a communal order would spell the end of the very causes of social problems and thus the need for coercion to enforce proper behavior.

The "withering away" of the state, as this concept came to be called, was given its classical expression by Engels in the following statement from his *Anti-Dühring*:

As soon as there is no longer any class of society to be held in subjection; as soon as, along with class domination and the struggle for individual existence based on the anarchy of production hitherto, the collisions and excesses arising from these have also been abolished, there is nothing more to be repressed which would make a special repressive force, a state, necessary. . . . The interference of the state power in social relations becomes superfluous in one sphere after another, and then ceases of itself. The government of persons is replaced by the administration of things and the direction of the processes of production. The state is not "abolished," it *withers away*.[2]

As the chief interpreter of Marxism for the Russian Bolsheviks, Lenin embraced this formula of Engels with the moving passion of a revolutionary idealist. He dramatically foresaw the day when the armed people would replace armies and police, when every baker would be as capable of such duties as a minister of state. His faith in the ultimate truth of the idea, "good man: bad social order," is illustrated in his comment upon withering: "The expression, 'the state withers away,' is well chosen, since it indicates both the gradualness of the process and its elemental nature." According to Lenin, people by habit "become accustomed to the observance of the rules of society necessary for them, if there is no exploitation or nothing of the sort that would evoke protest and rebellion or create the necessity of suppression."[3]

Without at all renouncing the ideal, Lenin was, however, also the practical revolutionary leader who immediately added a word of caution to any who might forget the essential union between theory and reality. He warned that "during the *transition* from capitalism to communism suppression is *still* necessary . . . ," although the situation in this case is not the same as that under capitalism. The special apparatus, the machine for suppression, is still necessary, but it is now a transformed state, not a state in the proper sense, said Lenin, "for the suppression of the minority of exploiters by the majority of yesterday's hired slaves is a matter so comparatively easy, simple, and natural that it will cost considerably less blood . . . , and it is combined with the spread of democracy to the suppressed majority of the population so that the need of a *special machine* for suppression begins to disappear. . . ."

Lenin was thus careful to point out that "for the complete withering of the state full communism is necessary," and he declared flatly that the dictatorship of the proletariat in the first stage would in fact seize the state machine to use as a "bludgeon" against its enemies. Only when exploitation "no longer exists in the world" will the proletariat finally "consign this machine to the scrap heap." The phrase, "in the world," could, of course, be held to imply that the state would remain until the victory of communism throughout the world. And yet he clearly did not mean to deny the point that, once the dictatorship of the proletariat was established, a gradual withering would begin and would proceed steadily until full communism were achieved. Indeed, he insisted that even in the earlier phase of the transition "a special apparatus of suppression is not needed." With the elimination of exploitation the causes of social problems are removed, and "with their withering the state also withers."[4]

Lenin would set no timetable for this process, but he was confident that, with the basic transformation of the social order under the dictatorship of the proletariat, the remaining prerequisite for communism would be the education of the people in the art of communal living. The state, he concluded, can wither fully at the time when society practices the rule: from each according to his ability, to each according to his need—that is, "when people are so accustomed to the observance of the basic rules of society and when their work is so productive that they will voluntarily work according to their abilities."

While it is impossible to say what Lenin would have done with these ideas under the impact of the need to build socialism in only one country, it is clear that in this as in most cases the theoretical heritage of the Soviet regime was open to various interpretations. Stalin, whose lot it was to use that heritage as he saw fit in building the modern Soviet dictatorship, proved just how far the technique of reinterpretation could be carried. He did not deny the obvious contradiction between his program of building socialism in one country and any withering of the state; on the contrary, he maintained that such a contradiction was precisely what was required by dialectical development. As he reported to the Central Committee in 1933, noting some confusion in some comrades' minds on this matter:

Some comrades interpreted the thesis on the abolition of classes, the establishment of classless society, and the withering away of the state to mean a justification of laziness and complacency, a justification of the counterrevolutionary theory that the class struggle is subsiding and that state power is to be relaxed. Needless to say, such people cannot have anything in common with our Party. . . . The abolition of classes is not achieved by the subsiding of the class struggle, but by its intensification. The state will wither away, not as a result of a relaxation of the state power, but as a result of its utmost consolidation. . . .[5]

Stalin, of course, reversed the earlier inclinations, in theories of education and law, for example, to expect that state institutions and controls would soon disappear. Instead he saw to it that all instruments of coercion, including not only police and the law but also courts and the lawyer, were made into monolithic instruments of his regime. But he also took the trouble to explain the theoretical basis of his actions, or at least to provide a rationalization of them in terms of a contrived reinterpretation of the theory.

Having asserted the claim that the class struggle did not abate but in fact was intensified during the building of socialism, Stalin concluded that therefore a classless society cannot come about spontaneously but rather must be built "by strengthening the organs of the dictatorship of the proletariat." Denouncing as Right deviationists those who thought otherwise, he held that a "dialectical" withering must be a progression of opposites and the movement from socialism to communism a dialectical "leap." So firmly did he hold to this position that not even the claim made in 1936 in connection with the adoption of the new Constitution that "there are no longer any antagonistic classes in (Soviet) society" could produce any modification. The achievement of socialism was merely described as marking "the transformation of the dictatorship into a more flexible and, consequently, a more powerful system of guidance of society by the state. . . ."[6]

Stalin in fact ultimately went so far as to deny the relevance of Engels' formulation of the theory of the state's withering. Chiding those who "memorized certain tenets of the doctrine of Marx and Engels about the state . . . (but) have not grasped the essential meaning of this doctrine," he declared that Engels' proposition is correct only on one of two conditions: (1) if the international situation is ignored, or (2) if it is assumed that "socialism is already victorious in all countries, or in the majority of countries, that a socialist encirclement exists instead of a capitalist encirclement, that there is no more danger of foreign attack, and that there is no more need to strengthen the army and the state."[7] Engels, said Stalin, proceeded from the second assumption, so his doctrine will be relevant only when these conditions are met. The important thing was the "capitalist encirclement" which might even make it necessary for the state to continue to exist, even under full communism.

Khrushchev's Synthesis

In his report to the Twenty-first Party Congress in January, 1959, Khrushchev went to some length to explain his position on the withering of the state, the transition to communism, and the importance of mass participation. Just as Stalin so often did, Khrushchev began his discussion of the theoretical problems of the "new stage in communist construction" by remarking that "some comrades" took an incorrect position, in this case by believing that full communism should be introduced right away without further preparation. In presenting his reasons why this is not yet possible, Khrushchev at first gives Lenin's rather than Stalin's prerequisites: that is, an abundance of material goods, and a population "prepared to live and work in a communist way." His description of how the transition will occur is also Leninist:

We must advance step by step, creating the material and spiritual requisites for a planned transition to communism. . . . It would be wrong, erroneous, to assume that communism will somehow appear suddenly. . . . The transition from socialism to communism is a continuous process. . . . If we approach it dialectically, the question of withering away of the state is a question of evolution of the socialist state toward communist public self-government.[8]

The Leninist Khrushchev thus spoke of a continuous process of withering in which "communist forms" are gradually taking shape. Even now, he promised, they are "opening the door to communist society," and with proper preparation it should not be so far off. This means, he said, that they are now preparing for the stage in which "the functions of public administration will lose their political character and will turn into management of society's affairs directly by the people." As a part of this trend, there is taking place "the utmost unfolding of democracy, the enlisting of the broadest strata of the population in the management of all affairs of the country." Under this development "many functions performed by government agencies will gradually pass to public organizations," which will provide the training ground for the new Soviet man:

The transition to communism requires not only a developed material and technical basis, but also a high consciousness on the part of all citizens of society. The higher the consciousness of the masses, millions strong, the more successfully will the plans of communist construction be carried out. . . . To attain communism, the most just and perfect society, in which all the finest moral traits of free man will unfold to the full, we must bring up the man of the future today. . . . We have learned . . . that revolutionary practice plays a decisive role in changing the conditions of life and the views of the people.

Life—our Soviet reality—is the best training school, the most exacting teacher. . . .

Having thus lauded the transfer of state functions to public organizations and the immanent transition to communism, Khrushchev then interestingly reverts to an only slightly modified Stalinist position to justify the continued presence of the state's power. He approaches his point gradually, first noting that "of course, definite functions will remain with the courts, the militia, and the Prosecutor's Office . . . in order to exert influence on persons who maliciously refuse to submit to socialist society's standards of behavior and are not amenable to persuasion." Therefore, the transition must be undertaken "without undue haste" and at first on the basis of "exploratory steps."

This, however, is not the only reason for going slow in relinquishing state authority to the people. Indeed, the withering of the state is not merely "like the turning of leaves in autumn." Even "under communism, too, there will remain certain public functions similar to those now performed by the state," said Khrushchev, for under existing conditions the withering process must "not at all mean weakening the role of the socialist state" and its security agencies whose task it is to block "the provocational actions and intrigues of our enemies from the imperialist camp."

The most important reason why the state machine must remain powerful is thus that it can wither away "only when the danger of an imperialist attack on our country or on countries allied with ours is completely removed." Khrushchev insists that Stalin was correctly criticized for his thesis on the intensification of the class struggle, and he declares that "the capitalist encirclement no longer exists." But, he cautions, the state and its functions can wither away only with the "complete triumph of communism," which means not simply that the Soviet Union can repel any attack by an enemy but also that all the socialist countries must be "guaranteed against the possibility of aggression by the imperialist states." Since all the socialist countries "will enter the higher phase of communist society more or less simultaneously"— a fact discovered by "new laws" of development "unknown to human society in the past"—the imperialist danger to all of them must be taken into consideration. Thus using Stalin's analysis of Engels' position, Khrushchev declares that as long as any possibility of attack from the outside exists "stringent control" must be maintained "by the state."

In this fashion Khrushchev synthesizes the Leninist and the Stalinist positions. He authorizes a significant development of public participation on the basis of the idea that the Soviet Union is moving gradually toward the stateless society, and at the same time he points out that the immediate purpose must be the strengthening of the state, partly because the educa-tion of the public will take time, but especially because the capitalist encirclement has not been entirely replaced by a socialist encirclement. The necessity of maintaining powerful security forces will make the withering of the state a gradual process. Moreover, it is the methods of control which will undergo this evolution and not control itself. In short, the building of communism will involve not less control but more efficient methods.

Others who have picked up Khrushchev's theme and elaborated upon it in the Soviet press have noted that the withering away of the state is a most complex process which will require not only the material and technical base and public consciousness but a whole array of changes which must accompany them. It is recalled, for example, that the achievement of economic abundance must also lead to the abolition of a money economy so that a free exchange may take place on the basis of the principle: to each according to his need. Moreover, full com-munism must mean the eradication of differences between various kinds of property so as to leave only "communist" property, the elimina-tion of differences between physical and mental labor and between city and country, and the removal of all class distinctions and any remaining traces of religious or national antagonisms. Finally, not only must "bureaucratism" be eliminated but, as Lenin said, everyone in the society must learn to do "everything." It is explained that the latter means only a basic knowledge of production principles, but this still leaves an enormous task of transformation at hand.

Practical Steps toward Communism

On the other hand, Khrushchev is evidently determined to prove that immediate, practical steps can be taken toward communism, or at least toward developing new methods justified by this end. The area significantly singled out for a trial in this regard is that of law enforcement. Boasting that the militia has now been "sharply reduced," Khrushchev declares that the people themselves are now ready to take over some of the tasks of "enforcing public order and the rules of socialist society." Already, he adds, "Our public organizations have no less adequate capacities, means, and forces for this than the militia, the courts, and the Prosecutor's Office!" This, of course, does not mean that the latter will lose any of their present significance. . . .

The criminal law will continue to operate much as before, but further development requires not only the elimination of crime but an end to all "antisocial phenomena." This, it is noted, is not something that police and courts can do alone. It requires the complete involvement of the population at large in the task, for there is more to the problem than formally defined and prosecuted crime. A way must also be found to deal with the behavioral problems conveniently lumped under the category of "the rules of socialist society." Even the most detailed criminal law leaves this area uncovered, but apparently it is precisely upon the extension of the "law" into the area of morals and attitudes that the transition to communism depends. It is not a question of the withering away of law, or police, but rather their extension under the guise of public participation. This is to be accomplished by way of a shift of emphasis from formal law at the lowest levels to the "rules of society" enforced by a new array of "public organizations," namely, comrades' courts and people's militia detachments whose function will be, in Khrushchev's words, "to spot a transgressor before he commits a misdemeanor or crime, when he first shows a departure from the standards of public behavior." . . .

Therefore, it was decreed that people's militia assistance brigades were to be established throughout the country at all enterprises, construction projects, institutions, farms, and apartment houses, with district and city headquarters staffs set up as command posts. The latter are to consist of representatives of Party and Soviet agencies, unions, Komsomol units, and individual brigade and detachment commanders, who in turn will recruit members "on a strictly voluntary basis" to take up patrol activities on the streets, in parks, theaters, public carriers, and the like. Working closely with regular state agencies, each detachment during its "free time" will seek to safeguard order, combat hooliganism, conduct "explanatory work," and in general let nothing "escape their vigilant eye." Relying mainly upon "persuasion and warning" to accomplish their tasks, each such civilian policeman will be given a special identification card and a badge.

Following the publication of this decree an intense campaign was begun in the press to popularize public enforcement of the rules of socialist society. Numerous articles proclaimed the remarkable success and democratic character of the militia-assistance detachments, hailing them as a "noble undertaking," and the beginning of an era of "exemplary order," "purity of life," and "peace and joy." At last an end of "filth and evil" was at hand because the people themselves were assuming the job of policing society at its most personal level. . . .

An equally, if not more, important step was then inaugurated by the Supreme Soviet, which apparently concluded that if the people could be policemen they could also be judges. . . . The uniqueness of these laws was noted in their being specifically designed for "the period of comprehensive construction of a communist society" during which all citizens would be drawn into the management "of all affairs of the state," thus receiving their "communist education" for life in the ultimately stateless society.

Under these drafts, comrades' courts are to be elected by the collectives of every enterprise, institution, organization, higher and specialized secondary school, state and collective farm, producer's cooperative, rural soviet, housing development, and street committee. In the first of these, they are to be under the direction of the trade unions and elsewhere under the direction of the executive committees of the local soviets. Members, all laymen, are to be elected from the collective body of workers, tenants, students, and the like for a term of two years by majority vote and may be recalled in the same manner. The comrades' court will hear cases after working hours with the chairman or vice chairman and at least two members taking part, and decisions will be taken by a majority vote of those participating.

The comrades' courts are not courts in the strict sense of the word but lay tribunals, nor are they a wholly new phenomenon, for similar courts had been organized as far back as the NEP period in housing cooperatives and some factories. What is new is that they are now to be established universally and, more important, that their competence and powers are to be enormously expanded. No longer limited to housing regulations or matters of labor discipline alone, they are to be given jurisdiction over an almost incredible array of offenses ranging from petty violations of law to "deviations from the norms of public behavior." The general criterion upon which the comrades' court's competence is to be based, apart from the pettiness of any actual crime involved, is whether the offender can be "reformed through the application of measures of public influence."

The recently elevated People's Courts, along with the Prosecutor's Office, will play an important role in keeping the comrades' courts within these bounds, but cases may also be brought before them by both public organizations and by individual citizens who are members of the offender's collective. Twelve categories of offenses are set forth to describe the comrades' court's jurisdiction, including labor discipline (lateness, intoxication, poor quality work, negligent attitude, and the like), nonfulfillment of parental duties, abusive language, spreading rumors, poaching, petty speculation, petty hooliganism, drunkenness, foul language, petty arrogance, illicit home distilling, property disputes under 500 rubles, and any antisocial acts referred to the court by the regular authorities. In most cases, a petty criminal offense must be the first such offense for the person so arraigned.

The penalties which can be imposed range from "comradely warning" to fines up to 100 rubles and recommendation of reduction in status and pay or dismissal from work. The comrades' court will turn serious cases and those resisting "re-education" over to the regular courts, and the latter may when they feel such treatment warranted turn an offender over to his fellow workers, with suspended sentence, for a year's probation under "collective custody." The only appeal provided is in the form of a rehearing or a challenge in the People's Court of the comrades' court's competence.

The New "Democracy"

All of the above new measures may be regarded as a part of the policy of decentralization being carried out under Khrushchev, ranging from the reorganization of the MVD and Ministry of Justice to the creation of "people's" organizations at the bottom of the scale. They are officially represented as providing for the broadening of democracy and the beginning of a transition to full communism, with the people more and more taking over the functions of the state through the "spontaneous" development of "independent" organizations like the people's militia and the comrades' courts. Clearly the idea is to confront the population with the necessity not only of obeying the law and leading an upright life oneself, but also of seeing that one's fellow workers and neighbors do the same. At stake is whatever may remain of the distinction between what is public and what is private, what is criminal and what is merely unrighteous. With every collective group sitting in judgment over its members for cases of "petty arrogance" or "foul language," all such distinctions must certainly be blurred if not destroyed. . . .

So that there may be no confusion regarding a supposed withering of the Party along with the state and so that the development of public organizations may not be regarded as something to be left to the spontaneous initiative of the people, it is made quite clear that the public organizations are to be instruments of the continuing Party dictatorship. They will in fact be used to pressure the apathetic into the proper mold of public spiritedness. Indeed, the closer communism comes, the greater is the need for Party control both to guard against "revisionist tendencies toward the view of spontaneous development" and to "unite and coordinate the multifaceted activity of the entire ramified system of public organizations." It is the Party itself which is "the highest form of public organization, and only it can give and does give correct political direction to the work of all other organizations."

Is the Party, then, to replace the state under full communism? At the moment this possibility is only implied not stated directly. What is emphasized is that any step toward "public communist self-government" is to be understood as increasing rather than diminishing the role of the Party. The more the "moral factor" becomes the guide to people's behavior, the more the "conscious element" takes over the earlier function of economic laws; the more that "democracy" of the masses supersedes state operations, the more the Party leadership becomes an "organic need."

Thus the vicious circle of contradictions is expanded. In recent months the Soviet press has shown growing concern over such problems as drunkenness, "parasitism," and hooliganism, and especially the ineffectiveness of efforts to indoctrinate the people in the communist outlook. Khrushchev's program is geared to solving such problems, but the methods are carefully identified with and justified by the slogans of popular democracy, the withering of the state, and pristine morality. If successful, Khrushchev could raise the techniques and efficiency of totalitarianism to new heights, but that there are serious obstacles in his path is equally apparent.

The transition to communism in any case is surely not to mean more real democracy if present developments are any indication. The innovations introduced are pointedly intended to strengthen the state, to reassert the dominant and pervasive role of the Party, and to produce more "transmission belts" for the dictatorship. Using the comrades' courts and people's militia to intensify the pressures of social conformity to established norms, the regime will try to prove the fallacy of "the assertions of bourgeois ideologists and propagandists that socialism has not changed and cannot change the mentality of man, that . . . the human mind does not change, that it is the 'fortress that no one can capture,' . . ." Upon this rests the claim of communism to the future. The gamble is that, in trying to prove it, the regime must popularize ideas which may in the long run be its own undoing.

NOTES

1 "Manifesto of the Communist Party, 1848," in M. Eastman, (ed.), *Capital and Other Writings by Karl Marx* (New York, 1932), p. 343.

2 K. Marx and F. Engels, *Selected Works* (Moscow, 1950), vol. II, p. 138.

3 V. I. Lenin, "Gosudartstvo i revoliutsiia," 1918, *Sochineniia* (3d ed., Moscow, 1935), XXI, p. 431.

4 *Ibid.*, p. 432.

5 J. Stalin, "The Results of the First Five-Year Plan," Report to the Central Committee of the G.P.S.U. (b), Jan. 7, 1933, *Problems of Leninism* (Moscow, 1953), p. 538.

6 J. Stalin, "On the Draft Constitution," Report to the 8th Congress of Soviets, Nov. 25, 1936, *op. cit.*, pp. 690, 698–699.

7 J. Stalin, "Report to the 18th Congress of the G.P.S.U. (b)," March 10, 1939, *op. cit.*, p. 793.

8 N. S. Khrushchev, Report to the 21st Congress of the G.P.S.U., *Pravda*, January 28, 1959, pp. 2–10; *Current Digest of the Soviet Press*, XI, no. 5 (March 11, 1959), 13.

31

The Asiatic Mode of Production
and Oriental Despotism

Michael Curtis

THE SEARCH for the Asiatic mode of production, and its political form, Oriental despotism, in the writings of Karl Marx and Friedrich Engels may not have lasted as long as the quest for the Holy Grail but it has had equally passionate devotees, heretics and disbelievers disputing the nature and even the existence of the quarry. Marx himself, in the original preface to the first volume of *Capital* in 1859, conscious of the provocative character of his work, was aware that inquiry into the nature of political economy summoned as "foes into the field of battle the most violent, mean and malignant passions of the human breast, the furies of private interest."[1] The concept of the Asiatic mode has aroused even more emotional turmoil and heated polemical exchanges than is customary in the normally turbulent world of Marxist exegesis.[2]

The heat engendered by the considerable debate about Oriental despotism and the Asiatic mode of production (AMP) emanates from two different sources. Some results from genuine differences in interpretation of the writings of Marx and Engels, some of it opaque, on the two issues. An unusually large variety of views has been presented about the AMP. It includes the AMP as a genuine socioeconomic formation unique to the Orient; a primitive society geographically widespread before the period of slavery; a variant of slavery or of feudalism; an "archaic formation"; a specific form of property ownership or of relations of production; a pseudo-concept really about the hypothetical origins of modern bourgeois society; a society with a state but without private property; the most general form of the evolution of primitive communist society; the most primitive form of the state, a concept that could define precolonial black African systems; an imaginative sketch to help analyze capitalism; the only Marxist non-Western type of society; a political structure without a class system; a transitory formation between a class society; a stagnant variant of the ancient mode of production; an important vehicle for Aesopian criticism of the despotic power of rulers. In light of the different and contradictory interpretations, some analysts in despair have argued that the term AMP be dropped or buried.[3]

Even stronger has been the critical, even hostile, view of the AMP. For orthodox Marxists a theory that implicitly argued that Western capitalist systems had been capable of positive benefit to colonies, that a bureaucratic group might be the ruling class, that no uniform pattern of historical development necessarily existed for all mankind, that productive forces were not always the primary element in a society, that progress was not inevitable, that societies might become modernized by external forces, and that geographical factors might limit the primacy of technology, was unacceptable. The concept of the AMP divided the Russian revolutionary movement at the end of the nineteenth century and in the early twentieth century; it was condemned by the Chinese Communists in Moscow in 1928 and by Soviet specialists in a celebrated meeting in Leningrad in 1931, and was regarded as nonexistent by Stalin in 1938.[4]

Neither Marx nor Engels wrote any sustained substantive, precise, or systematic analysis of the Asiatic mode or of Oriental societies or of Oriental despotism. Nor did they provide an account of any dialectical change from that mode to another in the process of historical development as they did for other economic and social systems. Compared with the thousands of pages by Marx and Engels on the history and societies of Western Europe and on the stages of capitalist development they wrote little about Asian affairs. They knew incomparably more about Europe, about Roman history, the medieval origins of the bourgeoisie, feudal trade and finance, the German Middle Ages, than about the East.[5] Their various commentaries and remarks on Oriental societies do not have the resonance or detail as did the long attempt to analyze the capitalist system.[6] Robert Tucker has acutely observed that Marx spent thirty years writing and rewriting one book on that system under a number of different titles.[7]

Part of that book, in its various guises, was clarification of the preconditions for the emergence of capitalism. In the *Grundrisse,* part treatise, part inchoate notes for the writing of *Capital,* Marx asserted that bourgeois society was "the most developed and the most complex historic organization of production."[8] By understanding the relations and the structure of that society one could gain insights into "the structure and relations of production of all the vanished social formations out of whose ruins and elements it built itself up." The bourgeois economy thus supplied the key to the ancient one.

Yet even acknowledging the disproportionate amount of space in their writings on European and on Asian affairs, it would be wrong to conclude that Marx and Engels were uninterested in Asia as such or that the study of the Asian societies was merely instrumental for tracing the movement toward or the understanding of the political economy of capitalism. In the 1850s their interest in the Orient and their scholarly immersion into its history became serious as their correspondence and their newspaper articles showed. One of the more amusing allusions to the growing interest was by Engels in his letter to Marx of June 6, 1853, where he informed his friend he had put off learning Arabic but had given himself a maximum of three weeks to learn Persian.[9] Engels later recognized that such economic science as "we possess up to the present is limited almost exclusively to the genesis and development of the capitalist mode of production" and that there was a need to study others.[10]

In the early writings of Marx and Engels the Orient is rarely mentioned: a few times in *The German Ideology* and a reference in Engels' 1847 *Principles of Communism*. Marx first alluded to "Asiatic despotism" in his *Contribution to the Critique of Hegel's Philosophy of Right*, written in spring/summer 1843, where he argued that the political body in early history was either a real concern of citizens who participated in it as among the Greeks, or was nothing but "the private caprice of a single individual so that, as in Asian despotism, the political state was as much a slave as the material state."[11]

The real, and continuing, interest in Asian affairs began with the usually short articles in the *New York Daily Tribune* in 1853 and the correspondence between the two writers on India and China during the time. The articles were concerned with the specific, empirical issues of the day: the renewal of the East India Company charter, the social system in India, British rule and its future in that country, the Taiping rebellion in China. These were not simply informative for serious newspaper readers. They, and the letters which overlapped in subject matter, also put forward striking generalizations about the history and character of Oriental societies and suggested important differences between Western and Eastern life. The dependence of Marx and Engels at this stage on particular sources for their information and for some of their more general opinions about Asia—writers like François Bernier, officials such as Sir Stamford Raffles, British government documents, and parliamentary debates—are clear. Later, their reading about the Orient and related matters would be more extensive, especially on the history of Asia, including the work on Asiatic monarchies by Robert Patton, and on early societies.[12]

Marx and Engels also absorbed and combined ideas from diverse nonspecialists on the Orient: Oriental despotism from Montesquieu whom Marx read in 1843; absence of political participation and economic backwardness from Hegel; its stationary nature from Voltaire; equivalence of rent and tax from Adam Smith and Richard Jones; and the general belief that India was the cradle of languages and cultures.[13] Interestingly, Marx in his early letter of May 1843 to Ruge had not at first appreciated Montesquieu's differentiation of a despotic state from a monarchy.[14] At that time Marx saw the terms "monarchy, democracy, and tyranny" as referring to a single concept denoting at best different modes of the same principle.

The continuing writings of the two never resulted in a concise treatise on Oriental societies. Analysis of their work therefore rests on a variety of sources: the occasional newspaper articles; letters to each other and to the many, mostly socialists, who sought advice; passages from the economic analyses of precapitalist and capitalist societies, and in their later years ethnological studies and notes. Two aspects of this are noticeable. Not surprisingly, writing at different times and in varying formats with different audiences in mind, they touched on different features of Asian societies and economic structures in particular writings, or they gave changing emphasis to the importance of specific factors in Oriental affairs with which they dealt. Also these writings alternate between empirical remarks on specific issues and current affairs, and theoretical and abstract analysis of the kind familiar in the major economic works.[15]

This is illustrated in the early newspaper articles and letters as Marx and Engels grappled with the subject for the first time in earnest. In those writings some of their views on Asian society emerged: the importance of separate village communities; the absence of private property in land; the Oriental despotism which, among other things, controlled water resources and undertook public works. Those views first appeared as Marx and Engels exchanged ideas in their close symbiotic relationship. Marx on June 2, 1853, informed his colleague that he could answer the question: "Why does the history of the East appear as a history of religions?" Depending on "old Bernier" who for Marx had correctly discovered the basic form of all phenomena in the East, referring to Turkey, Persia, and Hindustan, the answer was the absence of private property in land. "This is the real key even to the Oriental heaven." Engels on June 6, 1853, quickly agreed that this absence of private property in land explained the political and religious history of the East. But why was it absent? Engels' first explanation is that it was mainly due to the climate and the nature of the soil in the East, which for him stretched from "Arabia to the highest Asiatic plateaus."[16]

Engels also introduced two important factors: the need in Oriental countries for artificial irrigation, and the organization of Oriental governments into never more than three departments: finance (plunder at home), war (plunder at home and abroad), and public works (provision for reproduction). Marx was to use the same language about government in Asia "generally, from immemorial times," in his article in the *New York Daily Tribune* of June 25, 1853, written on June 10.[17] He also repeated the assertions of Engels that climate and territory in the East meant that artificial irrigation was the basis of Oriental agriculture, and that government in Asia had to provide public works.

In this article, *The British Rule in India,* Marx discussed the colonial role, which had dealt with finance and war, but not with public works, and its consequences about which he was caustic. He was even more caustic about the Indian system of villages, each with a separate organization, each forming a world of its own. Explaining the reason for the stationary nature of India, Marx gave two answers: the fact that public works were the business of the central government, and the reality that the whole empire, not counting a few towns, was divided into villages. Drawing on the 1812 British report of the Select Committee of the House of Commons on the Affairs of the East Indian Company, Marx used a long quotation to give a picture of the organization of a typical village community with its twelve different officials and its division of labor.

Both in the June 25 article, and in his letter to Engels of June 14, 1853, Marx made similar points about that village system. These village communities, "idyllic republics" in his ironic phrase, which still existed in parts of Northwest India, "had always been the solid foundation of Oriental despotism," or "the foundation for stagnant Asiatic despotism." He also remarked, in the letter of June 14, but without pursuing the matter, that "it seems to have been the Mohammedans who first established the principle of "no property in land" throughout the whole of Asia."

From the newspaper articles and exchanged letters, some general propositions about Asian society and politics had emerged. Between 1857 and 1862, Marx and Engels resumed writing on Indian and Chinese affairs—issues such as the Indian mutiny, the Anglo-Chinese war, British actions on land ownership changes and confiscation of land, trade with China, and the opium trade—and deepened their knowledge of Oriental matters. At the same time allusions to Asia were occurring in the major economic writings of Marx, especially as he compared precapitalist systems, including Oriental ones, with capitalism and the conditions necessary for its existence. These references to Asia, to Oriental economics and Asiatic societies as abstract concepts were now put in the context of discussion of theoretical issues: production, distribution, commodity exchange, division of labor, levels of production, the relation of rent and tax, state use of surplus labor, ownership of land, the relation of town and countryside, the individual and the commune, and Oriental despotism. The Oriental systems became part of the analysis of historical evolution when in 1859 Marx, in the preface to *A Contribution to the Critique of Political Economy,* indicated for the first time the existence of an Asiatic mode of production (AMP).

Marx provided an initial explanation of the historical development of mankind in his letter of December 28, 1846, to Pavel Annenkov. "If you assume given stages of development in production, commerce or consumption, you will have a corresponding form of social constitution, a corresponding organization, whether of the family, of the estates or of the classes—a corresponding civil society, (and) a political system."[18] Economic forms, in which man produced, consumed, and exchanged, were transitory and historical. With the change in new productive faculties came changes in the mode of production. At other times, Marx argued that the economic process started with "socially determined individual production," and that production took place at a definite stage of social development.

Throughout their lives the two Marxists presented their views of historical materialism or the materialist conception of history and of the concepts of the mode of production and relations of production in somewhat changing fashion and less starkly expressed in later years. The clarification of these views and concepts has given rise to a considerable cottage industry with diminishing intellectual reward. All might agree that Marx and Engels succumbed to what Ernest Gellner called "the charm of the world growth story; the image of a growing cosmos, of upward growth," and that they generally saw history as an entelechy, as a series of successive and connected stages.[19] Engels, explaining Marx's work, acknowledged that Hegel was the first to demonstrate there is development, an intrinsic coherence in history.

It had taken Marx fourteen years after his generalizations about historical development and categories of social and economic systems before he arrived at the AMP. That development Engels explained in an essay in 1859 "proceeds by jumps and zigzags, and by and large from the simplest to the more complex relations."[20] He had joined Marx, in their first set of analytical categories to explain world history, in *The German Ideology* written in 1845-46. Societies, they argued, differed most significantly according to their modes of production and the character of the social division of labor to which corresponded different forms of property. They outlined three forms of property ownership and social division of labor: tribal communal property ownership; the communal and state property ownership of antiquity; and feudal or rank property ownership.

In the first form, the undeveloped stage of production, a people sustained itself by hunting and fishing, by cattle raising or farming. Based on kinship groups, the very elementary division of labor in this form existed within the family, and the social hierarchy consisted of an extension of the family: patriarchal tribal chiefs, members of the tribes, and slaves. Slavery increased with the expansion of population, the growth of wants, and as a result of wars or barter.

The second form, originating in cities formed by the union of tribal groups and exemplified by the Greek city states and Rome, was based on slavery and communal ownership. That ownership would dissolve as private property became more important. The division of labor was more evident than previously, town and country were more differentiated, and a class system, free citizens and slaves, existed.

The third form, feudal property ownership in the Middle Ages, had a social communal organization based on the countryside, small-scale cultivation of land owned by feudal lords using serf labor, handicraft manufacturing and the guild system, and an armed nobility. This feudal system would lead to a fourth system, the bourgeois form, with the increase in private property, the separation of town and country, manufacturing, division of labor in the cities between production and trade, use of and greater concentration of capital, and the rise of a bourgeois class.

To help prepare for the *Communist Manifesto,* Engels in 1847 wrote the *Principles of Communism* in which he pointed out that one of the results of the industrial revolution was that the old system of industry founded on manual labor was destroyed in all countries of the world. "All semi-barbarian countries, which until now had been more or less outside historical development and whose industry had until now been based on manufacture, were thus forcibly torn out of their isolation." Those countries that for thousands of years had made no progress, for example India, were revolutionized, and even China was marching toward revolution.[21]

The first well-known and widely used Marxist statement on historical stages came in the *Communist Manifesto* of 1848. It presented three stages, different from those in the 1845 formulation, which were characterized by types of relations of production and class society: slavery in antiquity, feudalism in the Middle Ages, and the modern bourgeois society from which socialism would emerge in the future. All the stages reflected class struggles: free men against slaves, feudal lords against serfs, and capitalists against the proletariat.

But the tribal or patriarchal societies of *The German Ideology* did not appear, nor did Asia, in this European-centered version of historical change. Interestingly, Marx, in analyzing the role of the bourgeoisie, praised it for having drawn "all, even the most barbarian, nations into civilisation." The crucial passage relating to the non-European world was the conclusion: "Just as it has made the country dependent on the towns, so it has made barbarian and semi-barbarian countries dependent on the civilised ones, nations of peasants on nations of bourgeois, the East on the West."

The third version of historical change appeared in the *Grundrisse*, the very lengthy first draft of *Capital*, written in 1857-58 but not published until 1939. In the *Introduction* Marx wrote of the problem inherent in categorization.

Since bourgeois society is itself only a contradictory form of development, relations derived from earlier forms will often be found within it only in an entirely stunted form, or even travestied. . . . The so-called historical presentation of development is founded, as a rule, on the fact that the latest form regards the previous ones as steps leading up to itself. . . . It would be unfeasible and wrong to let the economic categories follow one another in the same sequence as that in which they were historically decisive.[22]

In the *Grundrisse*, Marx compared the precapitalist economic formations, the different forms of property ownership before capitalism, the development of private property, and the relations of production.[23] To this end he devised another set of categories to explain the alternative routes out of the primitive communal system, some favoring historical evolution and some not. Regarding slavery and serfdom as "secondary" forms of society, he concentrated on "primary" forms which included a variety of tribal and other communities.[24] Marx started with the earliest form of landed property, that of the tribal community, the natural common body. This original community was modified depending on various external, climatic, geographical, physical factors as well as on the character of the tribe. The community was, properly speaking, the real proprietor.[25] Politically, the emergence of the state power differentiated it from the primitive communal form of property. Economically, what existed was communal property and private individual possession.

This early kind of community could be realized in a variety of ways. Marx's classification was based on the different forms of communal and private property and the relations of production. He indicated four main forms: the Asiatic or Oriental; the Slavonic (which was not discussed but appeared to be a variant of the Asiatic); the ancient classical; and the Germanic.

This was the first time that Marx presented Asiatic or Oriental society as a distinct category. That presentation is at a high level of generality and abstraction. In addition, as Hobsbawm acknowledged, the writing in the *Grundrisse* resembles a kind of "private intellectual shorthand which is sometimes impenetrable."[26] But the general meaning is clear. Marx's first discussion of Asiatic or Oriental society is the starting point of his analysis of relations of production.

The Asiatic society was based on tribal or common property, in most cases created through a combination of manufacture and agriculture in the small communities which became entirely self-sustaining and contained within themselves all the factors of production and surplus production. Above these communities was "the all-embracing unity," which might appear as the higher or sole proprietor, while the real communities were regarded only as hereditary possessors. The unity was the real owner of property and the real precondition of common ownership, and could appear as something separate and superior to the many, particular communities. The individual was propertyless, or property might be a grant from the total unity to the individual through the intermediary of the particular community.

What Marx asserted, though not always in a clear manner, and repeated in later writings, was that property ownership was communal, stemming originally from group cohesion or tribal organization. More than one analyst has observed that Marx used the term *Gemeinwesen* to denote both common, tribal property and membership in a tribal organization.[27] Historically, for Marx, private property came later than communal property, not the other way around.

The despot appeared as the father of all the numerous lesser communities, thus realizing the common unity of all. The surplus product of the communities belonged to this highest unity. Oriental despotism therefore appeared to lead to a legal absence of property. Surplus labor was rendered both as tribute and as common labor for the glory of the unity, symbolized by the despot, who was also the imagined tribal entity of the god. A central feature of any socioeconomic formation in Marx's economic analysis was the way in which the surplus was appropriated from the direct producers. In the Oriental societies, as in other precapitalist societies, where surplus labor was not appropriated by purely economic means, by free exchange, but by other means such as force or sacred authority, it occurred through direct slavery, serfdom, or political dependence.

In the Asiatic form of society, variations could occur. Labor in the communal property could appear in two ways. The small communities could "vegetate independently side by side"; within each one the individual worked independently with his family on the land, while a certain amount of labor was performed for the common store. Or, the unity above the smaller communities could involve a common organization of labor itself which could be a formal system. Marx, somewhat confusingly, gave as examples of this latter system, countries and people as diverse as Mexico, Peru, the ancient Celts, and some tribes of India.[29]

Within the Asiatic form, the political character of the tribal bodies might also vary. The unity might be represented by a chief of the tribal group, or through the relationship among the patriarchs, the heads of the families. Therefore, the community could have a more despotic or a more democratic form. Above this was the higher unity, the despotic government which was poised above the lesser communities, responsible for the communal control of labor for irrigation systems, very important among the Asian peoples, and the means of communication. Economically, the tribal community was the "hereditary possessor" of property, but was subordinated to the state, the real owner.

Comparing the Asiatic or Oriental form with the other forms in his category, Marx asserted it "may appear as communal property which gives the individual only possession and no private property in the soil." The ancient classical form was characterized by a combination of state and private property. The Germanic form had private property supplemented by communal property.[30]

The Asiatic form was not only the original form of direct communal property. It also "necessarily" survived longest and most stubbornly. This resulted from its fundamental principles, that the individual did not become independent of the community and that the circle of production was self-sustaining. If the individual changed his relation to the community, he modified and undermined both the community and its economic premise. Though Marx held the Asiatic or Oriental form to be the original one, "historically closest to man's origins," because of the survival of the primitive village community in the wider social system, that form did not necessarily lead to any other form, nor did it become the starting point of the dialectical process of history.[31] Indeed, the forms in the *Grundrisse* did not appear to represent successive chronological historical stages nor any evolutionary process from one stage to another, nor a unilinear pattern of historical development, though they might represent changes in the evolution of private property.

In 1859, Marx again changed his categories of historical development in *A Contribution to the Critique of Political Economy,* the shorter, revised version of the *Grundrisse*. In the preface he briefly wrote: "In broad outlines, Asiatic, ancient, feudal, and modern bourgeois modes of production can be designated as progressive epochs in the economic formation of society." Using the category "mode of production" rather than "form" or "society," Marx for the first time designated an "Asiatic mode of production" as a separate concept. The German and Slavonic types had disappeared. It was nowhere explicit that all societies had passed or would pass through these four epochs. Nor was it apparent why the Asiatic mode was a "progressive epoch" when Marx and Engels saw it as static and stagnant.

Marx's terse list in the preface was preceded by a sweeping generalization: "No social order ever perishes before all the productive forces for which there is room in it have developed; and new, higher relations of production never appeared before the material conditions of their existence have matured in the womb of the old society itself." As a result of class struggles and the developing tension in each mode of production a logical progression from the ancient mode to socialism was presumed. The Asiatic mode, however, did not logically appear to lead to the ancient stage nor to any other. Nor was it located in any particular time or clearly confined to Asiatic space. Moreover, the preface did not, as Georges Sorel pointed out, "aim to furnish the rules for studying a particular period in history. It deals with the succession of civilisations; thus the word 'class' is not even mentioned."[32]

After the 1859 preface to the *Critique,* Marx did not formulate any further list of historical categories nor did he propose any other pattern of historical change. Marx and Engels, in a minor way, kept discussing aspects of Asiatic societies and Oriental despotism, and the destiny of the village community, partly because of their interest in the Russian mir, within the context of their general theoretical speculations in *Capital* and other works. In these works and in their unpublished statements and letters they often referred to terms such as "primitive communalism" or "primitive communal ownership" and the relationship between these socioeconomic forms and the AMP is not altogether clear.

One example of this is to be seen in the third of Marx's four drafts of his letter to Vera Zasulich in February-March 1881.[33] Primitive communities were not all the same. On the contrary, they constitute a "series of social groupings, differing both in type and in age, and marking successive phases of development." This general type, the "agricultural commune," included the Russian and German commune. The agrarian commune had developed from the more archaic type of community. The rural commune might also be found in Asia, among the Afghans for example. But it everywhere appeared as the most recent type in the archaic formation of societies.

Marx and Engels began to use the term "archaic formation" or "type," which appeared to include the four categories discussed in the *Grundrisse*, and the AMP, the most primitive of the early socioeconomic formations. Thus, the AMP was still an inherent part of the Marxian historical outlook even if referred to in a more oblique fashion. Certainly Marx and Engels refused to regard the AMP as a variant of feudalism.[34] Marx rejected the argument of the Russian sociologist M. M. Kovalevsky that India be regarded as feudal because three of the four characteristics of Germano-Roman feudalism were present there. Engels too in *Anti-Duhring* excluded the Orient from his discussion of feudalism.[35]

The change in terminology also reflected a change in intellectual interest. In *The German Ideology,* Marx and Engels had regarded the first form of ownership as tribal ownership. Influenced by Lewis Morgan and other anthropologists such as Henry Maine, John Phear, John Lubbock, and M.M. Kovalevsky, whom they studied in the latter part of their lives, Marx and, especially, Engels became more concerned with tribal social organization which was based on the gens, a social group sharing a common ancestry, and with the evolution of the family from the stage of savagery through barbarism to civilization.[36] In the *Grundrisse* early societies were said to be organized into clans or combinations of clans, communalities of blood, language, and customs. Membership of a naturally evolved society, a tribe, was a natural condition of production for individuals. Property meant belonging to a tribe.[37]

Engels went even further in his concern with ethnological issues, on which both of them had been reading. Commenting in his letter to Marx of December 8, 1882, on the similarity between ancient Germans and American natives, he wrote that "at this stage, the method of production is less crucial than is the degree to which old blood ties and the ancient mutual community of the sexes within the tribe are being dissolved." In his introduction to the 1888 English edition of the *Communist Manifesto,* Engels proclaimed that Morgan discovered the nature of the clan and its relation to the tribe: "the inner organization of this primitive communistic society was laid bare in its typical form." In *The Mark* Engels declared that two fundamental facts that arose spontaneously governed the primitive history of all, or almost all, nations: the grouping of the people according to kindred, and common property in the soil. And this was the case with the Germans who had brought with them from Asia the method of grouping by tribes and gentes. By the 1880s Marx and Engels were seeing the gens, the clan, as the earliest form of social organization. For Marxist analysis the problem then arose of whether the structure of the family or of kinship developed in an independent way according to its own laws or whether it resulted from the mode of production.

As a result of Morgan's works, Marx and particularly Engels tended to focus less on the Orient when dealing with earlier periods. In his *The Origin of the Family, Private Property and the State,* published in 1884 a year after Marx's death, Engels argued that early history could better be understood through studying American Indian tribes than through India. The American was the original form, and the Greek and Roman forms were later and derivative. The Asiatic mode did not appear in a work that discussed communal, antique, and feudal systems.

Engels, pursuing his revisionist view of "pre-history of society", corrected, in his 1888 English edition of the *Manifesto,* Marx's original bold statement, "the history of all hitherto existing society is the history of class struggles." Marx, of course, meant all written history.[38] Books by authorities such as August Haxthausen, who "discovered" common ownership of land in Russia, and G. L. von Maurer, who investigated the social foundation of all Teutonic races, now threw light on prehistory, showing that village communities "were found to be, or to have been the primitive form of society everywhere from India to Ireland." Engels found communal ownership of the land among all Indo-Germanic peoples at a low level of development, from India to Ireland, and even among the Malays who were developing under Indian influence.[39]

These categories of the AMP and communal ownership, in different terminological formulations, have troubled those who adhere to or assume the main Marxist orthodox position of the relations of class, politics, and society. Discussion of the AMP has, as one contemporary Marxist analysis suggested, raised questions not simply about the relevance of orthodox Marxist concepts outside the European context, but also about the Marxist views of class society, revolutionary change, and world history.[40] The implication of the AMP is that political power, Oriental despotism, is not the result of an exploitative class, but results from the nature of the society and from the performance of vital economic functions. Some fundamental tenets of Marxism appear to be challenged, if not contradicted, by the analysis of the AMP and its related factors: the importance of geographical factors rather than the primacy of productive forces, the existence of social stagnation rather than progress in a historical setting, the argument that change in Asia had to be induced from outside, the implication that social development from slavery to capitalism was essentially Western and that there was no uniform pattern of development for all countries.[41]

That debate is parallel to, though not equivalent with, the broader question about the very study of Oriental societies or politics, and indeed of all social and political systems that have for one reason or another lagged behind in economic modernization and political development. Discussion of this matter has become part of the contemporary controversy of whether Western intellectuals can objectively analyze non-Western systems, or whether that analysis can be other than a reflection of the imposition of power relationships.

The charge of Eurocentrism in the writings of Marx and Engels would, for adherents of political correctness in this discussion, be accompanied by accusations of racism, cultural chauvinism, and the ultimate evil of Orientalism. The Marxist outlook would therefore be seen as yet another manifestation of cultural hegemony, of the belief in the innate superiority of European peoples and cultures, and of a false ideological construction of the East, the Other.[42]

Without entering into the larger debate at this point, an initial issue, troublesome for some, can be discussed, the terminology used by Marx and Engels. Contemporary social scientists have been wary in their analysis of comparative politics. Marx and Engels, like other nineteenth-century writers, were more apt to make comparisons in terms of evolution and progress. A typical example might be the late preface in 1884 by Engels to *The Origins of the Family, Private Property, and the State,* where, following Lewis Morgan, he sketches the "picture of the evolution of mankind through savagery and barbarism to the beginnings of civilisation." The use throughout their writings of concepts such as "primitive societies" is not to be taken as moral condemnation by Marx and Engels, but simply as references to early history, and to stages in the production process.

It must be admitted from the start that Marx and Engels, critical though they were of bourgeois society and its values, were, like other nineteenth-century thinkers, conscious of the prominence of that society among the nations of the world. Influenced by Hegel's philosophical analysis of world history and of the development of the world spirit, Marx and Engels accepted, at first, some of his empirical views about the Orient as well as his belief that dialectic of historical change had been manifested in the progressive West. That historical movement allowed them to speak without difficulty of "higher" or "lower" forms of society. Whether to regard these views as "Eurocentric" or unconsciously imbued with conviction of Western superiority is open to question, but it does not logically follow that the theories of Marx and Engels were efforts to impose on and to dominate the East. The Hegelian doctrine of a historical mission to be performed by the West was never overtly stated by Marx and Engels even if sometimes implied at a time when only the Western nations were pursuing the road to industrialization in any significant way and dominating world trade. Besides, the two Marxists qualified their historical materialism on many occasions. "World history," Marx wrote to Kugelmann on April 17, 1871, "would be of a very mystical nature if 'accidents' played no part in it." In the first draft of his letter to Vera Zasulich he spoke of "historical twists and turns."[43]

The historical movement was complex as well as unpredictable. What were the historical paths to be followed? One can extract from the voluminous writings of Marx both a unilinear and a multilinear model of historical change. In the first, essentially the European experience, the line of Western development would be the norm for all nations, and the capitalist system would be the culmination of that development before it was transformed into the final stage of socialism or communism.[44] This would suggest a given, universal sequence of historical stages and types, from tribal property or ancient mode of production to capitalism in all societies. Each stage would appear, develop, and then give rise to the next phase in the sequence. This law of social development, seen by some Marxists as scientific socialism and occasionally as "inevitable" in Western Europe, could be the basis for decisions on revolutionary tactics in the transformation of societies.

But the AMP, if a distinctive socioeconomic form, did not fit into this universal perspective of social development. The AMP, if it were to be located anywhere in this schema, would probably be placed between primitive communism and the ancient (slave) mode of production.[45] Historical change could also be seen as multilinear with separate lines of development for different countries. Those countries with the AMP might have a different history from those experiencing slave or feudal modes of production. What preceded and what followed the AMP in the historical process? This remained unclear but Marx asserted that "A more exact study of the Asiatic, more especially the Indian, forms of communal property would demonstrate how, out of the various forms of natural communal property, various forms of its dissolution are brought forth."[46]

This more sophisticated second model, with the AMP as a prominent feature, brought certain consequences: viewing the history of societies as uneven, the inadequacy of the unilinear model for historical analysis and for political tactics; an interest in developing societies; rethinking the role of the peasantry in history and in contemporary politics for revolutionary activity; a recognition that the state was not simply part of the superstructure but might have a decisive political role in developing societies.[47]

Where does history go? In his graveside eulogy of Marx on March 17, 1883, Engels said his friend had discovered the law of development of human history as Darwin had discovered the law of development of organic nature. He had also discovered the special law of motion governing the present-day capitalist mode of production and the bourgeois society that this mode of production had created.[48]

These laws clearly stem from Marx's study of European history and change. In turn they helped make that history more comprehensible. One interesting exemplification of this was Engels' preface to the third German edition of Marx's *The Eighteenth Brumaire of Louis Bonaparte* where he stated that Marx's law—that all historical struggles were in fact only struggles between social classes, which in turn depended on the nature and mode of production and exchange—was the key to understanding the history of the French Second Republic.

Yet, these laws have to be treated with caution. Engels, in his preface to the 1888 English edition of the *Communist Manifesto,* made a revealing statement implicitly suggesting that early societies were outside the scope of these laws: "the whole history of mankind (since the dissolution of primitive tribal society, holding land in common ownership) has been a history of class struggles." Marx and Engels were both anxious that their laws not be interpreted as historical inevitability for all societies, though the very concept of precapitalist societies, including the Oriental, may have the implication that change has occurred in a particular, if not inevitable, direction. Engels wrote a number of letters in the last years of his life trying to clarify the point: the Marxist materialist conception of history meant that the ultimately determining element in history was the history and reproduction of real life, not that the economic element was the only determining one.[49]

Though Marx had proposed these various categories of historical development, from *The German Ideology* to the *Critique,* he was conscious of the perils of intellectual generalizations about history. In the early *Poverty of Philosophy,* published in 1847, he objected to Proudhon's simplifications of history proceeding in a categorical fashion. Later he, and Engels too, warned readers and correspondents on a number of occasions about wrong conclusions drawn from their theory of history.[50] Perhaps the clearest caution was given, paradoxically because it was not immediately sent for publication, in the draft letter to the editors of *Otechestvenniye Zapiski* written probably in November 1877 but not published until 1886. Written as a reply to his critic N. K. Mikhailovsky, Marx clarified his position, cautioning not "to metamorphose my historical sketch of the genesis of capitalism in Western Europe into an historico-philosophical theory of the general path every people is fated to tread." Marx denied he had sketched "an historico-philosophical theory of a Universal Progress, fatally imposed on all peoples, regardless of the historical circumstances in which they find themselves."

Again, in the first draft of his reply to Vera Zasulich who on February 16, 1881, had asked his views on the commune in Russia and its likely historical path, Marx returned the question: "Does this mean that the development of the land commune must necessarily follow the same lines under all circumstances? Certainly not."[51] In the second draft of the letter, Marx wrote he had shown the metamorphosis of feudal production into capitalist production taking place in Western Europe, but "I expressly *limited* this 'historical inevitability' to the countries of Western Europe." By implication, Russia, as well as Asia, might take a different historical path.[52]

The discussion of historical development and of unilinear or multilinear change has been of more than academic interest in two important policy areas: the role of developed countries, especially those that had colonial responsibilities, towards those lands that had lagged behind in modernization and development; and the use or disregard of the Marxist writings.

Not many would dare accuse Marx and Engels of being imperialists or colonialists. Their moral indictment of colonialism is evident.[53] Britain was waging an "unrighteous war" on China. Marx was caustic about the "Christianity-canting and civilization-mongering British government." He wrote of the "European despotism planted upon Asian despotism by the British East India Company, forming a more monstrous combination than any of the divine monsters startling us in the Temple of Salsette."[54] England had broken down the entire framework of Indian society. Marx criticized the history of English economic management in India as a history of futile and actually stupid economic experiments.[55] Near the end of his life, he wrote of the British in India: "the suppression of the communal ownership of land was only an act of English vandalism, which has brought not an advance, but a setback to the native peoples."[56] Similarly, in a letter to Danielson of February 19, 1881, Marx called the British appropriations from India "a bleeding process with a vengeance."

Yet, both Marx and Engels also wrote on a number of occasions about the benefits of Western colonial rule in helping non-European peoples develop, especially countries such as India and China that for thousands of years had made no progress. In an article of January 22, 1848, on the revolt of Abd-el-Kader against France in Algeria, Engels argued, as de Tocqueville had also done, that the French conquest was an "important and fortunate fact for the progress of civilization. . . . The modern bourgeois, with civilization, industry, order, and at least relative enlightenment following him, is preferable to the feudal lord or to the marauding robber, with the barbarian state of society to which they belong."[57]

More generally, Engels believed that because of Western industrialism, the old system of manufacturing or industry founded on manual labor was completely destroyed in all countries of the world. All semi-barbarian countries were forcibly torn out of their isolation. Marx spoke of the progressive role of the British rule over India. Britain had brought more changes than had the French Revolution and had upset more property relations in India than were upset in the whole of Western Europe since the French Revolution. British political and economic power had disrupted the small economic village communities.[58] English steam and free trade, English commerce as a whole, had a revolutionary effect on those small, semi-barbarian, semi-civilized communities as the low price of English goods destroyed the hand loom and the spinning wheel. Its intentions may have been vile but by its actions and its introduction of private property, Britain was causing a social revolution in India, "the only social revolution ever heard of in Asia." "Whatever may have been the crimes of England it was the unconscious tool of history" in bringing change, "the sine qua non" of Europeanization.

Summing up, Marx in his important newspaper article of August 8, 1853 indicated the "superior" British double mission in India. One was destructive in breaking up the native communities and industries; the other as regenerating. Britain had laid the basis for a new society. It had brought the electric telegraph and communications, trained a native army and a native administrative class, set up a free press for the first time in India, established political unity, and begun the system of private property, "the great desideratum of Asiatic society."

Marx also appreciated that colonialism in India did not come cheap for Britain. The colonial country had taken large sums from India. Yet, in objective articles in April 1859 about the financial crisis in India, Marx indicated the considerable deficit resulting from the British administration due to the greater permanent debt of Britain after the Indian mutiny, the high general military costs, over 60 percent of aggregate regular income, and the negative effect on the British home market. About the same time, in a letter of April 9, 1859, Marx argued, as he had done earlier on September 21, 1857, that only the British upper class and colonial administrators had benefited from British rule. India had the "privilege of paying English capitalists five percent for their capital. But John Bull had cheated himself, or rather has been cheated by his capitalists."

Similarly, Marx concluded after evaluating the pattern of Anglo-Chinese trade that Britain had a balance of trade deficit because Chinese imports of British manufactured goods had not increased whereas its exports to Britain had increased considerably.[59] "The consuming and paying powers of the Celestials have been greatly overestimated." In a number of articles Marx had the same explanation: the main obstacle to British imports into China, other than the opium trade, was "the combination of small scale agriculture with domestic industry," the same characteristics as in India.[60]

The second policy issue, the heat engendered by the considerable debate about the location of Oriental despotism and of the AMP in the historical process, emanates from mixed motives, as was discussed earlier. Some results from genuine differences in interpretation of the Marxist writings, especially of the more obscure passages, on these issues, which were also explained above. But some also arises from the use or manipulation of those writings for political or ideological advantage, for their possible relevance in commentary on past or existing social and political systems, or for political tactics.[61] In the nineteenth and early twentieth centuries the main controversy over the AMP centered on the obshchina, the Russian mir commune. At the same time the very linking of Russia to the AMP meant emphasizing its non-European features, which affected the polemics of the Russian revolutionary movement, especially the internal disputes among the Marxists.

In more contemporary times, discussion of the AMP was related to the Soviet and Chinese Communist regimes, especially to the years under the rule of Stalin and Mao. Criticism, and occasionally support, of those regimes has often been couched in Aesopian language, long familiar in such discussions, about the despotic power of the rulers.[62]

In the latter part of their lives, from 1873 and for a decade, Marx and Engels read a great deal on the origin of the Russian village commune and on Russian society, using the material both as a source of data and for analyzing a noncapitalist system. They made ambivalent statements about that society, its history, and especially about the destiny of the mir. They also occasionally interrelated Russian and Indian Oriental despotism. Both from time to time referred to czarist Russia as "semi-Asiatic" or "semi-Eastern," in its condition, manners, traditions, and institutions, and as a country held together with great difficulty by Oriental despotism.[63] In his article, "What is to Become of Turkey," of April 21, 1853, Engels wrote of the Russian autocratic system, accompanied with its concomitant corruption, half-military bureaucracy, and pasha-like extortion.

Marx found similarities between the Russian communal system and a section of the Indian communities in the nondemocratic but patriarchal character of their communal management and in the collective responsibility for taxes to the state. Engels wrote of the Russian and Indian village communities suffering under the fiscal oppression of the despotic state, "the finest and broadest basis of exploitation and despotism."[64] In *The Frankish Period*, written in 1882, Engels wrote of the state power, arising among the Aryan peoples of Asia and the Russians when the fields were still cultivated by the community for the common account and there was not yet private property in land, the state power appeared as despotism.

On the question of the destiny of the mir, Marx and Engels could not give an unequivocal answer to their various interlocutors, despite their attention to the issue and their reading in the Russian language. Essentially the question was whether the mir, a form of early common ownership of land, could pass directly to the higher form of communist common ownership, or was it necessary for Russia to go through the same process of historical development as the West had done including capitalism?[65] Using a picturesque metaphor, Marx wrote that the Russian commune, the only one that had continued on a nationwide scale to his time, incorporated all the positive acquisitions devised by the capitalist system without passing through its Caudine Forks.[66] He also saw the commune as similar to the AMP, holding that the isolation of the commune, the lack of connection between the life of one commune and another, "the localised microcosm," caused a more or less centralized despotism to arise on top of the communes.

The uncertainty of the Marxists is best shown by Marx's inability to give a clear and quick answer to Vera Zasulich's letter of February 16, 1881. Perhaps the clue to his indecision can be found in the four drafts, written before the final short, somewhat bland response of March 8. Marx explained the dualism in the commune between collectivism, common land ownership, and individualism, peasant cultivation on his own plot.[67] The direction to be followed would depend on the historical environment in which the commune finds itself. In the main, in the various articles and letters on the subject and taking into account certain differences between the two men, Marx and Engels appeared to conclude that internal change in Russian society and economics would be dependent on external factors, "a sudden change of direction in Western Europe."[68] A proletarian revolution in the West, accompanying a Russian Revolution, might mean that the Russian common ownership of land could serve as the starting point for communist development. But the final remarks of Engels in January 1894 on a subject about which he and Marx had been so inconclusive were that he could not say whether enough of the Russian commune existed for it to become, as he and Marx had hoped in 1882, "a point of departure for communist development in harmony with a sudden change of direction in Western Europe."[69]

The question of the future path of Russia and the desirable revolutionary tactics led to fierce debates among the Russian Social Democrats. At the 1906 party congress the controversy centered on Lenin's proposal for the nationalization of land. George Plekhanov, who saw Russia as semi-Asiatic, argued this was likely to strengthen the existing absolute government and to lead to Oriental despotism. Lenin, who usually, though not always, viewed Russia as "partly Asiatic" and essentially feudal, declared nationalization was appropriate for Russia's development if it took the road to capitalism. The debate among the Russian revolutionaries was closely tied to the perception of the AMP. Was it a mode unique to the Orient, and to Russia which also had communal property, or should it be regarded as the early stage in historical development as in the West?[70]

The implications of the question became clear in the Soviet Union when for a twenty-year period from 1931 on the Stalin regime prevented any publication about the AMP lest a comparison be made between that regime and Oriental despotism. In 1938 Stalin's own simplistic formula, in his *Dialectical and Historical Materialism,* of five stages of modes of production, without reference to any Asiatic mode, became doctrinal truth for the whole communist world. Only after his death and with the process of de-Stalinization did the AMP emerge for intellectual dissection, especially on issues such as state control by a bureaucratic group that did not own the means of production and therefore could not be considered a class in the classic Marxist sense, and on the question of the way of historical development.

A Distinctive Mode of Production

Though Marx and Engels never presented their own systematic analysis of the AMP, and though the emphasis on particular features of the mode changed in different writings, one can draw from the various references and passages devoted to Oriental affairs an interrelated syndrome of characteristic features that make it a distinctive economy and political system. One analyst has even argued that Marx's views on the AMP were well formulated and digested, and had found their organic place in the Marxian political economy and theory of history. Marx and Engels used the Asian and Middle Eastern countries of Turkey, Persia, China, and, above all, Mughal India as the basis for their generalizations about the Orient, even if later they seemed to widen the geographical boundaries of the AMP.[71]

The term was first used by Marx in 1859 and rarely appeared again in that form. Engels usually spoke of Oriental despotism or Oriental society. In a number of places they made clear, either explicitly or by inference, differences between the Asiatic mode and other modes of production or property arrangements. One such difference concerned ownership of the surplus product of the society: in the antique mode it went to the slave owner, in feudalism to the feudal lord, and in the AMP to the state or Oriental despot. The social and political features of feudalism—seigniory, estates and corporations, its system of fiefs, the personal dependence in relationships—all were absent from the AMP.[72]

Marx compared essential features of capitalism with those in early societies, including the AMP. Capitalist production rested on a complete separation of the producer from the means of production; the expropriation of the agricultural producer was the basis of the whole process.[73] In precapitalist forms, the laborer was tied to the community by patriarchal, tribal, or feudal bonds. Direct producers were not separated from the means of production. This unity between the worker and the conditions of labor had two main forms: the Asiatic communal system (primitive communism), and small-scale agriculture based on the family and linked with domestic industry.[74] Both were embyronic forms and both were equally unfit to develop labor as social labor and the productive power of social labor. Also, in all precapitalist forms, it was the landed proprietor, not the capitalist, who directly appropriated the surplus labor of other people. Rent appeared historically as the general form of surplus labor, of labor performed without payment in return.[75]

It is however more difficult to differentiate clearly between the AMP and other earlier societies, or even to define the exact geographical contours of "Asia." These analytical problems arise because one of the essential features of the AMP, communal ownership of land, is said to exist in those other societies outside Asia given different names such as "old community communism," or "primitive communal ownership or communism," or "tribal ownership."[76] Marx, in his discussion of the clan system in Scotland, even talks of "the ancient Asiatic family communities." At these times, and especially as the emphasis shifted to the discussion of tribal property and organization rather than state organization property in the later writings, the AMP may appear to be less a distinctive mode of production than a part of the category of primitive forms of society.

Yet for Marx the AMP was not a particular variant of the original communism at the beginning of history. It was different conceptually in at least two major ways: its villages were settled and engaged in agriculture and crafts unlike other societies which also engaged in hunting and gathering; and it had a political organization, the state, which was absent elsewhere.[77]

In the four drafts of Marx's letter to Zasulich, he discussed the differences between the various "archaic formations" of societies, the primitive communities and the agricultural commune, the most recent type. The primitive communities rested on natural kinship relations between members of the commune. The agricultural commune had emancipated itself from these relations, and thus could adapt and expand, and engage in contacts with strangers. In the agricultural commune the house and its complementary plot belonged to the individual farmer; in the more primitive communities communal housing and collective habitation was an economic base. In the earlier societies work was done in common and the common product was distributed among the members according to needs; in the agrarian type, the cultivable land was periodically divided among the members of the commune.

First, the question of communal ownership, its origin, and its priority in property forms. Marx was always concerned to counter the view that private property was the natural form. Marx in his letter to Engels of March 14, 1868, was enthusiastic that the German historian G. L. von Maurer had shown that private property in land was of later origin than communal property: "The view I put forward that the Asiatic or Indian property forms everywhere mark the beginning of Europe receives new proof here."[78] Two years later he reminded Ludwig Kugelmann, on February 17, 1870, that common property was of Indian, not Mongolian, origin and "may therefore be found among all European peoples at the beginning of their development."[79]

Engels evaluated Maurer's work in similar fashion, as "devoted to proving the primitive common ownership of the land among all civilized peoples of Europe and Asia and to showing the various forms of its existence and dissolution." He did, however, sometimes appear to qualify this generalization. In *Anti-Duhring,* for example, private property had existed though limited to certain objects in the ancient, primitive communities of all civilized peoples.[80] Wherever private property evolved it was a result of altered relations of production and exchange in the interest of increased production.[81]

But the ancient communes "have also, for thousands of years, formed the basis of the most barbarous form of the state, Oriental despotism, from India to Russia."[82] Both Marx and Engels repeated the same point about communal ownership in slightly different ways. For Marx, at one point it existed among the Indians, Slavs, and ancient Celts.[83] At another time, he found it in various places, including the Russian and the German type of "primitive community" as well as in the village community in Asia.[84] In a late letter to Edward Bernstein of August 9, 1882, the peasant exploitation was extended in space and in time: "From Ireland to Russia, from Asia Minor to Egypt" and "since the time of the Assyrian and Persian Empires."[85]

Engels also ranged geographically.[86] He saw communal ownership, the primitive form of society, "among all Indo- Germanic peoples at a low level of development from India to Ireland." He also could trace it historically among the Slavs, Germans, and the Celts.[87] He even, in two letters in 1884, wrote of the old community or primitive communism in Java, and of the original tribal form among the native American Indians. Engels too in the 1888 edition of the *Manifesto* wrote that the primitive form of society from India to Ireland included Russia and all Teutonic races.[88]

What about China from which fewer examples or illustrations were taken about the AMP? Did in fact the Asiatic mode include China? In some twenty articles, mostly in *The New York Daily Tribune,* written between 1857 and 1862, Marx addressed current issues especially on British foreign policy, and on Anglo-Chinese trade. He did not designate it directly as an Oriental despotism nor as a society that depended on state-controlled large-scale irrigation works. Appreciating that private land-holding, "the combination of minute agriculture with domestic industry" existed in China, Marx could not completely fit it into the theory of a mode of production based on communal ownership.[89]

If Marx and Engels were not wholly consistent in their remarks about China, their characterization of it was similar to their view of India. Engels in his 1847 *Principles of Communism* wrote of "isolated, unchanging China," and in a speech of November 30, 1847, commented on a country "which for more than a thousand years had defied progress and historical development" and was now being revolutionized by English machinery and drawn into the mainstream of European civilization.[90] Marx too in his July 7, 1862, article saw China as "a living fossil" in which the unchanging social substructure was accompanied by "unceasing change in the persons and tribes who manage to ascribe to themselves the political super-structure." In any case, change was coming there, as in India, as a result of outside contacts.[91]

At the end of the *Grundrisse* and in the *Critique,* Marx indicated the value of studying India to gain insight into historical development. On the matter of common property in land, India provided "an array of the most varied forms of such economic communalism, more or less dissolved, but still fairly recognisable . . . research would rediscover it as the starting point among all civilised peoples." From the study of Asiatic, and especially of Indian forms of common property, one could observe "how from the different forms of primitive common property, different forms of its dissolution have been developed."[92] India was the origin of communal ownership which could therefore be found among all European peoples at the beginning of their development. In all the speculation, geographical and historical, about communal ownership and Oriental despotism, India was always at the core. Partly this was the consequence of Marx living in London from 1849 until his death in 1883, and of Engels living in Manchester and London for an even longer period until 1895. Marx acknowledged in his preface to the *Critique* that London had been a favorable vantage point for the observation of bourgeois society, and in *Capital* that England was used as the chief illustration in the development of his theoretical ideas.[93] It was equally useful for Marx and Engels to reside in England, drawing on the work of British economists, official government reports, and parliamentary papers, to increase their knowledge and to formulate their opinions about Britain's major imperial possession at the time.

Throughout Marx's writings on Asia the influence of the British economists can be detected.[94] Adam Smith had written that water control systems were important, that public works including roads and canals were noticeable, that the economy of China was stationary and that the revenues of the rulers in many Asian countries came from a land tax or ground rents. James Mill, in his *History of India* had written of the "Asiatic form of government" as a distinctive type of system, different from feudalism, in which the sovereign was the supreme landlord.[95] John Stuart Mill in his *Principles of Political Economy* made some insightful comments on the bureaucracy of Oriental despotism.[96] From Richard Jones, lecturer on economics at the East India Company College at Haileybury, Marx took quotations on the unique access of the state and its officials to many important sources of income, on the monuments built by that income, and on the place of cities in Asia.[97]

Although Marx drew on these reputable sources and on a mass of official British government documents, his accuracy about Asia has been challenged by critics. Daniel Thorner argued that Marx was mistaken that communal property ever existed in either Mughal or post-Mughal India, or that common cultivation in villages was the norm.[98] Indeed, much of the argument about the self-sufficiency, equality, and isolation of the Indian village, on the importance of irrigation, especially by central government, and on the role of the bureaucracy has been challenged.[99]

Yet a necessary, if insufficient, retort to the critics is that the theory of the AMP, whatever the historical and factual errors, is not so much an abstraction of any real economic, social, or political system, as an ideal type with a particular set of characteristics. With this in mind the model proposed by Marx of a distinctive mode of production can be analyzed.[100]

The Features of the Asiatic Mode

The Village Community

In the AMP, and under Oriental despotism, people lived in "a social system of particular features," the result of two factors: the central government taking care of the great public works, and the domestic union of agricultural and manufacturing pursuits. It was a system of self-sufficient, isolated village communities, each with a unity of its own, forming "a little world in itself."[101] Though these communities might take different forms, they were "the solid foundation of Oriental despotism."[102]

This partly resulted from the little communication they had with each other. The inhabitants were bound to the village by custom, a bond that was strengthened by lack of an alternative. Each village produced what it needed, with the small surplus going "from time immemorial" as taxes to the central government in the form of compulsory labor and produce, the equivalent to rent. This surplus was used in turn by the government for public works.

In each village community the individuals maintained at the expense of the whole community included the "chief inhabitant" who was judge, police, and tax gatherer in one; the bookkeeper; legal prosecutor; the man who guarded the boundaries of the community; the water-overseer who distributed water for irrigation; the Brahmin conducting religious services; the schoolmaster; the astrologer; the smith, carpenter, potter, barber, washerman, silversmith, and from time to time the poet.[103] If the population increased, a new community was founded, on the pattern of the old one, on unoccupied land. Marx got many of his views on the village community from George Campbell's *Modern India,* published in 1852, and from a number of other writers and reports in the early nineteenth century. His list of village occupations is virtually identical, as Louis Dumont pointed out, to that in *The Philosophy of History* by Hegel who derived it from the 1806 report by Munro.

The villages all produced the same kind of output with a fixed division of labor. Marx, following the report written by Mark Wilks, the fifth report from the Select Committee of the House of Commons on the Affairs of the East India Company, 1812, outlined the list of officials and twelve occupations to be found.[104] That division of labor operated with "the irresistible authority of a law of nature," thus leading to a static condition.[105] Though Marx provided few other details about the functioning or the structure of the villages, he suggested that they sometimes differed, from the simplest procedure, land cultivated in common with the produce divided and spinning and weaving in each family as subsidiary activities, to those where the villagers tilled their own plots, and used common pasture land.[106]

The Unity of Agriculture and Manufactures

Economic life in each village community was based on the unity of small-scale agriculture and home handicraft industry. This economic pattern, which was reproduced regularly in the same form, maintained village life in its traditional form, the villagers being bound by economic interests, kinship ties, and custom. In *Capital,* Marx explained that the social division of labor was a necessary condition for the production of commodities, but the reverse was not necessarily true: "In the primitive Indian community there is social division of labor without production of commodities." The economy of the village and of the AMP was organized to produce self-sufficiency, not commodities.[107] Most products were directly consumed by the community itself for use, not for exchange. Only the surplus products became commodities, going as tribute to the despot and the state. Since they were spent by the ruler, these surpluses could not be accumulated as capital, the process that was at the heart of capitalism.[108]

Marx quoted Richard Jones to argue that no accumulation of capital took place. Since the most numerous part of the people of India was self-sustaining peasants, the means of labor and of subsistence never existed in the shape of a fund that was saved from revenue and therefore could contribute to accumulation. Also, labor was tied to the community. Wage labor arose from the disintegration of slavery and serfdom, or from the decay of communal property as among the Oriental and Slav peoples. It appeared as the dissolution, the destruction of relations in which labor was fixed in all respects, such as income, content, locality, and scope.[109]

In his analysis of the reproduction and circulation of social capital, Marx explained that in capitalist production all products were transformed into commodities which were then transformed into money. In the ancient Asiatic and other ancient modes of production, the conversion of products into commodities, and therefore the conversion of men into producers of commodities was of little importance, though it became more important as the primitive communities approached dissolution.[110] The methods of production in the AMP were extremely simple and transparent as compared with bourgeois society. Commodity production was limited as was exchange of commodities which could only come from external factors.[111] Usury could, in the AMP, persist for a long time without leading to anything more than economic decay and political corruption. Moreover, every division of labor that was well developed and brought about by exchange of commodities was founded on the separation of town and country.[112] The whole economic history of society was summed up in the movement of this antithesis. But the AMP was different: agriculture and handicrafts were not separated geographically, but were carried out in the same village community.

Though the portrayal of the combination of the two occupations was mostly based on Indian conditions, Marx also applied it to China where husbandry and manufacturing existed.[113] The difference between the two cases was that in India British control of landed property enabled them to undermine the self-sustaining communities whereas in China they were not able to wield this power.

Communal Ownership of Land

In their first newspaper articles and letters on India in 1853, Marx and Engels agreed that the key to the Orient was the absence of private property in land. An essential feature of Oriental society, and what was soon to be called the AMP or the "Oriental form," was communal property ownership, on which Oriental despotism was founded.[114]

Wherever common ownership existed, Engels wrote to Karl Kautsky on March 2, 1883, be it of land, women, or anything else, it would necessarily be primitive. The subsequent process of development consisted entirely in the gradual dissolution of this primeval common ownership.[115] Earlier in the *Critique,* Marx criticized the "absurdly biased view" that primitive communal property was a specifically Slavonic phenomenon. It was an early form which could be found among Romans, Teutons, and Celts, and of which "a whole collection of diverse patterns (though sometimes only remnants survive) is still in existence in India."[116] Engels in 1894 made a similar point that the common ownership of land was a form common to all peoples at a certain stage of development. He found it among all the Indo-European peoples in primeval times; it still existed in India.[117]

The two writers often made the point that common property, not private property, was the original historical form of ownership.[118] All Indo-Germanic peoples began with common property, according to Engels. This common property quietly persisted in India and Russia, under the most diverse forcible conquests and despotisms, and formed their basis. This was an exemplification of the general proposition made by Engels in his *Preparatory Writings for Anti-Duhring* that, although all states were based on force, social and political variations could be explained by the different productive forces and distribution in states.[119]

But who owned the land in the AMP—the despot, the higher unity, officials, the village communities, the tribes? The terminology on the issue changed in the different writings. Marx, in his article of June 7, 1858, acknowledged that differences of opinion existed among British authorities about land tenure and private property in India, but thought they all agreed that in India, as in most Asiatic countries, "the ultimate property in the soil was vested in the government." His argument in *Capital* about labor rent in Asia rested on the view that direct producers there were under "direct subordination to a state which stands over them as their landlord and simultaneously as sovereign."[120] The state was then the supreme lord. Sovereignty in Asia consisted in the ownership of land concentrated on a national scale. No private ownership of land existed, but there was both private and common possession and use of land. Engels provided a slightly different version: "In the whole of the Orient, where the village community or the state owns the land, the very term landlord is not to be found in the various languages. It was the Turks who first introduced a sort of feudal ownership of land in the countries conquered by them in the Orient."[121]

Yet the position is not altogether clear. In the *Land Tenure in India* article, Marx discussed the role of the zemindars, talookdars, or sirdars in the Indian economic system. Were they to be considered as landed proprietors or as mere tax gatherers?[122] Though Marx recognized that the claims of the zemindars and talookdars were to a certain extent legal, he appeared to favor the alternative view that "the property of the land was in the village corporations, in which resided the power of allotting it out to individuals for cultivation." In this view the two groups were only officers of the government, looking after the interests and collecting rent for the ruler.

A distinction was made between ownership and possession, between property rights held in an absolute sense, and rights held in a more limited fashion. "In the Asiatic mode (at least, predominantly) the individual has no property but only possession; the real proprietor is the commune, hence property only as communal property in land."[123] In that mode the individual never became a proprietor but only a possessor; "he is at bottom himself the property, the slave of him in whom the unity of the commune exists." The original form of property in the "Oriental form, modified in the Slavonic" was direct common property. Again, in *Capital,* Marx held that in India, "no private ownership of land exists, although there is both private and common possession and use of land."[124]

A somewhat different emphasis on the issue of common ownership derived from their interest in anthropology. Marx spoke of tribal or common property rather than the state property, in some passages in the

Grundrisse.[125] The tribal community was not the result but the precondition of common application and use of the soil. Engels asserted that in the early history of all civilized people, tribal and village communities existed with common ownership of the land, from India to Ireland. While giving in *The Mark* a short historical sketch of the primitive agrarian conditions of the German tribes, Engels generalized that "two fundamental facts govern the primitive history of all, or of almost all, nations: the grouping of the people according to kindred, and common property in the soil." He added that the Germans had brought the method of grouping people by tribes and gentes from Asia.[126]

Marx and Engels both recognized that if private property evolved in early societies, it was the result of altered relations of production and exchange brought about by external factors.[127] Barter with foreigners and more production of commodities for exchange, and increasing exchange within the communities themselves all led to inequality in property ownership and to the undermining of the ancient common ownership of the land. Ironically, Engels argued, for thousands of years Oriental despotism and the changing rule of conquering nomad peoples had not injured the old communities, but foreign large-scale industry competing with the primitive home industry had brought those communities closer and closer to dissolution.[128] The condition of individuals in the AMP was one of "general slavery," though this was not the kind of slavery to be found in Greece and Rome. This general slavery was the consequence of the binding ties, the umbilical cord, between individuals and the community, resulting from communal property ownership and Oriental despotism, the embodiment of the unity of the community. Essentially a matter of labor tribute to the ruler, this form of slavery was different from that of individual slavery in which the worker was one of the factors of production for someone else.

Communal ownership of the land may have been the original form, but it was a fetter, a brake on agricultural production.[129] Engels explained that the Russian peasant lived in and had his being only in his village community, which was his whole world: the Russian word "mir" means both "world" and "peasant community." The parallel with the AMP is clear. For Engels, a complete isolation of individual communities from one another was the natural basis for Oriental despotism in India and Russia.

Cities

Because the basis of the AMP lay in the village communities, cities were less important economically than in other societies, including earlier ones.[130] The Marxists pointed out the difference. Ancient classical history was the history of cities, but cities based on landed property and agriculture; the city there "with its attached territory . . . forms the economic totality." By contrast, Asiatic history is "a kind of indifferent unity of town and countryside." Marx had spoken in *The German Ideology* of the antagonism between town and country that could only exist in the framework of private property. By inference no such antagonism existed in the AMP.[131]

Following the influential Bernier, Marx wrote that the really large cities in the AMP must be regarded merely as royal camps, as an artificial excrescence on the actual economic structure. Towns like Delhi or Agra lived almost entirely on the army and were therefore obliged to follow the king if he went to war for any length of time. These towns were not like Paris, being little more than military camps and "only a little better and more conveniently situated than in the open country." Since in Asiatic societies the monarch appeared as the exclusive possessor of the surplus product of the countryside, entire cities arose which were really nothing but "wandering camps, through exchange of his revenue with the free hands, as Steuart (Sir James Steuart) calls them." Cities in the proper sense were set up only at exceptionally favorable locations for foreign trade or where the head of state and his satraps exchanged their revenue (surplus product) for labor.[132]

Rent and Tax

In Marxist analysis a central, usually crucial, factor was the way in which the surplus product in a particular mode of production was extracted and allocated. For the most part in that analysis the AMP was differentiated from other systems because the surplus was concentrated in the hands of the Oriental despot and because of the nature of the surplus. The principle revenue of Asiatic countries was in the hands of princes, landlords, in the form of rent.[133]

Marx spent some time reading and assessing the works on this issue by British economists, especially the book by Richard Jones, *The Distribution of Wealth and The Sources of Taxation.* He quoted extensively and presumably agreed with Jones that in precapitalist forms it was the landed proprietor, not the capitalist, who directly appropriated the surplus labor of other people. Rent appeared, especially among the Asiatic peoples, as the general form of surplus labor, of labor performed without payment in return.[134]

Rent and tax thus coincided. The reason stemming from the common ownership of property, was that the state was both landlord and sovereign. No tax existed that differed from the form of ground rent. The state taxes depended on the conditions of production that were reproduced with the regulation of natural phenomena. And this mode of payment tended in turn to maintain the ancient forms of production. An individual need not be politically or economically under any harder pressure than that common to all who were subject to the state, the condition already categorized in the *Grundrisse* as general slavery.[135]

The Need for Irrigation

Early in their writings on India, Marx and Engels pointed to the crucial need for irrigation and water controls in Asiatic societies. Engels first wrote on the subject in his June 6, 1853, letter with his statement that "Artificial irrigation is (in the East) the first condition of agriculture and this is a matter either for the communes, the provinces, or the central government." Marx repeated the argument in his article of June 25, 1853, with one significant difference.[136] Comparing the Orient with Western Europe, where voluntary associations, in Flanders and Italy, took care of the need for water, Marx wrote that in the East where "civilization was too low and the territorial extent too vast to call into life voluntary association," the central power of government was necessary. The function of providing public works devolved on all Asiatic governments, but Marx said nothing about decentralized political power in this regard. The need to provide large-scale irrigation works and water control required bureaucratic and managerial control by a state capable of organizing a hydraulic system.[137]

This functionalist argument—that the power of the ruler came from this functional necessity, rather than from ownership of land or possession of military force—for Oriental despotism, and for a state that is not merely part of the superstructure but which performs vital economic functions, has led to much of the controversy over the accuracy and value of the concept of the AMP.[138] Some cannot accept this activity by the state as a sufficient explanation for the origin or existence of a political and social structure. Orthodox Marxists may tend to see the AMP concept as a denial of or too strong a qualification of the materialist conception of history because of the absence of any recognizable class struggle based on the relations of production, which in theory gives rise to the political structure. Some of them therefore have exhaustively looked for evidence of the existence of classes in the AMP.[139]

Co-operation

The links among people in the labor process in early societies, including agrarian Indian communities, were based both on common ownership of the means of production, and also on the ties of individuals to the "navel-strings: of their tribes or communities, from which they had not been able to tear themselves free.[140] As a result, the links took the form of simple cooperation, different from the cooperation in capitalist systems which presupposed free wage laborers who sold labor power to capital, the essence of capitalism.[141] Marx at times appeared to differentiate cooperation and communal ownership in the AMP from that in other early societies where the sporadic application of cooperation on a large scale rested on direct relations of dominion and servitude. What Marx called the colossal effects of simple cooperation in the AMP could be seen in the gigantic structures in the ancient Asiatic, Egyptian, and Etruscan countries. Marx accepted the statement of Richard Jones in the latter's *Textbook of Lectures on the Political Economy of Nations* that Oriental states, after supplying the expenses of their civil and military establishments, had a surplus which they applied to "works of magnificence or utility, and in the construction of these, their command over the hands and arms of almost the entire nonagricultural population has produced stupendous monuments which still indicate their power."[142] In Asian monarchies, the despot was able to direct the masses to build the "palaces and temples, the pyramids, and the armies of gigantic statues of which the remains astonish and perplex us." The fact that revenues in the AMP went to one or a few people made these undertakings possible.

Stagnation

Running through all the Marxist comments on the AMP is the argument that it was inherently static or stagnant.[143] The Asiatic mode could not develop through internal mechanisms and therefore did not follow the dialectic of history as did other modes of production.[144] The "Oriental mutual complementation of agriculture and manufactures" and the self-sustaining circle of production meant the unchanging nature of the old forms of property in the AMP and of the community as a whole.[145] The small and extremely ancient Indian communities, some of which continued to exist, were based on the possession of the land in common, on the blending of agriculture and handicrafts, and on an unalterable division of labor.

The individual member of the village commune was "firmly rooted" to the community, and could not be independent from it.[146] Labor in the

AMP did not advance economic development, or serve, as did the urban labor of the Middle Ages, as "a preparatory school for the capitalist mode of production."[147] The very essence of the AMP was that the individual did not become independent of the commune with its unity of agriculture and manufactures, and self-sufficiency and self-sustaining character. Asiatic countries, China and India, were marked by an absence of fixed capital and machinery that were necessary for economic development. Production did not have a cyclical nature as in capitalism.[148] It was for immediate consumption, and not for exchange. Productivity was at a low level, as was circulation of money, and there was little connection between villages.[149] The interrelated factors—absence of accumulation because the surplus went to the Oriental despot, the lack of village initiative because there were no voluntary associations, the bondage of individuals to the soil, the absence of wage labor and the persistence of primitive conditions of production—explained the inability to develop.[150] In the Asiatic, as in the antique mode of production, exchange or what Marx termed "the transformation of the product into a commodity" was of secondary importance. Exchange could only result from external influence: "Commodity exchange begins where the communities end, at the points of their contact with foreign communities or members of foreign communities."

Marx and Engels saw the old primitive communities remaining in existence for thousands of years—as in India and among the Slavs—before change came as a result of contact with the outside world.[151] The Oriental empires always showed an unchanging social infrastructure coupled with continual change in the political leaders and tribes. China was seen as a mummy preserved in a hermetically sealed coffin.[152] Engels spoke of Oriental ignorance, impatience, prejudice, vicissitudes of fortune, and favor inherent to Eastern courts. Yet these old countries, India and China, that had made no progress for thousands of years were revolutionized as a result of the cheapening of Western products by industrialization. The only case where change was brought about by an internal despot rather than by external factors appeared to be czarist Russia under Peter the Great.[153] In Marx's analysis, Peter's transfer of the capital to St. Petersburg occurred because "the East was narrowly circumscribed by the stationary character and the limited relations of Asiatic peoples." He converted Muscovy into Russia by changing it from a semi-Asiatic inland country into the paramount maritime power of the Baltic.

Not surprisingly because of the static nature of the AMP and because of its low level of production, it was also a simple organizational structure though there were variations. Marx had suggested that all the forms of primitive communities were "extremely simple and transparent." The very simplicity in the AMP of the organization of production in the self-sufficient communities that constantly reproduced themselves in the same form and kept recurring was the key to the secret of the unchangeable character of Asiatic societies, in striking contrast to the constant dissolution and refounding of Asiatic states and changes of dynasty.[154]

Backward

The Orient was not only stagnant: it was also backward. In this, Marx, consciously or not, expressed Hegel's attitude about the East where "the principle of subjective freedom is lacking" and where despotism was appropriate to the "Dawn-Land of History." Engels in his 1859 review of Marx's *Critique* explained that his friend had struggled against Hegel's philosophical ideas and that Marx's "epoch making conception of history was the direct theoretical premise for the new materialist outlook."[155] Yet on Asia, Marx's implicit premises were close to the more explicit pronouncements of Hegel. The latter saw Asia as a moment in the movement of the World Spirit and as a place where the principle of subjective freedom was lacking.[156] It was fixed, stationary, isolated from the great trends of history, or even outside them. For Hegel, despotism was natural to Asia, though he qualified this in the case of China. India, however, was a "despotism without principles, without ethical or religious norms," the most arbitrary and dishonoring despotism. No consciousness of self, which might inspire the soul to revolt, stood in the way of Asian tyranny.[157] Everything was regulated, directed, and watched over from on high. Hegel also touched on a number of empirical features of Indian society, including one that was central for Marx, the permanence of its village structure, barely affected by the outside world. The fate of Asiatic empires was to become subject to Europeans.

In the *Principles of Communism* of 1847, Engels had referred to all semi-barbarian countries, including India and China, which until this time had been more or less outside historical development.[158] Again, in the *Communist Manifesto,* Engels and Marx, before they really knew anything of Asia, had spoken in a general way of barbarian and semi-barbarian countries and of the dependence of the East on the West. In one of his first writings on India, the article of August 8, 1853, Marx regarded India as a backward country with no known history. That history was merely one of successive intruders who founded their empires on the passive basis of an unresisting and unchanging society.

Earlier, in his June 25, 1853, article, Marx waxed ironic at the expense of "the idyllic village communities," which among other things restrained the human mind within the smallest compass, made it the unresisting tool of oppression, subjected it to tradition, and deprived it of grandeur and energies. He spoke in his strongest critical tone of "the barbarian egoism" that had witnessed the ruin of empires, unspeakable cruelties, and massacres. He saw in this Asiatic society "undignified, stagnatory and vegetative life," a passive sort of existence that evoked wild, aimless, unbounded forces of destruction and rendered murder itself a religious rite in Hindustan.[159] The religion of the Hindus had made them "virtuosi in the art of self-torturing; these tortures inflicted on the enemies of their race and creed appear quite natural (to them)."

The communities in India were contaminated by caste distinctions and slavery, and subjected inhabitants to circumstances. This led to a brutalizing worship of nature and to degrading man who "fell down on his knees in adoration of Kanuman the monkey, the Sabbala, the cow."[160] Other Asian countries exhibited the same backwardness. In Persia the European system of military organization had been engrafted on Asiatic barbarity.[161] Marx talked of China as "the rotting semi-civilization" and of Chinese nationality "with all its overbearing prejudice, stupidity, learned ignorance, and pedantic barbarism."

Oriental Despotism

During the time when Marx was working on his major books on economics, he wrote both to Ferdinand Lassalle on February 22, 1858, and to Engels on April 2, 1858, that he was planning six related books, one of which would be on the state. That book was never written and, in spite of the efforts of later epigoni, there is little theoretical discussion of political systems and their organizational characteristics in the original Marxist writings.

Marx had given a concise summary of the division of occupations in the village communities, but he had little to say about the political structure of the AMP once he assumed it was despotic.[162] He accepted Bernier's view that the king is "the sole and unique proprietor of the realm in the Mogul empire." The despotic ruler had sovereign power, especially over the court and his followers, though he had little contact with the villages themselves.[163]

These village communes, Marx suggested in the *Grundrisse,* varied politically: despotic when the head was chief of the clan family, democratic when power was shared. Above the communes and their political arrangements stood the Oriental despot who incorporates "the higher unity" and who wielded ultimate power in the political, economic, reli-

gious, and military areas. Marx referred to him as the "patriarchal authority, the only moral link embracing the vast machinery of the state."[164]
The stability of the AMP allowed that link to exist. In most Asiatic fundamental forms, the

> all-embracing unity which stands above all these small common bodies may
> appear as the higher or sole proprietor, the real communities only as heredi-
> tary possessors. Since the unity is the real owner and the real precondition
> of common ownership, it (may) appear as something separate and superior
> to the numerous real, particular communities. . . . The despot here appears
> as the father of all the numerous lesser communities, thus realising the
> common unity of all.[165]

Using different language, Engels in *The Frankish Period* made the same
point.[166] The continued existence of the nation, arising from the early
small village communities, depended on a state power that did not derive from these communities but confronted them as something alien
and exploited them to an ever-increasing extent.

The precapitalist forms of production, Marx argued in *Capital III,*
provided "a firm basis for the articulation of political life (and their)
constant reproduction in the same form is a necessity for that life."[167] In
those forms most of the surplus product went to the rulers: the slave
owner, the feudal lord, and in the case of the AMP the state, the Oriental
despot.[168] Again, political rule by the despot was linked to the economic
form. In Asia the fact that state taxes were chiefly composed of rents
payable in kind depended on the conditions of production which were
reproduced with the regularity of natural phenomena. This mode of
payment tended in its turn to maintain the ancient form of production.[169] It also helped explain the continuing political rule as with "the
conservation of the Ottoman Empire." Engels expressed this more simply in a letter to Bernstein of August 9, 1882: "The satrap, alias pasha, is
the chief Oriental form of the exploiter, just as the merchant and the
jurist represent the modern Western form."[170]

Engels tended for the most part to prefer the functional explanation
of the Oriental despot. Marx in an early article had stated that not conquest by itself but the performance of public functions lent authority to
the despots of the East and stabilized their rule.[171] Engels, in his *Anti-
Dühring,* after establishing that the exercise of a social function was
everywhere the basis of political supremacy, explained that organs of
authority, once established, made themselves more independent and more
indispensable. The person chosen as the servant of society gradually
changed into the lord, the lord emerged as an Oriental despot, or satrap,

or as the dynast of a Greek tribe or chieftain of a Celtic clan. Yet, however great was a number of despotisms that rose and fell in Persia and India, each was fully aware that above all the despot was responsible for the collective maintenance of irrigation throughout the river valleys.

Why Oriental Despotism?

Though they did not say so in any systematic fashion, Marx and Engels from time to time alluded to factors that would explain the basis of Oriental despotism or the reasons for its existence.[172] At bottom of course was the mode of production in the self-sufficient village communities that constantly reproduced themselves in the same form, or replaced themselves if they were accidentally destroyed. This was the key to the secret of the unchangeableness of Asiatic societies.[173] Marx quoted Sir Stamford Raffles, former governor of Java: "The inhabitants give themselves no trouble about the breaking up and division of kingdoms; while the village remains entire, they care not to what power it is transferred, or to what sovereign it devolves; its internal economy remains unchanged." With an unchanging social structure, the Oriental despot personified the state.

Only one fleeting reference to a psychological factor was apparent. Marx, borrowing a thesis and a phrase from the economist Richard Jones, remarked that peoples in different countries did not have the same predisposition towards capitalist production. "Some primitive peoples such as the Turks have neither the temperament nor the disposition" to it.[174] The implication is that they were not able to live in a regime without free labor.

Some brief, tantalizing references were made to other factors that might have had an impact on the origin and persistence of Oriental despotism. One is the size, and even the climate, of the area to be governed. Explaining the absence of landed property, even in its feudal form, in the Orient, Engels in his June 6, 1853, letter to Marx wrote that he thought it was mainly due to the climate, taken in connection with the nature of the soil, especially with the great stretches of desert which extended from the Sahara straight across Arabia, Persia, India, and Tartary up to the highest Asiatic plateau.[175] By contrast, the mother country of *Capital* was not the tropical region with its luxuriant reputation, but the temperate zone.[176] It was the necessity of bringing a natural force under the control of society, of economizing on its energy, of appropriating or subduing it on a large scale by the work of the human hand that played the most decisive role in the history of industry.

A second factor, never followed up or discussed analytically, was religion. In his June 14, 1853, letter to Engels, Marx remarked that it seemed to have been the Mohammedans who first established the principle of "no property in land" throughout the whole of Asia, in the context of his argument about the sovereign as absolute landlord.

A third factor, referred to from time to time, was tradition, which played a dominant role in affairs and economic relationships in early societies, and sanctioned the existing order as law. At one point in *Capital,* Marx remarked that the "ancient Asiatic and other ancient modes of production are founded either on the immature development of man individually, who has not yet severed the umbilical cord that unites him with his fellow men in a primitive tribal community, or on direct relations of subjection."[177] The more general argument, especially as provided by Marx in his article written on June 10, 1853, is that "the idyllic village communities, inoffensive though they may appear, have been the solid foundation of Oriental despotism." The sober picture Marx gave of the life and behavior of inhabitants, passive, subjugated, worshipping idols of the ruler, is already familiar. Marx insisted in a number of places that most of the surplus revenue from the village communities went to the state and its officers. They established the centers of distribution of the royal revenues, and moved the capital city from time to time, causing the population to move also. This explained the vanished capitals in Asia.

A fundamental characteristic of those village communities was communal ownership.[178] For Engels, primitive communism furnished in India and Russia, and also in Java, the "finest and broadest basis of exploitation and despotism." Discussing the state power in early small village communities, Engels made the point that the form taken by that power depended on the form of the communities at the time—where, as among the Aryan peoples of Asia and the Russians, when agriculture was cultivated by the community for the common account, when no private property existed, the state power was despotic.[179]

Elsewhere Engels gave a related explanation for the existence of Oriental despotism when discussing whether the obshchina, the village community system in Russia, might lead directly to a socialist regime.[180] It was the complete isolation of the individual communities from one another that created throughout the country similar, but the very opposite of common, interests, which was the natural basis for Oriental despotism.[181] From India to Russia this form of society, wherever it had prevailed, had always produced it and always found its complement in it.

In the afterward to the 1873 second German edition of *Capital* Marx confessed that in his chapter on value he had "coquetted with the modes of expression" peculiar to Hegel.[182] He certainly also did so in his most picturesque reference to the Oriental despot. The image was that of the "all embracing unity" the proprietor of land, which stood above the village communities.[183] These village communities sent their surplus, or most of it, in tribute and in labor, to "the higher community which ultimately exists as a person." This tribute and the common labors were performed for the "glorification of the unity, which is in part the real despot and in part the imagined tribal being, the god."[184]

This theological attribute of the despot was rarely mentioned elsewhere, but one interesting relevant passage appeared in Marx's discussion of the rule of Napoleon III where he put forward the generalization that the most trying governmental position was that of a civilian at the head of a despotic military state.[185] In the Orient, Marx continued, the difficulty was more or less met by transforming the despot into a god, above the level "common to himself and his swordsmen." Elsewhere, Marx had written that the state was personified in the Oriental despot, a personification that engendered a belief in his absolute power.

The most hotly disputed explanation for the existence of Oriental despotism is, of course, the functional one.[186] First Engels in his June 6, 1853, letter and then, quickly, Marx in response and in his article of June 25, 1853, saw the crucial need for irrigation systems and thus for a ruler, "the despotic government poised above the lesser communities." Marx, however, emphasized more than Engels had the role of central government to perform this function. Some structural Marxists have challenged the functional argument in two ways. They hold that crucial characteristics of the AMP, such as communal ownership and expropriation of the surplus by a higher unity, were not confined to those societies requiring irrigation. They also argue that large-scale irrigation controls were present not only in the AMP but also in non-Asiatic countries and areas such as Lombardy, Holland, Spain, and Egypt, as well as in India and Persia.

Both Marx and Engels argued that all Asiatic governments had the functions of providing public works.[187] Compared with their discussions of the various aspects of the AMP from a social and economic point of view, Marx and Engels had little to say on the political organization or structure of Oriental despotism.[188] Marx in the *Grundrisse* did refer to possible differences in governmental arrangements in tribal bodies, which could take either a more despotic or a more democratic form.[189] But the starkest commentary on Oriental government, given in 1853, was the statement on its simple organization. There had been, Marx said in a letter and an article, in Asia generally from time immemorable only three departments of government: finance or the plunder of the interior, war or the plunder of the exterior, and the department of public works.

Parenthetically, Marx argued that British rule in India had continued the functions of finance and war, but had neglected that of public works.[190] This helped explain the poor state of agriculture in that country. When the public works fell into disrepair, vast expanses once magnificently cultivated became arid, and were ruined, and trade was destroyed.

In another article of September 9, 1854, on *Revolutionary Spain,* Marx made another point about the centralizing character of Oriental despotism by allusion and comparison.[191] He explained that the absolute monarchy in Spain, unlike other European absolute monarchies, prevented rather than fostered the growth of common interests on which "alone a uniform system of administration and the rule of general laws can be created." Spain therefore resembled Asiatic forms of government not the other European ones. Oriental despotism attacked municipal self-government only when opposed to its direct interests, but was very glad to allow those institutions to continue so long as they took off its shoulders the duty of doing something and spared it the trouble of regular administration.

Over the last two centuries Marx and Engels had been among the more prominent of those writers whose ambition has been to make history intelligible by finding what Berlin called large patterns or regularities in the procession of historical events.[192] In these patterns they envisaged the Orient as a region with a historical background and a socioeconomic and political system qualitatively different from the West. Previous writers and analysts dealing with Asian countries tended to focus on the prominent role of the ruler, the Oriental despot, in the life of those countries. The two Marxists, in consonance with their general approach to analysis of historical development and contemporary societies, concentrated in their discussion of the Asiatic mode of production on socioeconomic features rather than on political factors or the relationship between the ruler and his subjects in the intellectual structure they created.[193]

Of course, they wrote, mostly in their newspaper articles on the empirical issues of the day, with considerable insight on a variety of topics, and on political and governmental policies concerning the Asian countries, especially India. Yet they never dwelt on theoretical analysis of political rule or compared Asian political institutions or the interrelationship between the individual and the state with Western systems in the same way or with the depth they exhibited in comparing socioeconomic formations or forms of property ownership. In particular, the role of the Oriental despot is made clear but little is revealed of the activities or nature of his political and administrative functions.

The contribution of Marx and Engels to the discussion of Oriental societies has been important not only for its insight and suggestive comments, but also for its effect on later Marxist theoreticians and activists. That contribution was the creation, with some qualification, of a coherent and consistent pattern of a distinctive form of society. To ideas and information they had garnered from previous writers, who influenced much of their work on Asia, and from contemporary documents on the region, Marx and Engels added their own reflections, sometimes changing emphases, and their general comparisons, making up a systematic overall theory of the AMP. Some of these comparisons were cast in negative form since the norm for explanation was often the essence and elements of the capitalist system. This is reflected in discussion of topics such as free labor, private property, division of labor, separation of the worker from the land, commodity production, degree of commodity exchange, use of money, capital accumulation, extraction of surplus value, temperate climatic zone. But other features of the AMP, especially the communal village system, the unity of agriculture and handicrafts, the stagnant society, and the Oriental despot, are attributes that are not necessarily related to Marx's primary concern with capitalism.

For disciples, epigoni, and the general literature on Marxism, the AMP has been important in at least two ways. First, it was an example of the complexities of historical analysis, illustrating or implying the possibility of different paths of development in the past or in the present. Equally important is that the AMP portrays a society in which political power appears to be autonomous and not the result, as in the main Marxist explanation of that power, of class conflict and domination by that class owning the means of production.

Partly because of its unorthodox nature the AMP has occasioned considerable critical comment from both Marxists and less ideologically oriented analysts. Some of the criticism is justifiable, but the extent of it is somewhat surprising. Gellner wittedly pointed out that commentary on classical antiquity or primitive tribalism are hardly crucial testing grounds for Marxism. Nor would one normally go to Marxist writings for such commentary if expert knowledge was sought.

Yet, cogent criticisms of the concept of the AMP are valid. Analysis of the AMP does not always have the clarity or easy comprehensibility one would like, particularly on the differences between the AMP and other early societies, and between state property and communal or tribal property. At times the very location of "Oriental" appears to go beyond normal geographical boundaries. A related problem is the changing emphasis on specific features of the AMP in different writings as Marx and Engels were influenced by research by others on their subject over a thirty-year period.[194] Nevertheless, in spite of a particular emphasis at one point or another, the essential features, whether it is the self-sufficient village, the method of extraction of surplus labor, the communal property, or the Oriental despotism, remain always as part of the analysis.

To what extent does the Marxian analysis correspond to the realities of Oriental societies, economies, and politics? Experts in the field of Oriental societies have pointed out the factual mistakes or too strong generalizations that cannot bear the freight of the empirical statements in the writings on the AMP, though they often stemmed from the works of British administrators in India and from government documents as well as from the general reading by Marx and Engels. Thorner, in particular, indicated factual errors; Marx was mistaken that communal property had ever existed in either Mughal or post-Mughal India. Others have made the point that there was neither a historical nor theoretical relationship between elements of the AMP such as absence of private property in land and need for state control of irrigation and Oriental despotism.[195] Anderson went even further by arguing that the whole Marxist picture of the Indian villages was inaccurate except for the union of agriculture and crafts, which in fact was common to all pre-industrial rural communities.[196] Moreover, the villages were not egalitarian communities but rather based on caste differences, a topic Marx mentioned but ignored for the most part.

Yet, Anderson's argument is too strong in suggesting that the AMP was essentially a generic residual category for non-European development.[197] Marx and Engels were not Orientalists in the sense of specialized scholars in the field of Oriental societies, but neither were they ignorant or lacking in perspective of that area and of a type of society and political rule, Oriental despotism, that was distinctive there. More apt is Dumont's comment that Marx, and the English historian Henry Maine, were the two foremost writers who had drawn the Indian village community into the circle of world history.[198] It may be excessive to hold that the views of Marx on the AMP are essential elements in his work and that without them the composition of *Capital* would have been unimaginable. A more modest claim is that the Marxist writings on the AMP have an important place in the perceptions of Oriental despotism by Western writers.

NOTES

[1]   Karl Marx, *Capital,* 3 vols. (Chicago: Kerr, 1909).

[2]   Joshua A. Fogel, "The Debates Over the Asiatic Mode of Production in Soviet Russia, China, and Japan," *American Historical Review* (hereafter *AHR*), 93, no.

1 (February 1988), p. 79; Anne M. Bailey, "The Renewed Discussion on the Concept of the Asiatic Mode of Production," in Joel S. Kahn and Josef R. Llobera, eds., *The Anthropology of Pre-Capitalist Societies* (London: Macmillan, 1981), pp. 89-107; Jean Suret-Canale, *L'Afrique noire occidentale et centrale, géographie, civilisations, histoire* (Paris: Editions sociales, 1958), p. 94; Barry Hindess and Paul Hirst, *Pre-Capitalist Modes of Production* (London: Macmillan, 1975), p. 178.

3 Among the more interesting of these discussions are: Jean Chesneaux, "Ou en est la Discussion sur le Mode de Production Asiatique," *La Pensée*, no. 138 (March-April 1968), pp. 47-57, and Chesneaux, "Le Mode de Production Asiatique: Une Nouvelle Etape de la Discussion," *Eirenne*, III (1964), pp. 131-169; Maurice Godelier, preface to *Sur les Sociétés Précapitalistes* (Paris: Editions Sociales, 1970), and Godelier, "Les écrits de Marx et d'Engels sur le mode de production asiatique," *La Pensée*, no. 114 (January-February 1964), pp. 56-66; Anthony Giddens, *A Contemporary Critique of Historical Materialism* (London: Macmillan, 1981); Heinz Lubasz, "Marx's Concept of the Asiatic Mode of Production: a Genetic Analysis," *Economy and Society* (1984), pp. 456-483; Ferens Tokei, *Essays on the Asiatic Mode of Production* (Budapest: Akadémiai Kiado, 1979); Maurice Bloch, *Marxism and Anthropology* (Oxford, Oxford University Press, 1983); Gianni Sofri, *Il Modo di Produzione Asiatico* (Turin: Einaudi, 1969); Stephen P. Dunn, *The Fall and Rise of the Asiatic Mode of Production* (London: Routledge and Kegan Paul 1982); Bryan S. Turner, *Marx and the End of Orientalism* (London: Allen and Unwin, 1978); Kimio Shiozawa, "Marx's View of Asian Society and His 'Asiatic Mode of Production'," *The Developing Economies*, IV (September 1966); Donald Lowe, *The Function of "China" in Marx, Lenin, and Mao* (Berkeley: University of California Press, 1966).

4 Leo Yaresh, "The Problem of Periodization," in Cyril Black, ed., *Rewriting Russian History*, 2nd ed. (New York: Vintage, 1962), p. 40; Teodor Shanin, ed., *Late Marx and the Russian Road* (New York: Monthly Review Press, 1983); Stephen Dunn, *The Fall and Rise of the Asiatic Mode of Production*.

5 Eric Hobsbawm, ed., *Pre-Capitalist Economic Formations* (London: Lawrence and Wishart, 1964), p. 23.

6 Pierre Vidal-Naquet, "Karl Wittfogel et le concept de 'Mode de production asiatique'," *Annales*, xix (1964), pp. 531-549.

7 Robert C. Tucker, *Philosophy and Myth in Karl Marx*, 2nd ed. (New York: Cambridge University Press, 1972), p. 204; and Robert C. Tucker, ed., *The Marx-Engels Reader* (New York: Norton, 1972), p. xxiv.

8 Karl Marx, *Grundrisse* (New York: Vintage, 1973), p. 105.

9 Engels to Marx, June 6, 1853, in Karl Marx and Frederick Engels, *Collected Works* (hereafter *CW*) (New York: International Publishers, 1975), vol. 39, p. 341.

10 F. Engels, *Anti-Duhring* (New York: International Publishers, 1939), p. 181.

11 Marx, *Contribution to the Critique of Hegel's Philosophy of Law, CW*, vol. 3, p. 32.

12 Norman Levine, "The Myth of Asiatic Restoration," *The Journal of Asian Studies*, 37 (1977), p. 75.

13 Maurice Godelier, *Sur les Sociétés Précapitalistes* (Paris: Editions Sociales, 1970), pp. 41-42.

14 Marx, letter to Arnold Ruge, May 1843, *CW*, vol. 3, p. 138.

15 Anne M. Bailey and Josep R. Llobera, eds., *The Asiatic Mode of Production: Science and Politics* (London: Routledge and Kegan Paul, 1981), pp. 1-2.

16 Engels, June 6, 1853, *CW,* vol. 39, pp. 335-342.
17 Marx, June 14, 1853, *CW,* vol. 39, pp. 346-348.
18 Marx, December 28, 1846, *CW,* vol. 38, p. 96.
19 Ernest Gellner, *Spectacles and Predicaments* (Cambridge: Cambridge University Press, 1979), p. 322; Gellner, *Thought and Change* (Chicago: University of Chicago Press, 1964), pp. 47-49.
20 Engels, "Karl Marx: A Contribution to the Critique of Political Economy," *CW,* vol. 16, p. 475.
21 Engels, "Principles of Communism," *CW,* vol. 6, p. 345.
22 Karl Marx, *Grundrisse,* pp. 105-106.
23 *Ibid.,* p. 107.
24 *Ibid.,* p. 490.
25 *Ibid.,* p. 472.
26 Eric Hobsbawm, *Pre-Capitalist Economic Formations,* p. 10.
27 Shlomo Avineri, *The Social and Political Thought of Karl Marx* (Cambridge: Cambridge University Press, 1969), p. 112.
28 *Capital,* vol. III, p. 791.
29 Marx, "Critique of Political Economy," *CW,* vol. 28, p. 401; *Grundrisse,* p. 473.
30 Hobsbawm, *Pre-Capitalist Economic Formations,* pp. 70, 83.
31 Hobsbawm, *Pre-Capitalist Economic Formations,* p. 38.
32 Georges Sorel, *Illusions of Progress,* translated by John and Charlotte Stanley (Berkeley: University of California, 1969), p. xii.
33 Third draft to Vera Zasulich, *CW,* vol. 24, pp. 364-367.
34 Hobsbawm, *Pre-Capitalist Economic Formations,* p. 58.
35 F. Engels, *Anti-Duhring,* p. 164.
36 Lawrence Krader, *The Ethnological Notebooks of Karl Marx,* 2nd ed. (Assen: Van Gorcum, 1974), p. 179.
37 Brendan O'Leary, *The Asiatic Mode of Production* (Oxford: Blackwell, 1989), pp. 94-95.
38 Engels, *The Origin of the Family, Private Property and the State,* 2nd ed., quoted in Tucker, *The Marx-Engels Reader,* p. 335.
39 Engels, "On Social Relations in Russia," *CW,* vol. 24, p. 46; also, Engels, letter to "Kautsky," February 16, 1884.
40 B. S. T., "Asiatic Thought" in Tom Bottomore, ed. *A Dictionary of Marxist Thought* (Cambridge: Harvard University Press, 1983), p. 32.
41 Leszek Kolakowski, *Main Currents of Marxism* (Oxford: Clarendon Press, 1978), vol. I, p. 350.
42 Brendan O'Leary, *The Asiatic Mode of Production,* p. 25; V. Kiernan, "Marx and India," in R. Miliband and J. Saville, eds., *The Socialist Register, 1967* (London: Merlin Press, 1967), p. 67; Helen Carrère d'Encausse and S. Schram, eds., *Marxism and Asia, 1853-1964,* (Harmondsworth: Penguin, 1969), p. 8; Maurice Bloch, *Marxism and Anthropology* (New York: Oxford University Press, 1983), p. 64.
43 First draft to Vera Zasulich, *CW,* vol. 24, p. 346.
44 Steven Lukes, *Marxism and Morality* (Oxford: Clarendon Press, 1985), pp. 9-10; Engels, *CW,* vol. 16, pp. 474-475; Donald Lowe, *The Function of "China" in Marx, Lenin, and Mao* (Berkeley: University of California Press, 1966), pp. 6-8.
45 Marian Sawer, "The Concept of Asiatic Mode of Production and Contemporary Marxism," in Shlomo Avineri, ed., *Varieties of Marxism* (The Hague: Nijhoff, 1977), p. 337.
46 Marx, "Critique of Political Economy," *CW,* vol. 29, p. 275.

The Asiatic Mode of Production   371

47   Shanin, ed., *Late Marx and the Russian Road*, p. 29.
48   Engels, "Preface to the 1888 English edition of the Communist Manifesto," *CW*, vol. 26, p. 517.
49   Letters of Engels to Joseph Bloch, September 21, 1890; to Conrad Schmidt, October 27, 1890; to Franz Mehring, July 14, 1893.
50   Haruki Wada, "Marx and Revolutionary Russia," in Shanin, ed., *Late Marx and the Russian Road*, pp. 41, 59.
51   The four drafts of Marx's reply were not discovered until 1911, and were first published in 1924.
52   Second draft to Vera Zasulich, *CW*, vol. 24, p. 360.
53   This is made clear in a number of articles written for the *New York Daily Tribune* (hereafter *NYDT*), especially those of January 23, 1857; April 10, 1857; and September 25, 1858.
54   Marx, "The British Rule in India," *NYDT*, June 25, 1853, *CW*, vol. 12, p. 128.
55   Marx, "The Turkish Question," *NYDT*, June 14, 1853, *CW*, vol. 12, p. 113; "The Future Results of British Rule in India," *NYDT*, August 8, 1853, *CW*, vol. 12, pp. 217-222.
56   *Capital*, vol. III, p. 451; Maurice Meisner, "The Despotism of Concepts," *China Quarterly*, 16 (November-December 1963), pp. 99-109.
57   Engels, "Abd-El-Kader," *NYDT*, January 22, 1848, *CW*, vol. 6, p. 472.
58   Marx, "The British Rule in India," June 25, 1853, *CW*, vol. 12, pp. 126-128.
59   Marx, "The Anglo-Chinese Treaty," *NYDT*, October 5, 1858, *CW*, vol. 16, pp. 31-32.
60   Marx, "Trade with China," *NYDT*, December 3, 1859, *CW*, vol. 16, pp. 536-539.
61   M. C. Howard and J. E. King, *A History of Marxian Economics: Vol. I, 1883-1929* (Princeton: Princeton University Press, 1989), p. 134.
62   Fogel, *AHR* (1988), p. 79.
63   Marx, articles on the Turkish question, *NYDT*, April 19, 21, 1853, August 5, 1853; Engels, *On Social Relations in Russia, 1875 and Afterword 1894*, *CW*, vol. 24, p. 50; Marx, "In Retrospect," *Neue Oder-Zeitung*, January 2 and January 4, 1855, *CW*, vol. 13, p. 559.
64   Marx to Engels, November 7, 1868, *CW*, vol. 43, p. 154.
65   Marx and Engels, preface to 2nd Russian edition of the *Communist Manifesto*, *CW*, vol. 24, p. 426.
66   First draft to Zasulich, *CW*, vol. 24, p. 353.
67   Derek Sayer and Philip Corrigan, "Late Marx: Continuity, Contradiction and Learning," in Teodor Slanin, *Later Marx and the Russian Road*, p. 89.
68   Preface to 2nd Russian Edition of *Communist Manifesto*, *CW*, vol. 24, pp. 425-426.
69   Engels, Afterword to "On Social Relations in Russia," *CW*, vol. 27, p. 433.
70   Ferenc Tokei, *Essays on the Asiatic Mode of Production*, pp. 20-21; Samuel Baron, "Plekhanov's Russia: The Impact of the West upon an Oriental Society," *Journal of the History of Ideas*, xix, no. 3 (June 1958), pp. 390-394; Joseph Schiebel, "Pre-Revolutionary Russian Marxist Concepts of Russian State and Society," in G.L. Ulmen, ed., *Society and History: Essays in Honor of Karl August Wittfogel* (The Hague: Mouton, 1978), pp. 318-323; Marx, letter to the editors of *Otechestvenniye Zapiski*, November 1877 (sent but not published until 1886).
71   Perry Anderson, *Lineages of the Absolutist State* (London: Verso Books, 1979), p. 484.
72   *Capital*, vol. III, p. 331; Marx, "On the Jewish Question," *CW*, vol. 3, p. 165.
73   First draft to Vera Zasulich, *CW*, vol. 24, p. 346.

74   Marx, "Theories of Surplus Value," in *CW*, vol. 33, p. 340.

75   *Ibid.*, p. 321.

76   Marx, "The Duchess of Sutherland and Slavery," *CW*, vol. 11, p. 488.

77   Krader, *The Ethnological Notebooks of Karl Marx*, p. 173.

78   Marx to Engels, March 14, 1868, *CW*, vol. 42, p. 547.

79   Engels to Kugelmann, February 17, 1870, *CW*, vol. 43, p. 434.

80   Engels, *Anti-Duhring*, p. 163.

81   *Ibid.*, pp. 149-150.

82   *Ibid.*, pp. 198, 203, 232.

83   Marx, Introduction to First Version of *Capital*, *CW*, vol. 28, p. 25.

84   Third draft to Vera Zasulich, *CW*, vol. 24, pp. 365-366.

85   Engels, letter to Edward Bernstein, August 9, 1882, *CW*, vol. 46, p. 301.

86   Engels, "Preparatory Writings for *Anti-Duhring*," *CW*, vol. 25, pp. 610-611.

87   Engels, "Afterword," *CW*, vol. 27, p. 421.

88   Engels, English edition, 1888 of the *Communist Manifesto*, *CW*, vol. 26, pp. 515-518.

89   Marx, "Trade with China," *NYDT*, December 3, 1859, *CW*, vol. 16, p. 538; Lowe, pp. 25-26; Benjamin Schwartz, "A Marxist Controversy on China," *Far Eastern Quarterly*, February 1954, vol. XIII, pp. 143-154.

90   Engels, "Principles of Communism," October 1847, *CW*, vol. 6, p. 345.

91   Marx, "Chinese Affairs," *NYDT*, July 7, 1862, *CW*, vol. 19, p. 216; Marx, "The Anglo-Chinese Treaty," *NYDT*, Oct. 5, 1858, *CW*, vol. 16, p. 32; Marx to Engels, Oct. 8, 1858, *CW*, vol. 40, p. 347.

92   *Capital*, I, ch. 3; Marx, *Economic Manuscripts*, *CW*, vol. 28, p. 29.

93   Tucker, *The Marx-Engels Reader*, p. 192.

94   Adam Smith, *The Wealth of Nations* (New York: Modern Library, 1937), pp. 348, 360, 362, 645, 687, 789; Umberto Melotti, *Marx and the Third World* (London: Macmillan, 1977), pp. 52-53.

95   James Mill, *The History of India*, 2nd ed., vol. I (London: Baldwin, 1820), p. 175.

96   John Stuart Mill, *Principles of Political Economy* (London: Longmans, 1873), p. 12.

97   Richard Jones, *Lectures on the Political Economy of Nations* (Hertford, 1852), pp. 77-78.

98   Daniel Thorner, "Marx on India and the Asiatic Mode of Production," *Contributions to Indian Sociology*, no. 9 (December 1966), p. 57.

99   Anderson in *Lineages*; Louis Dumont in *Religion, Politics and History in India* (The Hague: Mouton, 1966), pp. 112-132; Timothy Brook, ed., *The Asiatic Mode of Production in China* (Armonk, Sharpe, 1989).

100   Frederic Pryor, "The Asian Mode of Production as an Economic System," *Journal of Comparative Economics*, 4 (1980), pp. 420-442.

101   Marx to Engels, June 14, 1853, *CW*, vol. 39, pp. 346-347; Marx, *CW*, vol. 12, pp. 219-220.

102   Marx, "The British Rule in India," *CW*, vol. 12, p. 132.

103   *Capital*, vol. I, pp. 337-338.

104   Marx to Engels, June 14, 1853, *CW*, vol. 39, p. 347.

105   *Capital*, vol. I, pp. 374-376.

106   Thorner, "Marx on India and the Asiatic Mode of Production," p. 57; Marx, *NYDT*, Feb. 9, 1853, *CW*, vol. 11, p. 488.

107   *Capital*, vol. I, p. 49.

108   *Capital*, vol. II, p. 178; vol. I, p. 83.

109   *Capital*, vol. I, p. 625.

110   Tucker, *The Marx-Engels Reader*, pp. 223-4; *Capital*, vol. II, pp. 34-35.

111 *Capital*, vol. III, p. 325.

112 *Capital*, vol. I, p. 387; Tucker, *The Marx-Engels Reader*, p. 281.

113 Marx, "Trade with China," *NYDT*, December 3, 1859, *CW*, vol. 16, p. 539.

114 Marx to Engels, June 2, 1853; Engels to Marx, June 6, 1853; Marx, "British Rule in India," *NYDT*, June 25, 1853.

115 Engels to Kautsky, March 2, 1883, *CW*, vol. 46, p. 451.

116 *Critique of Political Economy*, *CW*, vol. 29, p. 275.

117 Engels, "Afterword," *CW*, vol. 27, p. 421.

118 Engels, "Preparatory Writings for *Anti-Duhring*," *CW*, vol. 27, p. 606.

119 *Ibid.*, p. 613.

120 *Capital*, vol. III, pp. 771-772, 790-791.

121 Engels, *Anti-Duhring*, pp. 164, 198.

122 Marx, "Lord Canning's Proclamation and Land Tenure in India," *NYDT*, June 7, 1858, *CW*, vol. 15, p. 547.

123 Engels, *Anti-Duhring*, p. 150; also *Grundrisse*, pp. 484, 493, 497.

124 *Capital*, vol. III, p. 791.

125 *Grundisse*, p. 400.

126 Engels, "The Mark," *CW*, vol. 24, p. 441.

127 Marx, *The German Ideology* (New York: International Publishers, 1960).

128 Engels, *Anti-Duhring*, pp. 149-150.

129 Engels, "On Social Relations in Russia," *CW*, vol. 24, pp. 46-47.

130 *Grundrisse*, pp. 406-407, 479.

131 Marx, *The German Ideology*, p. 70.

132 Marx, "Outlines of the Critique of Political Economy," *CW*, vol. 28, p. 401.

133 Marx, "Theories of Surplus Value," *CW*, vol. 31, p. 174.

134 *Ibid.*, vol. 33, p. 321.

135 *Capital*, vol. III, pp. 790-791, 798; vol. I, p. 140.

136 *CW*, vol. 12, pp. 126-128.

137 *Capital*, vol. I, p. 514.

138 Daniel Thorner, "Marx, India and the Asiatic Mode of Production," *Contributions to Indian Sociology*, IX (December 1966), pp. 33-66; Geoffrey de Ste Croix, *The Class Struggle in the Ancient Greek World* (London: Duckworth, 1981); Hindess and Hirst, *Pre-Capitalist Modes of Production*; Benjamin Schwartz, "A Marxist Controversy on China," *Far Eastern Quarterly*, XIII (February 1954), pp. 143-154.

139 Maurice Godelier, *Sur le "Mode de Production Asiatique"*; and Godelier, "The Asiatic Mode of Production," in Bailey and Llobera, eds., *The Asiatic Mode of Production: Science and Politics*, p. 273.

140 *Capital*, vol. I, p. 316.

141 *Capital*, vol. I, p. 366-367.

142 *Capital*, vol. I, p. 315-316, 349-350; vol. II, p. 26.

143 "Outlines," *CW*, vol. 28, p. 400.

144 *Grundrisse*, p. 486.

145 "Outlines," *CW*, vol. 28, p. 418.

146 *Ibid.*, p. 416.

147 "Theories of Surplus Value," *CW*, vol. 33, p. 356.

148 *Ibid.*, p. 368.

149 Pryor, "The Asian Mode of Production as an Economic System," pp. 420-442.

150 "Theories of Surplus Value," *CW*, vol. 33, p. 356.

151 Marx, "Chinese Affairs," *Die Presse*, July 7, 1862, *CW*, vol. 19, p. 216-218; *Capital*, vol. I, p. 358; Engels, *Anti-Duhring*, p. 167.

152 Marx, "Revolution in China and in Europe," June 25, 1853, *CW,* vol. 12, p. 95; Engels, "Principles of Communism," *CW,* vol. 6, p. 345; Engels, "Persia-China," *NYDT,* June 5, 1857, *CW,* vol. 15, pp. 278-280.

153 Marx, "Revelations of the Diplomatic History of the 18th Century," published in *The Free Press* (1856-57), *CW,* vol. 15, pp. 90-92.

154 *Capital,* vol. I, pp. 338, 352.

155 Tucker, *The Marx-Engels Reader,* p. xviii.

156 Umberto Melotti, *Marx and the Third World* (Atlantic Highlands: Humanities Press, 1977), pp. 50-51.

157 Hegel, *Lectures on the Philosophy of History* (New York: Collier, 1902), ch. 2.

158 Engels, *CW,* vol. 6, pg. 345.

159 Marx, "The British Rule in India," *NYDT,* June 25, 1853, *CW,* vol. 12, p. 132; "The Indian Revolt," *NYDT,* September 16, 1857, *CW,* vol. 15, pp. 353-356.

160 "The British Rule," *CW,* vol. 12, *ibid.*

161 Engels, "Persia-China," *NYDT,* June 5, 1857, vol. 15, pp. 279-282.

162 *Capital,* vol. I, pp. 337-338.

163 Krader, *The Ethnological Notebooks of Karl Marx,* p. 289.

164 Marx, "Revolution in China and in Europe," *NYDT,* June 14, 1853, *CW,* vol. 12, p. 94.

165 *Grundrisse,* p. 69.

166 Engels, "The Frankish Period," *CW,* vol. 26, p. 59.

167 *Capital,* vol. III, p. 732.

168 *Ibid.,* p. 448.

169 *Capital,* vol. I, p. 140.

170 Engels, August 9, 1882 in *CW,* vol. 46, pp. 301-302.

171 Marx, "The British Rule in India," *NYDT,* June 25, 1853, *CW,* vol. 12, pp. 125-126.

172 *Capital,* vol. I, p. 338.

173 *Ibid.,* p. 285.

174 "Theories of Surplus Value," *CW,* vol. 33, pp. 356-357, 369.

175 *Capital,* vol. I, p. 647-649.

176 *Capital,* vol. I, p. 649.

177 *Capital,* vol. III, p. 793; vol. I, p. 91.

178 Engels to Kautsky, Feb. 16, 1884, *CW,* vol. 47, p. 103; Engels, "The Frankish Period," *CW,* vol. 26, pp. 59-60.

179 *Anti-Duhring,* p. 203; Engels, *CW,* vol. 25, p. 168.

180 Engels, *CW,* vol. 24, p. 46.

181 Marx makes a similar point about Spain in "Revolutionary Spain," *NYDT,* September 9, 1854, *CW,* vol. 13, p. 396.

182 *Capital,* vol. 1, p. 29.

183 *Grundrisse,* pp. 472-473.

184 *Ibid.,* p. 473.

185 Marx, "Pelissier's Mission to England," *NYDT,* April 15, 1858, *CW,* vol. 15, p. 482.

186 Barry Hindess and Paul Hirst, *Pre-Capitalist Modes of Production* (London: Routledge, 1975), p. 207; Krader, *The Ethnological Notebooks of Karl Marx,* p. 274; Marian Sawer, "The Concept of the Asiatic Mode of Production and Contemporary Marxism," in Shlomo Avineri, ed., *Varieties of Marxism* (The Hague, Nijhoff, 1977), p. 340; Tokei, *Sur le mode de production asiatique,* Centre d'Etudes et de recherches Marxistes, Paris, 1963, pp. 85-86.

187 Engels to Marx, June 6, 1853, *CW,* vol. 39, pp. 340-341; Marx to Engels, June 14, 1853, *CW,* vol. 39, pp. 346-348; Marx, "British Rule in India," *CW,* vol. 12, pp. 126-128.

[188] Robert C. Tucker, "Marx as a Political Theorist," in Shlomo Avineri, ed., *Marx's Socialism* (New York: Atherton, 1973), p. 136.

[189] "Outlines," *CW,* vol. 28, p. 401.

[190] "The British Rule in India," *CW,* vol. 12, p. 127.

[191] "Revolutionary Spain," *NYDT,* September 9, 1854, *CW,* vol. 13, p. 396.

[192] Isaiah Berlin, *Historical Inevitability* (London: Oxford University Press, 1954), p. 5.

[193] O'Leary, *The Asiatic Mode of Production,* p. 134.

[194] Lucian Pye, *Asian Power and Politics: The Cultural Dimensions of Authority* (Cambridge: Belknap Press, 1985), p. 8.

[195] Godelier in a number of his writings, especially the preface to *Sur les Sociétés Précapitalistes.*

[196] Anderson, *Lineages of the Absolutist State,* pp. 488-489.

[197] *Ibid.,* p. 494.

[198] Dumont, *Religion, Politics and History in India,* p. 80; Tokei, *Sur le 'mode de production asiatique,* p. 9.

Selected Bibliography

The literature on Marxism is now voluminous in many languages. For convenience this selected bibliography is divided into biographical works, expository books, critical works, and books relevant to subjects in the four parts of this book.

BIOGRAPHICAL WORKS

Berlin, Isaiah, *Karl Marx*, 3d ed., Oxford University Press, London, 1966.
Carmichael, Joel, *Karl Marx, the Passionate Logician*, Scribner, New York, 1967.
Carr, E.H., *A History of Soviet Russia*, 7 vols., Macmillan, New York, 1950– .
Cole, G.D.H., *A History of Socialist Thought*, 5 vols., Macmillan, London, 1954–60.
Deutscher, Isaac, *Stalin: A Political Biography*, rev. ed., Penguin, Harmondsworth, 1966.
Deutscher, Isaac, *Trotsky*, 3 vols., Oxford University Press, New York, 1954–63.
Fisher, Louis, *The Life of Lenin*, Harper & Row, New York, 1964.
Frolich, Paul, *Rosa Luxemburg*, Gollancz, London, 1940.
Gay, Peter, *The Dilemma of Democratic Socialism*, Columbia University Press, New York, 1952.
Gray, Alexander, *The Socialist Tradition*, Longmans, Green, London, 1946.
Laski, H.J., *Karl Marx*, League for Industrial Democracy, New York, 1933.
Mayer, Gustav, *Friedrich Engels*, Knopf, New York, 1936.
Mehring, Franz, *Karl Marx*, University of Michigan Press, Ann Arbor, 1962.
Nettl, J.P., *Rosa Luxemburg*, Oxford University Press, New York, 1966.
Payne, Robert, *Portrait of a Revolutionary: Mao Tse-tung*, Abelard-Schuman, London, 1961.
Payne, Robert, *Marx*, Simon & Schuster, New York, 1968.

Ruhle, O., *Karl Marx: His Life and Work*, Viking, New York, 1935.

Souvarine, Boris, *Stalin*, Alliance Book Corporation, New York, 1939.

Treadgold, Donald, *Lenin and his Rivals*, Praeger, New York, 1955.

Wolfe, Bertram D., *Three Who Made a Revolution*, Dial, New York, 1948.

GENERAL WORKS ON MARXISM

Althusser, Louis, *Pour Marx*, Maspero, Paris, 1965.

Burns, Emile, ed., *A Handbook on Marxism*, Random House, New York, 1935.

Carew Hunt, R. N., *The Theory and Practice of Communism*, Macmillan, New York, 1957.

Cole, G.D.H., *The Meaning of Marxism*, Gollancz, London, 1948.

Drachkovitch, Milorad M., ed., *Marxism in the Modern World*, Stanford University Press, Stanford, 1965.

Gregor, A.J., *A Survey of Marxism*, Random House, New York, 1965.

Labedz, Leo, ed., *Revisionism: Essays on the History of Marxist Ideas*, Praeger, New York, 1962.

Lichtheim, George, *Marxism: An Historical and Critical Study*, Praeger, New York, 1961.

Lobkowicz, N., ed., *Marx and the Western World*, Notre Dame Press, Notre Dame, Ind., 1967.

Marcuse, Herbert, *Soviet Marxism*, Columbia University Press, New York, 1958.

Mayo, H.B., *An Introduction to Marxist Theory*, Oxford University Press, New York, 1960.

Meyer, Alfred, *Marxism: The Unity of Theory and Practice*, Harvard University Press, Cambridge, 1954.

Meyer, Alfred, *Leninism*, Harvard University Press, Cambridge, 1957.

Meyer, Alfred, *Communism*, 3d ed., Random House, New York, 1967.

Mills, C. Wright, *The Marxists*, Dell, New York, 1962.

Strachey, John, *The Theory and Practice of Socialism*, Random House, New York, 1936.

Ulam, Adam, *The Unfinished Revolution*, Random House, New York, 1960.

Zeitlin, Irving, *Marxism: A Re-examination*, Van Nostrand, Princeton, 1967.

SOME CRITICAL COMMENTARIES ON MARXISM

Berdyaev, Nikolai, *The Origin of Russian Communism*, Bles, London, 1955.

Brzezinski, Zbigniew, *The Permanent Purge*, Harvard University Press, Cambridge, 1956.

Crossman, Richard, ed., *The God that Failed*, Harper & Row, New York, 1965.

Eastman, Max, *Marxism, Is It a Science?*, Norton, New York, 1940.

Kelsen, Hans, *The Political Theory of Bolshevism*, University of California Press, Berkeley, 1949.

Koestler, Arthur, *The Yogi and the Commissar*, new ed., Macmillan, New York, 1967.

Lowenthal, Richard, *World Communism*, Oxford University Press, New York, 1964.

Parkes, H.B., *Marxism: An Autopsy*, Houghton Mifflin, Boston, 1939.

Plamenatz, John, *What is Communism?*, National News-Letter, London, 1947.

Popper, Karl, *The Open Society and its Enemies*, Vol. 2, Routledge, London, 1945.

Russell, Bertrand, *The Practice and Theory of Bolshevism*, Harcourt, New York, 1920.

Talmon, J. L., *Political Messianism: The Romantic Phase*, Praeger, New York, 1960.

BOOKS RELEVANT TO PART I

Bernal, J.D., *Marx and Science*, International Publishers, New York, 1952.

Dupré, Louis, *The Philosophical Foundations of Marxism*, Harcourt, Brace and World, New York, 1966.

Hyman, Stanley, *The Tangled Bank*, Atheneum, New York, 1962.

Mitrany, David, *Marx against the Peasant*, University of North Carolina Press, Chapel Hill, 1951.

Laqueur, Walter, and Leopold Labedz, eds., *Polycentrism*, Praeger, New York, 1962.

Schlesinger, Rudolf, *Marx, His Time and Ours*, Routledge, London, 1950.

Schumpeter, Joseph, *Capitalism, Socialism and Democracy*, Harper, New York, 1942.

Talmon, J.L., *The Origins of Totalitarian Democracy*, Secker & Warburg, London, 1952.

BOOKS RELEVANT TO PART 2

Bauer, Raymond, *The New Man in Soviet Psychology*, Harvard University Press, Cambridge, 1959.

Bigo, Pierre, *Marxisme et Humanisme*, Presses Universitaires de France, Paris, 1953.

Buber, Martin, *Paths in Utopia*, Beacon Hill, Boston, 1949.

Calvez, Jean Yves, *La Pensée de Karl Marx*, Editions du Seuil, Paris, 1966.

Fromm, Erich, ed., *Marx's Concept of Man*, Ungar, New York, 1966.

Kamenka, Eugene, *The Ethical Foundations of Marxism*, Routledge, London, 1962.

Novack, George, *Existentialism versus Marxism*, Dell, New York, 1966.

Petrovic, Gajo, *Marx in the Mid-twentieth Century*, Doubleday, Garden City, 1967.

Selsam, Howard, *Socialism and Ethics*, International Publishers, New York, 1943.

Tucker, Robert C., *Philosophy and Myth in Karl Marx*, Cambridge University Press, New York, 1961.

Venable, Vernon, *Human Nature: The Marxian View*, Knopf, New York, 1945.

BOOKS RELEVANT TO PART 3

Acton, H. B., *The Illusion of the Epoch*, Cohen & West, London, 1955.
Bloom, S. F., *The World of Nations*, Columbia University Press, New York, 1941.
Bober, M. M., *Karl Marx's Interpretation of History*, Harvard University Press, Cambridge, 1927.
Böhm-Bawerk, Eugen von, *Karl Marx and the Close of his System*, Kelley, New York, 1949.
Bukharin, N., *Historical Materialism*, International Publishers, New York, 1928.
Croce, Benedetto, *Historical Materialism and the Economics of Karl Marx*, Latimer, London, 1914.
Federn, Karl, *The Materialist Conception of History*, Macmillan, London, 1939.
Joseph, H.W.B., *The Labour Theory of Value in Karl Marx*, Oxford University Press, London, 1923.
Mandel, Ernest, *La Formation de la pensée économique de Karl Marx*, Paris, 1967.
Robinson, Joan, *An Essay on Marxian Economics*, Macmillan, London, 1942.
Rossiter, Clinton, *Marxism: The View from America*, Harcourt, Brace, New York, 1960.
Seligman, E. R. A., *The Economic Interpretation of History*, Columbia University Press, New York, 1961.
Wetter, Gustav, *Dialectical Materialism*, Praeger, New York, 1958.
Wolfson, Murray, *A Reappraisal of Marxian Economics*, Columbia University Press, New York, 1961.

BOOKS RELEVANT TO PART 4

Chang, S. H., *The Marxian Theory of the State*, Russell & Russell, New York, 1965.
Djilas, Milovan, *The New Class*, Praeger, New York, 1957.
Hayward, Max, ed., *On Trial*, Harper & Row, New York, 1967.
Hook, Sidney, *Reason, Social Myth and Democracy*, Day, New York, 1940.
Leites, Nathan, *A Study of Bolshevism*, Free Press, New York, 1953.
Milosz, C., *The Captive Mind*, Knopf, New York, 1953.
Moore, Barrington, Jr., *Terror and Progress*, Harvard University Press, Cambridge, 1954.
Plamenatz, John, *German Marxism and Russian Communism*, Longmans, Green, New York, 1954.
Schurmann, Franz, *Ideology and Organization in Communist China*, University of California Press, Berkeley, 1966.
Somerville, John, *Soviet Philosophy: A Study of Theory and Practice*, Philosophical Library, New York, 1946.

Index

Absolutism, 30
Accumulation of Capital, The (Luxemburg), 6
Acton, H. B., 27, 119
Address and Provisional Rules of the Working Men's International Association (Marx), 42
Address to the 3rd Congress of the Russian Young Communist League (Lenin), 112
Adler, Max, 99, 100
Alexander III, Tsar, 57
Alienation, 13–14, 39, 40, 42–43, 129–143
critique of, 131–143
Anarchism, 9
Anti-Dühring (Engels), 3, 24, 40, 111, 139, 160, 189, 191, 263, 316
Appeal, of Marxism, 9–10
Arendt, Hannah, 150
Aristotle, 94, 156
Atheism, Marx and, 155–163
Aventures de la Dialectique, Les (Merleau-Ponty), 147

Babeuf, François, 7, 251, 252
Bagehot, Walter, 205
Bakunin, Mikhail, 9, 46, 80, 84
Balzac, Honoré de, 113
Barran, Paul, 238
Bauer, Bruno, 131, 133, 140, 156

Bebel, August, 42, 46
Beer, Max, 201, 206, 296
Bell, Daniel, 12, 15, 38, 130, 131–143, 146, 147–150
Bergson, Henri, 24
Beria, Lavrenti P., 35
Berlin, Isaiah, 1, 14, 99, 104
Bernal, J. D., 113
Bernstein, Eduard, 2, 47–58, 88, 140
Blanqui, Louis A., 7, 81, 285, 287
Blanquists, 277, 285–295
Böhm-Bawerk, Eugen von, 11, 15, 217, 236
Bolsheviks and Bolshevism, 47, 57, 61, 110, 284, 298
Bonaparte, Louis, 243
Bottomore, T. B., 89, 97–104
Brinkley, George A., 304, 315–325
Buber, Martin, 134
Buckle, Henry Thomas, 186–187
Bukharin, Nikolai, 172, 309
Business cycles, Marxian explanation of, 229

Calvez, Jean-Yves, 131
Capital (Marx), 3, 13, 20, 31, 38, 47, 50, 51, 52, 82, 87, 88, 94, 101, 111, 137, 138, 140, 143, 148, 149, 150, 154, 175, 182, 187, 190, 213, 214, 221, 229, 230, 231, 232, 234, 236, 237, 238, 243, 246, 250, 270

Capitalism, 5–7, 27, 30, 37, 50, 52, 53, 109
Captive Mind, The (Milosz), 35
Carew Hunt, R. N., 107, 109–117
Castro, Fidel, 2, 62
Chang, Sherman H. M., 296
Change, gradual, 263–264
  ambivalence about, 280–282
  possibility of, 275–279
China, Communist, 12, 25, 62, 75–86
Christianity, Marxism and, 155–172
Civil War in France, The (Marx), 9, 56, 87, 248, 276, 277, 291, 295, 298
Class, 4–5, 11, 12, 243–244
  social, concept of, 245–253
Class conflict, 7, 243–244
Class Struggles in France, The (Marx), 42, 48, 81, 243, 250, 266, 276, 281, 283–284, 286, 288, 289, 297
Clemenceau, Georges, 81
Collected Works (Marx), 1
Collectivism, 10
Communism, primitive, 5, 27
Communist Manifesto, The (Marx and Engels), 4, 7, 25, 39, 40, 43, 48, 50, 75, 81–82, 109, 111, 113, 114, 137, 159, 188, 238, 247, 250, 253, 270, 276, 289, 290, 297, 299, 315
Communist society, future, 5, 9, 27
Comte, Auguste, 21, 23, 27, 28, 29, 30
Condition of the Working Class in England in 1844, The (Engels), 40
Consciousness, 20
Contribution to the Critique of Hegel's Philosophy of Right, A (Marx), 108
Contribution to the Critique of Political Economy, A (Marx), 40
Correspondence of Marx and Engels, 275
Coser, Lewis, 32–35, 129
Credo (Kuskova), 54
Crime and Punishment (Dostoievsky), 115
Criticism of Hegel's Philosophy of Right (Marx), 13, 157
Critique of the Gotha Programme (Marx), 42, 139, 294, 295
Critique of Political Economy (Marx), 26, 48, 148
Croce, Benedetto, 3, 14, 97, 179
Cuba, 62

Dahrendorf, Ralf, 98, 104, 244, 254–261
Daniels, Robert V., 15
Dehumanization, 13, 138, 150
Democracy, 50, 52–53
  Social, 49, 51, 53
Democracy and Socialism (Rosenberg), 287
Democritus, 92
Descartes, René, 192
Determinism, 88
  historical, 186
Deutscher, Isaac, 3
Dialectic, Marxian, 175–193
  Eastman's attack on, 177–185
  Simpson's defense of, 186–193
Dialectical materialism, 3, 24, 26, 92, 116, 144, 176
Dialectics, 3
Dialectics of Nature (Engels), 24
Dictatorship, 7, 11, 13
  necessity of, 283–284
  of the proletariat, 285–296, 297
Dictatorship of the Proletariat, The (Kautsky), 298
Diderot, Denis, 192
Dolci, Danilo, 167
Dostoievsky, Feodor M., 115
Drahn, Ernst, 296
Draper, Hal, 283, 285–296
Draper, John William, 187
Durkheim, Emile, 29, 98, 102

Eastman, Max, 154, 176, 177–185, 186–190
Economic determinism, 4
Economic and Philosophic Manuscripts of 1844 (Marx), 2, 37, 41, 42, 107, 135, 142, 144, 145, 146, 149, 175
Economics
  contribution of Marxism to, 213–239
  Marxian
    modern economic theory and, 215–228
    significance of, for present-day economic theory, 229–234
"Economism," 54–55, 57
Eighteenth Brumaire of Louis Bonaparte, The (Marx), 11, 188, 243, 276
Elliott, Charles F., 38, 46–59
Empiricism, 28

End of Ideology, The (Bell), 38
Engels, Friedrich
  on Christianity, 169
  death of, 47–48
  on dialectics, 176, 190–193
  on Marx, 245
  religion and, 159–161
  on revolution, 267–268
Ethics, Marxian, 107–127
Evolution of the Family, the State, and Private Property, The (Engels), 189
Exploitation, 41, 43, 138, 139

Fascism, 12
Fetscher, Irving, 146, 163
Feudalism, 5, 27, 29
Feuer, Lewis, 20, 45, 276, 279
Feuerbach, Ludwig, 92, 131, 133–134, 136, 137, 139, 140, 151, 153, 155–157, 162, 171, 178, 191
"Fideism," 26
Fougeyrolles, Pierre, 146
Freedom, 119–126, 133
French Revolution, 257
Freud, Sigmund, 42, 140
Frölich, P., 48, 58
From Hegel to Marx (Hook), 131
Functionalism, 97–98

Galbraith, John Kenneth, 238
Garaudy, Roger, 117, 251
Gay, Peter, 58–59
German-French Annals, 39
German Ideology, The (Marx), 26, 137, 139, 142, 153, 263
Germany: Revolution and Counter-Revolution (Engels), 243
Gerth, Hans, 141
Glaeserman, 311, 312, 313
Goethe, Johann, 134
Goldmann, Lucien, 132, 144
Gramsci, Antonio, 2, 84
Grillenberger, Karl, 295
Grundrisse (Marx), 2, 27, 148
Guerin, Daniel, 146

Haldane, J. B. S., 201, 206
Halévy, Elie, 19
Halle, Louis, 87, 154

Harrington, Michael, 130, 144–154
Hegel, G. W. F., 3, 4, 27, 28, 46, 108, 110–111, 118–120, 126, 133–137, 139, 140, 144, 156, 175, 177–182, 193, 270
Hegelianism, 3, 24, 28, 88, 99, 119
Hess, Moses, 131
Hexter, J. H., 196, 207–212
Hilferding, Rudolf, 7, 236
Historical determinism, 186
Historical materialism, 92, 195–212
History
  Marxism as a philosophy of, 197–206
  materialist conception of, 195–196
  nature of, 3–5
  social, new framework for, 207–212
History of Civilization in England (Buckle), 186
"History of the Communist League, The," 39
Hobbes, Thomas, 94
Hobsbawm, E. J., 100, 104
Hobson, J. A., 7
Hodges, Donald Clark, 38, 39–45, 88, 90–96
Holy Family, The (Marx), 42, 46, 88, 140, 188, 264
Hook, Sidney, 15, 117, 131, 132, 141, 176
Hoover, Calvin B., 304, 305–314
Horowitz, Irving Louis, 45
Housing Question, The (Engels), 292
Howe, Irving, 20, 32–35
Humanism, 144–154

Ideology, 20, 21, 22, 31
  role of, 32–35
Illusion of the Epoch (Acton), 119
Imperialism, 7
  Lenin's theory of, 56
Imperialism: The Highest Stage of Capitalism (Lenin), 7
Inadequacies, of Marxism, 10–12
Industrial Revolution, 257
Industrialization, 61
Intellectual Development of Europe (Draper), 187

Jacobinism, 7, 81, 82, 276, 300
Jaurès, Jean, 251

Kafka, Franz, 141
Kamenev, Lev B., 309
Kamenka, Eugene, 107, 118–127
Kant, Immanuel, 110, 125
Kautsky, K., 2, 23, 24, 29, 49, 51, 53,
    56, 58, 140, 169, 282, 296, 298–299,
    301
Keynes, John Maynard, 231, 235,
    238
Khrushchev, Nikita, 304, 315–325
Kierkegaard, Sören, 141
Knox, T. M., 126
Korsch, Karl, 12, 31, 99
Kuskova, Madame E. D., 54–55

Labor, division of, 14
Lafargue, Paul, 48, 49, 291
Landes, David, 279
Lange, Oscar, 214, 215–228, 231, 232,
    237, 238
Lassalle, Ferdinand, 294, 295
Left Wing Communism (Lenin), 32–33,
    109
Lenin, Nikolai, 2, 4, 8, 10, 12, 13, 23, 24,
    26, 30, 32, 46, 47, 51, 53, 56–58, 61,
    78–86, 88, 91, 95, 96, 109, 111, 113,
    114, 140, 141, 272, 283, 284, 298,
    301, 303, 306–307, 310, 316–317
    attack on Kuskova, 54
    concept of dialectic, 180
    on marxism, 1
    "Protest of the Seventeen," 55
Leninism, 12, 24, 277
Leontief, Wassily, 214, 229–234, 235, 237
Lewis, John, 116
Liberalism, 21, 25
Lichtheim, George, 19, 21–31, 62, 75–
    86, 276, 277, 278, 302
Liebknecht, Wilhelm, 42, 48–49, 53
Lipset, S. M., 264, 275–279
Living Thoughts of Karl Marx, The (Trots-
    ky), 265
Lobkowicz, N., 154, 155–164
Logic (Mill), 186
Lowenthal, Richard, 15, 61, 63–74
*Ludwig Feuerbach and the End of Classical
    German Philosophy* (Engels), 10, 87,
    139
Lüning, Otto, 288, 289

Lukacs, Georg, 2, 46, 58, 99, 100, 140–
    141, 147, 148, 149
Luther, Martin, 133
Luxemburg, Rosa, 2, 6, 47, 51–58, 284

Machiavelli, Niccolo, 116, 199
MacIntyre, Alasdair, 154, 165–172
Malinowski, Bronislaw, 98, 260
Mandeville, Geoffrey de, 211, 212
Mannheim, Karl, 100, 141
Mao Tse-tung, 2, 62, 75, 79, 80, 85
Marcuse, Herbert, 99, 104, 119, 142, 244
Marshall, Alfred, 217, 239
Martov, Julian, 278, 300, 302
Marx against the Peasants (Mitrany), 62
Marxism
    appeal of, 9–10
    consistency of, 37–45
    contribution to economics, 213–239
    ethics and, 107–127
    goal of, 43
    inadequacies of, 10–12
    introduction to, 1–15
    moral and ethical implications of, 13
    orthodox, 24, 25, 29, 31, 33
    as a philosophy of history, 197–206
    political modernization and, 61–62
    religion and, 153–172
    revisionism and, 37–38, 46–59
    revolutionary nature of, 12
    as a social science, 87–104
    sociological critique of, 254–261
    Soviet, 24
Marxism-Leninism, 62, 77, 80
Marxist methodology, 2–3
Marxists, The (Mills), 61
Mason, Edward, 279
Materialism, 26, 28
    dialectical, 3, 24, 26, 92, 116, 144, 176
    historical, 92, 195–212
Mayo, H. B., 196, 197–206
Merleau-Ponty, Maurice, 146–148, 150
Mill, John Stuart, 46, 94, 186, 187
Mills, C. Wright, 45, 61, 100, 142, 196
Milosz, C., 35
Mitrany, David, 62
Modernization, political, Marxism and,
    61–62
Monism, 24

Monopoly Capital (Sweezy and Barran), 238
Montesquieu, 199
Moore, Barrington, Jr., 61
Moore, Stanley W., 296
Morin, Edgar, 132
Mosca, G., 281
My Life (Trotsky), 307

Narodnichestvo, 30
Narodovol'tsy, 57
Nationalism, 11, 63, 196
Nero, 114
Niebuhr, Reinhold, 141
Nietzsche, Friedrich W., 24
1984 (Orwell), 35
Notes of a Publicist (Lenin), 82

Origin of the Family, Private Property and the State, The (Engels), 52
Orwell, George, 35
Ossowski, S., 243, 245–253

Pappenheim, Fritz, 45
Pareto, Vilfredo, 97, 98, 102, 217, 281
Paris Commune, 7, 56, 81, 82, 277, 278, 283, 291, 295, 298–299
Parliamentarianism, 50, 52
Parsons, Talcott, 259
Pensëe de Karl Marx, La (Calvez), 131
Petrovic, G., 13, 15
Philosophy of Right (Hegel), 126
Plamenatz, John, 213
Plato, 94, 175, 177
Plekhanov, G., 2, 23, 24, 26, 29, 82, 84, 92, 96, 140, 201, 206
Plutarch, 123
Political modernization, Marxism and, 61–62
Political power, Marxist view of, 7–9
Political theory, Marxism as, 19
Popper, Karl, 196
Populism, Russian, 30
Positivism, 27–30
Poverty of Philosophy, The (Marx), 3, 7, 12, 39, 44, 263
Power, political, Marxist view of, 7–9
Production, modes of, 4, 5, 11, 27, 31, 52, 213

Progressivism, 34
Proletarian Revolution and the Renegade Kautsky (Lenin), 298
Proletarian state, 297–302
Proletariat, 46
  dictatorship of the, 285–296, 297
  revolution and the, 265–274
"Protest of the Seventeen, The" (Lenin), 55
Proudhon, Pierre, 46, 111, 192

Radek, Karl, 47
Reason and Revolution (Marcuse), 119, 244
Reding, M., 155, 163
Religion, Marxism and, 153–172
Remarks on the Most Recent Prussian Instructions to Censors (Marx), 120
Revisionism, 37–38, 46–59
Revolution, 263–264
  proletariat and, 265–274
Ricardo, David, 214, 221, 225, 236, 252
Robbins, Lionel, 236
Robespierre, M., 58
Robinson, Joan, 228, 235, 238
Rosenberg, Arthur, 287
Rosenberg, Harold, 265–274
Rousseau, Jean Jacques, 46, 192

Saint-Simon, Claude, 27, 29, 102, 249
Samuelson, Paul A., 214, 235–239
Sartre, J. P., 2, 14, 100, 104
Schaff, Adam, 108
Schmidt, Conrad, 54
Schumpeter, Joseph, 13, 15, 227, 228, 238
Science of Logic (Hegel), 180
Scientific socialism, 3, 91–92, 96, 182
Seton-Watson, H. R., 64–74
Shibata, Kei, 215–216, 227, 238
Simmel, Georg, 140
Simpson, Herman, 176, 186–193
Slavery, 5, 27, 29
Smith, Adam, 236, 252
Social class, concept of, 245–253
Social Democracy, 49, 51, 53, 56
Social history, new framework for, 207–212
Social relationships, types of, 5

Social science, Marxism as, 87–104
Socialism, 9, 10, 22, 28, 51, 52, 53, 55, 88
    scientific, 3, 45, 91–92, 96, 182
    utopian, 46, 91
Socialism, Utopian and Scientific (Engels),
    190
Socrates, 114
Sombart, Werner, 29, 100
Sorel, Georges, 97, 274
Soviet Civilization (Webb), 10
Soviet Union, 10, 11, 12, 13, 305–325
"Speech at the Anniversary of the *People's
    Paper*" (Marx), 42
Spencer, Herbert, 29
Spengler, Oswald, 200, 238
Spinoza, Baruch, 192
Stalin, J., 2, 3, 10, 32, 83, 84, 92, 196,
    264, 283, 310–311, 313, 318
Stalinism, 20, 32–35
Starcke, C. N., 139
State
    future of the, 303–304
    Marxist view of the, 7–9
    proletarian, 297–302
    Soviet, 305–325
State and Revolution, The (Lenin), 8, 275,
    293, 296, 298, 301, 303, 306, 310
Steffens, Lincoln, 10
Stein, Lorenz von, 102
Structure of Social Action (Parsons), 259
"Substructure," 4
"Superstructure," 4, 30
Surplus value, Marx's theory of, 51
Sweezy, Paul, 236, 238

Taylor, Charles, 132
Technology, 28, 35
Theory, political, Marxism as, 19
Théses on Feuerbach (Marx), 139, 153, 156
Thought, Marx's interpretation of, 21–
    31

Tito, 2
Totalitarianism, 10, 11, 12, 35, 63
Toynbee, Arnold, 200, 202–203,
    238
Trade unions, 53–54
Troeltsch, Ernst, 29
Trotsky, Leon, 2, 12, 13, 83, 113, 183,
    264, 265, 284, 307, 308
Tucker, Robert, 7, 14, 15, 45, 87, 142,
    264, 280–282, 284, 297–302

Ulam, Adam, 61
Underdeveloped countries, Marxism
    and, 63–74
Unfinished Revolution, The (Ulam), 61
Universalism, 28
Utopian Socialism, 46, 91

Value, labor theory of, 236
Value, Price, and Profit (Marx), 237
Veblen, Thorstein, 100, 234, 238
Venable, Vernon, 117
Vico, Giovanni, 199
Voden, Alexis, 139–140, 143
Voluntarism, 24, 56

Watnick, Morris, 140
Webb, Beatrice, 10
Webb, Sidney, 10
Weber, Max, 29, 97, 100, 102, 141–142
Weil, E., 158, 163
Werke (Marx), 2
Wetter, Gustav, 176
Weydemeyer, Joseph, 288–290, 297
What Is to Be Done? (Lenin), 32, 55, 82,
    184, 272
Willich, August, 287, 288
Wischnewetzky, Florence Kelley, 139
Wolfe, Bertram, 15

Zinoviev, Grigori, 309